BETWEEN TWO HARBORS

Reflections of a
Catalina Island Harbormaster

Doug Oudin

BETWEEN TWO HARBORS
Reflections of a Catalina Island Harbormaster

iUniverse books may be ordered through booksellers or by contacting:

iUniverse
1663 Liberty Drive
Bloomington, IN 47403
www.iuniverse.com
1-800-Authors (1-800-288-4677)

Cover photo by the Santa Catalina Island Conservancy

ISBN: 978-1-4917-0064-8 (sc)
ISBN: 978-1-4917-0063-1 (hc)
ISBN: 978-1-4917-0062-4 (e)

Library of Congress Control Number: 2013913280

Print information available on the last page.

iUniverse rev. date: 8/30/2013

Dedication

To my adorable wife Maureen, our sons Trevor and Troy, and daughter-in-law Lauren. Thank you.

Acknowledgements

Special thanks to Vicki Miller and Sharon Bison for all your help and support. Thank you as well, to all those individuals with whom I worked, played, and got to know during our thirty-two years on the Island. Your fellowship and friendship will forever keep me smiling.

Table of Contents

Introduction

CATALINA ISLAND. THE NAME ITSELF conjures images of paradise. Located, as the song goes, a mere 'twenty-six miles across the sea', Santa Catalina Island has a magical allure that captures the imagination of the masses.

In the spring of 1978, my future wife Maureen and I packed all our worldly possessions onto a boat and headed across the channel to Catalina, a life-altering move.

Moving from the quaint little beach town of Hermosa Beach, California—where I was a self-employed carpenter and part-time commercial fisherman and Maureen worked for a BMW car dealership in Santa Monica—to the shores of Catalina Island (the Island) turned out to be much more than we envisioned.

Thirty-two rather amazing years, two children, and a lifetime of wonderful, challenging and interesting experiences later we left the Island. Along the way there were a multitude of memorable times, personal and professional events, and a lifetime of unique stories to tell.

There were harrowing storms, exciting rescues, a few tragedies (including the death of actress Natalie Wood), dozens of encounters on the ocean and in nature, and many unique experiences that can occur only on an island where, even though it is only an hour from metropolitan Los Angeles, it is a world away from mainland life.

Some of these recollections and reflections will undoubtedly be told with a certain amount of 'literary license' since the vast majority of the details will be conjured-up from the recesses of my memories and perceptions. If errors with timelines, references, or any personal information occur, please forgive the blunders. And for the many individuals that were a part of it all please forgive any omission or oversight of 'monumental significance' that occurred but are not included, in describing the life of a Catalina Island Harbormaster.

1. The Big Move

IT WAS APRIL 1, 1978, a grey, overcast morning that was typical along the coast of southern California. With me were my girlfriend Maureen, my brother Dave and my sister Vicki.

And yes, somehow it did seem fittingly appropriate to be moving to an island on April Fools Day.

As we approached San Pedro, the fluorescent lights of the waterfront cast an eerie glow over the warehouses and wharfs of Fish Harbor in the busy back bay of the Port of Los Angeles, where I kept my boat docked. Even though it was not yet daybreak, the hustle and bustle of the commercial basin was already teeming with activity as dockworkers went about the tasks of loading and offloading fish, supplies and cargo from the ships tethered to the docks.

We wanted to get an early start to the day, realizing that it would be long and that there would likely be a few unknowns to deal with along the way. As I backed my old Dodge pickup truck as close as possible to the dock where my boat *Little Smoke* was tied, my thoughts flew randomly from the present to the past, realizing that the move we were making was vastly different from the norm, and that the lifestyle that we were accustomed to living was likely going to change rather dramatically. Nonetheless, my senses soared with anticipation and my energy level was running at a feverish pace.

Climbing out of the truck cab, I looked around for a dock cart. The bed of my pickup truck was loaded with the last of our belongings. I located a cart next to the Port Police building and wheeled it over to the truck. Dave, Vicki and Maureen were already moving the boxes and assorted personal items from the bed of the truck onto the ground. There wasn't too much left to move; we had loaded most of the larger belongings that we were taking onto the boat the day before.

Working as a team, it wasn't long before the last boxes of clothing were stuffed into the bulging forward cabin of my old boat and everything stacked around the deck was tied-down and secured in anticipation of the ocean crossing we would soon make.

I parked the pickup outside of the gates along the side of Front Street, instructing Dave to park his vehicle nearby. We headed back to the dock where the boat was tied, climbed aboard and made preparations to depart.

Little Smoke, an old Hansen designed New England style lobster boat, was built in 1954. Her ribs were bent oak and her planks Philippine mahogany. She measured thirty-two foot in length, had an eleven-foot beam and was powered with twin six cylinder Chrysler Ace engines—classic old workhorse marine engines of the forties and fifties. My brother Mike and I had bought her in a state of sad disrepair about two years previously, and I had spent the past two years restoring rails, decking, cabin, and interior, while Mike and his good buddy Jimmy Watts rebuilt the engines and repaired and upgraded the electrical system. We set her up for commercial fishing, purchased a commercial fishing license, and did a limited amount of rod and reel rock cod fishing once she was running. Since the fishing endeavor was minimal, at best, and the expenses of maintaining and docking her in Fish Harbor was a burden on Mike's limited personal budget, he had expressed no problem with me moving and taking the boat to Catalina Island.

I re-checked the oil and cooling system, inspected the bilges and fired-up the engines. They both started on cue, we cast off the lines, and pulled away from the docks. We were on the way to our new life on Catalina Island.

As the sharp semi-displacement bow of the *Little Smoke* knifed across the smooth, oily surface of the bay, tiny flecks of phosphorescence danced outward on the bow wake. Plumes of white, misty steam spewed from the stacks and industrial pipes dotting the shoreline, eliciting a vapory rainbow of color from the vast array of lights emanating from the waterfront. Passing through the narrow, rocky breakwater that leads into the outer harbor, I reached out and pushed forward on the short bronze levers of the twin throttles, increasing our speed to a steady ten knots. *Little Smoke* purred like a heartily stroked kitten.

Maureen came alongside where I was seated on the captain's chair and placed her hand on my forearm. "I can't believe we're really doing this!" she stated.

I looked at her, smiled, and answered, "Well, it's true. We are on the way, and I can't wait to get there and start our new lives together." She squeezed my arm affectionately. I flashed back briefly on the day we had met.

Maureen and I had been living together in a small cottage in Hermosa Beach. We had met one night at the 'Poop Deck', a small pub located on the strand in the little beachside town. I was tossing darts with my current girlfriend's brother, Ron Stuerke. I looked over at the pool table and saw a cute little blonde preparing to make a difficult shot. The cue ball was on the far side of the table from where she stood and she needed to reach out and try to make the shot from the near side. In order to reach the cue ball with her cue stick, she had to stand on one foot, lift her right leg up onto the edge of the table, and stretch outward. When I saw her perform that maneuver, I almost choked on my beer.

Ron laughed, fully understanding my reaction. "Pretty nice, eh?" he commented. "Would you like to meet her?"

"Sure." I gulped.

He introduced us. When I reached out to shake her hand, a slight but very noticeable jolt of current passed through my body as our fingers touched. I gripped her hand and looked into her sparkling blue eyes. Her touch continued to send tiny little waves of titillation through my system and I was momentarily stunned. I had never experienced anything quite like that, and I think I held onto her hand and gazed into her eyes for a prolonged amount of time. When I finally realized that I was caught in a trance, I grinned sheepishly and felt my cheeks flush. She smiled back, giving my hand one final squeeze before letting go. Both of us were very aware of the spark that had occurred.

We played a game or two of pool, and a few weeks later I dumped my girlfriend and we moved in together. Now here we were on a boat heading off to live on a remote island.

There wasn't much boat traffic yet, and visibility was limited because of the gray canopy of a heavy marine layer that hung over the water, but we could see and feel an occasional boat wake as we ploughed toward the entrance at Angels Gate, the outer breakwater of Los Angeles Harbor. Rounding out around the L.A. Light, I checked the compass heading and steadied the boat onto a course of two hundred seven degrees, heading for the Isthmus of Catalina. I felt very comfortable about our compass heading, having purchased and installed a brand new Navigator Compass earlier in the week.

Once outside of the harbor entrance a slight southwest swell lifted and lowered the boat as it chugged seaward. Seagulls cawed in the milky darkness, ready to begin their insistent quest of hunting for food in the vast expanses of the surrounding sea. Not more than a mile from the breakwater entrance we became engulfed in the murkiness of a developing twilight, augmented by the presence of the persistent marine layer. It was a relief to know that daylight was not far away; there is always something disconcerting about cruising on the ocean in darkness, a noticeable sense of not knowing what is out there.

I was seated on the captain's chair with a small padded 'lift box' set atop the seat so that my head poked out above the cabin hatch, thus giving me improved visibility. I kept a close eye on the compass, depending upon it to steer us toward our destination, some twenty miles away.

Maureen and my sister Vicki kept up a steady diet of chatter as we motored to seaward, while Dave and I sat quietly in the two helm seats pondering our own thoughts as they chatted. We all pondered the unknowns about our new adventure and what we might expect to encounter once we were settled.

Maureen filled Vicki in on how we had come to the decision to move to Catalina.

"We were really just looking for something new and exciting to do," Maureen explained. "Initially, we looked into moving to the Marquesas Islands, a US territory that was actively seeking American citizens to invest or simply move to and work in the islands. It appeared that there was an abundance of opportunity for a young couple and we thought very seriously about going there. But it was a long way from home, family and friends, and so when we heard about a job opening on Catalina Island, we decided to look into it."

Vicki interrupted her and asked, "How long ago did you hear about this?"

"Less than a month ago," Maureen continued, "Doug has a friend, a couple that lives on a boat and they went to work on the Island for the summer. When they left the Island and returned to Redondo Beach, they got together with Doug and told him about a job opening for a bookkeeper at the Isthmus. I phoned, got an interview with Doug Bombard and his son Randy, the people who manage the Island operation, and they liked me. I was offered a job that same day."

"What about Doug?" Vicki asked. "How does he fit into the picture?"

"Well, that was interesting," Maureen chuckled. "When I told them about him, that he was a carpenter, did boat work and commercial fished, they said that he sounded just like the kind of person they needed on the Island. They told me he 'could come along'. So a couple of weeks ago they invited us to the Island for the weekend to look things over. We stayed at the Banning House Lodge, looked at housing, and basically just checked everything out. When we got back home we gave notice to our employers and started preparing to move. Now here we are on the boat heading for our new home."

"Wow!" Vicki exclaimed, "Sounds like you guys don't mess around when it comes to making big decisions."

"Well, like I said, we were feeling stagnant and just needed a change in our lives. We're going to give it a try for a while. We're thinking that we will stay for one year. It will certainly be different, but we are excited and looking forward to the change."

About that time, the first vestiges of daylight were lightening the morning sky. As the light improved, a silvery glow began to spread across the sea surface, its metallic looking sheen casting rippled shadows on the subtle undulations of the moderate southwest swells. When the sun climbed over the eastern horizon, its muted rays cast a fiery glow onto the mirrored sea surface. The marine layer was thick enough to prevent the sun from being wholly visible, but its presence was marked by a spreading brilliance causing all aboard the *Little Smoke* to squint and don our sunglasses.

We were about an hour out of port, a little less than halfway to our destination. I lifted the engine hatch to check the bilges. The steady throb of the engines filled the cabin with a mild roar. Everything looked in order in the bilge, so I closed the hatch cover and returned to the helm. Visibility was still quite limited, although the advent of daylight lent a more comfortable feeling to all aboard.

About that time a pod of several hundred dolphins suddenly appeared around the boat. From all sides the cavorting mammals raced and leaped from the gray-blue depths, their shimmering bodies soaring out of the water and then gracefully splashing back into the ocean. Dave, Vicki and Maureen ran out onto the foredeck to watch the spectacle, while I climbed up onto the lip of the cabin hatch in order to get a better view, steering the boat with my feet. All around, the beautiful animals swam, leaped and danced, their antics generating 'oohs' and 'aahs' from all of us. At the bow of the boat, two of the playful animals glided gracefully on the small wake of the prow, one on each side, and their powerful tails flicked only slightly to maintain their position. Occasionally they turned onto their side, their large black eyes seeming to glance upward to acknowledge the presence of the three humans standing on deck watching them swim. Periodically the dolphins rose to the surface and ejected a spout of seawater from their blowhole while releasing a sharp squeal in the process. The dolphin pod stayed with us for close to fifteen minutes before disappearing into the enveloping gray shadows that clung tenaciously to the surrounding ocean surface.

Another hour passed and I began to wonder why we had not yet seen the Island. We were now more than two-and-a-half hours from port and I fully expected to see land popping out of the misty gray. I slowed the engines to idle forward and spoke to the others.

"We really should be seeing land by now," I told them. "Why don't you all go out on deck and see if you can see or hear anything."

As the others went out onto the foredeck, I shut down the engines. An all-encompassing quiet engulfed the boat. Only the muffled sounds of the rippled sea surface gurgled against the hull. A gull could be heard squawking somewhere in the gray, but we could not see it through the low hanging shroud. Above us the sky glowed pale blue, an indication that the marine layer was burning away, but at sea level the visibility remained less than a mile. As we all looked around and listened, I caught a brief flash of something off our port stern. Gazing in that direction I recognized the vague outline of what appeared to be a small boat.

"Hey, guys, there's something over there," I called out, pointing in the direction of the muted shadow that had caught my attention. "I think it's another boat. I'm going to head over that way and see if we can find out where we are."

Restarting the engines, I put *Little Smoke* into gear and motored in the direction where I had spotted the other boat. As we moved closer it soon became obvious that there was a small fishing boat drifting on the small, undulating swells. When we neared the boat, I put the engines into neutral and drifted nearby calling out, "Good morning." We seem to be a little lost in the fog. Can you tell us where we are, or where Catalina is?"

We could hear chuckles coming from all three men onboard as they looked at each other, obviously thinking that we must be idiots to be 'lost' at sea. One of the men spoke out. "You're about two miles from the West End," he informed us, pointing toward the east. "You can see the outline of the Island over there."

Sure enough, when I looked in the direction he was pointing, I could see a very vague outline of the Island above the low cloud layer. I think all of us were focusing too much on the sea surface while looking around and did not recognize the outline of the ridge top of the Island.

"Great. Thanks for your help. Good luck fishing," I told them.

Back at the helm station, I shoved the two cast-iron bars of the gearshift levers into forward and turned the wheel toward the tip of the Island. Soon we were rounding 'Lands End' on the western tip of Catalina and cruising along the leeside toward the Isthmus.

Our little fiasco of 'getting lost' on our move to the Island was ultimately one of the little 'lessons of the sea' that would serve me well in later years.

As mentioned previously, I had purchased and installed a new compass about a week prior to our departure. When I attached it to the console top in the main cabin, I presumed that it would perform properly—after all, it was brand new and the salesman at the West Marine store assured me that it was more than adequate for my boat. What I did not know at the time is that magnetic forces from metal objects can affect the performance of a compass, and even though I was aware of deviation tendencies from magnetic to geographical north, I was not aware that the influence from metals could significantly alter a compass' reliability. As a consequence, when I installed the compass, I mounted it directly forward of the helm station, where the operator could see it easily. Unfortunately, the gear levers on the *Little Smoke* were cast steel levers, painted gray, and about eighteen inches long. When engaged, the levers moved to within six inches of the compass, thus exerting metallic influences onto the magnetic field of the compass and throwing the actual heading off by nearly thirty degrees. I had not taken the boat out since installing the compass, and so the deviation from my presumed heading put us way off course. I moved the compass to a less affected location a couple of weeks later, learning a valuable lesson along the way.

Later in my career, when I began giving 'Discover Catalina' seminars to groups on the mainland, I was to use that embarrassing story as one of my informative lessons for new boaters.

Once we were inside of the lee of the West End, the Island terrain became beautiful, covered in a lush layer of spring green grasses in the lower reaches and dotted with thick, dark green foliage in the higher elevations. Along the ridges a burnished red soil, peppered with patches of the dark green bushes, gave the scenery a vision of stark and artistic beauty. Along the shore, steep cliffs tumbled into the majestic blue waters where thick patches of floating kelp beds wafted lazily upon the calm sea surface. As we moved eastward, the cliffs ended quite abruptly, replaced by an expanse of a long pebbled beach that rose gradually toward low rolling hills. There was a small boat moored on a single mooring tucked into a tiny little cove nestled behind a low rocky cliff. Two small tents could be seen situated on another low bluff nearby. Dave pulled out the chart guide for the Island and informed us that we were looking at Parsons Landing and Starlight Beach.

Continuing eastward we passed the steep, bold promontory of Arrow Point, the rocky headland that breaks the incessant onslaught of the prevailing westerly winds and swells. Rounding that point, the calm seas laid down even more, flattening to a mirrored surface that brightly reflected the rays of the early morning sun.

Rounding Lion Head Point, a bold promontory that clearly resembles the head of a lion when approaching from the south, we passed by Cherry Cove and Fourth of July Cove, and then entered Isthmus Cove, with its two hundred forty-nine moorings and the small paradise that would become our Island home for the next thirty-two years.

Isthmus Cove is one of two primary recreational destinations on Catalina Island. Avalon, near the eastern end of the Island is the busiest, existing on the one square mile of publicly available land that can be bought and sold by the general public. The Wrigley family, who own the Island, deeded most of the remaining eighty-six thousand acres in

1976 to the privately operated, non-profit Catalina Island Conservancy, to be 'maintained and managed in its natural state in perpetuity'. The remaining parcels of land (excluding Avalon, which was deeded by the Wrigley family and incorporated as a city) are owned and operated by the Santa Catalina Island Company, at that time under the leadership of William 'Bill' Wrigley.

William Wrigley Jr. purchased the Island from the Banning Brothers in 1919. He served as chairman of the board in those early years, and envisioned the Island as a prime recreational destination for southern California boaters, residents and visitors. His vision was to make Catalina a resort destination where 'the everyday person' could share and enjoy the Island that he cherished so dearly.

Two Harbors, or the Isthmus as it was more commonly referred to in those days, is a boater's destination featuring nearly four hundred moorings in the immediate area, a campground, general store and one restaurant. It was managed by Doug Bombard, who served as president of the operation and agent for the Santa Catalina Island Company.

Doug Bombard had assumed leadership of the Isthmus in the mid-fifties, moving from Avalon with his family and taking over the operation from former manager Press Taylor. The Bombard family has a long and distinguished history on the Island. Doug's father, Al Bombard, had served as Mayor of Avalon, started-up the storied Catalina Speed Boat operation in Avalon, and was deeply rooted into the Island community.

Doug and his delightful wife Audrey had four children, Randy, Greg, Wendy, and Tim. All four of them moved to the Isthmus when he took over the operation and all were working in one capacity or another when we arrived on the Island. Our interaction and relationship with all of the Bombards' helped to shape our future on the Island.

We pulled into the floating dock and were greeted by one of the resident Harbor Department employee's, Tim Taylor. Tim was one of the prototypical individuals that made his way to the Island and found a niche working in the Harbor Department for a few years. As with many of the hundreds of other people we met and worked with during our thirty-two years on the Island, he worked and lived and enjoyed island life until it was time to move on to other things. There are not a lot of other residents who stayed on as we did, but there are a few who have outlasted us and are still there.

As we unloaded our belongings onto the dock, one of the maintenance crewmen, Chris Peterson, met us on the pier with a pickup truck to help move our belongings to our new house.

On our introductory visit to the Island to check things out we were offered the choice of moving into a two-bedroom mobile home located in the small employee housing complex near the upper shop, on the west side of the tiny community, or a small, one-bedroom house just up from the beach on the east side of the cove. We asked to see the one-bedroom house first and after seeing it, we told them we did not need to look at the other. The little one-bedroom house was perfect!

Built as a bathhouse for a movie crew working on the original 'Mutiny on the Bounty' film, the small house was converted a few years later into a tiny five hundred-fifty square foot housing unit. It was later expanded to about seven hundred square feet with the addition of a 'living room' a few years before we moved in, and then underwent numerous changes during our years living there. It was approximately seventy-five steps from the beach on a short bluff overlooking Isthmus Cove. When we saw the views from the living room, porch and yard, we were entranced. The entire bay was visible from our vantage point, with the two tiny 'islands' of Bird and Ship Rock projecting out of the clear blue waters as the silent sentinels that mariners look for on their approaches into the cove. We felt a little like modern day versions of Swiss Family Robinson, cast upon the shores of our own little island in the sea.

The house required some immediate attention, having been damaged several weeks previously when a large eucalyptus tree crashed onto the kitchen corner of the house during a particularly vicious late January storm. That storm, packing winds of close to one hundred miles per hour, did considerable damage throughout the community. In addition to the tree that crushed the corner of our 'new home', it also damaged several other homes, blew down one of the exterior walls at the restaurant (Doug's Harbor Reef—the only restaurant 'in town'), ripped away part of the roof of the Isthmus Yacht Club, damaged part of the roof of the Banning House Lodge (the former home of the Banning Brothers who owned the Island prior to the Wrigley family), knocked over fences, blew down trees, and generally made a mess of the tiny hamlet of Two Harbors.

Steve and Gladys Porter, the couple Maureen and I were replacing in the house, had managed to patch things up enough to keep the house livable, but it still needed some serious attention. One of the first jobs I worked on with George McElroy was to dig out the kitchen corner of the house, jack it up with a portable fifteen-ton hydraulic jack, and place concrete blocks under the corner for support. That support job served to last through our entire tenure in the house, but the foundation slowly collapsed through the years to the point where anything round that fell onto the floor rolled immediately toward the eastern wall. The drop in the floor was so extreme that when Maureen, who stands five-feet two inches tall, stood at the high end of the kitchen, and I, at six-feet tall, stood at the lower side we were looking eye to eye. She relished the opportunity to stand 'on the high spot' when we had 'serious discussions' about anything—it gave her a heightened sense of advantage.

As often occurs on the Island, Maureen and I moved into the house and took over the positions of the two people we were replacing. Gladys Porter worked in the accounting office and her husband Steve worked in the Harbor Department. They were a very nice couple that had simply had enough of island life and moved on to other venues.

Maureen's job and position were of utmost importance to the company. She brought a solid bookkeeping background into the job and her talents were sorely needed as the company prepared for the busy summer season. She had a lot to learn about many aspects of the job and what it takes to operate a self-sustained, privately run community, but she possessed the basic fundamentals of bookkeeping and administration through her previous work experience in the auto industry. She jumped into her new job with eager enthusiasm and very quickly proved herself to be capable, reliable and trustworthy.

When I started working, my first job was to help repair the damages from the hurricane force winds that had wreaked havoc a few weeks previously. I started working for George McElroy the General Foreman of the Catalina Cove and Camp Agency.

George was a mountain of a man, strong as an ox, a devout family man and more versatile and talented than any man I have ever known. He was married to Doreen McElroy, Doug Bombards' sister, and had moved to the Isthmus from Avalon in the mid 1950's when Doug accepted an offer from the Santa Catalina Island Company to move to, and oversee the entire Isthmus operation. In Avalon, George had owned and operated a bakery, but when the opportunity arose to move to the Isthmus, he accepted the move immediately. George had four children with Doreen, David, Ann, Stephen, and Kim, and another daughter Pam from a previous marriage. All but Pam lived on the Island and worked, or would later work for the company. The McElroy's and the Bombards formed the heart and soul of the Isthmus community and their two families combined to build the dynasty that would oversee the Isthmus operation for more than forty years.

I cannot say enough about George McElroy and his talents and character. He could build, repair, maintain, and engineer anything and everything that was needed in the entire 'town'. He operated the heavy equipment, maintained the machinery, installed, repaired and maintained all of the plumbing, electrical, and physical structures of the operation, and oversaw all of the dozen or so departments that kept the small town running.

As a boss, he was firm and demanding, and yet fair. Despite his outwardly gruff exterior, he also had a real soft spot for kids, family and friends. He, more than any other man I have ever known (my own father died when I was fifteen), served as a father figure for me throughout the many years that I worked with and alongside of him. He taught me how to do many things, but even more importantly, he instilled in me the work ethic that I believe helped me to achieve my role as a manager, leader and reliable employee during my years on the Island. His overall philosophy was simple, "Give me an honest day's work and I'll stand behind you." He did that from the very beginning and stood behind me until his retirement in 1992.

His 'sidekick' and good friend Roy Clark worked alongside George during my early years. Roy's strongest talent was electrical, but he, like nearly everyone who stayed for any length of time on the Island, learned to be versatile and multi-talented. Roy and another maintenance employee, Ken Danek, were to be my primary co-workers during my first year.

As mentioned previously, the damages caused by the big January storm wreaked havoc throughout the little community of approximately eighty year-round residents (the population was to double to about one hundred-sixty year-round residents during the next three decades). I started working for George to help with the repairs and rebuilding of the damaged homes and other structures.

One of the first projects I worked on was to help replace the roofing material torn off of the old Civil War Barracks which had housed the Coast Guard in World War II, served as a Girl Scout facility, housed Hollywood filmmakers through the years, and was currently converted into the Isthmus Yacht Club. I began working with George and Ken, first ripping off the old, torn roofing material, and then replacing it with new. One of my first impressions of George and his brute strength was when he grabbed two of the heavy (about sixty pounds each) rolled roofing packages, and climbed up the ladder carrying one on each shoulder. I thought I would try to emulate him by picking up two of my own rolls, but found that it was all I could do to lift and carry one of the rolls up the ladder and onto the rooftop.

About halfway through the project, while Ken and I kneeled on the plywood sheeting driving nails, I suddenly felt the plywood collapse under my knees and I crashed down through the rotten wood and onto the struts supporting the inner ceiling. My legs were straddling one of the beams with my feet dangling through broken drywall and into one of the rooms of a club member. Ken called for help and George and Roy helped get me out of the predicament by removing the rotten piece of sheeting on the roof and lowering down a rope harness that they then used to pull me back up onto the rooftop. I suffered a few scrapes and bruises, but fortunately was not seriously injured. Discovering the rotten plywood added a few extra days of work to the roof repair.

Following the yacht club job, we moved on and made a similar repair to the Banning House roof, replaced and modified the wind-wall that sheltered the outside patio of the restaurant, worked on a few homes and repaired a few fences. During one of those jobs, the modification of one of the small houses just up the hill from our house, I recognized the true ability of Roy Clark's electrical talents.

We were working on the little house where Johnny 'Pop' Vaughan had been living. It was a tiny one-bedroom cottage where 'Pop' had lived for several years. He had just moved back to the mainland and the house needed some serious attention. In its living room, the large front window hinged upward on a pulley system to open-up the front room to the great outdoors. The window hinges were decayed, the pulley system frazzled, and the window trim rotten. We planned to replace it with a standard picture window. Additionally, we planned to move a small shed structure alongside the house, open up the west wall, and attach the shed to the wall to add a second bedroom to the house.

In the process of doing that work, we ripped out nearly all of the wiring throughout the entire home. Roy then replaced the wiring, fixtures, switches and fuse panel. When the job was completed, we hit the light switch in the living room and the light did not go on. 'Darn', I thought to myself, 'Roy is going to have a heck of a time trying to trace out that problem'

To the contrary, he did not hesitate, stating simply, "The light bulb must be burnt out."

Skeptical, I looked at him and smiled. In my mind it was far more likely that something in the process of replacing and splicing-in all the new wires must have gone wrong, but when Roy replaced the light bulb, the light came on right on queue. I never questioned Roy's talents after that.

2. A Step Back in Time

WE DISCOVERED THAT LIVING ON an island is very different. There are no streets, no concrete, no traffic lights or stop signs, no malls, shopping centers, movie houses, hardware stores, or anything except one little general store and one restaurant. If you are socially dependent on anything except family, friends, and the great outdoors, it is not the place for you. On the plus side, there is almost no crime, no traffic, no noise, except some boat noise, weekend rowdiness in the summer, and plenty of fresh air and scenic beauty. We did not lock our house, we left the car keys in the ignition, we had about thirty 'mothers' to keep an extra eye out for our kids, and the company did, or at least paid for, most repairs and maintenance to our house. Life, we soon learned, was simple and easy—in most respects—a lot like it was when I was a kid growing up in the fifties. It truly was like a step back in time.

Maureen and I were adjusting to Island life. For me, the adjustment was easy; I absolutely loved living on the Island. For Maureen, however, the adjustment was more difficult. She missed the conveniences of mainland living—the shopping, the entertainment, and her friends. It was radically different living on a remote island where there was only one tiny general store, one restaurant, and very limited resources for traveling to and from the Island. In addition, it was somewhat difficult to get accepted into the tiny community. The locals were very nice and welcoming, but due to the transient nature of the community, which saw the population fluctuate dramatically from summer to winter, the permanent population tended to be somewhat aloof and was reticent to embrace 'newcomers' until they had lasted at least a year.

Even though the adjustment to Island life was somewhat difficult, we were enjoying ourselves. There were some epic parties. Because of the relatively youthful orientation of the residents (most were in their twenties), the party atmosphere was considerable. On any given weekend, you could depend upon at least one party per night, often lasting into the wee hours of the morning. There was an unwritten code for the partygoers, 'party hearty but show up to work'! For the most part, that code was adhered to diligently, but it was not too uncommon for someone to arrive at work on time, but then be sent home to 'sober-up'.

We were also beginning to meet and get to know some of the regular boaters that made the Isthmus their favorite getaway. Each weekend, hundreds of boats headed out to the Island for a day or two, or more. Many of those visitors made the journey on a regular basis, some of them every weekend of the summer. The diversion of having those visitors helped Maureen's adjustment to the remoteness of island living a little easier.

We spent many a warm summer evening at the outside patio of Doug's Harbor Reef Restaurant, listening to music, mingling with both locals and visitors, and enjoying the party atmosphere that occurs every weekend night of the summer. Among the first of our many interactions with regular visitors was the friendship we developed with one of the Seal Beach Yacht Club members, Ed O'Conner and his wife Joan. Ed was a real character who loved to sing and play his tiny little brass flutes and whistles while leading everyone around him in song. He was the life of the party and always kept everyone entertained.

That first year for us went quickly, both of us working, learning the ins and outs of the operation, and adjusting to our new lives. When fall arrived and the seasonal ritual of visitor traffic slowed, Maureen got her first real taste of 'Island Fever.'

Being so cut off from the mainstream flow of daily life, she desperately needed to get off the Island and reconnect with both mainland friends and family. She hopped aboard the *Catalina King*, currently the only cross channel carrier, and took a weekend off to go 'overtown' and revisit her previous life. I stayed on the Island and worked. The getaway worked wonders for her and, when she returned home, her appreciation for the Island was reestablished, at least for a while.

To clarify the 'over-town' reference, the locals have developed three names to distinguish the difference between going to the mainland, to Avalon, or to the Isthmus itself. 'Over-town' refers to the mainland, 'In-town' refers to Avalon, and 'Downtown' refers to the Isthmus proper. Those idioms were words we came to use on a regular basis and will apply henceforth.

Somewhere along the way, after we were on the Island for a few months, we made plans to be married. In the latter stages of summer and leading into the fall months, Maureen was preoccupied with putting together the plans and logistics for our Island wedding.

Getting married on an Island is not an easy undertaking. There are the transportation issues, housing and accommodation arrangements, weather to consider, and most challenging, the logistical process of getting all the things needed in order to put together a 'respectable' wedding in a remote locale. We both come from large families, eight children in mine, six in hers. While I was without parents or grandparents, Maureen had her father, an eighty-year old grandmother, and a sixty-one year old uncle to accommodate.

Somehow she managed to pull it all off, and on a lovely fall day on October 14, 1978, we were married in the courtyard of the Banning House Lodge overlooking Two Harbors. Or at least we thought we were. As it turned out, much to our chagrin some twenty-years later, we discovered that our wedding vows were never officially recorded. It turned into one of the many stories in our lives that we recall with mixed emotions.

Avalon Minister Dr. Bob Burton, an erstwhile minister of the esteemed Universal Life Church, performed the ceremony. The only problem, we discovered years later, was that Dr. Bob had neglected to register our marriage with the Los Angeles County Registrar's Office, and when Maureen tried to find our wedding certificate to provide proof of our marriage, the Registrar's Office told us that we were not legally married.

With two children, twenty years of life together, and both of our lives entwined with the links of that holiest of institutions, we were quite surprised—to say the least—to discover that we were not 'officially' married.

To try and rectify that dilemma, we made a trip overtown to the County Registrar's Office in Norwalk. When we arrived at the County building, we encountered another surprise; the employees were all on strike. Marching around the perimeter of the site, the strike workers presented a picket line that attempted to keep anyone from crossing. Inasmuch as we had taken a day off, made the long boat ride from the Island, and could not wait for the strike to end, we crossed the picket line to see if anything could be done.

Arriving at the front doors of the building, we encountered a few people standing around seemingly waiting for something to happen. Maureen began talking with one of the ladies, telling her about our situation. A few minutes later a gentleman in a suit approached Maureen and asked if she would mind explaining our predicament to him again. Somewhat confused, Maureen agreed to repeat what she had said.

The man asked her to wait just a moment, waved over another man who was holding a large movie camera, and set up a tripod. "Okay," he commented, "Now would you please explain your predicament for our viewers?" He was a reporter for Channel 5 News.

Maureen, thinking that not too many people watched the Channel 5 news at around nine a.m., repeated our story on camera, explaining what had happened with our wedding papers, and the ordeal that we had to go through in order to try and rectify the problem. She was quite surprised to receive several phone calls later from friends who had seen her on the news.

Eventually we resolved the problem, and received a certificate with our actual wedding date inscribed, but not before we had to secure signed affidavits from a couple of friends and relatives who attended our wedding, getting a judge and a notary to sign-off on the paperwork, and resubmitting the documents to the Registrar's Office. For both of us it was a relief to finally obtain the proof that we were indeed legally married and that our kids were not illegitimate.

As for the wedding itself, quite surprisingly, it went off smoothly. Most of our guests traveled to the Island on the Catalina Cruise Line boat, but Grandma Mary, Uncle Bud and a couple other family members flew across on the seaplane. In 1978 the seaplanes were still operating and flying to and from the mainland on one of the old Grumman Gooses was quite an experience for all.

Another highlight of the wedding, for me anyway, was when I climbed aboard one of the stabled horses that were available to rent and took my young niece Monica, my sister Sheri's youngest daughter, for a ride around the Banning House grounds—in our wedding clothes. That moment of 'horsing around' did not set real well with Maureen, but it did become one of the stories from our wedding that would be retold at family gatherings over the years.

Following the wedding, we settled in as newlyweds to spend our first winter on the Island. It was quite different living in a place where there were no roads, very little concrete, and therefore plenty of mud. When it rained, the dirt roads and paths turned into a gooey quagmire of thick, sticky ooze that became very difficult to drive, or walk upon. It was something that we learned to deal with from the very beginning, and a reality that still exists today.

We learned rather quickly that the elements of nature are felt and seen much more vividly when living on an island. From our vantage point overlooking Isthmus Cove, we marveled at the beauties and power of nature when storms blew in. Northeasters, the powerful Santa Ana winds that scour southern California during late fall and winter, are particularly threatening for residents of the Island. I would get to know them quite well in coming years. Southeasters, the rain producing systems that affect Island shores, are a blessing for the Island's limited water resources, but often create chaos and bedlam when the strong systems develop. Westerly winds, Northerlies, Southerlies, they all have their own unique effects on the Island and for those who work on the water, the inevitable wind related problems and challenges. I was to learn those lessons very personally.

3. *Of Whales and Other Tales*

ON ONE PARTICULARLY CALM AND warm Saturday in late February, Maureen and I decided to take our boat, the *Little Smoke,* out to the west end of the Island on a whale watching excursion. We packed up a lunch, grabbed binoculars and the camera, and headed west. It was peak season for whale watching on the Island, with the California gray whale migration in full swing. We had seen several spouts from our living room window while gazing out to sea, and decided it was time to get a closer look. I had made several whale watch trips in the past, on the mainland, and so I was familiar with the rules and guidelines for approaching the whales.

Cruising comfortably along the front side of the Island, we marveled at the beauty and tranquility of the Island and its surrounding waters. The green patina of spring grasses spread a verdant glow across the hillsides, and the shimmering blue waters of the Pacific lent a magical sparkle to the balmy mid-morning air. Along the ridge tops, and in several clearings, we spotted both wild goats and feral pigs foraging for sustenance. Dozens of sea lions and a few harbor seals sprawled leisurely along the rocky shoreline, or popped their shiny heads from the kelp beds as they deftly sought unsuspecting prey. Nature engulfed us in its splendor, overwhelming our senses and instilling us with awe.

Rounding the tip of the Island, a prevailing ground swell met the land mass and surged into the steep rocky shoreline creating a swirl of thick gray foam around the sharp pinnacles that jut from the ocean at land's end. That swell was noticeable as we rose to the crest and dipped into the trough, but it was so widely spaced—at about eighteen seconds duration—that once we were clear of the headland, it was barely perceptible.

We were not more than a mile from the tip of the Island when I spotted the distinctive spout from a whale. Turning to Maureen, I pointed toward the spout and headed in that direction. It was perhaps half a mile away and, as we got closer, the whale spouted several times and I realized that there was something a little odd about the way it looked. When we got to within a couple of hundred yards, I slowed the engines to idle forward and turned the helm to a heading that I considered to be in sync with the direction the whale was traveling.

After a couple of minutes, it rose to the surface not more than one hundred yards off our bow. At that point, I became very confused. Rather than rising to the surface in a slow, methodical surge, the medium sized leviathan seemed to be churning the surface in an agitating manner as it rose to spout. When it fluked, I blinked and shook my head in confusion. Something looked very wrong.

"I'm not sure what we are seeing," I said to Maureen. "Either that is not a gray whale, or there is something really different about it. Get ready with the camera so we can take a picture the next time it surfaces."

I was aware that when a whale flukes, it usually means that it is diving down deeper, often to avoid the presence of a pursuing boat. I suspected that it might alter its course, swim off in another direction, and resurface in another location. I shifted the boat into neutral and waited, gazing around in a full circle to try and spot the spout once again. Sure enough, the whale had changed its course quite radically, emerging about a quarter mile to our port side. I altered course and headed in that direction. Arriving in the vicinity I again shifted into slow forward, holding a steady course in the direction that I thought it might resurface. Moments later the whale spouted, not more than fifty yards to port.

I recognized the whale as a medium sized gray, but there was definitely something different about the way it looked. There was a whitish glow along its tail section, and it seemed to be thrashing unusually as it rose to the surface to breathe. I told Maureen to be ready with the camera. Two or three times it rose up and spouted, and each time I tried to look closely and ascertain what was so different about its appearance. I realized that the whale appeared to be swimming on the surface in a back and forth motion, rather than the normal up and down manner that most whales use. Then it spouted again, surged higher out of the water, and fluked. Maureen was ready for the motion and snapped a quick picture. My jaw dropped open when I realized that we were looking at a whale without a tail!

Dumbfounded, I turned to Maureen. "Did you see that?" I asked incredulously. "It didn't have a tail!"

"That's what I thought," she responded questioningly, "How could that be?"

"I don't know," I answered, "But that explains what looked so odd."

We gazed at the spot where it had sounded; pondering the unusual sight we had just seen. After a moment, I suggested we wait and watch for it to resurface again so that we might get another picture, hoping to capture the presence of the white angular stump where the tail should have been.

When we returned home, I was anxious to have the pictures developed to see what we might have captured on film. We made a special trip into Avalon, dropped the film cartridge off at the photo shop and did some grocery shopping. When we were done, we went back to the shop to see if the pictures were ready. They were, and two of them had caught the whale as it fluked, clearly and remarkably confirming that the whale was tailless.

I contacted the American Cetacean Society in San Pedro and told them about our experience. They asked if we could send the photos, and since we had made double copies, I agreed to send them over.

A few days later I received a phone call from a young girl who was very familiar with whales, and we talked for nearly an hour about the oddity. She told me that it was indeed very rare to witness such a spectacle, but it was not the first time they had seen a tailless whale. They had six other photos of whales existing in the wild without tails. She went on to explain that the one we had seen, and likely all the others, had probably gotten their tails wrapped in either fishing lines, or nets, and dragged those lines or nets around behind them for several weeks, or months. As the lines or nets contracted with the up and down swimming motion, the damaging material slowly but inexorably tightened around the base of their tail until all circulation was cutoff and the tail rotted away and fell off. As an adaptive means of survival, the whales then learned to swim in a side-to-side method, like a fish. She told me that they were posting the photos in their archives, and identifying it as the 'Catalina Tailless Whale'.

As that first winter came to a close, I was beginning to feel restless and frustrated. I had moved to the Island with the hope of working on the water, and yet I was still working for the maintenance department. Most of the big projects of repairing the damages from the previous year's storm were completed, and so I was working on more mundane, routine repair and maintenance tasks. When I talked with George about moving into the Harbor Department, he said he would look into it for me.

For several more weeks I continued with the maintenance crew, roofing another house, converting a small shed into a tiny little cottage for our friend Laura LaFlamme to live in, and building some plywood cabinets for another house. Needing a break, I talked with George and was given a couple of weeks off. Then one afternoon I bumped into Doug Bombard in the Isthmus plaza and he asked me what I was doing.

"Well, I'm currently taking a couple of weeks off," I hesitated, and when he did not respond immediately, I continued, "I was really hoping

I might be able to find some work on the water. That was my goal when I moved here, to work on the water. It's been great working with George, but I think we have most of the repairs finished that were needed, and if there is anything I might be able to do to get out on boats…well, that's kind of my dream."

Doug chuckled and looked at me, "I'll talk with Randy. We'll let you know if there is anything available in the Harbor Department."

Randy was Doug's oldest son. He had recently returned from the mainland where he had worked for Briles Helicopter Services in San Pedro, and had taken over the duties of Harbormaster when his brother Greg moved off the Island. A few days later Randy stopped me as I was walking on the pier and he told me that he had a job opening in the Harbor Department, if I was interested. I jumped at the opportunity and my career in the Isthmus Harbor Department began.

Operating boats came easily to me. As a longtime fisherman I had spent a lot of time on the water, primarily on small skiffs. But I also had learned to operate the twin-screw fishing boat that we had brought to the Island. I took to running the Harbor Patrol boats like a duck takes to water. I also picked-up rather quickly the basics of performing the various patrol duties that were in place, collecting mooring fees, assisting boats onto moorings, responding to radio traffic, and learning the basic administration duties of a harbor patrolman.

Laurie 'Flea' Andreson was serving as manager of the Harbor Office during my first year in the Harbor Department. Working with Laurie, I learned the basics of contracts administration, the intricacies of leasing and overseeing the Mooring Sublease process, and the somewhat complicated method of issuing and renewing the seven-hundred-twenty moorings that were available around the Island for members of the boating community to lease and use.

At the time, there were two 'types' of moorings in the scope of our operation, 'private' and public. The 'private' moorings were 'owned' by individual boaters and the public moorings were leased to members of the public on a one-year renewable basis. That process was to change dramatically in 1982 and become a contentious battle between the private owners and the California State Lands Commission—with us caught in the middle—for years to come.

For me, as a rookie Harbor Patrolman, the distinction between the private and the leased moorings was simple. We rented the leased moorings (sixty-five percent of the seven hundred twenty) to the general boating public when they were not in use by the Sublessee, and we ignored the users of the private moorings. Both types of moorings were serviced by our Mooring Service crew but the private moorings, identified as No PTR (No Permission to Rent) moorings, were not under our jurisdiction. About thirty-five percent of the moorings were 'privately owned' and were scattered throughout the eleven coves within our operation.

The primary duty of a patrolman was to relocate transient boats on moorings for a Sublessee who had reserved their mooring for themselves or a guest, and to collect mooring fees from the guests and the transient boats using the moorings. If a boat was on one of the private 'No PTR' moorings, we ignored it completely; even if the 'owner' of that mooring complained to us that there was another boat on their mooring. Since they had not given the company their permission to rent it to the public, the company was not obligated to move any other boats off those moorings. In a couple of the coves, Moonstone Cove and Howlands Landing, the shore-based yacht club (Newport Harbor and Los Angeles Yacht Club, respectively), 'policed' the coves with their own cove steward.

Keeping track of records of the moored boats was rather lax and relatively easy in those early days as a patrolman. We used printed sheets with mooring reservations written in by hand, and sometimes, when the office girls were unavailable, we even used erase-it boards to keep track of transient boats. In addition, commercial fishing boats, all transient boats that picked-up No PTR moorings, and quite often other boats that just picked up empty moorings on their own, did not pay mooring fees simply because of the lack of record keeping.

I was really enjoying my new career on the water, operating boats every day and interacting with the boating public. It didn't pay much, right around minimum wage, which at the time I think was around six dollars an hour, but I was working on the water, driving boats, meeting a lot of great people, and was very happy with my new and lovely little bride. I also experienced my first taste of winter duties and storm response.

———— ⟋⟍⟋⟍ ————

In our early years we also learned to cope with, and learn how to provide for ourselves, when living on a remote island.

Seafood was abundant, and being a fisherman at heart, I was living in a dream world. Having the *Little Smoke* to go out fishing in was a real plus. In those days fuel costs were not really an issue. Gas was around eighty-five cents a gallon and I went fishing whenever I could. Halibut, calico bass, rock cod, bonito, yellowtail, and even the highly prized and elusive white seabass were abundant at different times of the year, and we enjoyed the spoils of catching and eating all of them.

Additionally, both abalone and lobster were readily available in season. I quickly discovered that during the winter months when neap tides were in evidence, we could go out onto the rocks at several locations and pop-off abalone with ease. Abalone were so abundant in a few remote Island locations, that several residents went out at those low tide periods and gathered gunny-sacks full of the prized mollusks which they then sold to Avalon or mainland fish markets. Similarly, lobster populations were so thick that a set of one or two traps could result in a trap bulging with the spiny crustaceans. We ate so many abalone and lobster in those early years that Maureen got 'sick' of eating them.

We also discovered that obtaining other foods and personal items was not very easy. There was the little general store 'downtown', that stocked basic dry goods and other essentials, but rarely had anything fresh, and everything was very expensive. The general store was known as 'Dottie's Deli' at the time, in deference to its manager Dottie Peterson. Dottie and her husband Pete were fixtures in the community, a delightful couple who had lived there for many years. Dottie ran and operated the store and Pete worked at the time for the Mooring Service. They were a wonderful couple and would enrich our lives and give us some great memories for years to come.

Shopping for fresh produce, meats, and nearly all other household necessities, required a trip to Avalon or the mainland.

Getting to and from Avalon was an ordeal. It was 'roughly' a twenty-five mile drive over dirt/mountain roads to the town of Avalon. It took a minimum of an hour each way to get there, and required solid driving skills. The roads were steep, winding and bumpy, and when it rains they often became impassable. In addition, they were prone to periods of severe fog or heavy low clouds that often hovered on the mountain peaks and made driving even more difficult

In the beginning, the trip to and from town was an exciting adventure and we marveled at the size, beauty and impressiveness of the Island's interior. As time went on, the trip would sometimes become more of a necessary evil, although it was truly a spectacular journey when it was done either for recreational pleasure or when time and the elements were not a factor.

I shipped my old Dodge pickup truck, affectionately known as Mr. Truck, to the Island soon after we moved. Having a vehicle available was an absolute necessity. That old truck served us well for about ten years before finally succumbing to the ravages of the roads and was eventually buried in the old dump up above Wells Beach. Of course, that was back in the days when you could still get away with that sort of disposal.

We became friends with David McElroy and his brother Stephen. David was married at the time to his first wife Laurie, and they had their son Nicholas, one of only a few children in the community in those early years. The only other families with young children were Randy Bombard and his second wife Debbie with their children Britain and Brian (little Doug), and Ty and Patty Ewing with their son Ricky.

David, Stephen and I fished together a lot, and David, Laurie, Maureen and I did quite a bit of exploring, hiking and enjoying the

Island's rugged interior together. I also started playing golf on a regular weekly basis with a few Island buddies.

Golfing for me was to become a passion that I alternately enjoyed, cursed, avidly pursued and could never master. There was a group of us that played together for years, nearly every Monday. We hopped into our pickup trucks and assorted other vehicles at daylight, drove across the Island to Avalon, and played the Avalon links religiously, but never well. We had some great times together and I will always cherish some of the memorable times we had playing golf, including a regular series of matches against a group of Avalon golfers. The group included Avalon Harbormaster John Phelps, who would later play a very big role in the future of Two Harbors, his good friend and cohort Paul McElroy, who was the Avalon Baywatch Captain at the time, and several Avalon harbor patrolmen.

Concerning my golf game, another good friend that I played with on occasion, Kim Everson, a member of Fourth of July Yacht Club and good family friend, once told a gathering of our mutual friends that, 'I was the only golfer he knew that could be struck by polio and it wouldn't affect my golf swing at all'. He is probably right about that; I must admit that my swing is unorthodox.

After a couple of years of living on the Island and having an old, wooden thirty-two-foot boat to take care of, we decided that it was simply too much work and effort to keep *Little Smoke*. At the time, as an employee, I got a free mooring for the boat, but even so, it was an ordeal and a financial burden to keep and maintain a boat of that size.

Several times during those first two winters I had needed to go out in the middle of the night to check on the boat and make sure it was secure during storms. On one particularly cold, wet and windy night, when I had the boat moored in Cat Harbor, the mooring started dragging and the boat was in jeopardy of going ashore. I went out in pelting rain and howling wind and set the anchor from a small skiff.

I deployed a twenty-pound Danforth with about thirty-five-feet of three-eighth-inch galvanized chain. I played-out about eighty-feet of scope, in about ten-foot depth, and the boat stopped dragging. I stayed out on the boat for about two more hours to ensure that it was secured, and then returned to our house. That episode, along with several others not quite as severe, prompted us to put *Little Smoke* up for sale.

I sold it about a month later, with the help of Augie and Joe Camello at Colonial Boat Works in San Pedro. I sold it for twenty-five hundred dollars, realizing a five hundred dollar 'profit' after having poured about two thousand dollars of repairs into her. It was one of those emotional moments in the life of a boat owner that adhered closely to the old saying; 'Selling a boat is the happiest, and the saddest day of a boat owner's life'.

Not long after selling *Little Smoke*, we purchased a small runabout from Johnny Vaughan. That little fiberglass boat was a fourteen-foot Glaspar. It had a twenty-five horsepower Evinrude outboard motor, and Johnny had owned and used the boat for several years. Those old Glaspar's were solid little boats and Johnny had taken it back and forth to the mainland on numerous occasions. We named the boat *Little Mo*, and kept and enjoyed her for several years.

4. A Growing Family

A COUPLE OF YEARS AFTER our wedding, we began the joyous pastime of trying to get pregnant. Despite our most diligent and ardent efforts, it didn't seem to be working. Maureen decided that since our effort wasn't an immediate success, she would get me a dog.

One afternoon she brought home a furry little black 'mutt' with a splash of white on his tiny little chest. The offspring of an Australian shepherd and a Pit Bull, we named our little dynamo Buddy. A few days later, Maureen discovered that she was pregnant with our first son, Trevor. We kept Buddy anyway, and he became a big part of our lives.

Gratefully, Buddy took on the temperament and character of his mother—the Australian shepherd—rather than the Pit Bull. He was a small dog, only about the size of a standard sized Beagle or Cocker Spaniel, but he had the distinctive chest and powerful jaw structure of the Pit Bull. The shepherd heritage helped to make him gentle and playful. As Buddy grew, he began to exhibit an incredible ability to catch tennis balls in midair. A joy for all of us, his ball-chasing and catching exploits were really quite extraordinary. Buddy could leap at least three or four times his height, twist around and grab a tennis ball out of the air, and land on all fours. He loved for us to throw the ball for him, and he had the stamina to do it for hours on end. If we weren't able to throw it for him, he would carry one down to the beach—despite our efforts to keep him contained in the fenced-in yard—and find some kids, or adults to toss the ball for him. On those days when there was nobody on the beach, he trotted over the hill to the east of our house and found someone at the campground that would play catch with him.

We had a fence about five-feet high surrounding our little front lawn—intended to keep the buffalo and pigs out of the yard. Buddy could always find a way to jump over, dig under, or somehow find a way to escape.

One afternoon when Buddy was about three-years old he escaped the yard. I checked the beach but he was not there. I was about to head over to the campground when I saw him heading down the trail from the campground, moving unusually slowly. As I watched him moving down the hill—he usually ran or trotted—I could see that he was not walking normally. I headed up the trail to meet him. When I got near, I could see that he was hobbling on three legs. I reached his side and he looked up at me with his normally bright puppy-dog eyes, and they looked sad. That was very unusual.

When I looked down at his foreleg, I could see that it was swollen to about twice its normal size. I reached down and picked him up, and then carried him home. Back at home I looked his leg over carefully, trying to see what might be wrong. I could see nothing obvious. I knew that there was no vet in Avalon at that time, and that if he needed treatment, it would have to be on the mainland. I carried him down to Baywatch, and I believe it was John McKay or John Stonier who noticed two puncture wounds on the tender inside of his right thigh area; the distinctive red-ringed marks of a rattlesnake bite.

I quickly got things together with the boat and Maureen and I headed across the channel in the *No Mo*, our twenty-two-foot Grady White, to try and get him to a veterinarian. Maureen held Buddy on her lap all the way across. It was obvious that he was in pain, and couldn't seem to understand what was happening.

Arriving on the mainland at around noon, we found a veterinarian office nearby in San Pedro and took him in for treatment. After an initial assessment, the doctor said he would see what he could do. He told us to take a seat in the waiting area. We waited uneasily. About fifteen minutes later, the nurse rushed out and said to us. "I think there's a problem. You might want to come with me."

When we reached the treatment room, Buddy was lying on his side atop a white sheet. He was not moving and his eyes were closed. "What's wrong?" I asked anxiously.

"He seems to have stopped breathing," she told us.

"Where's the vet?" I questioned her.

"Well, he went to lunch."

"What?" I asked incredulously. "He went to lunch?" I could not believe what she was telling me. Our poor little dog was lying on the operating table with a severely swollen leg from a rattlesnake bite and the vet had left him to go to lunch! I looked around frantically, completely befuddled and growing angry.

"Well, do something!" I demanded. "There must be something you can do?"

"Well, I suppose we could try CPR," she replied quietly.

"Then let's do it! I know CPR, I'll help!" I informed her.

She positioned herself on one side of the table. I took the other side. Reaching out to adjust his position so that we could work on him together, the nurse handed me a rescue-breathing mask and suggested that I might try to fit it around his muzzle. I wrapped the device around Buddy's nose and jaws, pulled the outer edges tightly against his snout and breathed into the opening of the mouthpiece. I could hear air escaping around the outer edges of the device. I closed it tighter and tried again. That time, I could feel that the majority of the air I was delivering was going into his chest cavity, and I began timing my breathing with a slow count, giving him a rescue breath every few seconds. At the same time, the nurse was thrusting gently on Buddy's chest, trying to stimulate his heart. We worked together for about ten minutes, but to no avail. Buddy was dead.

Numbed, befuddled and exhausted, I looked up at Maureen. Her face was stained with tears and her head was dropped low onto her chest. I shuffled over to where she was standing and wrapped my arms around her. We stood together sobbing for a while.

Eventually, we pulled ourselves together and I asked the nurse, "Now what?"

She was obviously disturbed also, and unsure of what to do or say. She looked at us with compassion for a few moments, and then asked, "Do you want us to dispose of the body?"

"No!" I responded immediately. "I will take care of that myself!"

In a disbelieving trance, we went about the process of wrapping Buddy's inert body into a white bag, something similar to a pillowcase. I carried him out to our car and we headed back to the boat. Neither of us spoke until we reached the dock, and then Maureen asked, "What are we going to do?"

I had already decided that I was going to give Buddy a burial at sea. I told her my intentions. She shook her head in acquiescence and we loaded him into the boat and headed out. About halfway across the channel I stopped the boat and shut off the motor. We sat there in the warm sunshine, breathing deeply in the salt air and contemplating the situation. After a few minutes, I turned to her. "Ready?" I asked softly. She shook her head in affirmation.

I reached down and lifted the white bag from the deck cushion where I had laid him down. Lifting the bag to the rail, I rested it momentarily on the gunwale and then opened the flap. I picked the closed end up into the air and let Buddy's body slide out of the opened end of the bag and into the water. I watched Buddy drop into the purple/blue depths. It was a serene and almost beautiful sight as the jet-black sheen of his fur slid into the depths, but my vision blurred through the tears. I stared into the depths for a long time; long after Buddy's lifeless form was gone.

Eventually I looked back over at Maureen, went to her side and held her tightly. After a while, I moved back to the helm, started the engine and headed toward the Island, and home.

A few minutes later, Maureen reached out and held my free hand. She talked quietly to me, reliving some of the most precious moments we had shared with our little dog. Her calming and almost cheerful recollections were soothing and reassuring and it helped me begin the slow healing process that always accompanies a personal loss.

About a week later we received a bill from the veterinarian for a hundred-forty dollars. I think we were both still in shock, because for some inexplicable reason, we sent them a check. A week, or so later, I realized that it was completely wrong to have received an invoice for their ineptitude, and that we should probably instigate legal action of our own against them. But the whole ordeal was simply too overwhelming for both of us, and we just let the matter drop. But we will always remember our little dog Buddy and all the joy and pleasure that he brought into our lives.

Maureen was extremely happy and a glowing mother-to-be. She carried our first son with pride and womanly pleasure and was very anxious to deliver.

Of course there were certain aspects of a pregnancy and giving birth that would prove to be a challenge because of the 'Island Factor'. Doctor's visits were not easy. Each checkup required a trip to the mainland, a two-day endeavor no matter how it was done. Even making the channel crossing was sometimes difficult because of rough seas. A two-and-a-half-hour boat ride in a pitching, rolling swell is tough on many people, especially a pregnant woman.

When the big day loomed closer, Maureen went to the mainland about two-weeks prior to her due date. She most certainly did not want to take the chance of being stuck on the Island when the time came for delivery. She stayed on the mainland with good friends Johnny 'Pop' Vaughan and his bride Elaine, who were to become godparents to both of our sons. I stayed on the Island working. It was near the end of August, the busiest time of the year in the harbor, and I was sorely needed. She phoned me daily, keeping me updated on her status and just to chat.

In the wee-hours of darkness (around one a.m.) on August 30th, 1981, Maureen called me to tell me that her water broke. Sleepily, and somewhat frantically, I shook the cobwebs from my head and asked her, "What does that mean? Are you delivering right now?"

"No," she laughed lightly, "It only means that I should expect to deliver within a few hours. But you don't need to worry or rush right over. It will probably be at least six to eight hours before it happens. Go ahead and go back to sleep and maybe you could head over in the early morning on the *Little Mo,* after the sun comes up."

"Okay," I told her, "I'll head over at daylight."

We had discussed how I would get to the mainland when the time came. If the timing turned out to be right, I would hop aboard the Catalina Cruise boat. If her delivery time came when the boats were not available, I would take *Little Mo* over—presuming the weather was mild enough to cross the channel in the little fourteen-foot skiff.

I put my head back onto the pillow, closed my eyes for a moment, and then popped upright. There was no way I could go back to sleep! We were having a baby. She was on the mainland and I was 'stuck on the Island'. I sat up, went out and turned on the VHF radio (I had a radio setup at the house so that I could monitor the harbor when necessary) and listened to the marine weather forecast. It was typical for August, 'late night and early morning coastal clouds, with winds light and variable night and morning hours, becoming westerly five-to-fifteen knots in the afternoon. Southwest swells two-to-four-feet at a fourteen second duration', nothing unusual.

I turned on the teapot, had a big cup of Instant Folgers Coffee, ate a bowl of Cheerios, took care of my morning constitutional, pulled out my traveling bag, which I had packed ahead of time, and headed down to the pier.

It was about three-thirty a.m. by the time I was ready to go. I hopped into a work skiff and went out to the stringline—a row of moorings designed for small boats—and climbed into *Little Mo*. I towed the work skiff back to the dock and headed out of the harbor toward the distant mainland.

It was a dark, moonless night. The faint glow of the lights of the Isthmus spread a grayish luminescence within the mooring area, but as I headed out of the harbor, the muted lights faded into a thick and misty darkness. Above me, the low hanging shroud of a heavy marine layer obscured all of the stars. Phosphorescence sprayed from the bow and sides of the boat, leaving a silvery blue streak in the boat's wake.

Tucked behind the molded plastic windshield of the *Little Mo*, I focused my attention on the compass, adhering to a determined course of zero-two-two degrees, which I trusted would put me at the entrance to Angels Gate. The outboard engine purred along smoothly. I had filled both six-gallon fuel tanks, changed the lower unit oil, put in new spark plugs, and inspected all the hoses and fittings during the past few days.

The seas were flat, the minimal southwest swell barely perceptible. Gazing through the filmy plastic of the windshield, everything looked a little distorted. I felt as if I were looking into a dark tunnel where shadows moved strangely back and forth, animalistic looking shadows with long necks and tails. After a while my mustache drooped with moisture. I wiped it periodically with the sleeve of my jacket.

My thoughts flashed back and forth between concentrating on maintaining a steady compass course and the fact that I was heading across the Catalina Channel to meet my wife who was having a baby. Wow! A baby! I was thirty-five years old, quite a bit older than most men are when they have their first child, and I wondered if I was ready. But I also realized that, ready or not, the time was here. Before the day was done I would be a father.

I was about half way across, making good time when a warm breeze began to blow off the mainland. It wasn't strong, only about five-to-ten knots, but it quickly created a mild surface chop. The breeze was slightly east of my heading and within a few minutes I was feeling some light spray stinging my cheeks. I slowed down a little, dropping my rpm's from thirty-five hundred to twenty-eight hundred. That speed kept the *Little Mo* on a gentle plane, but slowed the boat enough to keep the spray from getting me wet—at least for a few minutes.

As I continued on, the breeze picked up a little more, blowing steady at about ten-to-twelve knots. That increase in winds also caused the chop to build and my little fourteen-foot boat began to pound gently as it lifted and dropped from the wind chop. I slowed a little more, but that caused the boat to plow into the wavelets, tossing increasingly wet sheets of water over the bow. I tried to speed up again to get onto a plane, and that helped a little with the spray, but caused the boat to start pounding again. I had a decision to make; either pound into the slight swells and get a little wet, or slosh into the swells and get a lot wet. I decided to pound onward.

I was about seventeen miles out of the Isthmus, roughly five miles from my destination, thumping steadily into the mild southeast breeze that was causing me to get increasingly soaked. It was mild, the air temperatures in the low sixties and the ocean temperature in the high sixties, so it wasn't too cold, but being wet and heading into the wind gave me a chill.

When I reached Angels Gate, I ducked inside of the long low breakwater in an effort to seek more protected waters. That worked well, and soon I was back up on a full plane cruising along toward the east end of the eight-mile long, Long Beach Breakwater and into the entrance of Alamitos Bay, with an ultimate destination of Naples Marina, where I had made arrangements to tie-up in a slip belonging to a good personal friend.

That slip belonged to Mike Campbell, an avid sailing enthusiast and regular Island visitor that I had gotten to know soon after moving to the Island. Mike owned a flourishing warehouse business that supplied the upstart Trader Joe franchise, among other businesses. He would remain a lifelong friend with whom we partied, golfed, and enjoyed a friendship with he and his future wife Veronica for years to come. I found his slip easily despite the fact that it was still dark and it was my first time into that area of that particular harbor. I secured *Little Mo* in the slip and walked up the gangway to his house, a classic Naples Beach house built right on one of the Naples Canals. Mike was waiting at the top of the ramp for me, along with Johnny Vaughan and Mike's girlfriend at the time, Cindy Cummins. They invited me inside for a cup of hot coffee. I was still drenched from the sea-spray.

I sipped on a cup of hot coffee, munched on a bagel with cream cheese and began telling Mike and the others about my channel crossing. The phone rang. It was Elaine Vaughan, Johnny's wife. She said a quick hello and then passed the phone over to Maureen.

"Hi," she greeted me cheerfully. "So, you made it over okay?"

"Yes. No problems at all, although it did get a little choppy and I got pretty wet. But all is good now. I'm having a cup of coffee and a bagel."

"Well," she said to me, "I'm about four minutes apart in my contractions. You might want to think about heading to the hospital if you want to be here when the baby arrives."

She groaned suddenly at that point, going into another contraction and Elaine came back on the line. "Yes, I think you'd better come quickly," she told me rather matter-of-factly.

I gulped down a final swallow of coffee and turned to Johnny, "Well, Johnny, I guess it sounds like I'd better get there right away. Are you ready to go?"

"Sure. Let's go," Johnny grinned.

I thanked Mike and Cindy and grabbed my small carrying bag and we headed for the hospital.

Once we arrived at Long Beach Memorial Hospital, we asked a nurse for directions to Maureen's room and headed for that location. We found the room easily. Elaine was sitting on the edge of the bed chatting casually with Maureen. I rushed to Maureen's side and blurted, "Wow! I guess I made it in time?"

She laughed lightly, just as a contraction arrived. She grimaced, moaned lightly and clutched at her bulging stomach. It was difficult to see her that way. She appeared to be in severe pain and I reached over and grabbed her hand. With glazed eyes she looked up at me and smiled wanly. "It's okay," she whispered stoically, "It was a mild contraction. I'm fine."

I had rushed to the hospital because I was expecting her to deliver the baby imminently, but that was not to be. She remained in labor for nearly twelve more hours.

Birth is a miracle that compares to nothing else, but honestly, not one that I enjoy. We had gone to classes during her pregnancy and I thought I was prepared for the big day. I wasn't. Most of the women, and many of the men that I spoke with during our 'birthing classes', ensured me that the entire birthing process is said to be something to look forward to with eagerness and joy. But when the time came, I did not enjoy it at all.

For me it was a painful and troubling ordeal. I did not like seeing Maureen in pain. The lessons that we had learned together in the birthing classes simply didn't work for me. When she went into contractions, I had been taught to gently massage her scalp, shoulders, or arms, hold her hand and give her gentle, soothing words of encouragement.

When she convulsed, my techniques of massaging went haywire and my 'words of encouragement' turned into tense mumbles that sounded stressful and worried. I was tense and anxious and my 'gentle massages' turned quickly into a frantic, intense rubbing. It was so extreme that she finally blurted out, "Get him away from me!"

Stunned and dumbfounded, I backed away from the bed. Elaine took my place at her side, giving her the gentle, soothing touch that she needed. I stood in the corner of the room wringing my hands together and wishing the ordeal would end.

When our son Trevor finally arrived, I felt as though I had just gone through one of the most trying and difficult days of my life and the comfort of knowing that everything had gone okay, despite my ineptness, was a huge relief.

Seeing a newborn child is an amazing and wonderful thing. But for me, the first few months of a child's life is not the greatest. They sleep, they cry, they dirty their diapers. Sure, they are kind of cute and warm and cuddly, but the 'big moment' of being a father didn't really hit me until many months later, at that moment when he looked up at me for the first time, obviously recognized me, and cooed. From that point on, fatherhood became a joy and a pleasure.

Maureen also realized that I was not ideally suited to be her coach and companion during the delivery process, and so when our second son Troy was born seven years later, she chose Elaine as her coaching partner and I sat in the lobby watching a Lakers playoff game during his birth, keeping the doctor updated on the score.

Two days after the birth of our son Trevor we returned to the Island. We were met on the dock by a nice gathering of friends and a big banner draped across the end of the pier saying 'Welcome Home Trevor'. It was a touching welcome and we both really began to feel the warmth and caring of the Island community.

Trevor's arrival was one of four births that occurred around the same time and was the beginning of the 1980's 'baby boom' at the Isthmus. In addition to Trevor, John and Ann Marie Ermatinger delivered their son Paul, Sea and Bill Peterson's son Colin was born, Debbie and Louie Latka gave birth to their daughter Nicole, and Robin and Dave Coiner saw the arrival of their son Martin—all within the space of a couple of months. It was perhaps the biggest baby boom the Isthmus had ever known.

Two days after returning home we packed a picnic lunch, an umbrella, beach blankets, extra diapers and headed for Emerald Bay for an afternoon of beach play. At four days old, Trevor was probably one of the youngest babies to ever spend the day on Sandy Beach.

I swam and snorkeled in the crystal clear water. Maureen waded out to about waist deep. She was not much for going into the water except on those rare occasions when the sea temperature climbed above seventy degrees. It was a fun little outing and a lesson that Maureen used to affirm that our outdoor lifestyle and adventures could continue even with an infant in the household.

As the summer of 1981 faded toward fall, the Island was slammed with a steady succession of northeast winds. It became a consistent pattern for me to have to go out in the middle of the night in response to strong winds and heavy seas developing in Isthmus Cove.

Anytime visiting boats were in the harbor, we did our best to secure them in the manner that would give them the best chance of riding out stormy conditions without encountering problems; most significantly, to assist them with 'turning their boats around' so that their bows pointed seaward.

In Isthmus Cove, as opposed to all other mooring fields around the entire Island, the moorings are designed to face toward shore. This mooring process works best about eighty percent of the time in the Isthmus because of the prevailing 'Isthmus Fan' that blows across the narrow expanse of land that separates Catalina Harbor on the backside of the Island and Isthmus Cove on the front side. During the summer months in the Isthmus, it is much easier and more comfortable for visiting boats to pickup and moor with their bows facing toward shore. In all other coves, where the winds typically prevail from the west, the mooring fields are designed to face with their bows to seaward. Conversely, in Isthmus Cove during the off-season, when contrary winds develop, it is a standard practice to moor boats 'backwards', or with their bows pointing toward the mainland.

While this practice helps when northeast winds develop, it is not the only step that should be taken in an effort to keep boats as safe and secure as possible. We always advised boaters to install chafing gear around the mooring lines and especially on any rails or gunwales that have 'sharp' edges. Additionally, we advised them to not get too tight on the mooring—a concept that few people understand. In heavy seas, if a boater pulls the mooring lines in tightly, and then wind and swells develop, it tends to put excessive strain on the mooring lines and ground tackle, chafing-through lines that might then break and/or drag mooring weights. If that occurs, the boats are subject to dragging ashore, breaking loose, wrapping-up on severed lines, and suffering a multitude of similar problems.

As a patrolman, I quickly learned that it is not easy to assist boats with mooring problems when winds and seas pickup, especially during the middle of the night when it is cold and dark; the most common timeframe for northeast winds to develop.

That fall and winter taught me a lot about operating boats in heavy seas, towing boats in distress, securing our company boats and equipment, and coping with adverse conditions. I spent many a night in a small patrol boat with penetrating winds chilling me to the bone as I tried to prevent injuries or damages during the worst of the numerous storms that occurred. We did have a couple of boats go aground that year despite our efforts. All but one was salvaged.

I also decided about that time to apply for and try to earn my Coast Guard's Masters License. Having a license would allow me to operate shoreboats, carry passengers for hire, expand my knowledge and training, and enhance my benefit to the company. After looking into the licensing requirements, I knew that I had more than enough of the seven-hundred-twenty days of documented sea-time that was required to qualify for testing. All I needed to do was pass the test.

I got together with three other Island employees who all wanted to earn their license; Richard Brown, who worked with the Mooring Service, Ray Lyman, a member of the Harbor Department, and another employee whose name I cannot recall, who left the Island shortly after obtaining his license. We rented a couple of motor homes and drove to San Diego to enroll in a two-week course at the Mariners License Preparation School. Studying under the expert instructional tutelage of Frank 'Chief' Gaines, we spent two intense weeks studying Rules of the Road, Navigation, Right of Way, and all of the fundamental areas of marine information necessary to obtain the Masters License.

The four of us managed to have a little fun along the way, but for the most part, we hit the books, memorized the Rules of the Road, and plotted courses that would ultimately lead all four of us to obtain certification. It was a very gratifying day for each of us when we walked out of the Coast Guard offices with a Masters License under our belts.

With some sea-time that I had earned on a one-hundred-forty-seven-foot boat cruising for six months through Central America and the Western Caribbean, I qualified for a one-hundred ton license, along with a towing endorsement, and it provided me with more than enough certification to enhance my career on the Island.

After Trevor was born, Maureen took a few months off of work. Realizing that it was very difficult to live comfortably, much less get ahead solely on the wages I earned as a harbor patrolman, Maureen decided to go to work in the restaurant.

Art Nielson was restaurant manager at the time and agreed to give her an evening position as a waitress. That way, she could care for our son during the day and I could take over parenting duties at night, after my shift in the harbor ended. For the most part, that arrangement worked okay for a couple of years, although there were a few times when I was called out to respond to a problem in the harbor and had to either quickly find a baby-sitter or drop our young son off at the restaurant.

Working in the restaurant proved to be a nice change for Maureen in some ways, because she was able to make new friends and interact with more people. She worked alongside some very nice young women, Christy LaFlamme, Michelle Mileski, Kitty McElroy, Tina Quinn, and others. She also enjoyed working with the head chef, Yeoung Yu, a cantankerous old gentleman from Korea who was a very good chef and ran a very tight ship but tended to be a bit cranky at times. Maureen, however saw beyond his gruff exterior and they got along very well.

One night while she was working and I had experienced a very trying and tiring day on the water, our one-year old son Trevor was in an equally troubled mood. I think maybe he was teething, but whatever the cause, he was not happy unless I was holding him and walking around holding him in my arms.

Our house, as mentioned, was tiny, about seven-hundred-fifty square feet after we had added on Trevor's small bedroom. I created a walking path across the living room floor, through our small bedroom, around the corner into the bathroom and then back into the kitchen, before returning to the living room. Walking kept Trevor calm and quiet, but I was tired. Walking that much was wearing me out. Each time I attempted to put Trevor down, he cried, loudly. His crying wore on my nerves as much as the walking wore out my body. After several hours of walking I could go no more. I put him down beside me on the couch. Immediately he started crying again. After a few minutes I struck out in frustration, slamming my hand down on the coffee table. I broke two fingers.

Holding Trevor in my left arm, I walked down to the restaurant and told Maureen what had happened. She was not happy.

Fortunately she was not extremely busy that night and so she took Trevor home while I drove into Avalon and had my hand set in a cast. About the only good result of the incident was that it helped get me out of doing some household chores and changing diapers. It also taught me a humbling lesson about keeping my temper under control—at least most of the time—I suffered no more broken bones, but I do still tend to swear, on occasion.

Working with a cast on my hand proved to be a lot easier than working with a cast on my foot.

After healing from the hand injury I started playing basketball with some of the guys. One afternoon I went up for a rebound and came down on the foot of another player, breaking my right ankle. I took about a week off from work, then returned on limited duty. I could operate the boats so I continued with my general patrolman's duties.

5. The Death of Natalie Wood

IT WAS ALSO IN NOVEMBER of 1981 that one of the most tragic and devastating deaths in the fabled history of Catalina Island occurred in Isthmus Cove; the death of Natalie Wood.

I have often looked back on that tragic incident with a certain amount of regret. Similarly, I have often second-guessed my personal involvement in the tragedy and felt rueful about the actions that I took during the sequence of events that ultimately led to her drowning. It was slightly more than thirty years ago when her death occurred and the details and memories of that fateful night have faded significantly in my mind. However, I did make notes during and immediately following the incident, and I think the best narrative I can provide to describe my involvement in the situation is to present the self-written document that I put together immediately following the heart wrenching ordeal.

Following is my perspective on the death of Natalie Wood based upon my notes taken during, and a few weeks after, the tragic accident:

Natalie Wood—
The Tragedy That May Have Been Prevented

I was the acting harbormaster at Two Harbors, Catalina Island when Natalie Wood drowned while visiting the Island on Thanksgiving Weekend 1981. As acting harbormaster, I was the first one contacted after her disappearance and I coordinated the search efforts to find her when she was reported missing.

In retrospect, there is one aspect surrounding Natalie Wood's tragic death that has remained very obscure in the public's eye; her death quite possibly could have been prevented. Bureaucratic decisions stemming from L.A. County Baywatch Search and Rescue cutbacks related to Proposition 13 prevented Catalina Island's trained professionals from responding in a timely manner to the scene of the incident. Had they been called immediately, as they should have been, the chances are good that Natalie Wood might be alive today.

Over the years, since her drowning, I have contemplated my decision not to call Baywatch in the early stages of the search for Natalie Wood. In referring to my notes taken shortly after the incident occurred, I feel that my decision was logical and justifiable, but I have often second-guessed myself as to whether things would have turned out differently had I made that phone call.

The following is my perspective on the story of Natalie Wood's death.

On Saturday, November 28, Splendour, the sixty-foot Bristol motor yacht belonging to actors Robert Wagner and Natalie Wood, motored into Isthmus Cove on Catalina Island to secure a mooring. Being on duty at

the time, I stood by while Splendour pulled up to and secured mooring O-1-Isthmus Cove. Since the Wagner's leased another mooring in nearby Emerald Bay, it was not necessary to collect fees or sign them up for the mooring usage, as they were entitled to a reciprocal use privilege. I wished them a pleasant stay and went about other business.

Later that afternoon, Wagner, Wood, their boat guest actor Christopher Walken and their captain Dennis Davern went ashore for dinner and drinks at 'Doug's Harbor Reef Restaurant' (the only restaurant in the tiny community of Two Harbors). According to staff members and other diners, the group drank rather heavily and became quite loud. Some reports indicated argumentative and disruptive behavior amongst the group. Those who were in the restaurant that I spoke with did confirm that they were quite boisterous. They reportedly departed the restaurant sometime after nine-thirty p.m. to return to their boat.

It was a cold and blustery night for southern California with temperatures in the fifty's and the tempestuous northwest wind whipped-up small whitecaps in the normally placid waters of Isthmus Cove. Heavy silver/black layers of clouds scuttled overhead, periodically obscuring stars and the sliver of a waxing moon. A weak weather system had blown in from the west earlier in the day, bringing scattered showers and chilling winds that lingered into the night.

At about one-fifteen a.m. my wife Maureen shook me awake. "Doug, Doug, there's someone at the door. I think its George" (She was referring to General Foreman George McElroy). Grabbing my blue robe from its hangar, I stumbled to the door, tripping over one of the rainwater pans strategically placed below our leaking rooftop.

Standing at the door was Don Whiting, a fellow employee of the company, who lived aboard the vessel Almitra in Catalina Harbor.

"What's wrong?" I asked.

"Natalie Wood is missing," he responded.

"What do you mean she's missing?"

"Splendour put out a call on VHF channel 16 (the emergency radio frequency for boats) a while ago and said that Natalie Wood and the dinghy from Splendour were missing. I think somebody should check it out"

"Okay," I said. "I'll meet you at the pier in a couple of minutes."

I had been up for much of the previous night helping with the search for a lost catamaran and was not really excited about going out again, but duty called and so I hastily dressed and hurried to the Harbor Office located on the end of the Isthmus Pier. In the process, I was thinking to myself that it was more than likely not a serious situation; it was not at all uncommon for dinghies or individuals to be missing for a short while. They often went out for 'harbor cruises' or to visit friends on other boats. On the other hand, the fact that it was late, and a cool blustery evening, made it seem unlikely that anyone would be out for a 'joy ride'.

I called Splendour on channel 16, identified myself and asked if everything was all right.

Robert Wagner responded, "No. She's not here. We need help.'

He was difficult to understand, sounding either sleepy or intoxicated. It proved to be the latter. In fact, all three men aboard the yacht were difficult to talk with—acknowledging they had been drinking heavily since early evening. That alone was not unusual for visitors to the Island; people go to the Island to party and have fun, and drinking is commonplace for almost all visitors.

While Don Whiting and I were pulling alongside Splendour, co-worker and resident Paul Wintler called on the radio to inform us that he was operating Shoreboat #6 and initiating a search through the mooring area. Paul had been monitoring the radio and overheard the transmissions.

Once we were aboard the Splendour, my first effort was to try and establish some basic information, including the size, type and color of the dinghy. How much fuel was aboard? Could she operate the skiff? Did they have friends on other boats that she may be visiting? Might she have tried to go back to Avalon? Did they hear her leave?

Their responses were initially difficult to follow due to their obvious state of insobriety, but we soon established that there was not anyone she might be visiting nearby. She did know how to operate the dinghy, but they did not hear it start and she would certainly not go out alone at night, or attempt to go back to Avalon or go out for a 'joy ride'. There was plenty of fuel aboard, as they had filled the dinghy soon after arriving in the cove that afternoon.

Robert Wagner did ask me to keep the situation low-key in order to avoid unnecessary or sensational attention from the news media.

After gathering as much information as possible, asking them to change channels and listen on VHF channel #9, and suggesting they brew a pot of coffee, I returned to the Harbor Office to initiate further action. Back in the Harbor Office, my initial thought was to call in Baywatch Isthmus. But just the night before, they had declined to respond to an overturned catamaran with two people in the water about three miles out to sea. They were under heavy pressure from their Los Angeles County administrators to reduce their budgets by limiting their overtime responses. If they would not respond to a capsized vessel with two people in the water in November, it seemed much more unlikely that they would respond to a report of a missing person in a dinghy. So instead of calling Baywatch, I called Coast Guard Long Beach, leaving it to their discretion as to whether Baywatch should be called in or not. It was 0326 (three-twenty-six a.m.) when I made the call to the Coast Guard.

First Petty Officer Gallagher took the report, making note of our conversation that he had overheard a short time before with our staff and the crew of Splendour, and of our intended search procedures. Officer Gallagher also informed me that he would be dispatching the Coast Guard Cutter Point Camden, but that it would be approximately two-and-a-half to three hours before they would arrive on scene.

This was the critical time for deciding whether or not to involve Baywatch in the search and rescue effort, and the Coast Guard did not comment on their status or involvement.

I then made a few more phone calls to step-up the response efforts by calling in additional personnel to assist in the search.

A search pattern was established with all available patrol units, as well as a couple of vehicles to initiate a shore search on the local dirt roads overlooking the harbor. Harbor Unit #10, with Paul Wintler now at the helm, continued to run a series of search patterns through the mooring area. Paul, who worked in the maintenance department, was also an *experienced boat operator. Curt Craig, a night-shift patrolman and the only 'regular' harbor patrolman involved on the water, was dispatched west, toward Arrow Point and along shore. Don Whiting, the bartender who first reported her missing, operated Harbor Patrol Unit #6 with Bill Coleman, another restaurant employee. Shawn Caise, an expert scuba diver who worked with the mooring service, also helped in the search, operating Unit #1, running a zigzag pattern toward the north and east. At that point, the Splendour sent out a radio call suggesting that the search should continue farther out to sea. Considering the sea conditions, the direction of the wind, and the prevailing currents, it was highly unlikely that an inflatable would be pushed out toward sea. We continued the search along the shoreline.*

For the ensuing few hours the search continued with no results. Each unit called in frequently to the Harbor Office for updates and instructions. I informed all to pay particular attention to any and all little nooks and crannies along the shoreline as well as the sandy beaches that dotted the leeside shores. I also dispatched one of the units to check nearby Bird Rock and Ship Rock.

Then, at precisely 0515 (five-fifteen a.m.), Don Whiting on Harbor #6 made a call reporting that he had located the missing dinghy and that it was empty. Natalie Wood was not aboard. It was found floating in a kelp bed in an area known as Blue Cavern Point, approximately half a mile from the Harbor. Whiting reported that the skiff appeared intact, everything aboard seemed to be in order and the engine was turned off with the key in the ignition. There was nothing at all to indicate any presence of Natalie Wood. I instructed all units to proceed toward that location and for everyone on scene to periodically shut-off their motors, shout out, and listen for any possible calls for help.

At that time I also phoned L.A. County Sheriff's Deputy Bill Kroll, my employer Doug Bombard, and Baywatch Isthmus, advising them that we now considered the missing person's report a life and death matter. All responded almost immediately to join in the search. Paul Wintler then climbed into a four-wheel drive vehicle and departed for the area above the cliffs at Blue Caverns in the event that she might have climbed ashore at that point.

After organizing those actions, I took a patrol boat out to the Splendour to inform Wagner of our discovery. He, along with Captain Dennis Davern, returned with me to shore, leaving Walken aboard the Splendour. Wagner, now painfully sober, was visibly shaken, continually asking questions. "Why is this happening? What is going to happen? Why hasn't she been found? What can I do?"

Mustering a positive response, which I did not really feel, I attempted to reassure him. "We'll find her," I stated, "She's probably walking back from the point where we found the dinghy. It's dark, but we have personnel on the way to the area on land, as well as more units responding on the water. She may be sitting somewhere in a safe spot waiting for daylight. It will be light soon and that will make it easier for all of us."

He stood forlornly at the rail of the pier, head between his hands, staring at the black water below. "She hates the water," he murmured, "She's terrified of the water. She doesn't even like to swim in the water. It scares her" All I could do was nod my head.

When Sheriff Kroll and Baywatch members Roger Smith and (I think it was) John Stonier arrived, I brought them up to date on the situation. They immediately began to interrogate Wagner and Davern, and then took them back out to the Splendour to perform their own search to ensure that Natalie was not on board.

At that point, Doug Bombard, who ran the Isthmus operation, took over the helm of Unit #10, while Sheriff Kroll dispatched to assist in the shore side search. Bombard headed directly for the area where the dinghy had been discovered, near Blue Cavern's Point.

With Baywatch Isthmus now on scene, search capabilities increased dramatically. Equipped with powerful searchlights, capable of lighting up a broad area, the odds of locating Natalie Wood improved considerably. Also, soon after Baywatch joined in the search, the Coast Guard Cutter Point Camden arrived on scene.

All units onshore and on the water continued to search for the missing woman, all desperately hoping to bring a happy ending to the developing drama.

Then, at precisely 0752 (seven-fifty-two a.m.) *on the morning of November 29, 1981, Doug Bombard, operating Isthmus Harbor Unit #10, made the dreaded announcement. "You can call off the search."*

Natalie Wood was discovered floating face down in a kelp bed not more than two-hundred yards from the spot where the Zodiac had been discovered earlier, near Blue Cavern Point. Her body was pulled from the water in front of a cavernous opening known ironically as 'Perdition Cave'; which means 'Cave of the Lost Soul'.

For years I have asked myself; What if? What if I had called Baywatch earlier? Would it have made a difference? Would they have found her alive, clinging to the dinghy? Those questions will never be answered.

Many people who were aware of my involvement in the death have also asked me, 'What do you think happened'?

I am convinced that it was a sad and tragic accident. I believe she was trying to sleep in her cabin and the dinghy was slapping on the side of her berth. She grabbed a coat to ward off the cold and went out on the aft deck to retie the dinghy. In the process of untying the skiff she slipped on the swim-step, perhaps sustained minor injuries as she fell, and went into the water. She then clung courageously to the sides of the dinghy for hours, and I can't imagine what went through her mind during that dreadful time. But based upon the reports of her arms being bruised and discolored with rubbery markings all along her inner arms, I have no doubt that she was alive for a long time, clinging to the Zodiac. Also, a body submerged in the water will drift completely differently than a dinghy floating upon the surface. They would not have been anywhere near each other had she not been holding on.

Sadly, had she been more water-savvy, she could have probably climbed up into the dinghy by moving to the transom of the skiff and use the trim tabs on the outboard engine as a purchase point for her foot. Also, because the transom is lower, it makes it a much easier place to pull oneself out of the water. It is extremely difficult, even for a strong, proficient athlete to pull himself over the rounded pontoons of a large inflatable.

As for my involvement in the incident, I have often reflected on whether I made all the right choices, decisions, and actions in coordinating the search and response effort. In retrospect, I probably should have called Baywatch and the local Sheriff immediately, but the controversy in Baywatch's administrative circles was very intense and from my perspective, something to avoid. Also, the regular local Sheriff, Robert Murcott was not available that weekend for some reason, and I did not really know his replacement well. Had Bob Murcott been there, I would not have hesitated to call him, and his involvement may have helped to change the outcome.

Now, thirty years later, as I reflect back on the tragedy, I still feel somewhat troubled by the decisions that I made that night. The age-old question of 'what if?' looms heavily in my mind and my memories. 'What if we had a patrolman on duty that night? What if I had called the Baywatch team in the early stages of the search? What if some of our regular, more experienced patrolmen had been available and involved in the search? What if, what if, what if?' Those 'ifs' will forever linger in my thoughts whenever I reflect on the incident, but they will never be answered.

It is likely that no one will ever know exactly what happened that fateful night, regardless of the fact that the Los Angeles County Sheriff's Department reopened the case thirty-years later in response to allegations made by 'Captain' Dennis Davern. His assertions that foul play may have been involved are, in my mind, very unlikely. I saw the torment and anguish that permeated Robert Wagner's demeanor during the search and after she was found dead, and those human reactions are not something that even a gifted actor can fake. I firmly believe that it was nothing more than a tragic accident, but one that might possibly have had a different outcome if not for the relevant influences of governmental bureaucracy that existed at the time.

Regarding Baywatch and their role in the incident, they were not called solely because of histrionics involving administrative cutbacks. Prior to those cutbacks, and shortly after the Natalie Wood tragedy, they resolved their administrative conflicts, but not before Captain

Roger Smith was transferred off the Island and back to the mainland. Prior to, and soon after Natalie Wood's death, the Baywatch team could always be counted upon to be there when called upon—day or night. They are dedicated, professional, and deeply committed to their duties and to the Island community. Had it not been for the political climate at the time, I know they would have been there if asked.

Ironically, and for some strange and inexplicable reason, at the time of Natalie Wood's death, I was never contacted or interviewed by the investigative team, even though I was first on scene and coordinated the search. I kept my notes, fully expecting to be called upon for information, but for thirty-years, nobody asked.

When the case was reopened in 2012, purportedly as a result of insinuations included in a book written by Captain Dennis Davern, I was finally contacted by one of the investigators. I spent more than an hour on the phone with detective Kevin Lowe of the Los Angeles Homicide Division, discussing my involvement in the incident and sharing my insights with him. He expressed surprise about the fact that I was never contacted during the initial investigation and asked that I send him my notes and documentation concerning the incident. I e-mailed him my account of the night's events and a copy of the original notes detailing timelines and names of those involved in the initial search. He expressed his appreciation for the information supplied, and informed me that he was grateful for my cooperation.

I have heard nothing further about the investigation, and I suspect that the case will ultimately be closed for good, with no further insight into what actually happened that fateful night. It is my firm belief that Natalie Wood is the only person who really knows what happened the night she died at Catalina Island, and sadly, her version of the tragedy can never be told.

Natalie Wood, Robert Wagner, and Christopher Walken were not the only celebrities that frequented the Island on a regular basis. Catalina is and always has been a magnet for the rich and famous. During my thirty-two year tenure on the Island, I had the privilege of meeting and interacting with dozens of notable celebrities.

I was fortunate to meet and shake hands with John Wayne a few years before he passed away. George Hamilton leased a mooring in the Isthmus and was a frequent visitor. Actor Doug McClure and I had a memorable interaction one afternoon when he pulled into Isthmus Cove on a busy holiday weekend in search of a mooring and had to be turned away because no moorings were available. I had the pleasurable opportunity to play golf a few times with Don Felder, one of the original members of the popular band, the Eagles. In an embarrassing moment, I met and spoke with Paul Newman, but didn't even realize who he was at the time. Rod Stewart, David Crosby, basketball stars Bill Walton and Sasha Vujacic were all frequent visitors to the Isthmus. In addition, I had the wonderful opportunity to know and interact with William Wrigley, California Governor George Deukmejian, renowned woman sailor Peggy Slater, and dozens of other noted celebrities and public figures as a result of the position that I held on the Island. Those interactions all contributed to making my years on Catalina memorable and enjoyable, and helped to shape and define my position as harbormaster.

6. Mooring Turmoil

DURING THE FALL OF 1981, as the Harbor Department prepared for the renewal of the Mooring Subleases, we were made aware of some political maneuvering that was destined to have a huge impact on the mooring 'ownership' process on the Island.

The Catalina Mooring Service, as the agent for the Santa Catalina Island Company, held a long-term lease with the California State Lands Commission to administer the submerged lands around most of the Island. Avalon Harbor held a grant of the tidelands, through the City of Avalon and was, therefore, exempt from State Lands Commission oversight.

With the twenty-year lease that was in place nearing its end, two individual business entities, the Wrather Corporation and Pioneer Chicken Corporation, decided that they would like to obtain the lease rights for the Island concessions. Both corporations, working with affiliated Island entities, submitted bids for the lease rights to the Catalina mooring operation—outside of Avalon. What ensued was a two-decade long, 'nightmare of negotiations' that ultimately went in favor of the Catalina Island Company, but not before a lot of 'blood and tears' were shed.

Rather than attempt to report all of the brutal negotiations, emotional drama, and personal financial losses that resulted from the battle, I will try to summarize the overall process and ultimate results of the 'mooring ownership issue'.

As I alluded to in the early part of this manuscript, the Santa Catalina Island Company (with a 'silent' partnership with the Santa Catalina Conservancy) oversees the control and usage of seven-hundred-twenty moorings in eleven individual parcels around the Island, from Emerald Bay in the west, to the Whites Landing area, Gallagher's Cove, and Toyon Bay to the east, including Cat Harbor and Little Harbor on the backside of the Island. The Master Lease with the State Lands Commission also includes several coves along the front side of the Island that do not have public moorings and are operated by the upland camps.

Of those moorings, in 1982 when the Master Lease was due for renewal, two-hundred-thirty-four of the seven-hundred-twenty moorings were considered 'privately owned moorings'.

When the lease went out to bid, the State Lands Commission, in their ultimate wisdom, determined that the general public could not own State lands. They advised the bidding entities, and those individuals who 'owned' moorings, that ownership of the submerged lands was in violation of existing State stewardship, and therefore, illegal.

A long drawn-out and long-winded document was then released defining the concept of 'ownership' and advising the 'owners' of their options to divest themselves of their holdings. The 'mooring owners' were given fifteen years to either make a single, 'one-time only' transfer of the mooring (the right to sell), or to amortize their investment over that fifteen-year period at a lesser sublease rate. At the end of the fifteen-year period (1997), all mooring 'ownership' would cease and the 'owners' would become leaseholders on a one-year renewable basis.

That decision by the State created a significant battle with the 'mooring owners' and the State Lands Commission, with the Catalina Island Company and Catalina Conservancy caught in the middle. It also put the Harbor Department into the heart of the battlefield.

For the next fifteen-years, the 'ownership' issue remained contentious, caused considerable strain between the 'mooring owners', the Catalina Island Company, and the harbor operation. It also put me, as Acting Harbormaster into a difficult position.

From a personal perspective, the political battle was both a boon and a burden. On one side of the coin, I benefitted professionally from the process, learning to interact with both the governmental agencies and the powerful leaders of the 'mooring coalition' that formed to fight the State Lands Commission on the issue of ownership. On the other hand, it made my job and interaction with our customers more difficult.

While I sided with the 'owners' on their objections to having the State take away their 'property' and resultant loss of investment (some of the moorings were 'worth' as much as one-hundred-thousand dollars on the open market before the State's intervention), I also needed to remain as neutral as possible from a professional perspective.

I commiserated with numerous 'mooring owners' who had their life savings tied-up in their moorings and were facing a direct loss of money by being forced to sell at a reduced value. Without the opportunity to resell, the inherent value of the moorings was considerably lower than it had been before the State took action. Several people that I knew were financially devastated by the new policy. On one of the trips I made to Sacramento for a State Lands Commission hearing, one couple I knew explained that they had paid thirty-thousand dollars for their mooring only a year previously and with the new policy in effect, they were able to sell it for only five-thousand dollars. Their pleas to the commissioners were systematically ignored. Similarly, I watched the State Lands commissioners ignore the petitions and submittals from numerous 'owners' that pleaded their cases of long-standing support of the Island operations, the Catalina Conservancy, and of the boating community. 'Private ownership' was destined to end, and the State Lands Commissioners adamantly refused to modify their decision.

Another direct result of the Master Lease renewal was a significant increase in prices to be charged under the new lease. Ironically, the two 'outside' companies that attempted to take over the Master Lease, Wrather Corporation and the Pioneer Chicken Company, had submitted poorly designed prospects for assuming control of the operation and effectively managing the lease.

The Wrather Corporation submitted a plan to operate the lease by utilizing a huge floating barge to manage the harbors, the shoreboats, a fuel dock, a restaurant, trash disposal, and all of the other services required under the auspices of the Master Lease.

Pioneer Chicken proposed to manage the lease by operating out of Avalon—eleven miles away by water—and twenty-five miles by land.

The land rights, owned by the Catalina Island Company and the Catalina Conservancy, were not available for either outside entity. For the State Lands Commission to even consider the submittals from the other two companies was, by nearly all accounts, outrageous.

Regardless of those factors, when all was said and done, the boating public would ultimately face an increase of fees nearly triple the pricing formats of the previous Lease.

It also created complications in enforcing the new policies inherent in the new Master Lease. For me, and for the entire Harbor Department, enforcement of the new rules regarding 'ownership' proved to be a problematic ordeal.

All of those moorings that were previously 'No PTR' (No Permission to Rent) by the 'owners' were now under the jurisdiction of the Harbor Department, and some of the individual 'owners' did not appreciate the new rules. For some of those 'owners' the idea of the general public having access to their 'personal property' was not acceptable. They believed that they, and their personal guests and associates, still retained the exclusive rights to use their moorings as they saw fit, without any intervention from the Harbor Department. As a consequence, there were a few heated interactions and rather ugly situations that developed. In one of those, which occurred in Cherry Cove, one of the young female employees of the Harbor Department was very nearly physically assaulted.

Deva Santoro, a strikingly beautiful and wholesome young girl about twenty-years old at the time, was working one afternoon as the Harbor Patrolman in Cherry Cove. She approached a 'transient' boat to collect its mooring fees. That boat was a regular guest of the 'mooring owner' and the captain knew that that particular mooring was designated as one of the 'No PTR' moorings and therefore not subject to mooring fees. He was unaware of the new rules in the Master Lease.

When Deva attempted to explain the new policies, the man steadfastly refused to pay the newly required fees or get off the mooring. After a few frustrating attempts to gain his cooperation, Deva called me on the radio for assistance. I asked her to pick me up at the dock.

Arriving on scene, with Deva at the helm, we approached the boat with the intention of gaining his cooperation. As we neared the moored boat the man aboard hollered out quite menacingly, "Don't come near my boat! This is my personal property and I refuse you permission to come near!"

Taken aback by his belligerence, I turned to Deva and advised her to standoff while I make an effort to explain the new policies to the man. She told me that she had already tried, but that he was 'a real jerk and completely unwilling to cooperate'.

Patiently, I told her that I understood her frustration, but wanted to try to gain his cooperation. She maneuvered the patrol boat into position a few yards from the other vessel and shifted into neutral, drifting.

When I started to explain our change in policy to the man, he stated, "Shut up. I don't want to hear a damn thing about it. Just get the hell away from my boat."

"See," Said Deva. "I told you he was a jerk."

I tried to placate her. "It's okay," I said quietly, "Just let me try again."

Turning again to the man, I calmly told him, "Sir, I understand that you're upset, but we have new rules that went into effect and all visiting boats must now pay mooring fees. We'd like to come alongside and collect the fees that are due."

At that point he grabbed an oar, stood up on the side deck brandishing it menacingly, and blurted, "You come near my boat and I'll bash your bloody head in! And that little blonde bitch's too!"

At that point, Deva completely lost her cool and began berating him back. Speaking her mind quite forcefully, she told him in no uncertain terms just what she thought of him. I don't believe I have ever heard any female use some of the language that flowed from Deva's lips.

"Deva," I said to her, pulling her back from the rail where she was standing as defiantly close as possible to the other boat, "Calm down. There's nothing we can do. I'm going to go get the sheriff." I moved to the helm, shifted into forward and called out as we were pulling away, "We'll be back with the Sheriff soon."

Heading out of Cherry Cove toward the Isthmus, I made a radio call to Harbor Base, advising them that we needed the Sheriff ASAP. They said they would make the call.

As we approached the pier, I could see the Sheriff's patrol jeep parking near Visitor Services. Officer Bob Murcott met us at the pier. Murcott was a heck of a good Sheriff. With a background in ghetto work, and a member of the tactical K9 squad, his training and experience had made him an officer that should not be messed with. On the other hand, his humorous character and strong sense of humanity was perfect for the isolated and relatively 'crime free' Isthmus community.

I advised him of the situation, our attempts to do our duties, and the response and threats that were made. Deva began swearing and belittling the man loudly, at which point Murcott tried his best to calm her down. It wasn't easy. Deva was reacting angrily, obviously upset by the man's attitude and behavior. By the time we neared Cherry Cove, Deva had unleashed the strongest of her anger and Murcott pleaded with her to stand to the side and not say anything.

As I approached the moored boat, Murcott did not waste any time in stating his intentions. "We're coming alongside. Don't move. Sit right where you are and keep your hands visible."

The man stood and yelled back. "Don't come near my boat! This is private property and you have no right to invade my personal property!'

Murcott turned to me, unbuckling his gun belt in the process. "Pull alongside," he instructed me, and then quickly turned back to the man. "You threatened these two patrolmen. I'm coming aboard and if you know what's best for you, you will sit back down and put your hands on top of your head."

The man looked at him defiantly, an angry glare emanating from his twisted facial features. But there was something even more menacing about Officer Murcott's appearance, and the man slowly stepped away from the rail and sat down in the cockpit of his boat.

"Put your hands on top of your head," Murcott said coldly. The man complied.

We pulled alongside and in one smooth motion, Officer Murcott leaped onto the deck of the other boat, his right hand wrapped snuggly around the handle of his pistol. The man glanced at the gun, looked up into Murcott's face and said, "I'm cooperating."

Murcott stood stoically above him, seemingly a little disappointed with the man's reaction. I had the impression that he was hoping that the man would remain defiant so that he could take the matter into another direction.

Murcott stood watching him for a long moment and then asked, "So, are you still refusing to pay your mooring fees?"

The man looked up and said, "No, not at all. How much do I owe?"

Murcott looked toward Deva and me with a questioning look.

Recognizing the boat as approximately thirty-six-foot long, I responded, "The fees are nine dollars per night."

"Not a problem," the man stated, starting to stand and reach into his pants pocket.

"Hold on!" Murcott advised him sternly. "Turn around!"

When the man turned, Murcott made a thorough visual inspection of his rather tight fitting Levi's and, satisfied that there was no weapon of any kind visible, spoke again to the man. "Before you pay your fee, I think you owe these two patrolmen an apology."

The man balked momentarily, casting an unfriendly glance toward Deva and me. But almost as quickly, he turned back to Murcott and stated. "I apologize."

"Not to me," Murcott told him. "Apologize to these two patrolmen."

Somewhat reluctantly the man turned toward Deva and me and mumbled, "I'm sorry."

"Yeah, you sure are, you ass hole," Deva told him. "You're a real f...."

Murcott cut her short. "Okay Deva. We understand. Are you satisfied with his apology, or do you intend to press charges for his threatening you?"

I looked at Deva and nodded an encouragement. She thought for a long moment and then said, "Okay. I'll accept the apology, but he's still a jerk."

Murcott then stood by as the man pulled out his wallet and handed me a ten. I wrote a quick receipt, gave him a dollar change, and Murcott climbed back into the patrol boat.

As we pulled away, Deva couldn't avoid blurting one more comment, "And don't ever give me any crap again!"

The man just stood and glared.

That episode was perhaps the worst of the reactions we had as a consequence of the policy changes, but it certainly wasn't the only one. As time went on, the negativity diminished, although many of the 'mooring owners' held negative attitudes about their loss of ownership for as long as I remained in my position.

7. Buffalo

LIFE ON CATALINA ALSO BROUGHT about some very unique nature experiences. There are not too many places where buffalo (bison) roam freely through local neighborhoods.

In 1924, reportedly for a silent film based upon the Zane Grey book *'The Vanishing American'*, Hollywood filmmakers shipped a small herd of about fourteen bison to the Island to be used for visual effects in the making of the movie. Upon the films completion (reportedly the bison footage went unused in the finished product), the herd of bison was left to propagate on their own, freely and contentedly roaming the lush hills of the Island without much intrusion into their blissful existence. By the time we moved to the Island in 1978, the herd had grown to somewhere between six or seven hundred animals.

When we first arrived, as most new residents and visitors do, we snapped dozens of pictures of the large brown beasts as they roamed through the hills and often into the residential areas of the community. We took a lot of pictures with bison in our yard, on the local beaches, in the local campground, and even walking in and around the main plaza 'downtown'. Later, sometime around 1990, the Catalina Conservancy built a fence across the Island about a mile from the Isthmus residential area and herded all of the bison to the east of that tall chain-link fence.

During the years when they roamed freely on the Island, it was particularly inspiring to see a herd of buffalo grazing on the grasses in and around our yard, but they did tend to destroy plants and tear-up our small lawn.

One July weekend my sister's, Sheri and Vicki, were visiting for a few days. It was unusually warm and they decided to sleep on our small front porch on lounge chairs. Before going to sleep, Sheri had seen a row of ants marching along the side of the patio. Shortly after daybreak she awoke in that odd state of mind that can often occur when you are sleeping in a place other than your own home and you awaken unsure of your surroundings. Emerging from a deep sleep with the strange feeling that something was snoring beside her, she believed that it was coming from unusually loud ants. Opening one eye as she tried to orient herself, she heard a distinct snorting sound. Her other eye flew open when she realized that she was staring directly into the huge brown eye of a mature, perhaps seven-hundred-fifty to eight-hundred pound bull buffalo. It was standing alongside the porch, not more than four-feet from her bed.

Completely and utterly daunted by the size and proximity of the huge animal, she called out to our sister Vicki sleeping a couple of feet away, and asked her what to do. Vicki advised her to remain quiet and not move. Petrified, Sheri forced herself to remain perfectly still.

The buffalo was looking directly at them with his big black left eye, unmoving and trying to figure out what he was seeing. They could see a large drop of gooey eye mucus at the corner of its eyelid and the black knob of its nose also dripped a slimy substance from its large nostril. The thick, kinky black/brown fur along its neck and under its chin was matted with tufts of shrubs and thorn bristles. The muscles in its massive shoulders shuddered a couple of times as it tried to shrug-away several pesky kelp flies that buzzed around its head. After a few moments it apparently lost interest in the four bulging blue eyes of the women gazing back at it, and it lowered its head and began munching on the lawn.

Eventually the huge animal sauntered off in search of more luxurious grass to feed upon. When the buffalo moved approximately fifteen feet away, they rolled quickly off their beds, jumped up and rushed into our house petrified. Their motion caused the buffalo to momentarily stop eating and turn its head to see what the commotion was all about. Satisfied that there was nothing to be concerned with, it lowered its head once more to continue munching its morning meal.

Shortly after that episode we decided to construct a fence around the perimeter of our yard. Living where we did, on a small knoll at the eastern edge of the community, our house was the last cottage on the perimeter of the housing area, with twenty-five miles of rolling hills as our side yard. An area about twenty-by-forty feet was level and covered with grass, so we decided to fence in that area. I poured concrete footings with steel brackets and then attached about fifteen four-by-four's as uprights. Between those posts I added two-by-four inch studs, thus creating a ranch style fence. At the upland side of the fence I built a solid gate.

That fence worked well to keep the buffalo out, although wild pigs could easily crawl under the lower studs and get into the yard to dig up plants as they foraged for food. Deer simply slipped inside the openings between the studs. Several years later we added white vinyl lattice between the studs and that proved very effective in keeping nearly all of the wild animals out of the yard.

However, one morning not long after the fence was constructed, I left the side gate open. A short while later, as Maureen stood at the kitchen sink washing dishes and gazing out the window, she saw a large female buffalo enter the gate, walk directly to her newly planted flowers and basil plants, and start munching away.

"Doug!" she called out frantically to me, "There's a buffalo in the yard eating my new plants!"

I was seated in the living room gazing out the front windows at the harbor when she hollered. I stood and looked into the yard and sure enough, the large cow buffalo was nonchalantly eating her new garden.

"Do something!" she ordered me, "Get it out of the yard!"

"Okay, I'll try," I responded, not really sure just what I could do to persuade the buffalo to go back out the open gate.

I opened the front door and walked the few short steps to the edge of the porch. The buffalo was about ten feet from where I stood and it stopped its eating and looked up at me. "Get!" I shouted. "Get out of here!"

The buffalo stared back at me as if I was some kind of idiot. It chewed on its cud, tilted its head to the side as if trying to get a better focus on what, or who I was, and then began eating Maureen's flowers once again.

I thought, 'Okay, that didn't work very well. I need to try something a little more forceful'. I wasn't about to confront the animal physically with a stick or anything like that, so I decided to pick up a metal garden tool and a metal planting container that were lying on the porch. Taking those objects again to the end of the porch, I firmly banged the two metal objects together and yelled at the top of my lungs, "Hyaa! Get out of here!"

The buffalo startled, jumped slightly sideways and for a moment I thought it might charge at me. I back-pedaled rapidly toward the door. But the buffalo turned suddenly in the other direction, charged across the yard, lowered its head and crashed through two of the two-by-four's, splintering both of them into several small pieces.

Standing there staring at the splintered fence, I turned to Maureen as she walked up to my side. "Well," I asked her, "How was that?"

She looked at me blankly for a long moment and then began to laugh. We both laughed. It was really quite comical, and it didn't take too much effort to pick up the mess and attach a couple of new boards to the fence. After that, we did a better job of keeping the gate closed.

Another rather amazing buffalo incident took place one day while we were both at home. On that occasion, a very large herd of perhaps seventy-five to one-hundred buffalo were grazing peacefully on the hill adjacent to our house, perhaps eighty yards away. We had watched the herd slowly assemble on the hill and I intended to grab the camera for a few photos, but Maureen stopped me.

"We already have a few hundred pictures of buffalo. Do you really think we need more?"

I thought that she was probably right, but there was always something within me that called out whenever they wandered near— 'take pictures!' I restrained from getting the camera and after a few minutes of watching them grazing, we lost interest.

A short while later we heard an unusual grunting noise emanating from the hillsides. Anytime the buffalo herds were nearby, there was a distinctive huffing noise that accompanied their feeding. But this time the noise was louder and somehow different sounding than we were accustomed to hearing. Maureen looked over at me and commented, "That's kind of a strange sound don't you think?"

"Yes. It is kind of odd. Let's see what's going on."

We walked out onto the porch and looked up on the hill. Everything seemed normal at first; the herd of buffalo were grazing casually, seemingly indifferent to their surroundings. But then we noticed two large bulls that appeared to be facing off. Something about their posturing and animal demeanor looked somewhat threatening. Their heads were bobbing unnaturally, their nostrils were flaring and the hair on their backs and necks looked like a dog with its hackles up.

Puzzled about this posturing, we watched them for a few minutes. As we watched, their aggressive dispositions became more evident. Both animals were snorting toward each other, their nostrils spewing streams of secreted foam. They faced each other in a threatening stance with their powerful forelegs beginning to paw in the red clay, sending small clouds of disrupted soil into the still, eerily quiet afternoon air. All of the other buffalo had stopped feeding and turned to stare at the two bulls that were obviously confronting one another.

Maureen and I watched in fascination as the two animals assessed each other. One was quite a bit larger than the other, older looking and heavier. The other appeared to be younger, leaner, and obviously in its prime. As we watched, the confrontation escalated. Soon the two animals were thrusting their sharp horns at each other, dropping their massive heads low to the ground and lunging upwards in a menacing gesture as they jostled for a preferred position. Several times their heads thumped together, their sharply curved horns clanking noisily on contact. With each thrust, both bulls attempted to twist their massive heads into an advantageous position, obviously trying to maneuver to administer a damaging blow. But both animals were also wary, quick and strong, and neither could outmaneuver the other.

As the escalating battle continued, the noise and clamor from their efforts became louder and more extreme. Soon a white foamy froth was streaming from both of their nostrils and mouths and their grunting and bellowing grew progressively louder.

We saw our neighbor uphill from us, Chris Ryan come out onto his porch to see what all the commotion was about. Also, Paul Wintler, our neighbor to the west came out to watch the spectacle. It was quite obviously a battle for supremacy. The two large bull buffalo were fighting for the domination of the herd; the young bull challenging the reigning master.

While the battle raged, all of the other buffalo continued to stand on the hillside, intent on watching the conflict unfold.

There was an intensity and sense of violence palpable in the warm afternoon air and the two combatants were oblivious to everything around them. They parried and thrust at each other, with both of them managing to inflict damaging slashes from their horns. With their horns locked together they violently shook their heads back and forth, twisting and jerking in an effort to gain the upper hand and cause damage. The sound from their clashing horns and butting heads wafted loudly on the hillside. Soon blood was oozing along their flanks and shoulders. The smaller bull had a deep gash below its left ear that allowed dark red blood to seep slowly down its neck and mingle with the saliva that was flowing from its mouth and nose.

The confrontation was taking place on a rather steep hill, with an incline of perhaps twenty degrees and consequently, their constant jostling caused them to move inexorably down the slope toward the deep ravine that served as a watershed at the base of the hill, about twenty yards from our doorstep.

We watched in fascination as the younger bull gained the uphill advantage over his older adversary and wisely shifted his torso so that he maintained the superior position.

Realizing the mistake that he had made, the older bull recognized the predicament. The young bull was now positioned above him with the chasm of the deep, rocky ravine looming closer. Knowing that the young bull could now drive him backwards with ease, the old bull struggled mightily to shift its body to a more favorable position, but it was impossible. His hooves could not gain a good hold, and he continued to be driven backwards toward the looming, cactus-covered crevice that would likely inflict severe injury if he allowed himself to be driven over the edge. The moment of judgment was imminent. Either he must surrender or suffer the consequences of being driven over the ledge. The old bull dropped to one knee, lowered its head and cowered in defeat. Standing defiantly above him, the younger bull stood proudly, stomped insistently on the hard, dry soil and snorted and tossed its massive head in a display of control and domination. It then let out three loud bellows and glared down at the cringing old bull.

After a few tense moments, the old bull slowly and ponderously stood on four legs, keeping its head low in a cowering position and slunk sideways away. The young bull watched warily, making numerous aggressive thrusts of its head as the older bull skulked off.

Proudly, the young bull stood imperially along the hillside, glancing possessively at the harem that it now controlled. As the old bull shied away, it glanced back furtively at its conqueror, realizing that the defeat would bring an end to his domination and would ultimately lead to the inevitable exile that accompanied all of the old bulls that had suffered a similar fate. Eventually the old bull reached the dirt road at the top of the hill and moved slowly off to nurse its wounds.

Back on the hillside, all of the other buffalo, the cows, the yearlings, the young bulls and the newborn, went back to grazing.

Maureen and I looked at each other, and turned and looked at our neighbors who had watched the spectacle. It was truly a moment out of National Geographic, and we had watched it unfold on our doorstep.

8. Boats, Planes, Drugs, and Bombs

DURING OUR FIRST COUPLE OF years on the Island, the only cross-channel transportation available was either the Seaplane service or the Catalina Cruise boats. Operated by Crowley Maritime, the Catalina Cruise vessels were steel-hulled passenger boats that could carry up to seven hundred passengers. They were slow, taking about two-and-a half hours to make the crossing, and they tended to roll heavily in large swells. The boats ran a regular schedule in the summer months into the Isthmus, but discontinued all service into Two Harbors from late October through mid-February. During those 'dead' months, the only way to get to and from the mainland was by seaplane or driving into Avalon to catch a boat. One of the fun things that occurred each February, when the first boat of the season arrived, was to see people out on the pier pointing and cheering 'Da Boat, Da Boat', in reference to the old television sitcom 'Fantasy Island' that aired at the time.

In 1981, Doug Bombard initiated a longtime vision by starting up the Catalina Channel Express. Doug hired his son Greg, and Greg's good friend and former Catalina Mooring Service employee Tom Rutter, to help run the operation. Bombard began a cross-channel service that would provide a more reliable and faster year-round service into the Isthmus and to Avalon.

Beginning with a single fifty-six passenger vessel named the *Checkmate,* later re-named the *Channel Express*, the new service cut nearly an hour off the travel time of the Catalina Cruise boats. It wasn't an easy beginning, with an engine-room fire that nearly ended their effort, but perseverance, determination, and a vision of succeeding eventually led to the highly successful Catalina Express fleet that dominates the cross-channel service to this day.

Doug Bombard initially served as President of the company, with Greg, his second oldest son, as General Manager. Tommy Rutter served as Operations Manager and all three, as well as Doug's youngest son Tim, served at various times as captains. As the operation grew, several other Island residents and former employees were to join the firm, including Ray Lyman, Johnny Vaughan, Chris Ryan, Richard Brown, and Gary Huntington, to name just a few.

All of those men began their maritime careers on the Island, and their experiences in the Harbor Department and with the Mooring Service paved the way for their successes with the Catalina Express.

For the residents of the Isthmus, having a dependable year-round cross-channel service was a real blessing. No longer did one have to always suffer the challenging drive across the rugged Island roads in order to catch a boat from Avalon, or pay the increasingly high fares of taking the seaplane or a helicopter. The service also increased visitor counts at the West End by bringing more and more customers into the local campgrounds, Banning House Lodge, and local kid's camps.

With Doug Bombard dedicating a lot of his business hours to the Catalina Express operation, Randy Bombard assumed a more active role in the Two Harbors operation. With Doug spending more and more time on the mainland, Randy, Tim, and their sister Wendy, assumed more administrative duties within the Isthmus operation

Wendy was married to Gary Adams, a delightful guy from the State of Maine whose strong east coast accent helped add flavor and charm to his daily dialogue. Gary took over the management of the Harbor Reef Restaurant when Art Nielson retired, and brought a new fresh look. Gary and Wendy, like all of the Bombard family members, worked long hours and completely immersed themselves into running a smooth operation where Island visitors could find fun-filled, relaxing enjoyment and quality service. They also depended upon several other key individuals to help run the various departments, including George McElroy and his offspring.

David McElroy followed in George's footsteps by becoming an extremely gifted mechanic and heavy equipment operator. Stephen put his highly talented marine skills into good use by operating the Mooring Service boat the *Kingfisher*, and Ann, who had married Dave Luchau, worked in both the accounting department and the restaurant.

Doug Bombard also counted on Dottie Peterson to manage the General Store. Her likeable husband Pete served with the Mooring Service and later the shoreboat operation, Ty Ewing managed the Isthmus Boat Shop, and Nancy Rinehart managed the campgrounds and the Visitor Services center. It was a tight-knit family operation and everyone knew that they could depend upon each other to back them up and provide support wherever and whenever needed.

This was a great time for Maureen and me. She started working again in the Accounting Department, drawing upon good friend Laura Peterson for day-care service for our son Trevor. I loved my job and was thoroughly enjoying the opportunity to fish, golf and spend quality time with the family.

By far the most defining moments on the Island were the innumerable boating situations and incidents that took place. In one of my earlier involvements, I vividly recall the unusual act of towing an airplane onto a mooring in the summer of 1982.

During the first several years we lived on the Island, Catalina Seaplanes ran a regular service into Avalon, with less regular but occasional flights into and out of Two Harbors. In our first year, I seem to remember the cost of flying one-way was around twelve dollars and fifty cents per person. That cost rose considerably as the years went by until the seaplane service stopped after two fatal accidents.

The first seaplane service actually began in 1919 when Syd Chaplin, half-brother of Charlie Chaplin, initiated a flight service that lasted about two years. Service discontinued after that until 1931 when Phillip K. Wrigley started the Wilmington-Catalina Airline Service.

Following Wrigley's involvement, several other seaplane businesses kept the seaplane service in operation until 1989 when those two fatal crashes led to a complete termination of the service.

On that memorable afternoon in the summer of 1982, one of the seaplanes had taken-off from the seaplane ramp in Catalina Harbor, outbound for Wilmington Harbor. As it banked around Cat Head and rose above the gap in the Island that forms Two Harbors, it encountered a mechanical problem. The captain contacted the Harbor Office on VHF Channel 9, informing them that he was going to land in front of Isthmus Cove so that he could try and ascertain the source of the mechanical issue. Aligning his heading into the wind, the Seaplane Captain made a smooth landing out near the Isthmus Reef. Once it was down, the plane taxied to an area just outside of the Isthmus mooring field and then shut down its engines and the Captain requested a tow onto a mooring.

I was standing-by during the landing and overheard the radio request. I headed toward the aircraft and approached it upwind. The Captain climbed out of the cockpit and stepped down onto one of the landing pontoons. From there he called out to me to maneuver ahead of his position and toss him a tow-line, which he informed me he was going to secure to the forward pontoon stanchion. I followed his directions and heaved a towline, which he retrieved from the water with what appeared to be a broom handle, tied a bowline around the stanchion, and directed me to begin the tow.

Proceeding forward at a slow, steady pace so as not to put too much pressure on the stanchion, I made way for a mooring. When the plane neared the mooring buoy, I took the patrol boat out of gear and let the plane glide ahead on its minimal forward motion. Surprisingly, the Captain was able to grab the mooring wand and pull up the bow hawser on the first effort. He released my towline and asked if I could transport his passengers to shore while he worked on the mechanical problem. I suggested he try to secure the sand line of the mooring to another point near the tail of the plane so that the plane would not swing in circles on the mooring. He walked aft with the sand line,

74

wrapped it around the stern stanchion of the pontoon and made it secure.

I maneuvered around the expansive wings and positioned my patrol boat near the rear portion of the starboard pontoon and grabbed the forward stanchion to keep my boat in position. The Captain then escorted six passengers out of the plane's main cabin and assisted them onto my waiting patrol boat. I took the passengers to the main float and dropped them off.

That was one of the most unusual tows and transports that I made during the years, and I regret that I did not get a picture of the experience from a boating friend who told me that he had taken several. It would have been a nice photo for my scrapbook.

I'll also never forget the experience of flying on the seaplanes. We had several opportunities through the years to ride aboard the planes, and each flight was exciting. There's nothing quite as exhilarating as the roar and shudder of the old Grumman Gooses as they revved their engines and roared noisily across the water in an effort to gain the speed needed for takeoff. Similarly, the rush of adrenalin that comes with liftoff, when thunderous sheets of seawater pound against the aluminum hull as the plane takes to the air, is enough to send shivers down the spine of even the saltiest sailor. Landing is every bit as exciting and nerve-wracking as you watch the sea surface getting closer and closer until that moment of impact when the pontoons touch the surface, obscuring all sight of everything except the water encapsulating the windows, the engines whining in a convulsive throb while the plane throttles down.

We personally never had any problems on any of our flights, but we talked with several people who told us they felt that it was the scariest plane ride they had ever taken.

Boating Catalina waters is a relatively easy pastime. In southern California, the weather is exceptional and boaters can enjoy the generally placid Pacific Ocean on a year-round basis (avoiding the occasionally stormy periods). Similarly, there are few hazards or sea-faring dangers to worry about near the Island, provided you do some basic research and learn the fundamentals of safe boating before heading out.

When we moved to the Island, we became aware of one of the few boating hazards that existed in the vicinity of Isthmus Cove, the notorious Isthmus Reef. That primarily submerged underwater reef lies directly landward of Bird Rock, a roughly one-acre island that juts impressively from the blue depths of the ocean to provide a starkly visible landmark for incoming boaters. About one-hundred yards from the perimeter of Bird Rock, heading toward the Island, the Isthmus Reef rises from a depth of nearly one-hundred feet, to a shallow area that is partially exposed at low tide. The remainder of the reef averages between six and twenty feet in depth, and generally does not present any danger. However the high point on the reef, an area about the size of a large powerboat, was notorious for causing boats to run aground, sometimes resulting in total losses.

In the early eighties the only navigational aids in place for the reef were a series of five mooring buoys, placed semi-strategically along the northerly side of the reef. Those markers were stenciled with the words REEF, but because of challenging underwater topography in the vicinity of the high spot, the buoys were positioned quite a distance from the danger zone—perhaps fifty-feet from the most dangerous spot. Also, the omnipresent seagulls used the buoys as landing pads from where they could rest and watch for prey. As is their wont, seagulls are notorious for their ability to build layers of guano wherever they choose to roost. As a result, the buoys were often covered with so much bird droppings that the REEF lettering was covered with a thick, blotchy coating of bird poop, obscuring the inherent danger of the reef markers.

As a consequence of all those factors, numerous boats struck the mostly submerged reef. The Harbor Department kept a chalkboard on the outer wall of the Harbor Office to record the number of boats that hit the reef each year. The average annual number of strikes was about thirty-five.

One day in the summer of 1982, a thirty-foot sailboat struck the reef dead-on, punching a gaping, three-foot hole into the port bow of the sailboat at, and below, the waterline. Within minutes the boat bounced off the reef and then sank in about sixty-feet of water. Four people were on board, and fortunately all four were plucked from the water without injuries. Insurance adjusters hired a dive service to inspect the boat and wrote it off as a total loss. To hire a commercial salvage company from the mainland to refloat and patch the hull, and then tow it to the mainland for repairs, was not worth the time and effort. The boat was named *Big Sky*.

Pete Peterson, who was working in the Mooring Service, discussed a possible salvage effort with George McElroy and together they decided to salvage the boat. Pete worked with his mooring crew to attach air filled lift-bags to the hull, float the boat to the surface and then tow it into the shallow waters in Isthmus Cove. He then worked with George McElroy to build a cradle for the hull and pull the boat from the water using the D-8 Caterpillar. The salvage effort went smoothly. Pete and George then worked together for a few months patching the hull, getting the engine flushed-out and running, rewired the boat, and performed an overall cleanup and restoration of the boat's interior. Afterward they put it up for sale and made a tidy profit!

That sailboat was one of many boats that hit the reef. A few of them are still submerged in the deep water surrounding the reef. Others suffered only the ignominy of having their pictures posted on the Harbor Office wall as they sat high and dry atop the reef waiting for the tide to float them free.

Finally, the Coast Guard decided that enough was too much, and sent a crew of Army Engineers to the Island in the early eighties to construct a tower directly on top of the high point of the reef. That navigational tower, clearly marked on four sides with large bold letters stating REEF, effectively put an end to most reef accidents. I say 'most' because it did not completely put an end to boats hitting the reef. At least half a dozen boats have struck the reef since its installation. Most of those boats commented that they were looking for the reef when they went aground. One boat, a twenty-one-foot outboard runabout belonging to a local resident, crashed head-on into the tower when returning from Avalon one dark summer night. That collision caused semi-serious physical injury to the operator of the boat and the boat sustained considerable bow damages. For the most part, the saga of the Isthmus Reef came nearly to an end with the construction of the Reef Tower.

Working as I did on the water, day after day, season upon season, there were a lot of odd and sometimes rather amazing things to see. Several people that I've known through the years have commented to me, "Boy, in your position I'll bet you've seen it all."

My response has always been the same, "Nope. I've seen a lot, but I've not seen it all. There will always be some new surprises."

There were funny things, tragedies, oddities and just about any descriptive adjective that can be used to describe the multitude of marine related events that I saw or was involved with through the years. One afternoon I was operating a shoreboat, returning from the USC Wrigley Marine Science Center in Big Fisherman's Cove, and the only other person on board was Kathleen Rinehart, who worked with me at the time as Contracts Administrator in the Harbor Office.

Kathleen 'Kathy' (later King) was the daughter of Nancy Rinehart, who served as manager of the Isthmus Visitor Services office. The Rinehart family had deep roots in the Island community, with family members in both Avalon and Two Harbors.

When I pulled away from the dock at Big Fisherman's Cove and headed for the Isthmus, Kathy moved up to the forward bulkhead of the shoreboat to talk with me and inadvertently leaned onto the microphone button. Our conversation was broadcast to the entire harbor. Fortunately we did not discuss anything too personal or controversial.

There were also several occasions when rather embarrassing moments occurred 'in the line of duty'. More than once I pulled alongside a boat to collect mooring fees, only to interrupt a personal action—or interaction.

In one of those situations, our good friends Candy and Kevin Cloud were visiting the Island aboard their eighteen-foot inflatable. They were in-between cruising boats at the time (switching from a thirty-foot Chris Craft cruiser to a thirty-four-foot trawler), and rather than forsake visiting the Island, they purchased and outfitted the inflatable boat with as many comforts as can be accommodated in an eighteen-foot center-console, rubber inflatable. They installed padded cushions for sleeping on the forward decking, with a canvas covering to enclose the bow section of the boat. In addition, they equipped the small boat with a Coleman stove for cooking, a large ice-chest, extra storage compartments, and a five-gallon portable toilet with seat.

Early one morning I was making runs through the cove, checking moorings, and I saw Candy on the foredeck. Thinking that she was merely sitting there enjoying the morning view, I pulled alongside to say hello. When I maneuvered near and reached out to secure a hold on their rail, I glanced over at Candy and realized that it was not a good time to visit. Lamely uttering my apologies, I diverted to another duty. After that, I always tried to avoid making my early morning runs in the vicinity of their boat.

Another time, shortly after I had obtained my Masters License, I was on my day-off and Maureen and I had planned an outing on our boat *Little Mo.* That is the little Glaspar that I took to the mainland for my son's birth, and at fourteen-foot it qualified to tie to the dinghy docks.

I pulled into the dock to pick-up Maureen, our infant son Trevor, and our gear. Putting the boat into neutral but leaving the engine running, I proceeded to climb up over the low plastic windshield to get to the bow. In the process, my right knee hit the gearshift lever, pushing down on the throttle and slamming the outboard engine into gear. That clumsy action caused the boat to propel forward, hit the dinghy dock, and ride up onto the deck planks. It was stuck there with about one-third of the hull on top of the dock, the outboard screaming at high rpm's.

It also caused me to fall forward onto the dock. So, there I was, a newly appointed one-hundred ton captain, lying across the planks of the dinghy dock with the bow eye of the boat hung up on the rails and the outboard engine in gear, screaming at high rpm's. To make matters even worse, the entire Baywatch crew was on the nearby main float at the time, undergoing a personnel transfer, and all of them, along with dozens of other people offloading from the Catalina Express, watched the entire incident. They clapped for me when I climbed up onto the impaled boat and shutdown the engine. Thankfully, they were gracious enough to help me lift the boat off the dock.

On another occasion I was rock cod fishing with my brother Dave, on the *Little Smoke*, out in front of Long Point. We were doing well, hauling aboard several nice rock cod, while fishing in about three-hundred-fifty-feet of water. I was cranking up a rig with two large Boccaccio (often called Salmon Grouper) when one of them popped off the hook.

Rockfish caught in deep water almost always pop their air bladders when pulled from the depths. Their bladders fill with air as they are reeled toward the surface and the pressure change causes the bladder to protrude out of their mouths like a big fat tongue. They then float to the surface.

I looked out and saw the unhooked fish floating about fifteen yards from the boat. I told Dave I was going to start-up the engines and head over to recover the fish. As I maneuvered into a position where I could gaff the floating fish, I saw the telltale dorsal fin of a large blue shark, estimated at about nine-feet long, slowly circling the floating fish. I shifted into neutral and rushed out onto the aft deck to grab the gaff. The boat slid perfectly into position with the rock cod floating about six feet off the starboard rail, at the exact time that the blue shark turned toward the fish and opened its jaws to grab the easy meal.

I leaped up onto the starboard deck and reached out with the gaff in an effort to reach the fish before the shark could gulp it down. At that precise moment, the wake from another boat struck our port side, rocking the *Little Smoke* sideways and I felt myself losing my balance. Desperately, I reached out with my left hand to try and grab the rail atop the main cabin, but missed. I looked down into the deep blue water, seeing the shark slide directly beneath me as I fell overboard, the gaff clutched tightly in my right hand.

I think I felt my left leg hit the shark as I plunged into the water and went under. Terrified, I kicked upward, looking around frantically as I broke above the surface. I could not see the shark, but I assumed it was still there and that it was likely not very happy about having a man land on top of it and disrupt its intended meal.

"Help me!" I called out to Dave.

He was standing in the aft cockpit laughing. "Don't just stand there laughing," I called out to him. "Help! Help me get out!"

The freeboard on the *Little Smoke* was not high by most standards, but at about two-and-a-half feet above the surface of the water, it was too high for me to reach and pull myself up. I still had the gaff in my hand and I reached out to snag the rail cap with the hook end. At the same time I continued to swivel my head back and forth, looking for and expecting the shark to make its move.

On board the boat, Dave continued to stand there and laugh. "Come on, Dave!" I pleaded, "Help me get out of here."

Still laughing, he moved to the rail and grabbed hold of the handle of the gaff, just above the hook. He pulled upward while I clutched the long mahogany handle with both hands. As I rose up to the rail of the boat, I managed to grasp the rail cap with my left hand. I then released the gaff with my right hand and swung my left leg up onto the rail. Dave reached down, still laughing, and helped me roll into the cockpit. Looking back over the side of the boat, Dave then reached out and gaffed the rock cod, which was still floating a couple of feet away. He pulled it aboard.

I looked out, trying to locate the shark. It was long gone. More than likely it had been frightened away when I fell overboard and landed on top of it. Of course I had no idea of that when I was in the water; all I knew was that I had fallen in with a large, menacing looking shark and couldn't get out. Dave continued to chuckle about the incident and I decided we had enough fish for the day and headed for home, my pride slightly wounded.

The vast majority of boating incidents that occurred during my career on the Island happened to visiting boaters.

The simple process of mooring a boat could sometimes turn complicated. More than once I watched helplessly when someone attempting to secure a boat onto a mooring fell overboard. On one of those occasions, a very nice older couple that I had become good friends with over the years became a victim of the mooring process while they attempted to secure their boat to their own mooring. George and June Ross, aboard their boat *June's Good Risk*, a forty-two-foot Uniflite, were in the process of picking up mooring K-2 in the Isthmus. I was fueling my patrol boat about twenty yards away from the mooring and saw them make the approach.

George and June were in their late seventies, but both were still healthy and spry, and visited the Island often. George was an avid scuba diver and loved to spend time exploring the kelp forests and nearby reefs. His granddaughter, Jana Love worked for a brief time on the Island, and she was on the pier watching as they pulled into the cove.

June Ross was on the bow as George motored slowly into position. The Isthmus fan was blowing, as usual, at about twelve knots and there were boats on either side of their mooring. June grabbed the pickup pole as she always did, pulling it up over the stanchions and preparing to reach down for the bow hawser. At the same time, George shifted into reverse in an effort to keep the boat from overshooting the mooring can. Unfortunately, he applied a little too much power and the boat began to back too quickly. Determined to get the lines on, June held tightly to the pickup pole, expecting George to take the boat out of reverse so that she could loop the hawser over the bow cleat. George did not adjust in time, and I watched helplessly as June's thighs pressed against the bow stanchion and, still clutching tightly to the pickup pole, she was pulled headfirst over the rail and into the water.

Fortunately, George had the good sense to shift into neutral and drift, rather than pulling forward toward his wife who was floating in the water near the mooring can, still holding onto the pickup pole.

I quickly discontinued my fueling, castoff from the dock and headed for the site. When I reached the mooring, I called out to June, asking her if she was okay.

"Oh, I'm fine." She smiled sheepishly, and looked up at me from the water, "I just feel so foolish"

I leaned over the rail of the patrol boat and clutched her by the wrist, holding her in position alongside the boat. It's not easy to pull a body from the water, so I waited until one of the Baywatch guys, Kevin Marble pulled alongside my boat, stepped aboard, and helped me pull her up over the rail. Assessing her condition, Marble determined that she was okay, suffering only a slight rope burn to her right hand and wrist. We headed over to *June's Good Risk* and I dropped both her and the Baywatch crewman off on the swim step. Marble then stayed aboard and helped George pickup the mooring while June went below to dry off and change clothes. Both George and June were real troopers and laughed-off the incident in good spirits.

I saw that same scenario happen several more times through the years, and fortunately there were never any serious injuries from any of the episodes. But there were a couple of mooring-related incidents that did have tragic results.

One of those occurred late one night when a woman boater was attempting to perform the simple task of climbing aboard her own boat.

On that fateful night, after returning to her boat from Doug's Harbor Reef Saloon, Vicki Guy, a regular Island visitor aboard her twenty-six-foot powerboat *Miss Sociable*, rowed her small inflatable from the dinghy dock to the side of her boat. She was moored on R-1, the closest mooring to the dinghy docks and not far from the pier. Pulling alongside the swim step, she was in the process of climbing over the transom when she slipped on the wet aft deck.

Her boat was equipped with a dinghy-davit, a system of stainless steel brackets designed to allow the boat owner to secure a small dinghy in place on their swim step for easy transportation. One of the brackets, about four-to-six-inches long, serves to help secure the dingy in place once it is pulled up onto the step. That bracket is about the diameter and shape of a five-eighth-inch rod.

When she started to climb aboard, her foot slipped on the wet combing on the rail and she fell sideways, her body striking the side of the boat and then bouncing off the swim step. At the same time, she turned her head to the side and her right eye came down directly onto the stainless rod, impaling the bracket several inches into her eye socket.

In extreme pain and unable to move, she moaned and tried to call out for help. It was close to two a.m. and everyone on nearby boats was asleep. Fortunately, our graveyard patrolman Mark Woolery was in the Harbor Office at the time and he heard Vicki's plaintiff moans. Walking out onto the end of the pier, he looked out to try and determine what had caught his attention. From his new vantage point he could see that something was amiss, but he was unsure of just what had happened. He climbed into his patrol boat and headed over to the mooring.

Arriving alongside her boat, he encountered one of the most gruesome and terrifying sights that he had ever seen. Vicki was mostly submerged in the water, with only her head and shoulders positioned above the swim step. At first he could not tell what he was looking at, but as he knelt down along the side of his boat he could see the metal bracket thrust deeply into her eye socket. There was a lot of blood.

Realizing that there was extreme danger in attempting to pull her free, Woolery had the good sense to seek Baywatch help. Fortunately a nearby boater had also heard the commotion and arrived on scene to help. Leaving that individual with Vicki, Woolery hurried to the Harbor Office and called Baywatch on the landline. They were on scene within minutes and took charge of the situation, very carefully lifting her from the water and pulling her free from the steel bracket stuck in her eye socket.

Immediately and professionally the Baywatch crew dressed her wounds and arranged transport for her to a mainland trauma facility. She lost her right eye and was several months in recovery, but the accident did not prevent her from continuing to visit the Island that she loved so dearly.

Another terrifying and unfortunate incident took place one afternoon when a large powerboat was in the process of mooring in the Isthmus.

On that occasion, I once again was standing on the fuel dock when the vessel *Kaneokakai* pulled into the cove to pick up its mooring L-1, the third mooring row on the fairway on the east side of the main dock.

Harry Harper, a wonderful man and his charming wife Linda, were maneuvering into the mooring field on a busy summer weekend. When Harry shifted the boat out of gear and begin the close-quarters maneuvering process required to moor smoothly, the transmissions did not disengage. There was something wrong with the shifting mechanism and the boat continued moving forward.

Confused and daunted by the boat's failure to respond, Harry reached over and pushed down on the throttles, thinking that perhaps the boat's forward propulsion was not responding properly because there was not enough fuel going to the engines. Because the engines were locked into forward, the increased throttle caused the boat to propel forward even faster. There was another small boat pulling away from the main float and heading directly toward the *Kaneokakai*. In a desperate effort to alter course, Harry swung the helm to port, an action that caused his boat to swerve directly into the path of another boat moored nearby.

Kaneokakai crashed into the side of the forty-two-foot sailboat that was moored there, knocking the man seated in the cockpit overboard.

The *Kaneokakai* continued to plough forward, moving inexorably toward the man in the water.

Popping back up to the surface after being knocked out of his boat, Sandy Sinclair, a fellow mooring lessee and owner of the moored sailboat, watched in terror as the big powerboat approached him as he treaded water. He thought to himself that his only chance was to dive down below the surface in an effort to avoid being run over. He dove below the surface and swam downward as the big boat continued onward. Running out of breath, Sandy looked up and saw the big twin propellers churning round and round not more than five feet above his head. The out of control powerboat continued onward, just a few feet from his submerged location. When it finally passed by, Sandy surged to the surface, gasping for air. Fortunately he surfaced completely unharmed.

Meanwhile, the out of control powerboat continued onward, with Harry frozen in place at the helm. When the *Kaneokakai* reached the boat moored on M-1, it passed between the bow of the boat and the mooring can, snagging the bow hawser on one of its prop's and effectively killing one engine.

With a lot of weight behind it, the boat continued onward for a short distance, dragging the mooring and the boat on M-1 along with it. The two boats, now pinned side by side, continued to move slowly through the mooring field, their bows pointing in opposite directions. The man aboard the moored sailboat leaped up and climbed the ladder to the bridge of the *Kaneokakai*. Reaching Harry Harper's side, the man reached down and pulled the engine kill-switches, shutting off all power to the engines and stopping the carnage.

The resultant damages were rather extreme, with three boats, not including the *Kaneokakai* sustaining damages in the tens of thousands of dollars. Amazingly, and very fortunately, there were no personal injuries.

While those incidents described above were quite distressing and dramatic, it always surprised me that there were not more similar accidents. Oh, there were others, and some of them resulted in both damages and injuries, but overall, considering the number of boats that visit the Island on any given summer weekend (more than twelve-hundred boats might visit the West End on a busy holiday weekend); serious boating accidents were few and far between.

One afternoon while on duty, we overheard a radio call indicating that a small airplane was having engine problems and was going to attempt to make an emergency landing on the Cat Harbor road. That dirt road, which runs between Catalina Harbor and Isthmus Cove, is around one-thousand yards long and is adequate for landing a small plane. Doug Bombard, who flew on a regular basis between the mainland and the Island, has landed on the road on numerous occasions.

Looking up into the eastern sky, we watched for the plane to make its approach. When it appeared from the east, rounding the point at Blue Caverns, it was obvious that it did not have enough altitude to clear the palm trees and other structures in the Isthmus. The captain of the plane called out that he could not gain altitude and was going to put her down in the water in Isthmus Cove. Watching in fascination, we saw the plane gliding dangerously close to the mast of an anchored sailboat and then drop slowly from the sky until it splashed down in front of the Isthmus mooring area, near the prominent headland at Fourth of July Cove. The landing looked completely smooth and easy and the plane glided to a stop about fifty feet from H-7, the westernmost mooring in Isthmus Cove. I was in a patrol boat and immediately headed for the scene.

Upon arrival alongside the small airplane, one of the passengers had opened his cabin door and stepped out onto the wing. Another passenger aboard the plane, a woman, stepped out onto the wing directly behind him. I maneuvered into position near the wing of the plane and the two people stepped onto the bow of my boat. Another man climbed out and onto the wing, passing out several bags of luggage. The luggage was put into the boat and the man stepped aboard. As the pilot stepped onto the wing carrying two more bags, the plane started to dip and go under. He quickly handed up the two bags he was holding just as the wing slipped below the surface and the plane glided underwater and toward the bottom. Treading water, the pilot dog-paddled over to the side of my boat and we helped him climb up over the rail and aboard. Three of the passengers, along with their luggage had gotten out dry and unscathed, only the pilot got wet.

The following day, the mooring service dove on the submerged airplane, connected a series of air bags, and floated the plane to the surface. They then towed it to the east side of the main Isthmus Beach where a plan to haul it out of the water was in effect. Unfortunately, in the process of towing the plane onto the beach, a line connected between the plane and the tractor that was towing it out of the water snapped, and a lead mooring weight still attached to the line flew back and struck Tim Bombard in the shin, breaking the bone.

Tim, Doug Bombards' youngest son, was serving as Harbor Director at the time, overseeing all departments in the harbor operation, including the harbor, mooring service, boat shop, fuel dock, and the other smaller departments within the operation.

Tim was a very hands-on manager. He held his own Masters License and is a very knowledgeable mechanic. He moved from department to department, filling in where needed and working tirelessly to keep things running smoothly. His easy-going temperament served him well during his tenure in the operation. I always appreciated his calm, cool and collected demeanor when dealing with difficult employees, customers, or situations. He, like all of the Bombards, is also a skilled and professional boat operator and I always knew that he could be counted upon to perform at the top level of the boating spectrum during storms and adverse conditions.

I have a photo in one of my family albums with Tim, the Harbor Director, and myself, the Harbormaster, seated atop one of the dock boxes on the pier with each of us sporting a knee-high cast on our right foot. The photo serves to remind me of one of the unusual episodes that we shared while working together.

Another event that occurred about that time was the discovery of dozens of waterproof bundles of Thai Sticks—tightly rolled packages of high-grade marijuana—that began washing up on several Island beaches one fall afternoon. The first bundles were discovered in Big Fisherman's Cove at the USC Wrigley Institute. Two thirty-pound packages wrapped tightly in sealed plastic were found rolling around in the surf by one of the employees of the Marine Science Center. That person then called the local Sheriff and he in turn called the Drug Enforcement Agency (DEA) in Los Angeles.

Within an hour, two large Sikorski Helicopters circled around and landed on Isthmus Beach, adjacent to the pier. It was low tide and the beach served well as a temporary landing site. Soon there were nearly a dozen high-speed Sheriff and Coast Guard boats patrolling West End beaches, stopping occasionally at selected locations to put crewmen ashore to recover bails of the pot that had been discovered. Before the afternoon was over, more than forty bails of the high-grade marijuana were piled along the Isthmus Pier, under the watchful eye of an armed DEA officer. Local Sheriff Bob Murcott assisted the federal agents in the recovery effort, giving his knowledgeable and insightful advice on where he thought additional bails might be found. He pulled several bails from the water while assisting in the search and recovery effort.

Apparently, from the information dispensed by the agents on scene, they suspected that a drug smuggling ring had made a night drop from an airplane near the Island's West End and a boat was scheduled for the pickup. The location of the transaction was near the tip of the Island in the vicinity of Starlight Beach, a small cove about three-quarters of a mile from the West End on the front side of Catalina. Unfortunately for the drug smugglers, there is an offshore rock, Johnson's Rock that lies about a quarter mile from Starlight. It appeared that the pickup boat struck the partially submerged rock and broke apart, allowing the bails of Thai Sticks to drift away and end up scattered on beaches all the way from Starlight to near Long Point.

Federal officials, to the best of my knowledge, were never able to make any arrests or identify any of the individuals involved in the smuggling operation. Rumor has it that several Islanders benefited from the incident, discovering one or more of the bails for themselves.

Another unique boating situation occurred one winter day when a report came into the Harbor Office about a boat partially submerged but still afloat a few miles west of Catalina Harbor. A small commercial fishing boat reported the situation, calling in to state that he was attempting to tow the semi-submerged boat into Cat Harbor.

When I heard the radio report, I contacted Sheriff Murcott and we hopped into a patrol boat and departed Cat Harbor, heading for the coordinates we were given. Approximately two-miles southwest of Ribbon Rock, we spotted an old Monterey-style commercial fishing boat slowly towing a partially sunken vessel. The boat appeared to be about sixty-foot in length, and from what we could see below the surface, appeared to be a very nice private boat. It was ninety-five percent submerged with only about five feet of the bow section floating above the surface.

Maneuvering into a position near the towing vessel, Murcott called out and asked if they wanted us to take over the tow.

"No way!" bellowed one of the two fishermen visible aboard the rust smeared fishing boat. "We have salvage rights. There's no way we're giving up this tow!"

Murcott looked over at me and chuckled. "Well," he commented wryly, "Let's see if they make it all the way into the harbor before that thing goes to the bottom and takes them with it!"

There must have been a sealed bulkhead in the forward section of the submerged boat because it remained afloat for the remainder of the three-hour tow into the harbor. The plan of the commercial fishermen was to tow the boat as far into the back of the bay as possible so that it would go aground and could then be assessed and salvaged.

They maintained the tow into the harbor, staying in the narrow fairway on the west side of the Cat Harbor mooring field, until the submerged boat grounded on the muddy bottom of the bay. It was a moderately high tide, standing at the time at about four-and-a-half feet. When the boat came to a stop, the fishermen informed Murcott that they intended to remain on sight until a salvage representative arrived to assume oversight, and agree to salvage compensation.

Murcott agreed to their demands, with the understanding that he would be diving on the boat to ascertain the condition of the hull and to inspect the interior for the possibility of bodies.

I took him ashore to gather his dive gear, waiting at the dock for him to return.

About an hour later Murcott returned in his wetsuit, loaded his tanks and assorted dive gear into the patrol boat and we headed back out to the site. By that time the tide was dropping rapidly and the fly bridge of the sunken boat was now exposed. The bridge and helm station appeared to be in very good condition and the name painted onto the side of the bridge was visible, *Black Sheep*. As I pulled alongside the boat one of the fishermen walked out onto the foredeck of his boat and called out to us, "You'd better not take nothing! We have salvage rights!"

"Don't worry," Murcott called back, "I'm merely checking for bodies and inspecting for damages. I have no intentions of taking anything off the boat."

Seemingly satisfied, the grizzled looking fisherman sat down on the lazarette of the fish hold to watch Murcott perform his duty.

I reached out and held my patrol boat alongside the fly bridge and wrapped a deck-line around the stanchion of a heavy-duty arch that supported antennas and a radar unit. I secured the line to a side cleat on the patrol boat and then assisted Murcott with his tanks and dive gear.

He then seated himself on the rail of the patrol boat, adjusted his weight belt and fell backwards into the water. Rising briefly to the surface, Murcott took a couple of breaths on his regulator, gave me the 'thumbs up' and slid below the surface.

Sitting there alongside the sunken boat gave me a strange feeling. It was very weird holding onto the top of a boat and looking down into the murky water at the visible portion of the cabin and decking. It obviously was a very nice boat, heavy and well built, with the basic design of a Nordic Tug. There were a few items beginning to float to the surface as the tide fell, dislodging a couple of cushions and deck boxes from their normal storage space. I thought about releasing my hold on the boat and cruising around to pick up the loose items, but did not want to leave with Murcott still in the water. I kept thinking about the boat, and why and how it managed to be submerged. I considered that it was very possible that Murcott would come up and tell me that he had discovered a body, or bodies inside of the boat.

Suddenly, breaking into my reverie, Murcott burst through the surface holding a brownish cylindrical shaped object and yelled, "Let's get the hell out of here! This thing is wired with pipe bombs!"

Shocked by his sudden appearance and the tone in his voice, I yanked my hand away from the overhang of the side of the fly bridge that I was holding onto, grabbed the object and tossed it into the water. I looked down at my hand as if it was damaged, as I realized what Murcott had said. He was still in the water, unsnapping his weight belt and tank and making an effort to climb up into the boat.

I reached down and pulled his dive tank and harness from his back, grabbed onto his weight belt and dropped it onto the deck. I then reached over and assisted him in rolling over the rail and into the cockpit. Once he was in the boat he turned to me and insisted, "Let's get the hell out of here, that thing is loaded with bombs. In fact we'd better evacuate the entire back harbor."

I started to pull away when Murcott told me to go over and tell the commercial fishing boat to move farther away. When I pulled alongside the boat, both men were standing on deck watching our approach. I told them the boat was wired with multiple pipe bombs and suggested they relocate.

"Nope," one of the men stated. "We ain't going nowhere! This is our salvage and we're staying right where we are until the salvage man gets here."

I started to say something when Murcott interrupted. "Listen asshole. There are at least four big pipe bombs wired to both engines on that boat. I don't give a damn if you want to kill yourselves, but you're not going to do it in my jurisdiction! Now start your engines and move out of this back bay or I'll put you both under arrest!"

The two men stared at Murcott for a long moment, and then Murcott said coldly, "Now! Start your engine and get out of here!" The tone of his voice seemed to trigger the right response and one of the men went into the cabin and started the engine. Murcott turned to me, "Okay, now who else is on a boat nearby?"

There was only one other occupied boat in the vicinity, one of the employees who worked in the General Store. I cruised over and told him that there was a problem with the sunken boat and that he needed to move his boat out of the back of the harbor to a safer location. He complied immediately. I then took Murcott back to shore and he instructed me to remain on the dock and make sure that nobody be allowed to go near the submerged boat. He climbed into his vehicle and drove off toward the Isthmus.

I stayed on the patrol boat tied to the dock. A couple of people wandered down the pier intending to go out to their boat moored near the sunken boat. I informed them of the problem and they stayed with me on the end of the dock until the Sheriff returned.

About an hour later Murcott returned to the dock and advised me that members of the Los Angeles County bomb squad would be arriving soon by helicopter. Within a few minutes we heard the distinctive roar of the big Sikorsky police helicopters beating toward the Island. Two of the big choppers landed on 'buffalo field', the cleared area at the base of Cat Harbor where we played softball. Having two big helicopters land there attracted a lot of attention in the community, both from their noise and from the massive red dust plumes that flew into the air. Soon there was a steady procession of residents in vehicles, on bikes, and on foot headed for the Cat Harbor pier. One of the members of the bomb squad instructed Murcott and a couple of the Baywatch crew that were now on scene to clear the Cat Harbor pier and setup a no-pass boundary about halfway down the Cat Harbor road.

A short while later, a dive team from the bomb squad was suited up and heading for the sunken boat. They asked me if they could use the patrol boat because they did not want any civilians to get too close. I complied with their request.

Anxiously we waited at the baseball field, watching from afar while the dive team inspected the sunken boat. After about forty-five minutes, the dive team surfaced, loaded a few things into the patrol boat and returned to the dock. They stayed on the end of the dock apparently working on the items pulled from the boat.

Eventually they gathered all of the things they had taken off the boat, loaded them all into big black duffel bags and headed back toward the helicopters. None of the bomb squad crew would talk with anyone except Sheriff Murcott, but two investigators remained on the Island to gather more information. After the helicopters had departed Bob gave us all a rundown of what they had found.

He informed us that the boat was unoccupied but that there were six three-foot long pipe bombs wired to the engines, three on each. All of the petcocks and saltwater intake valves were opened and the hoses either removed or cut. All of the portholes and hatches below deck were left open and the bulkhead doors unlatched in the open position.

Obviously it was an insurance job. Unfortunately for the person, or persons, responsible for the scuttling effort, the pipe bombs were wired to the engines with a timer. When the timing mechanism got wet because the water intruded into the engine room too quickly, the bombs could not explode. To make matters worse for the culprits, the forward lazarette had a watertight bulkhead that held a large void area and formed an air bubble that served to keep the boat from sinking completely.

Federal investigators questioned the commercial fishermen and learned that they had seen a small Whaler type skiff motoring rapidly toward the mainland from the vicinity of where they first found the partially submerged boat. We learned later that the owner of the boat had phoned-in a stolen boat report several hours before it was discovered off the end of the Island.

Salvage crews managed to refloat the boat a few days later. It was then towed back to the mainland. A few years later we saw the boat again on the Island, after it was salvaged, repaired and reportedly sold for about half its market value by the insurance company.

We also heard that the two men on the commercial fishing boat received a ten-thousand dollar salvage disbursement for the five-hour tow that they performed.

We never heard whether anyone was ever held accountable for the aborted attempt to sink and blowup the boat, but Officer Murcott did report that the owner was under investigation on charges of violating the RICO statute (Racketeer Influenced Corruption Organization) Act.

9. Pig Hunting

ONE DAY WHEN TREVOR WAS about two years old, Maureen and I headed out into the hills for a hike, taking our young son with us. We drove out Isthmus road to the 'bump gate' at Deer Valley. There were several bump gates on the Island in those days and a bump gate is exactly what it sounds like—you pull up to it and bump it to make it open. They were in place on the Island to try and keep the buffalo out of protected areas. The gates are set on large spring-coiled hinges with bars across the front and two or three rubber tires bolted to the steel bars. A driver pulls up near the rubber tires, slows or stops, and then rolls forward with enough speed to hit the tires and make the gate swing open. Hit it too easy and the gate does not swing open enough to pass through. Hit it too hard and it swings open quickly and then bounces back quickly.

Quite a few cars or trucks on the Island were marked with the scars from mistiming the bump.

We parked near the bump gate and hiked up the western ridge of Deer Valley to the 'bone yard', the old carcass dumping grounds near the top of the ridgeline. Trevor was sitting on my shoulders, as he usually did when we went out into the hills, holding onto the top of my head with his pudgy little fingers entwined in my hair. On the way back down the hill we were winding our way along a narrow pathway between thick patches of cactus and sugar bush, when an extremely loud, raucous squealing erupted directly in front of us. I looked down and jumped backward a little bit when a small wild pig about the size of a football rushed out from a patch of cactus and was headed directly for my legs. It was squealing at the top of its lungs, short, repetitive squeals that pierced our ears loudly. I quickly spread my legs about a foot apart and the little pig ran right between them and continued up the path.

The commotion really freaked poor little Trevor out and he began screaming and pulling really hard on my hair. He had never seen, or heard anything quite like that before and it really troubled him. He screamed loudly for a few moments until Maureen reached our side and pulled him off my shoulders to console him. His screams gradually turned to deep, wracking sobs and it took her quite a few minutes to calm him down. Eventually he settled down and we continued on back to Mr. Truck and returned home.

That first experience with a pig was Trevor's most traumatic, and sort of set the stage for many more wild pig stories. By the time he was eight or nine years old, he and his good buddy Nicholas McElroy, who was about three years older, regularly caught little baby pigs while hiking out in the hills. They also caught baby goats, tiny little quail and an assortment of Island snakes. The two boys had a real affinity with the Island's wild side and did their utmost to get out into the hills whenever possible. Most of their animal exploits resulted in fun or exciting stories, but many years later, Nicholas did suffer a compound fracture of his leg during one pig hunting expedition when a large wounded boar charged at him out near Parsons Landing and caused Nicholas to stumble into a deep ravine, where he shattered his tibia when he landed on the rocks. It happened about twelve miles from the Isthmus and it took several hours before he received medical attention. That ordeal was a brutal one for the young man.

Wild boar and wild goats were prolific during our early years on the Island. Thousands of wild boars, progeny of animals brought by coastal traders and early Island inhabitants, roamed the hills and valleys in abundance. Spanish goats also proliferated wildly, and herds of several hundred goats roaming the hills were quite common.

For us, and for most Island residents and visitors, the opportunity to see, photograph, hunt and just be around those wild animals was a real treat. As a family, we played a game whenever we drove in and out of Avalon, guessing which animals we would spot first, and how many. On numerous drives in and out of town (a roughly twenty-five mile excursion, each way), we might count more than fifty animals along the route. Buffalo didn't really count in the game; they were just considered a common sight and didn't really create much excitement, except perhaps when they were breeding and when the babies arrived.

Unfortunately, the Catalina Island Conservancy did not want the wild animals on the Island. They considered them a nuisance and harmful to the Island ecology. In the late 1980's the Catalina Conservancy initiated an eradication program that would ultimately eliminate all of the Island goats and pigs, a controversial program that caused a great rift between the Conservancy and many Island residents, and visitors. Even though I was not an avid hunter, I really liked having wild animals on the Island and relished the times we had while they were still around.

When the Catalina Conservancy built their 'Animal Control Fence', a wire fence that stretched across the Island from near the USC facility, to the point above Catalina Harbor, they herded all of the buffalo out of the west end, and systematically killed off all of the wild pigs and goats, it brought the end of an era to Catalina Island. There are few places in our modern society where nature and wildlife could be seen and appreciated like it was in those early years on the Island. We feel very fortunate that our children, especially Trevor, had the opportunity to live and experience that wild side of nature on a daily basis. Few people anywhere have had those types of exposures or adventures, and sadly those days are now over.

Many Islanders are avid hunters, but not I. However, on one occasion I went out pig hunting with good buddy David McElroy early one spring. We drove out the old dump road above Catalina Harbor toward the West End. Parking on the high summit that leads down into Bouchette Canyon (above Emerald Bay), we headed down the steep, thickly forested hillsides just as the first vestiges of daylight began to illuminate the dark green valley. From our vantage point at the apex of the steep ridge we could see nearly the entire canyon below us. Not far from our location, perhaps two-hundred yards to our left, a small plateau blanketed in spring grasses was surrounded by thick sugar bush and clusters of scrub oak. David pointed toward the clearing and silently signaled me to move with him toward that small pasture.

Crouching stealthily and walking softly so as not to make any noise, I followed him through a thicket of scattered cactus and sugar bush until we reached a pile of rocks that formed enough of a mound to hide behind. Ducking down, David indicated that I should kneel at his side. I knelt and peered out into the clearing, watching. At first, I could see nothing but the grass and thick, dark vegetation, but a moment later a subtle movement caught my eye and I saw three small white pigs foraging below the canopy of a scrub oak on the far side of the clearing. David put his finger to his lips, indicating quiet, while pointing slightly to the left of the three small pigs. Partially concealed behind the stump of the oak, I could see the haunches and rump of a rather large, white and black sow.

Using hand signals, David advised me to ready my gun, a Marlin 30-30 that I had purchased from another Island friend about a year previously.

I put the gun to my right shoulder and waited. After a few moments, the larger pig moved out from behind the trunk of the small oak. I started to lift the rifle into firing position when suddenly another larger, darker animal plunged out of a nearby thicket, standing momentarily broadside near the other animal. I looked to David and he nodded rather emphatically.

Placing the butt of my rifle firmly into my right shoulder, I lifted the barrel up and focused into the scope. I could not see a thing. I shifted my head slightly to the left, peering at the animals with my eyes and assuring myself that the rifle was pointing in the right direction and not blocked by any obstructions. Everything was clear and in full vision. I looked back into the scope, but could see nothing but a dark gray shadow.

At that point, the big mottled boar sensed our presence, because he suddenly turned rapidly in our direction, and crouched onto his haunches. David whispered emphatically, "Shoot! Shoot!" I glanced over at him with a dumbfounded expression and the big boar bolted from the clearing and back into the bushes.

David, kneeling next to me, looked at me perplexed, and turned his palms upward as if to say, 'What's wrong with you?' I shook my head stupidly and shrugged.

At that moment, the other pigs, the three small ones and the mother, also seemed to sense our presence and turned to run off. Instinctively, David pulled his own rifle to his shoulder, aimed, and squeezed off a round. The sow jerked, stumbled, and fell to the ground. After a moment, it rose awkwardly to its feet and stumbled into the scrub oak, wobbling like a drunkard as it disappeared into the nearby thicket.

David turned to me and blurted. "That was a really nice boar! Why didn't you shoot?"

I shrugged my shoulders and shook my head as I told him lamely, "I couldn't see it."

He shook his head and ran off into the clearing toward the bushes where the sow had disappeared. Approaching the thick bushes cautiously in case the sow was wounded and angry, David made a slow circle around the thicket. I reached his side and he pointed toward the opposite side. "She's in there," he informed me. "I'm not sure if she's dead or just wounded. Be ready in case she charges."

With that, he stepped over a pile of downed branches and moved carefully into the center of the mass of vegetation where the pig had gone.

I watched mesmerized as David climbed through the thick bushes, my rifle lifted into a hip-firing position in case the animal charged out at me. After a few minutes, David emerged from the morass of plants, vines and bushes, dragging the sow out by its hind legs. He tromped and dragged the dead animal until he was out of the clustered vegetation and into the leafy mulch in the canopy of the scrub oak.

Walking to his side, I stared down at the sow. She was a healthy looking animal, about ninety pounds.

"Nice job David," I commented.

He looked over at me and grinned casually. "Why didn't you shoot it, or the big boar? You had a clear shot at both."

I shrugged again and told him simply, "I couldn't see them." I paused, and then clarified my statement, "I could see them standing there under the tree, but when I looked into the scope, I couldn't see anything at all."

He reached out and grabbed my rifle, commenting, "Let me see that."

Looking the rifle over carefully, David paused when he turned the scope upward and gazed into the top of the lens. Reaching down into the lens with his pointer finger, David started laughing when he pulled his finger out and it was covered in a thick, gray covering of dust.

I realized what the problem was. I had stored the rifle behind the door in our bedroom closet, butt downward, and because of the super abundance of dust and dirt in the Isthmus, the lens was covered with a nearly quarter-inch thick coating. It made it completely impossible to see through the scope.

Needless to say, I felt thoroughly chagrined and humbled. I had never professed to be much of a hunter, and that morning I really proved my ineptitude. Fortunately, David showed his skills to be just the opposite, and so we returned home with a bountiful harvest of wild pig for the freezer. After that episode I gave up hunting and left that exploit to my sons Trevor and Troy, both of whom proved to be adept at the sport.

The winter of 1982 proved to be a wet one—one of the wettest in recent history. By year's end, the Island received an incredible thirty-two-point-seven inches of rainfall (the average is about twelve). Heavy rainfall of course meant powerful storms. Most of that winter's storms were of a southeast variety, generated from southern latitudes by the force known as El Nino. The rains started early in the season, in mid-September, and continued off and on well into late spring. It seemed like it rained nearly every day, but in actuality, there were several prolonged breaks between storms, it just didn't seem that way.

Several of the storm systems lasted for days on end, and the rains were prolific. More than six inches fell during one three-day span, creating major flooding and washing out roads.

During one of those rain systems, the interior roads washed out between the 'Airport in the Sky' and Avalon, effectively closing the only road into Avalon for interior residents. That road closure created significant hardships for local residents, including the children who attended Avalon schools.

With the roads closed, the school bus could not get the interior kids to school. There were about six kids from the Isthmus, a couple from Empire Landing, and a couple from Middle Ranch that all attended either the Avalon elementary, middle, or high school.

To resolve the dilemma, the Isthmus Baywatch crew stepped in and agreed to transport the kids in and out of Avalon by boat until the roads were reopened or another solution could be found. The bus ride was slightly over an hour—each way—while the ride on the water only took about thirty minutes, with good weather. For the kids, the Baywatch boat was not only a 'really cool' method of getting to and from school, but was also faster.

It took about three months to repair the roads, although a 'drive at your own risk' alternative was available for residents after about a week. That alternative at least allowed interior residents the ability to get in and out of town for groceries and essential business.

The Conservancy reluctantly allowed for 'essential' road travel, with a stipulation that nobody could drive through the interior to recreate. That edict almost put a crimp on our weekly golf excursions, but after some head-butting with one of the Conservancy Rangers who discovered us carrying golf clubs in the back of the truck, they relented—as long as we were shopping or conducting other business on the same day that we played golf. I guess that old idiom about a golfer's determination to 'play a round', regardless of obstacles, was clearly demonstrated with our dedicated group of hackers.

A few days preceding one of the particularly strong storms that hit that winter, the Harbor Department received a telephone call from a group of nine boats that called themselves the 'Newport Rough Water Sailors', informing us that they intended to undertake a cruise to Catalina Harbor the following weekend. The weather forecast for the upcoming weekend was dire, with gale force winds and heavy seas in the forecast. When I heard about the impending cruise, I made a telephone call to try and dissuade the group from coming.

It's not often that I, or anyone, would discourage visitors from going to the Island, but based upon the weather forecasts, it really did not sound like a good idea for them to make the crossing. I was informed that their club relished the idea of challenging the elements, and they were perfectly capable and competent to fend for themselves in the event of severe conditions. With a portent of dread, I wished them good luck on their venture.

On Friday morning the winds were howling out of the southeast, gusting above thirty-five knots. There was no rain yet, as often happens during strong southeasters'; the winds fill in from the east/southeast ahead of the rains. That pattern usually lasts about four to six hours and then begins to shift more southerly in advance of the rain. By noon, the first rainsqualls hit the Island bringing brief periods of heavy rain and stronger winds, with gusts exceeding forty knots.

I was preparing to head home after working all day at about four-thirty p.m., when the Harbor Office received a radio call informing all concerned that a couple of the boats in the Rough Water Sailing Club were encountering severe weather problems on the backside of the Island and requesting help. Their radio transmission was broken and spotty and we could not determine where they were. Regardless, our two patrol boats in Catalina Harbor at the time were a sixteen-foot and a nineteen-foot Seaway outboard, adequate for providing service inside of the cove but woefully inadequate for responding outside of the cove in gale conditions. We transmitted a message (not knowing whether the distressed vessel could hear the call) that they were on their own, at least until they entered the harbor. We also transmitted that we would be passing along the distress call to the Coast Guard, fully realizing that it would be several hours before the Coast Guard could reach that general area along the backside of the Island.

After talking with the Coast Guard about the developing situation, they informed me that they would dispatch a cutter, but that under the current conditions, it would be at least four to five hours before they could reach that area.

I stayed on duty, expecting another call from the sailing club. About an hour later we received a call that the first boat in the group of seven (two boats had turned around and returned to the mainland) Rough Water Sailors was rounding Cat Head and hoping to pick up a mooring. I advised the boat that we would meet them in the mooring area to provide assistance.

Donning my foul weather gear and mud boots, I headed out to Cat Harbor with Dave Coiner. He possesses very strong boating skills and is one of the best and most versatile and reliable men that I ever worked with on the Island. I felt good about having him at my side in that situation, because I knew I could count on him to perform at the highest level possible.

We took the Harbor Department pickup truck out to Cat Harbor. Getting to the harbor was not easy. The Cat Harbor road was a gooey quagmire of mud and the winds and driving rain made the short drive even more difficult. Our tires spun and slipped on the road, and we slid radically back and forth on the slippery surface.

When we reached the pier, regular Cat Harbor patrolmen Warren Lynch and Steve Slaughterback met us at the dock. We spoke for a few minutes about a basic strategy and headed out to sea.

I elected to work with Warren Lynch on the smaller boat and Dave worked with Steve Slaughterback on the larger boat.

Pulling away from the dock we were immediately struck by a severe blast of wind of at least fifty to sixty m.p.h. We heard it coming ahead of time, sounding like a freight train heading in our direction. Looking up we saw a wall of white water—spindrift—whipped off the surface of the bay. When it struck, the wind and water stung our faces like hundreds of tiny whips lashing our skin. We did our best to cover our faces and hold the bow steady into the wind. It wasn't going to be easy, or much fun.

After that first blast had passed, a brief lull developed and we headed out into the mooring field. The first of the seven boats to arrive was a thirty-eight-foot Swan, sleek, low profile and solid. They had dropped their sails after rounding Cat Head and entered the cove under power. Dave and Steve met that first boat, and had little trouble assisting them onto a mooring just before another strong squall hit the cove.

That next squall lasted for nearly fifteen minutes, arriving with a roar of wind and spindrift that whipped us around and dumped copious amounts of rain. On my boat, we grabbed a mooring line and hung it off the bow, hunkering down behind the console to try and ward off the penetrating wind and stinging rain. Dave and Steve tried to ride out the squall by keeping their bow pointed into the wind and holding steady with a light throttle. Several times, between the sheets of spindrift, I could see their boat pushed sideways and rolling in the short steep swells.

Soon after that squall passed, two more of the sailboats rounded the entrance to the cove and headed into the bay. One of those boats informed us over the radio that his engine was not working and that he would require assistance. That boat was a Hunter forty-six-foot, and the captain informed us that his deckhand was extremely seasick and virtually incapable of helping.

Dave and I spoke over the radio. With the larger boat, he offered to assist the Hunter, while Warren and I would provide assistance to the other boat, a thirty-five-foot Erickson.

The Erickson was under its own power and we stood by while he dropped his main sail and started heading for the mooring field. Dave and Steve were approaching the Hunter. At that moment, I looked out toward Cat Head and heard and saw another squall line heading in our direction. I called on the radio and informed both boats that they would need to heave-to for a few minutes until the incoming squall line passed by. The Captain of the Erickson turned to seaward, bow into the wind and awaited the squall. The Hunter was caught with its sail half-lowered and working alone, the captain was overwhelmed.

When the wind hit, the Hunter went out of control. Within moments it was broadside to the wind and swell with the mainsail flapping wildly and lashing back and forth, snapping in the wind with a sound like gunfire.

We helped the Erickson moor without any problems and headed over to help with the Hunter.

For a moment we lost sight of the boat. We were coping in our own defense from the storm, trying to keep the bow pointed into the wind, while at the same time trying to avoid striking any of the several boats that were moored. Violent blasts of wind and rain lashed across the surface. When I next looked up and saw a brief opening in the dark wet sheet that blanketed the night sky, I caught a glimpse of the Hunter. It had drifted dangerously close to another boat that was moored near

Ballast Point. I headed in that general direction, crab-walking the boat in an effort to keep from turning completely broadside to the wind.

Reaching the Hunter I screamed out to be heard. "Get to the bow and I'll try to get a line on you," I wasn't sure if he heard me, but a moment later I saw someone crawling on hands and knees toward the bow.

Positioning my patrol boat a few feet off the bow of the Hunter, I attempted to maintain a steady course, watching and waiting for the man to reach the bow. I instructed Warren to be ready with the towline. When I saw the man reach the bow and kneel, I hollered to Warren to heave the line. He did, but it fell short, splashing ineffectively into the water. Realizing that I would need to get more upwind from the boat so that the wind would not hinder the throwing of the towline, I began to move the boat into a better position. At that time I heard a loud CRUNCH when the Hunter slammed broadside into the bow of a thirty-four-foot powerboat moored nearby.

"Are you okay?" I screamed out.

"Yes. But please, help me!" I heard his plaintiff wail.

The Hunter pivoted away from the boat that it had struck and started moving through the mooring fields once again. I moved into position to try another heave of the towline. When I was ready again, I instructed Warren to heave the line once more, and that time it was successful. The towline draped across the safety rail on the port bow of the Hunter and the man aboard was able to grab the loop spliced onto the end of the line and drop it over a cleat.

Carefully I powered forward until there was tension on the towline and then proceeded to give more and more throttle in an effort to tow the sailboat out of danger and out to a mooring.

The thirty-five horsepower Evinrude roared at full rpm, its propeller casting a foaming rush of white water behind the transom. We were standing still, perhaps sliding backward. I continued to hold the throttle at full bore, spinning the helm when needed to keep the bow into the wind and swell. Finally, after several minutes, I detected some slight forward motion from the sailboat. I held firm, slowly, steadily dragging the boat toward a nearby mooring.

We reached the nearest mooring just before another powerful blast of wind hit. The man on the bow managed to grab the tip of the pickup pole, pull up the hawser and drape it over the bow cleat. We ducked down and braced ourselves for the blast of wind and water. Fortunately that blast was a brief one and we told the man on the bow to cast off our towline. I hopped aboard the man's boat to help him walk the sand line down the side of the boat, attach it to the stern and lash down the loose mainsail. In the driving rain and gusting wind, it was not easy, but we managed to accomplish the task. We then went looking for Dave and Steve in the other boat. During the chaos with the Hunter, I had lost track of our other patrol boat.

It turned out that another of the boats had entered the harbor without calling and Dave and Steve diverted to assist it onto a mooring. Dave told me later about their situation, and it sounded as if it was as harrowing as ours.

A few minutes later two more boats entered the harbor, requesting assistance onto moorings. We experienced another lull in the weather and had little difficulty in helping those two boats moor. During those assists, the winds were steady at around twenty-knots, with gusts to around thirty, but under those conditions it was not too difficult. Dave 'Fudley' Erwitt and Mike Latka had also responded to Cat Harbor to assist with the problems, and they worked with us to try and get the boats safe and secure.

There were still two boats due to arrive. We tucked behind the California Yacht Club dock on Ballast Point and waited. By that time, we were all shivering with cold and weary with exhaustion. None of us relished the idea of going through that again.

Finally the two boats arrived. The first one entered the harbor during another lull in the storm and we were able to get them onto a mooring with relative ease. Assisting the last boat turned into another nightmare.

That boat was a Spindrift forty-six-foot, a heavy cumbersome vessel that did not maneuver easily. The captain aboard that boat was competent and capable, but unfortunately, just as we were helping him pickup a mooring, a loose sheet from one of his deck winches fell into the water and caught on his propeller. Powerless, the boat began drifting toward the back of the harbor and directly into the path of several other boats. We did not have much time, the wind was pushing the boat sideways rapidly and it could endanger other boats.

Dave shot out ahead of the boat and called out for them to grab his towline. A crewman ran to the bow and caught the line that was heaved and secured it to a cleat. Dave started towing, but the boat wasn't moving. He powered with everything he had, but it was no go, the boat was not budging. Something didn't seem right. I could understand how my small boat would have trouble towing the other boat, but Dave's boat had considerably more power and should have been able to tow the Spindrift as long as the winds were not too strong, and at that moment they were relatively light.

I maneuvered into a position behind the Spindrift and discovered that not only had they wrapped on their own mainsheet, but that they had caught either the sand line or the stern hawser of another mooring in their prop at the same time. Why that line was on the surface was unclear, but they were obviously wrapped up on a mooring and unable to move.

Dave was forced to hold the bow in position by keeping a steady strain on his towline. If he were to release tension, the sailboat would swing around and slam into the boat off its stern. It was a major dilemma.

I called out and asked if anyone on board could go into the water. The swells were not too bad at that point and a qualified diver could probably cut loose the lines without too much difficulty. But they did not have anyone aboard who could dive.

At that point, Dave called me on the radio and suggested I pick him up on my boat. He would go in the water and try to cut the boat loose.

He turned the helm over to Dave Erwitt and explained how he wanted him to keep the boat in position, but be prepared to slack off and let the boat drift back slightly if he needed slack to get the wrapped lines out of the prop.

Dave needed to get a mask and snorkel, which he got from the powerboat that had been struck by the other sailboat and overheard our conversation. Donning the mask and snorkel and stripping down to his blue jeans, Dave went into the frigid, inky black water and initiated the dive. It wasn't easy, working without scuba gear, in the dark, with choppy seas and periodic gusts of wind that rocked the boat in the swells. To make matters worse, the prop wash from the patrol boat created a current that complicated the effort, but Dave is a talented and highly qualified diver and succeeded in cutting both lines loose.

I held position while Dave climbed back into the smaller patrol boat, and then towed the Spindrift out of that danger area and helped them secure to a mooring.

We had helped all of the boats onto moorings with as little damage as possible and no injuries. Still, we needed to spend about another hour stretching safety lines from each boat onto a secondary mooring, or in the case of the Spindrift, setting his anchor because there was no adjacent mooring available for a safety line. By the time we had completed those tasks we were all completely and thoroughly wiped out and exhausted. We dropped Warren off on his boat and were preparing to head back to the dock when another roar began to develop.

"Oh, Christ," Steve Slaughterback bemoaned, "Here comes another squall!"

We turned the bows of the boats into the wind. We were close to each other, perhaps twenty feet apart. Looking up we saw another high wall of wind spray heading in our direction and we ducked behind the console.

When the wind hit, it obviously was one of the strongest blasts of the night. The wind screamed wickedly, striking the boat like a sledgehammer at the same time that a torrent of rain dumped from the sky. Suddenly another loud noise occurred, a shuddering, metallic sound that pulsated through the dark stormy air like a tin drum that was being pounded upon by sledgehammers. I looked up, wondering what could possibly make a noise like that.

Between sheets of rain, I watched in morbid fascination as one approximately twenty-by-sixty-foot aluminum roof panel on the

California Yacht Club facility lifted into the air and, like a gigantic one-winged bird, flew up into the stormy black sky, pivoted, and knifed downward toward us.

"Look out!" I screamed, just as the framed aluminum sheeting knifed into the water about ten feet from our boat, halfway between our boat and Warren's own thirty-six-foot Grand Banks. A moment later we heard another tearing rip, and the second half of the roof soared into the air and disappeared into the darkness. That second roof section was never to be seen again.

It was extremely lucky that nobody was hurt that night, either from the ripped off rooftop, the process of mooring the boats, or even the overall power of the storm. I will always be grateful and appreciative for Dave's actions and for the assistance and efforts of Steve, Warren, Dave Erwitt and Mike Latka.

Upon returning to the Harbor Office I called the Coast Guard, informing them of our success in securing all of the boats to moorings. The cutter that they had dispatched was only about ten miles out of L.A. Harbor and was encountering powerful winds and fifteen-to-eighteen-foot seas. He turned them around. Later we learned that wind gusts that night exceeded eighty-knots—the limit of the anemometer on board one of the boats in Cat Harbor. In reality, the winds may have been higher than that.

There were other similar weather episodes of that nature that we dealt with through the years, but the Rough Water Sailors storm was undoubtedly one of the worst and most memorable.

10. Expanded Duties

As THE YEARS WENT BY, my responsibilities increased in the Harbor. I'm not really sure exactly when I fully assumed the position of Harbormaster. Like Doug Bombard told me on the day I retired, "You just sort of melded into the position." Regardless, I was assuming more duties and gradually becoming the leader of the Harbor Department team.

As one of the key employees of the Harbor Department, I was expected to provide guidance and training for rookie employees. One of the first disappointments in my early career was my inability to teach one of our shoreboat operators to effectively operate a boat without casualties. That employee, who will remain nameless, arrived at the Island with a fifty-ton Masters License. One of the surprising things about Coast Guard License issuing, is that an applicant does not have to demonstrate the ability to operate boats—he/she merely needs to submit adequate sea-time, pass a physical, pay the appropriate fees, and pass the Coast Guard exam.

This particular shoreboat operator had accumulated all of his sea-time during a three-year stint aboard a Cruise ship working as a cook's assistant. During his three-years at sea, he never operated a boat or even stood a helm watch. Even so, he diligently studied the materials needed to pass the exam and after passing the tests, was issued his license.

When I interviewed the young man, he seemed competent and capable, and I assumed that he could be trained to operate a boat effectively. I started working with him on a daily basis, showing him the fundamentals of safe and sensible boat handling, and did my utmost to teach him how to pull up to boats and docks without causing damage. It was frustrating. Some people just do not have the ability to perform certain things, and driving a boat was something that this young guy had a lot of trouble trying to learn. After about two-weeks working with him on a daily basis, we decided to turn him loose and see how he could do on his own. We started him off with the easiest, most basic duties—like making the camp runs.

With those runs, he only needed to pull up to the camp docks, load the kids aboard and return to the main docks in the Isthmus. On his first effort everything went okay until he pulled back into the Isthmus float and neglected to take the boat fully out of gear after pulling into the dock. His boat crept slowly forward and struck the stern of a patrol boat, causing minor damage.

I worked with him again to try and impress upon him the need to be diligent and aware of all aspects of the boat handling process and sent him back to work. Later that afternoon I received a radio call informing me that he had damaged the rail on a sailboat while attempting to pick up a passenger. I assessed the damages, assured the owners that we would work with them to make repairs, and went back to work with the young man in an effort to improve his operating skills. After a few more hours of working with him, I felt that maybe, just maybe, he was starting to get the picture.

A few hours later, shortly before he was scheduled to get off work, he was returning to the dock from a pickup when he cruised between the A-row and the B-row in the Isthmus on his way to the dock. Those two rows are relatively tight together and require a certain amount of caution when maneuvering between them. As he passed between the two rows, with boats moored on every nearby mooring, he swung his bow around to make his approach to the dock. As most boat operators know, when you turn your bow to one side or the other, the stern of your boat swings in the opposite direction. He failed to notice that factor, and without even looking back at his stern, made the turn and his transom swung into the dinghy davits of the classic old sailboat *Bos'n,* moored on A-1.

The boat belonged to a wonderful old gentleman who was in his mid-eighties named James McDonald. Jim, as we knew him, was a longtime fixture in the Isthmus and a good friend to many employees and regular Island visitors. He was a truly remarkable old guy who had wonderful stories to tell about his career with the Walt Disney Company. During his years with Disney, Jim McDonald helped design and develop the sets and visual effects for the animated movies Fantasia, Alice in Wonderland, Snow White, and many other films. He also served as the voice of Mickey Mouse for many years.

Jim was seated on a small bench seat near the cockpit of his boat, gazing out to sea as he so often did. He did not notice the shoreboat turning behind him and when the shoreboat crashed into his dinghy davit it knocked him to the deck breaking his hip.

We fired the young shoreboat driver that afternoon. After that, I never promised anyone a job until they demonstrated the ability to operate a boat with at least a semblance of professionalism.

I had numerous employees tell me over the years that I completely intimidated them during the 'boat handling' test that all prospective employees had to take prior to being hired. I tried to be easy-going and encouraging during the testing process, but I know that I was also demanding and critical. I firmly believe that a professional boat operator must have the skills to perform at a high level of competency and possess the willingness and aptitude to learn quickly. I believe that I helped a lot of people get started on becoming good boat operators, and that for the most part, those individuals appreciated my methods of instruction and perhaps severe expectations.

That spring I had an unusually high number of female applicants for summer employment. Prior to that year, very few females worked in the harbor. Kelly Suggs, (to my knowledge the first female shoreboat operator), had worked in the harbor for several years and had proven herself to be a completely competent and professional boat operator. I had no reservations about bringing other females into the crew.

Deva Santoro was already scheduled to return for the summer and when I looked over the short stack of employment submittals, I realized that young women had submitted a high percentage of the applications. Working as a Harbor Patrolman was still one of those bastions of male domination and although there were a couple of female patrolmen who had worked in the harbor over the years, the vast majority of harbor employees were men.

After completing the first phase of the interview process I called four females and two males to undergo the boat operation process of the hiring program. All four of the young women demonstrated a combination of adequate operating skills, or at least a fundamentally sound background on the water and a willingness and ability to learn.

I thought to myself, 'It actually might be kind of fun to have a crew of healthy young women working in the Harbor. They might add a touch of levity to the job'.

Those five girls, including Deva, did make for an interesting summer.

All five of the girls were good looking, wholesome and vivacious young women in their late teens or early twenties. They tended to attract an unusual amount of attention from the local male residents and many of our boating friends. In addition to Deva, there were Lori and Danenne Posey, two of the daughters of Nadine Posey and John York, who also worked for the company and lived on their boat in Cat Harbor (Another daughter, Kathy also lived on the Island and worked for Dr. Bob Givens at the USC Marine Science Center). There was Linda Fagan, whose brother Pete lived and worked in the Isthmus, and Debbie Galvin, who shared her time between the office and the harbor and was a little older than the others. Her husband Gary worked in the Purchasing Department.

All five of the young women proved to be solid, reliable boat operators and did a good job performing the variety of duties that are expected of the harbor crew. They also did add a certain amount of levity and fun to the summer, although it was not always easy for me. While it was kind of fun and refreshing to have a bevy of pretty young girls working together, it wasn't the easiest summer of my career, administratively.

In addition to the girls that we hired, we also had Dave Coiner, Jimmy the 'Night Stalker' Walker, Chris 'Hey Jack' Hajak, Dave 'Santana' Amatisto, Don Blakeman, Curt Craig, and Rob Johnson on the Isthmus Harbor crew.

During the winter months the Harbor Department serviced and repaired the fleet of boats that serve the operation. There were about a dozen patrol boats, five shoreboats and several work skiffs that needed to be maintained. Each boat was hauled out and painted, patched and re-worked as needed. We also worked with George McElroy and the maintenance department in servicing, painting and repairing all of the floats and docks, as well as the Isthmus and Cat Harbor piers.

When Pete Peterson moved from the Mooring Service to the Harbor Department, he became the lead shoreboat repairman, performing and overseeing the patching and painting of the five shoreboats. He came to be known as the 'Bondo King' for his propensity to fix the majority of the hull and interior damages with copious amounts of Bondo. He worked feverishly and intently, often jogging from the shop to the General Store or warehouse to pickup parts or supplies. Working with Pete was often quite interesting.

On one occasion, when we were working on the dinghy dock ramp, Pete was operating the boom truck—an old International truck that was converted to a piece of machinery used for lifting heavy items and equipment. He and I were working in Cat Harbor, finishing up repairs on one of the old wooden ramps that served as a gangway on the Isthmus Pier. We bridled the ramp to the lift cable on the boom truck, and he started driving down the Cat Harbor road, heading back to the Isthmus to make the annual seasonal installation. The Cat Harbor road was rather rough and bumpy that spring, scarred by the tracks of vehicles during winter rains, and necessitated slow and cautious driving to avoid problems. But Pete was in a hurry and he began driving way faster than I thought prudent. I was following him in his old Toyota Land Cruiser. He continued to pick up speed on the long straightaway leading toward the Isthmus and I watched in astonishment when he ran over a deep rut in the road, then watched helplessly as the ramp that we had just finished repairing slowly lifted off the bed of the truck, floated like a big white butterfly about twenty feet into the air, and came crashing back down onto the bed of the truck. It splintered into dozens of fragmented pieces. He stopped and I caught up to him. He jumped down from the cab of the truck, looked over the shattered remains of the ramp and commented, "Lousy piece of junk. I've been telling them they needed to build a new one for years."

Soon after, David McElroy and welder Jimmy Ristau built new aluminum ramps for the pier that are still in use today.

On another occasion that I heard about but did not witness, Pete was working on the mooring boat *Kingfisher* with Stephen McElroy. If I recall Steve's version of the episode correctly, the two men were finishing up their day and ready to head for home, when a sailboat wrapped its mooring lines in their propeller. Anxious to get home, Pete did not want to take the time to go back to the Mooring Shop for his dive gear, and so he stripped naked, dove under and unwrapped the boat, and climbed back aboard the *Kingfisher* and took over the helm. Stephen had to remind him to put his clothes back on. Pete was quite a character, told great stories, and was a true fixture in the Isthmus community for many years.

In addition to my normal winter duties of patrolling the coves and affecting repairs to the various boats, docks and floats, I also spent a couple of winters rebuilding and resurfacing the inside and outside bars of the Harbor Reef Restaurant.

Doug Bombard was aware of my carpentry background and had seen a few of the pieces of furniture and cabinetwork that I had done, both for personal use and on the patrol boats and shoreboats. One winter he asked if I would help restore or rebuild the two bar tops at the restaurant.

I explained to him my thoughts for the project and he went along with my ideas, only substituting teak for oak on the outside bar top. Working with maintenance employees Mike Esch and John Ermatinger, we purchased enough teak and oak to resurface both bar tops and the side paneling. Esch and I then spent the better part of the early spring installing a solid teak top on the outside bar, a new teak reception desk at the front door of the establishment, and a solid oak top on the inside bar. Both of those bar tops remain in use today, and I always felt a certain amount of pride and accomplishment whenever I visited the restaurant and saw the finished product.

Another time I participated in a tow that did not go very well.

When we first moved to the Island, the company operated an old converted LCM Landing Craft as the primary vessel for shipping supplies and materials to and from the Island. After many years of service, the old *Pacific Harvester*—the original barge—was scheduled for replacement with a newer and larger landing craft that Doug and Randy Bombard had located for sale in San Diego. After they had finalized the contract for purchase, Doug dispatched Jim Morrow, as operator of the barge, Richard Brown, from the Mooring Service, Gary Huntington and me to San Diego to tow the new barge (which was destined to become the *Island Supplier,* and is still in service today) back to the Isthmus with the *Pacific Harvester* as the tow vessel.

I flew down to San Diego with Doug in his personal plane and he oriented us with the new barge and equipment. He had also purchased several very large, two-hundred to seven-hundred pound steel Navy anchors, which were loaded into the well deck of the *Pacific Harvester.*

We plotted a course, rigged the towlines and headed out of San Diego Bay at around three p.m. with a destination of Catalina Harbor. Everything went well in the beginning. Our speed over the water was slow; we were making less than three knots. At that speed we calculated our tow would take approximately forty-five hours. We had plenty of fuel to get us to our destination, but would not have a lot to spare. That should not have become a factor, except for one little problem that occurred.

Our daylight shifts were easy and uneventful. Nothing out of the ordinary took place. The seas were calm, with only a slight two-to-three-foot westerly swell, and the winds were light and variable, increasing to only about twelve knots in the afternoon. There was a moderate marine layer, with visibility about a mile, but that did not, and should not, have presented any problems.

Cruising along in tow there was not a lot to see or do. From the outset, we saw only one or two fishing boats along the way. We passed through several large schools of playful dolphin and that was a nice diversion. We spotted a couple of whales spouting in the misty distance but they were not close enough to provide any serious stimulation. We read, we talked and we watched the water roll slowly past.

The dawn of the second day turned out to be a carbon copy of the first and we all settled into the humdrum of a low-speed tow. We watched the water, saw a few dolphins, seagulls, and a couple of big Navy ships cruising silently on the western horizon.

When nightfall arrived, the four of us got together and exchanged course information. Jim Morrow and Gary Huntington were to serve the first four-hour night watch and Richard Brown and I were scheduled for the second.

Richard and I lay down on the deck of the wheelhouse and tried to get a few hours of sleep. Sleep wasn't easy with the deep rumbling engine noise and occasional thumping of the steel hull on the sea-surface, but we did manage to rest. At midnight, Morrow woke us to take over the watch, advising us of our presumed dead-reckoning position and informing us that there was nothing else to report.

Richard and I took over the watch, holding a steady course that should put us a couple of miles southwest of the backside of Catalina Island. Shortly before four a.m., a few faint lights appeared in the distance off of our port beam. We presumed those lights to be the nightlights of the commercial fishing fleet. When Morrow and Huntington arose to take over the early morning watch, we pointed out the lights in the distance, and they agreed that it must be from the fishing fleet. (Later we figured out that those lights were probably the distant glow from the naval base at West Cove, San Clemente Island).

By eight a.m., on our third morning at sea, we were all up and anticipating sight of the Island. Unable to see anything from inside of the wheelhouse, we went out onto the outer deck to avoid the glare of the windows. Looking around, we could see nothing except a few lazy seagulls.

That was odd. Our calculations put us at a position about two miles southwest of China Point, about five miles south of Cat Harbor. We continued to cruise westward. About thirty minutes later we still had seen nothing. We talked briefly and decided to shutdown and try to look and listen for anything that might give us an indication of our current position. Also, we were running somewhat low on fuel. We shutdown and drifted, all four of us looking and listening for anything that might help. We could see nothing but an endless ocean merging with a canopy of gray clouds. It was glassy calm. The two barges were tethered together drifting on a silvery smooth sea surface surrounded by a shadowy white mist. Except for the slap and gurgle of the flat steel hull on the rippled sea surface, there was not a sound to be heard, nor anything but a few dark shadows on the backside of the minimal swells to be seen.

Puzzled, we all looked at each other and shrugged. We couldn't be too far off course, could we? Our plotting and dead reckoning techniques were universal and all of us were licensed captains with adequate navigational skills. We did not have radar aboard the vessel, nor did we have a GPS unit. All we had was the compass, but it was a good one and we had all adhered diligently to our course heading during the previous forty-plus hours. So why were we not seeing or hearing anything?

Suddenly, Morrow called out, "Hey! There's a boat over there." He was pointing toward the northeast. Sure enough, a medium sized ship that appeared to be a cargo carrier appeared in the distant gloom.

Morrow said he was going to try and make contact with the vessel. Entering the wheelhouse, Morrow picked up the VHF microphone and called out on channel 16. "Calling the vessel off our starboard quarter," he said. "This is the vessel *Pacific Harvester*, undertow about one mile off your starboard beam. Do you copy?"

A brief pause ensued and then the radio crackled. A voice transmitted, "This is the *SS President Polk*. We have you spotted off our starboard beam. You appear to be two small barges, one in tow."

"That's correct" Morrow smiled in relief. "Can you give us your exact coordinates? We are inbound for Cat Harbor and have no visual sight of the Island."

Another pause, and then the voice clicked back on. "I am at position…. (He then gave us his coordinates).

Taking a quick look at the charts and pointing to the approximate position where he placed his vessel, Morrow responded, "That's impossible!" It showed us as being in a 'no-man's land' several miles southwest of Point Dume (at the north end of Malibu). We double-checked our plot and Morrow called back. "Are you sure you have us identified correctly?"

After a brief pause, the voice called back. "We've identified you as a light brown barge, resembling a landing craft connected to a larger, dark gray landing craft. Is that correct?"

"Yes," Morrow responded. "And will you reconfirm your coordinates?"

The voice called back, reconfirmed the coordinates to reflect a minute correction based upon his distance traveled since his last report. Morrow thanked him and discontinued the transmission.

We put our heads together and discussed the dilemma. Even if we had improved our speed over the ground due to either a current, or increased engine speed, it still seemed impossible that we could be in the location that he had placed us. We also discussed the fact that if we were where he placed us, we would have passed under the flight path from LAX (Los Angeles International Airport) and should have seen planes passing overhead. We had seen nothing.

Still perplexed, we decided to call the Isthmus via the marine operator and advise them of our situation. By all accounts, we were lost. After contacting the front office, they advised us to standby while they contacted Doug Bombard. A few minutes later Bombard came onto the line and we explained our situation. He told us he would drive up to the airport, get into his plane, and come looking for us.

We drifted. And we waited. About two hours later we heard and then saw the image of a small plane coming into view to the east of our location. Bombard flew low over our heads, circled a couple of times and then called on his handheld VHF radio. "Is everything alright?"

"All is fine," Morrow responded, and then asked, "Where are we?"

"You are about twelve miles southwest of Cat Harbor, between San Clemente and Santa Barbara Island. How is your fuel?"

"We're down to about thirty gallons. It should be enough to get us back, but I'm not sure."

"Okay," Bombard called, "Start heading toward Cat Harbor and I'll phone ahead and have a shoreboat head your way with some extra fuel."

Bombard continued to circle, and when we got underway, he headed off on a course heading that would take us into Cat Harbor. Every few minutes he would make a big wide circle and then go back onto course in an effort to lead us in the right direction.

After about an hour, Bombard circled over us again and assured us that we were on the right heading and advised us to maintain a vigilant focus on our course heading. He was running low on fuel and needed to return to the Island. He asked if we needed him to refuel and return so that we could follow him, but we assured him that would not be necessary.

A short while later, Shoreboat #6 came into view and pulled alongside with two fifty-gallon drums of diesel fuel lashed to the seats of the boat. The operator carried a centrifugal hand pump and we transferred about one-hundred gallons into our tanks as a precaution. We could see the outline of the Island at that point, and after another three, long and frustrating hours, we pulled into Cat Harbor and moored the two boats.

Later we discovered that the compass on the *Pacific Harvester* had been thrown off during the loading of the big Navy anchors into the well deck. The yard where they were loaded used a heavy electro-magnet on a crane to lift and lower the anchors, and the magnetic field had knocked our compass out of whack. It explained the reason that we went off course, but did little to relieve the embarrassment and mortification that we felt over the fact that four licensed captains had become lost at sea.

It was a humbling experience for all four of us.

11. A Wild Ride

ONE OF THE MOST FRIGHTENING things that our young son Trevor did as a youngster was to go on a wild ride on a jet ski. He was about two-years old and he and Maureen were hanging out on the beach. I was at work, and for lunch I met them on the beach for a burger from the snack bar. After finishing lunch, Maureen asked me if I wanted to see Trevor do something really cute. She walked over and spoke with Ted Bauer, a friend who worked as a bartender at Doug's Harbor Reef Saloon and who had his own jet ski. There was a gray jet ski, or more accurately a Waverunner, floating at idle speed in the surf line. Maureen thought the small PWC (personal water craft) belonged to Bauer, when in actuality the one at idle belonged to resident Sheriff Bob Murcott, who was standing nearby chatting with a friend. When Bauer asked him if he could borrow it to give Trevor a brief ride along the beach, Murcott agreed; he knew that Bauer was an experienced PWC user and therefore believed the activity should be perfectly safe.

Watching with curiosity, I saw Ted pick Trevor up, place him on the seat of the jet-ski, and then move behind him to climb onto the machine and take him for a slow ride back and forth along the waterfront. It was an innocently fun beach activity that Ted had performed with Trevor and several of the other Island kids on numerous occasions. But that particular time, something went completely wrong.

When he placed Trevor on the seat of the machine and moved around to climb aboard behind him, Trevor reached out and grabbed the handles of the steering bar and throttle controls. Immediately the

Jet Ski shifted into gear and Ted was tossed off the back end, falling onto his face in the sand.

Dumbfounded, I stood there watching my two-year old son heading away from the shore all alone on a jet-ski moving at about thirty miles per hour.

Momentarily stunned and baffled, I glanced over at Maureen. She screamed, "Ted! Someone! Do something!"

Refocusing, I thought to myself, 'He's going to fall off! Everyone falls off when they first try jet skiing. He can't swim. I need to get to him!'

I started running toward the water, discarding my hat, sunglasses and shirt. I ripped my shoes from my feet as I reached the water's edge, dove in and started swimming. The jet-ski with Trevor still perched securely in the center of the seat continued to power away, passing between several boats moored on the R, A and B rows. I was swimming as hard and fast as I possibly could, expecting at any moment for him to fall off, or crash into one of the many moored boats in the area. I continued to swim.

The Jet Ski was moving rapidly and I realized that swimming after it was an action of futility, but kept thinking to myself, 'He's going to fall off', so I plunged onward.

When the watercraft reached the C-row, it suddenly stopped. Trevor had released the throttle. I was two rows behind him and continued to swim. Looking up, I saw a man dive off his sailboat and swim over to the stationary craft. He had watched the spectacle from the deck of his own boat, and when he saw the jet-ski stop, he dove in to help. At about the same time, Shoreboat #7 with Harrison Hall at the helm arrived on scene and was standing by. Moments later, the Baywatch boat, which happened to be in the process of getting underway and had witnessed the scene and responded, pulled into the area and John Stonier dove into the water, reached the side of the craft and lifted Trevor off the seat and into the waiting arms of fellow Baywatch member Bill Barker.

Still swimming, I watched with huge relief as I saw the scene unfold in front of me. When I finally reached the site, exhausted and anxious,

I glanced up at Trevor, who was seated on the aft deck of the Baywatch Boat, covered in blood.

"Oh, my God!" I gulped. His entire chest and stomach was covered in pinkish blood and a darker, thicker swath trickled from his chin, a consequence of striking the console when he released the throttle.

"It's alright" Stonier called down to me. "It is only a small cut on his chin. It just looks bad because he is wet and the blood looks bad because it is mixed with water."

I climbed up onto the swim step and leaned over to inspect the cut. It was not too severe. I watched as Stonier and Barker donned their gloves, treated the wound, cleaned up his chin and wiped away the blood with a towel. That task completed, they headed back to the dock to drop us off. Maureen was waiting there, looking surprisingly calm and collected. When we told her that Trevor was fine, she picked him up, thanked the Baywatch guys and we headed back to the beach.

A short while later, Murcott came up to us and told us how relieved he was that Trevor was not injured. He also informed us, tongue-in-cheek, that he would not press charges against our son for grand theft. His levity helped to ease the anxiety that we both still felt.

I was quite impressed with Maureen's calm and cool composure before and immediately following the wild and dangerous ride. I was feeling pretty shook-up, but extremely relieved. The incident did not seem to faze Maureen at all. I was perplexed, but it helped me to calm down and gain composure. I stayed with them for a while and then returned to work. I located the Baywatch guys and the fellow on the sailboat that had responded, thanking them all profusely. Later that evening, while we were at home cooking dinner, I heard a muffled sob. Looking over at Maureen, I could see tears streaming down her cheeks.

Walking over to her, completely baffled by her sudden breakdown, I wrapped my arm around her shoulder and asked quietly, "Maureen, what's wrong?"

"He could have been seriously hurt, or killed!" I glanced around, thinking there might be something nearby that she was referring to, and then realized she was thinking about Trevor and what had happened earlier in the day. I laughed lightly. She looked up at me in anger. "It's not funny! He could have been seriously hurt, or...." She let the comment dangle.

"It's okay," I tried to console her. "It's over. He's fine. It was only an accident and it all turned out fine. There's nothing to worry about."

She continued to weep, deep wrenching sobs that wracked her torso. Baffled by her delayed reaction, I stood at her side, holding her tightly and comforting her.

For me, the episode was now nothing more than a distant memory—a vivid and grateful one—but just a memory. I tried to understand why Maureen was reacting now, several hours after the incident took place, but I gave up. It was one of the puzzling enigmas that serve to differentiate the contrasts between men and women.

My brother Mark is a fanatic fisherman. Not an avid fisherman like I am, but a *fanatic*. He bought a little seventeen-foot aluminum boat shortly after we moved to the Island that he named *Aluminum Joe*—or *Aluminium Joe*, as he liked to say. Mark was married at the time to his first wife Nancy and she wasn't much into fishing. Mark would run his little boat out to the Island to fish on a regular basis, pounding along day or night and getting drenched on nearly every crossing. To him it didn't matter, he just wanted to fish.

For most people, a fishing excursion is usually a few-hour outing, unless you might be in a bigger boat going out for marlin or other exotics. However for Mark, a fishing trip was almost always an all day and sometimes all night adventure. He would arrive at the Island usually late in the evening after having worked all day and then launched his boat in Huntington Harbor and headed across. After sleeping for a few hours, he would awaken before daybreak and head out to fish. He'd then fish until dark, sometimes bringing in some impressive catches of local fish, and on occasion, during the late summer or fall, bringing back some of the exotics; yellowtail, tuna, and dorado. After making several dozen trips out to the Island, he had pounded the bottom of the little aluminum skiff so severely that it could not be repaired.

I'm not really sure how much of a factor it was that his first wife was not really into fishing, but a few years later they were divorced and Mark remarried a younger woman who loved to fish. Sara, a perky little blonde about fifteen years younger, was willing to go out fishing whenever and wherever he wanted. They would take their new boat, a twenty-five-foot aluminum Crestliner down to San Diego to fish Mexican waters, up to Morro Bay to fish albacore, out into the tuna grounds near the Cortez and Tanner Banks, it didn't matter. Wherever the fish were, that is where they would go. And they continued to visit us at the Island.

Usually their fishing trips involved a weekend on the Island, but Mark saw little land. He was always out on the water looking for another hookup. When he and Sara had kids, Mack and Valerie, they would leave the kids with us (or rather with Maureen because I was always working on the weekends) and Mark and often Sara would be gone all day. Despite the fact that we saw Mark for only a short duration when they visited the Island, we still had some truly fun times.

My brother Dave and his second wife Linda, and then his third wife Deborah also visited us quite often through the years. Dave, like me, is an avid fisherman—bordering on fanatic. He and Mark fished together a lot, but I think it was more of Marks influence than Dave's fanaticism that kept them out all day long on their trips together.

My entire family, Bob, Mike, Dave, Sheri, Mark, John, and Vicki are all avid fishermen. We all fished together, sometimes on our own individual boats, sometimes together. For several years we put together a 'locals only' halibut tournament. In those mini-tournaments, each angler tossed-in an entry fee of twenty dollars and the pool was distributed between first, second and third place for the largest halibut caught. It was always great to get together with my brothers and sisters and all my nieces and nephews. Afterward we held a big fish fry on the beach, or at our house, barbecuing or frying-up part of the day's catch. It was some really good times and one of the many things that helped to make my family a close knit one.

Leasing a mooring on Catalina Island is a highly sought after opportunity. Wait Lists to lease a mooring were established sometime in the mid-sixties and then refined and brought up to date when the Master Lease went out to bid in 1982. A few years later, we implemented a minimal fee to sign-up for and maintain a position on the lists.

In a couple of the coves, Cherry and Fourth of July Coves notably, the wait for a mooring could be as long as thirty plus years. In other coves the wait averaged closer to fifteen to twenty years, perhaps a little less in Cat Harbor.

In the winter of 1983, I was helping issue new Mooring Subleases. Each December the Subleases were up for renewal and those few moorings that were relinquished returned to the Mooring Wait List pool for reissue.

I made a phone call to a man who had been on the list for close to twenty-years and when I told him that a mooring was now available he was ecstatic. The man was Mike Daniels, at the time a producer for CBS Channel #2 News. He did not hesitate. "Of course I will take the mooring!" he responded immediately, the excitement in his voice palpable. "Can I come out to the Island and take a picture?"

I paused for a moment. I had never heard anyone make that request before and it momentarily set me back. "Well, sure," I told him. "Are you thinking about coming out on your boat?"

"No" I was thinking that I would just jump on the Catalina Express and head over so that I could take a picture. Is there any way that my boat name could be put on the mooring can?"

I laughed. People often became excited about getting a mooring lease at the Island, but I had never interacted with anyone quite as thrilled as Mike. I explained to him that there were a couple of problems with trying to accomplish his requests. First, it was a Tuesday morning and there were no cross-channel commercial boats into the Isthmus on Tuesdays or Thursdays, and that on the other days of the week, they only laid-over for about twenty minutes to load and offload. If he were to try and head over, the best opportunity would be on a Friday when they made two runs. Additionally, I told him, the Mooring Service did not begin servicing the moorings until January and so it would not really work to have his boat name painted on the mooring buoy until they began rigging.

Undaunted, he asked me, "If I hopped on the Wednesday boat, could you take me out to the mooring and let me take a picture and then get me back in time to catch the boat back?"

I chuckled again. This was definitely the most excitement I had ever seen from anyone about getting a mooring. "Sure," I told him. "I think we could do that without any problem."

"Great! I'll be there on the noon boat tomorrow. I'll bring a check with me."

"Okay," I replied, "But you don't really need to bring the check too. You can complete the lease arrangements with Wendy or Kathy later. Wendy Adams and Kathy Rinehart were processing the mooring contracts that year.

"No, no," he responded enthusiastically. "I'll bring the check tomorrow!"

"Okay, Mike. See you tomorrow."

That phone call was the precursor to a long and wonderful relationship with Mike Daniels. I met him on the dock on Wednesday afternoon, and took him out to the mooring, K-15 in the Isthmus. I had spoken with one of the members of the Mooring Service (I think it was Dan Deinlein) about the new Lessee and he graciously went out and painted the name *Gran Cru* onto the mooring. When we arrived at the mooring and Mike saw his boat name painted on top of the buoy, he actually had a tear in his eye. He snapped several pictures and I took him back to the dock. He submitted his check, signed the eight-page contract and hopped back aboard the Catalina Express as a proud new Mooring Sublessee.

On Memorial Weekend he made his first trip to the Island to use his own mooring. I met him on arrival and thoroughly enjoyed watching his joy.

Mike then established a summer ritual of taking his boat to the Island and leaving it on the mooring for the entire summer. He was on board as much as possible, having to return to the mainland for work or personal business on weekdays, but was back aboard nearly every weekend. After a couple of weeks, Mike came up to me and asked if he could 'help out' in the harbor. I asked what he had in mind. He told me, "Well, I've been watching you guys work and realize that especially on Friday and Saturday mornings you are all really busy. I know that you cannot be everywhere at once and I might be able to help arriving boats find their assigned mooring location or try to moor, especially if they are inexperienced."

Somewhat reluctant to put someone into a position where he might be exposed to injury or possible boat damage and not be covered by insurance, I explained my reservations to him.

He assured me that he would never put himself into a position where he might be injured or cause anyone else injury or damage, but that he would merely lead new boaters into moorings and standby and offer mooring advice and instructions if it was needed.

I thanked him for his offer and told him that we would give it a try. For the next twenty-five years, or so, Mike became an 'unofficial harbor patrolman', showing up nearly every Friday and Saturday morning during the peak season in his little inflatable dinghy, *Petite Cru*, to help guide boats into moorings and onto the stringline, giving them advice and often pushing their boat around with the bow of his inflatable if they needed a little help. He also maintained a vigilant radio connection with the crew, delivering cold water or soda when we got thirsty. In addition, he maintained a packet of money on board his dinghy, providing the patrolmen with change if they ran out of small bills or quarters. (Mooring fees at that time included pricing at twenty-five-cent increments). His help, friendliness and good nature endeared him to the entire crew and he became a favorite friend with many of our visitors.

At times I felt that perhaps we were taking advantage of him, but when I mentioned that to him he rejected the idea emphatically. He told me that he 'truly enjoyed being out on the water and helping in his own little way'. It wasn't much, but I rewarded him with an invite to all of our Harbor parties and gave him his own Harbor Department hat each season. He encountered health problems in 2009 and was forced to give up his boating lifestyle, but his legacy was very special to me and to many, many people that he knew and 'worked' with through the years.

Another person who left an indelible legacy on the Island community was 'The Admiral', James 'Jimmy' Walker.

Jim arrived on the Island in the spring of 1981, about a year after I began my career in the Harbor Department. He arrived aboard his thirty-four foot trawler *SeaView*, which was outfitted in the unorthodox bright orange canvas and trim that was his personal trademark.

Jimmy Walker was from Manhattan Beach and had served, at various times, as a real estate magnate, an 'oil baron', a city councilman, and reportedly the Mayor of El Segundo. He was thought to be independently wealthy and really didn't need a job, but the magnetism and allure of living on Catalina Island prompted him to apply for a position in the Harbor Department.

There was only one position still available at the time, the graveyard spot, and after completing an interview and testing, he was offered the position.

For the next couple of years, Jimmy Walker served faithfully as 'The Night Stalker', covering the ten-thirty p.m. to seven a.m. shift in the harbor. One morning, after coming into work and discovering that he had rescued a boat from the Isthmus Reef, pulled a drunken man from the water at the dinghy dock, assisted Baywatch with a medical emergency in Cherry Cove, helped a fleet of six boats from Santa Barbara Yacht Club secure moorings in Cherry Cove, and recovered two missing dinghies that had gone astray, I informed him that he did an 'admirable' job. His good friend and another unforgettable member of the Harbor Department, Harrison Hall, picked up on the 'admirable' reference and Jimmy's moniker of 'The Admiral' was initiated.

After a couple of years on the graveyard shift, Walker sought to try and enjoy a little more sunshine. He applied for and obtained his Coast Guard License and switched to a daytime shift as a Shoreboat Operator/ Harbor Patrolman. In order to make things easier for Isthmus residents needing a Notary Public, he obtained that certification. He then became a minister in the Universal Life Church and began performing wedding ceremonies for both local residents and boating friends. Somewhere along the way he decided to try his hand at being a bartender and went to work on a part-time basis at the Harbor Reef Saloon.

But perhaps his biggest contribution to the little village of Two Harbors was to serve as the 'ambassador of goodwill' for the Isthmus employees, and for Island visitors.

Jimmy had a wonderful personality and a gregarious disposition. He loved to stay busy, do new and different things, and develop entertaining diversions for his friends on the Island. One of his most enjoyable pastimes was water skiing. He had a little eighteen-foot outboard that he setup with a ski-bar and he and good friend Bruce Wicklund—a fellow harbor patrolman—skied religiously nearly every morning all summer long (and often during the winter). Jimmy offered a standing invitation for all Isthmus employees that he would take them skiing in the morning if they would simply meet him at the dock at six a.m. He would then proceed to take as many people as showed up out for a ski around the bay, usually buying them breakfast after the exercise.

Another thing Jimmy Walker introduced was the Two Harbors Epicurean Society. A fancier of good food and drink, Jimmy initiated the small club as a fun diversion for local residents. The society expanded to include many of our boating friends, and an annual Epicurean Hors d'oeuvre Contest was established that allowed all those submitting a hors d'oeuvre to vie for the opportunity to enter the society by winning the contest. That proved to be a big hit, especially with members of Cherry Cove Yacht Club, and soon the society had expanded to several dozen members. It continued to be a popular event for many years.

By far Jimmy Walker's most significant contribution to the Island community was his innate ability to ingratiate those he met. He befriended everyone he came in contact with, cultivated friendships and made everyone he met feel comfortable and welcome. For the seasonal employees, his friendship and interaction helped many adjust to the often quite difficult transition from their homes on the mainland into the very different lifestyle on a remote island. He made it a point to introduce himself to all new employees—which could be as many as one-hundred per season, remembering each of their names and complimenting them on the various duties they performed. For many of those young employees, his friendship and guidance helped them succeed and become valuable employees of the company.

Jimmy also began the traditional Jimmy Walker Buffalo Chip Contest that still takes place each Labor Day Weekend. His idea, the Buffalo Chip Toss—flinging a dried buffalo poop the farthest—is always a real hit with Island visitors.

He also emceed the entertainment for our annual employee parties, Buccaneer Days events, the Children's Festival, and numerous other special events for the company.

Jimmy 'The Admiral' Walker was a legend and a true Catalina icon that left an indelible mark in the community during his unforgettable years living with, and nurturing the people of Two Harbors.

Probably the absolute best fishing I experienced during our many years on the Island occurred in the winter of 84'-85'.

On the heels of a powerful El Nino year in 1983, when the Island received over thirty-inches of rain, the sea temperatures remained warm throughout the entire following year. As late as December the sea temperature continued to hover in the mid-sixties, and pelagic red-crabs swarmed local beaches in great quantities, often washing up on the beaches to create wide swaths of dead and dying crabs. The seagulls had a feast, as did all predatory fishes.

Beginning in late December, squid spawns began to develop all around the Island. Commercial fishing boats were harvesting thousands of tons of the highly lucrative 'market squid' and selling it to the 'Forty Thieves' fish markets in San Pedro. Whenever the weather allowed, the purse-seine fleet descended upon the squid grounds on the backside of the Island and set their nets. On the 'frontside' of the Island, commercial fishing was allowed only with hand braille nets. When another consistent spawn developed between Lion Head Point and Emerald Bay, the smaller commercial fishing boats began harvesting that area with their handheld nets.

Early one morning I was making a routine patrol to Emerald Bay when I noticed a deckhand on one of the small commercial boats fishing with a rod and reel. His rod tip was bent heavily and it appeared that he had hooked into something large. After a few minutes of battling the fish, I watched him reach out with a gaff and haul aboard a large, perhaps thirty-pound white seabass.

Later that day I told David McElroy about the catch and we decided to go out the following morning to try our luck. We headed out early, around four-thirty a.m.

Arriving in the general area where I had seen the fish caught, we setup anchor in about eighty feet of water. Using frozen squid, we tried our luck for several hours—to no avail. We did see one of the other two boats that were anchored in the vicinity haul aboard another big white seabass, and it was obvious that he had caught it using live squid for bait.

Later that evening David and I, along with Gary Adams, went out and 'made squid' to use for bait the following morning. In 'making squid', the technique is to setup high-powered lights and hang them over the rails of the boat to attract the spawning squid to the surface. Often the squid schools will 'float' to the surface in massive volume, which can then easily be scooped from the water using hand nets, and kept alive in circulating live bait tanks. At other times we dropped down 'squid rigs' and jigged the bait one or two at a time from under the boat. On that particular night the spawn was extremely heavy and the squid floated to the surface within minutes of our hanging the lights over the side. We filled our bait tank quickly and then filled several five-gallon buckets with fresh squid to freeze for later use.

The squid were amazingly thick that night. Hundreds of tons of squid, all swimming in the same general direction during their spawn, created a massive spinning vortex that spun our boat around in a slow, steady circle in the center of the squid biomass. Hundreds, perhaps thousands of hungry seagulls fed on the floating squid, their insistent caws pealing loudly in the misty shroud of a heavy marine layer. Many of the seagulls were so stuffed with squid that they landed and floated on the ocean surface, seemingly unable to take to the air. On the outside perimeter of the lights several dozen sea lions fed voraciously on the spawning squid, barking occasionally in obvious delight.

We had expected to spend several hours making bait, but we were done within an hour. However, the experience of witnessing the impressive squid spawn was so exhilarating that we stayed out for a few more hours, drinking beer and watching the spectacle. Eventually we hoisted anchor and returned to the Isthmus to get a few hours' sleep.

Heading out early in the morning, at around four-thirty a.m., the heavy marine layer had lowered and turned into a thick, engulfing fog. Visibility was less than fifty feet in the gray darkness of pre-dawn, and we had to 'feel our way' through the moorings and out to the squid grounds.

When we arrived in the general area, we setup anchor and dropped down a live squid. We were fishing in about fifteen fathoms (ninety-feet) and there was little current. We waited. When 'the grey' arrived—that time between the first vestiges of daylight and the rising of the sun—I felt a distinctive tug on the end of my line. Tensing, I waited a moment until I felt a heavy pull on the rod tip. Counting slowly to three I lowered my rod a little, leaned back and set the hook. My rod bent double. For a moment nothing happened, but then slowly and steadily line began to peel off of the reel. I was fishing with twenty-five pound test monofilament and using a short Sabre rod with an old reliable Penn Jigmaster reel.

The fish made a long, uninterrupted run, peeling away perhaps eighty yards of line—typical of a big white seabass. I kept moderate, steady pressure on the drag, waiting for the fish to slow. When it slowed, I began short-stroking the rod, raising the tip up and then fast-reeling down to retrieve as much line as quickly and efficiently as possible. About halfway back to the boat, the fish darted off again, peeling off about twenty yards of line. I waited for it to stop, then resumed pumping. Twice more the fish made short bursts away from the boat and then hunkered straight down below the boat. I lifted and pumped until I saw a distinctive silver flash in the oily black water under the boat. "Color", I called out.

David was ready with the gaff. He leaned over the side of the boat as the fish floated to the surface, yanked the hook into the fish's belly and swung it over the rail. A beautiful thirty-five-pound white seabass lay thumping on the deck.

A few minutes later David hooked-up. He fought the fish for about ten minutes and also brought a big seabass to the boat. I gaffed that fish and we had two hefty seabass on board. For the next hour, it was nearly nonstop action. Gary hooked and landed the next two fish, then David another at the same time I hooked-up. We landed both and then caught another. By the time the sun began to peek above the distant horizon we had caught full limits of white seabass—three fish each—and they ranged from twenty-seven to forty-two pounds. We headed back into the dock.

We created quite a stir in the local community when the crew showed up for work. The nine white seabass were laid across the end of the pier for a picture and everyone was impressed.

That was the start of the most remarkable and consistent winter of fishing I have ever seen. We repeated that scenario numerous times in the ensuing weeks; catching so many white seabass that all of the freezers in the Isthmus were stuffed with frozen filets, and dozens of ice-chests packed with fish had been taken to the mainland for family members.

In addition to the white seabass, several big halibut and quite a few yellowtail were hooked and landed in the same area. On one of the mornings, Chris King caught his limit of three seabass, a thirty-eight-pound halibut and a thirty-pound yellowtail. Jimmy Ristau landed a huge, forty-two-pound yellowtail. David and I also caught and released two black seabass (a protected species). That same morning, we pulled back into the dock with our nine fish limit of white seabass, four big yellowtail and two big halibut. We were back at the dock and ready for work by eight o'clock. It was truly some epic fishing.

For some reason, that year was the only time that I ever saw that location produce like it did. We tried it periodically in following years, when the area held spawning squid, and managed to catch another fish or two, but unlike most 'hot spots' that produce year after year, that spot never got 'hot' again. We felt fortunate for having discovered that 'once in a lifetime' experience.

Two other sidebars to that fishing adventure occurred later that spring. One of them was on Easter Weekend when my good friend Johnny Vaughan decided to give the hot seabass fishing a try. Johnny was not much of a fisherman. He had never gotten into it like so many other Islanders. He was on the Island for the weekend along with another good friend Greg Bombard. Greg, Johnny and I went out on Greg's boat to try and 'make some bait' for the following morning. We worked and worked at trying to 'make bait' but it just wasn't happening. After about five hours of jigging, trying to net bait, and waiting, we had a total of seven live squid in the tank. Normally we would fish with a full scoop or two of bait, maybe one-hundred-fifty to two-hundred squid. To expect much success with only seven pieces was unrealistic.

I told Johnny and Greg to use them since I needed to get up and be at work early in the morning anyway.

At around eight-thirty the following morning I was at work and heading into the dock on one of the patrol boats when I saw Greg maneuvering his boat up to the main float. Johnny was stepping off of Greg's boat with a silly grin on his face. I tied up and walked over to them.

"How'd you do?" I asked. "Any luck?"

"Yeah," Johnny answered in his typically low-key manner. "I got one."

"Great," I responded, "Is it a good one?"

"I think it's pretty good," he commented casually. "I'll show it to you."

He stepped back onto the boat, opened the deck hatch and reached down to pull out the biggest white seabass I had ever seen! When we weighed it on the official scale in the Harbor Office it weighed in at a whopping sixty-five pounds! It was the first white seabass Johnny had ever caught and he landed it on an old rental-type fishing rod using a wire barracuda leader! He basically did everything wrong, but he caught a white seabass that was much bigger than any I had ever caught.

He mounted the fish and hung his 'bunny bass' (because it was caught on Easter Sunday) on the wall at the Isthmus Bar for many years, until the Bombards' left the Isthmus. It's now on his wall at home.

Yet another episode in that epic year of fishing took place one afternoon when Phil Kerr and I went up to Emerald Bay in a work skiff to help the camp councilors with a problem on their docks. They required our assistance and a work skiff to help reattach and reposition their docks after one of their camp boats had crashed into one of the dock sections.

Phil was working with me in the Harbor Department at the time. After helping the camp councilors readjust their docks, Phil and I were cruising slowly back to the Isthmus in the work skiff. That old skiff is one of three plywood skiffs that one of the Isthmus 'old-timers', Bill McDermott, had built for the Harbor Department a few years previously. I was at the helm, motoring along at about five knots when something caught my attention about a hundred yards off our starboard bow. I stared at the spot where I had seen a flash of silvery-white and then it appeared again. "Hey, Phil" I commented to him as I pointed. "Look over there. What do you think that is?"

He looked, and after a moment caught sight of what I had pointed toward. "I don't know," he responded, "But let's head over and check it out."

Altering course and heading toward whatever it was on the surface that we had seen, I motored in that direction. We lost sight of it a couple of times, but then it would pop back up again. When we got close enough to see it clearly, we both blurted, "Holy shit! It's a white seabass." We spoke almost in unison and ironically used the exact same words.

I slowed and shifted into neutral. Assessing the situation, we watched as the big fish floundered on the surface, trying to swim down but unable to do so. Immediately I thought to myself, 'It was hooked and was brought to the surface from deep water and its air bladder has popped. It can't go back down'.

I turned to Phil. "I'm going to pull up to it on our starboard side. You get the tail and I'll get the head."

"Right," he commented, intent on getting himself ready for the maneuver.

I shifted back into gear and angled the bow toward the fish. When I reached the point where I anticipated we could drift close, I swung the bow hard to port and slid up to the side of the rail. The fish was pointing with its head toward the stern of our skiff, where I was kneeling, and the tail was dragging behind it toward Phil. I leaned over, stuck my left hand into its gills and lifted. At the same moment Phil reached down and grabbed the fish by the tail and we swung it into the boat. It began to flop, thudding its thick, heavy tail on the plywood flooring.

As I had thought, a strand of monofilament fishing line hung from its tooth-lined jaws, attached to a number two hook. The fish's air bladder protruded from its open mouth, bulging out like an overinflated white balloon.

Phil and I high-fived each other, laughing and staring at our remarkable 'catch'. It's not often that anyone hauls in a forty-five pound white seabass using his bare hands.

On those rare occasions when I found myself with little or nothing to do, one of my favorite pastimes was simply to stare out my living room windows. Our little house was not more than fifty yards from the shoreline in Isthmus Cove. The windows on the tiny cottage wrapped around two sides of the home, affecting sweeping views of the harbor, the distant open ocean and the rolling hills that lead into the interior. Sometimes our house was referred to as the fishbowl because of the expansive windows.

Seated at my living room window, the view looking out to sea was incredible; it was like a vast painting that was always changing. I could sit for hours—if time allowed—staring out at the shimmering water, the white sheen of Bird Rock. Farther out, about one mile north of the Isthmus Pier, the rocky, jagged promontory of Ship Rock stands like a tall sentinel of defiance, silhouetted against a soothing aquamarine sea and a subtle azure sky that blends the ocean and the sky into a vibrant blue horizon.

Those moments of reverie did wonders for my soul. There was something warming and fulfilling in my musings, a sense of magical wonder and inner serenity that filled my mind with peace and warmed my heart with happiness. Often I felt the ocean as a warm womanly presence, soothing and motherly. At other times I felt its essence to be more like a lover, its glowing surface radiating the wantonness and beauty of the female body. During storms, when it became tempestuous, it helped me to realize that it is quite comparable to the feisty temperament of a troubled woman. There is something about the ocean that is both all-encompassing and all-consuming and I was blessed to have it there, within reach, within sight, and within sound for so many wonderful years.

I made it a habit during the warm months of the year to go for a swim at least once a day. After work, beginning usually in early or mid-May until early or mid-October, I almost always headed straight for the bedroom, stripped down and donned my swimming trunks, then walked down to the beach for a swim. I usually swam out to the stringline, about thirty yards off the beach, then swam along it, fixing downed pickup poles or untangling and re-tying broken lines along the way. Usually I wore a facemask and snorkel, so that I could dive underwater to recover broken lines or retrieve items dropped overboard from visiting boats. I found a variety of items during those swims, from towels to sunglasses to knives to fishing tackle. On occasion I even found money—never a lot, but a few fives, tens, and even a twenty or two.

Often I swam out to my boat, which I kept moored on the J-row a few yards farther out in the bay. I would sometimes climb up out of the water and perform a little cleanup on the boat, wiping down the dirt and dust that always accumulates on boats moored in Isthmus Cove. At other times I would go out in the boat for a brief run around the bay, or head out for a short fishing trip.

On one of those fishing excursions, I headed out to Ship Rock around five p.m. to try and jig a few live baits to use for white seabass. It was early June and the early summer seabass bite was just starting to manifest. I quickly caught five medium sized greenback mackerel and decided to drop down a mackerel right where I was drifting, about fifty yards from the reef at the southern edge of Ship Rock. I was dropping my bait toward the bottom, in about eighty-feet of water when my line began peeling from the spool. My heart started racing, as it usually does when I anticipate the thrill of hooking into a big fish. I counted to five, reared back and set the hook. My rod bent double and I knew I was hooked into a nice seabass. It took me about ten minutes to haul the fish in, gaff it and haul it aboard. It had taken me no longer than twenty-minutes from the time I left the mooring to snag bait, land a thirty-six pound white seabass and head back for the dock.

As I neared the mooring field, Stephen McElroy was heading out to go fishing in his Boston Whaler. Stopping nearby he called out, "Hey, I thought you were going fishing?"

"I did. I already got one," I told him.

"You're kidding? I just watched you go out a few minutes ago. You couldn't have caught one already?"

I reached down and lifted the seabass from the deck, holding it high so that he could see it. It was still quivering, its silvery sides lit-up with the metallic gray stripes that often appear when a seabass is hauled from the water, before it dies and fades to a duller gray. "I still have four baits left in the tank, I only used one. Do you want them?"

"Sure," he responded. I pulled alongside his skiff, transferred the bait over to his tank and headed for home. After hauling the fish up to my house, I looked back out at Ship Rock and saw Stephen's boat bobbing on the rippled currents that were swirling around the reef. Picking up my binoculars—which I always kept near my living room recliner—I focused in on Stephen. He was standing, his rod bent over as he pumped on a fish. Soon I saw him bend down and grab the gaff, and reach over the side to haul a hefty seabass over the rail. He started his engine, stowed his rod and reel and headed back into the harbor. It had taken him perhaps fifteen minutes from the time he left the cove until he was pulling back into the bay with his own thirty-plus pound white seabass. It was not always that easy, but on that particular day it was. Stephen caught up with me the following day and thanked me for setting him on the right course. It was a gratifying fishing experience that we both cherished immensely.

12. Island Life

I'VE MENTIONED THE SANTA ANA winds that can wreak havoc on the north-facing coves of the Island. Late in the spring of 1984, Dave Amatisto, one of our more experienced Harbor Patrolmen, came into work for his early morning shift. As we usually do, we were listening to the marine weather forecasts on VHF weather #1. He walked in the door and listened to the droning voice of the broadcaster from the National Weather Service as he pronounced Small Craft Advisories with northeast winds twenty to twenty-five knots with occasional gusts to thirty-five, and combined seas six to eight feet. I reached over and shutoff the radio.

Amatisto, thinking that he had heard the inner-waters forecast, which included Catalina Island, had actually been listening to the outer-waters forecast for the northern Channel Islands and Point Conception. Trying to be proactive, and without my being aware of his action, Amatisto then proceeded to go out on his patrol boat and go from boat-to-boat in Cherry Cove advising dozens of moored boats of impending strong Santa Ana conditions and advising them to head for home.

A while later, Doug Bombard walked out to the pier, stopped me on the ramp as I was heading to my patrol boat and asked me, "Doug, why are so many boats leaving the harbor?" I looked up and saw a steady stream of boats pulling out of Cherry Cove and heading for the mainland.

"I don't know. Let me make a radio call."

I hopped aboard my patrol boat and called Amatisto on the radio. "Hey Dave, what's going on over there in Cherry? Got any idea why so many boats are pulling out of the cove?" On a Friday morning, one would expect an influx, not an exodus of visiting boats.

"Oh, yeah," Amatisto responded. "I heard the weather forecasts this morning for strong Santa Ana winds and I have been going around advising people that they would be wise to head for home."

Doug Bombard overheard the transmission and barked at me in exasperation, "What is he talking about? The forecasts for the weekend are mild. There is no Santa Ana forecast for the Island. What in the heck is he doing?"

I called him back on the radio, advising him to 'switch'. (To 'switch' is a request between boats to switch from channel #9, our standard operating channel, to channel #19, with the assumption that we could communicate more privately). We switched channels and I asked him what had prompted him to take the action he had taken. He informed me that he heard the marine forecast and it was calling for the Santa Ana condition. When I informed him that he must have heard only the outer-water forecast and that our inner-water forecast was mild, he apologized profusely. Several of us then went from boat to boat informing them that there had been a mistake and that there was nothing to worry about. It soothed the people on the remaining boats and stopped the exodus. But the damage was done, and Doug Bombard initiated an order that no one should ever again advise boats to leave the harbor without his personal direction.

Dave Amatisto was understandably chagrined, but accepted his new nickname 'Santa Ana Amatisto' with affable humility.

One afternoon in mid-summer of 85', Harbor Patrolman Ray Smith called in on the telephone that a commercial fishing boat was pulling into Cat Harbor with a large Great White Shark on board. He was requesting help. Ray called on the landline because he did not want to broadcast the news of a big shark over the radio. Island leaders are quite sensitive to negative publicity about the Island and the announcement of a Great White Shark was not something they wanted publicized.

I spoke to Ray on the phone and he told me that the fishermen had caught it near Santa Barbara Island and that it was wrapped and tangled in their gill net. They were hoping to get help hoisting the big shark onto the Wells Beach Pier so that they could more easily manipulate the shark and untangle their gear. Otherwise they would need to cut the net—an expensive measure that would also require 'down time' to make repairs. I phoned David McElroy and he agreed to head out to Wells Beach and help the fishermen hoist the fish with the crane on the end of the pier.

The news of the big shark spread quickly through the little community and by the time we arrived at the pier there were already about a dozen curious spectators. David and a couple of guys from the

Mooring Service tossed down a long, one-inch braided polypropylene rope to the fisherman and they tail roped the big shark.

As the crane began to hoist the fish, the fishermen played-out the loose end of the tangled net, trying to keep it clear. We could hear the crane straining and the pier creaking under the weight of the shark and when it was about halfway up to the top of the pier the polypropylene line snapped and the fish crashed down onto the deck of the fishing boat and then rolled into the water. Fortunately the fishermen were standing clear—not under the fish—and were uninjured. David tossed down another section of line and told them to double it up. On the next lifting effort the massive shark rose from the side of the boat and with the help of about five guys, David swung it around and lowered it to the deck of the pier.

We all stared down in amazement. It was monstrous! The huge Great White Shark measured seventeen-feet long, was approximately eight feet in diameter at its widest girth, and was estimated at near three-thousand pounds. Lying across the deck of the pier, its dark leathery torso looked and felt thicker than the leather on a pair of boots, and its impressive dorsal fin rose nearly four feet above its back. From the corner of its massive jaws a small, partially regurgitated sea lion hung about halfway out of its mouth. Mixed with thick and slimy saliva, and the juices secreted from its belly, the mass of regurgitate created a foul and pungent odor. Row after row of razor sharp, serrated teeth lined its inner jaws. Its big black, oval-shaped eyes seemed to have a vacant look, hidden behind a thin, opaque layer of film. It was truly an amazing spectacle and frightening to think that creatures that menacing could really be out there swimming around in nearby waters.

With the shark on top of the pier, the fishermen were able to lift it in sections and work the tangled net free. After the net was cleared we took lots of pictures. The shark was so massive that when I sat down on it for a photo, with my legs straddling its back, my feet did not touch the ground. We sat four-year old Trevor onto its back holding a lightweight-spinning rod that we hooked into the sharks jaw, had him pull up as though he were reeling in the fish, and snapped a photo.

That picture is one that graces his scrapbook with a certain amount of awe.

There were times on the Island that just flat out made me feel good. I loved it when I greeted a new boater, helped them onto a mooring and saw the same fascination and awe manifested in their eyes that I felt when I saw the Island for the first time. Catalina is called the 'Island of Romance' for several reasons, partly because it instills an atmosphere of romance in couples that become enraptured with its aura, but also because it instills in others a sense of love and appreciation of the beauty, tranquility, and serenity that prevails on its shores and in its entirety.

For us, living the Island dream was an everyday joy. Even at those times when things were difficult or challenging, the Island has a way of soothing your soul and calming your frustrations. I often told an employee who was having a difficult time with something, whether work related or personal, to try a technique that always worked for me; 'Just look up. Everywhere you gaze, the beauty and tranquility of the Island is surrounding you. Things cannot be too bad when you look up and see these marvelous surroundings.' I could take a pause, let the sights I was seeing envelop me, and return to the problem at hand feeling refreshed and energized. It usually worked for them, and always worked for me.

Similarly, it was gratifying to be able to share bits and pieces of our Island knowledge and insights with others. It always gave me a certain amount of happiness to take friends and relatives out into the interior to see its splendor. The animals—especially when the pigs and goats were still roaming the hills—always fascinated both our guests and us.

Just seeing the rugged interior, the vastness of nearly eighty-six-thousand acres of untouched, unspoiled nature is a rare opportunity. There is something fascinating about hiking a ridge line and gazing out over lush valleys smothered in the fresh green grass of spring, or sitting upon a rocky knoll gazing out over hill and valley, ocean and sky. Marvelous sunsets, fog shrouded canyons, fields of wildflowers and bold rocky escarpments, all combined to create visions and memories that will last a lifetime.

For me, the most indelible memories are probably those associated with the ocean. The simple vistas from the windows of our home, the moonlit nights with a silvery path leading to a Catalina full moon, the incredible panorama of a million stars stretching from horizon to horizon on a dark night at sea when the moon is on the other side of the planet. Those times, as well as the thousands of hours I spent working and playing on the water, will forever last in the memories of my own living dream.

In the fall of 1985, after extensive research into the options available in the small boat market, Maureen and I decided to buy a new boat. We had concurred that our little boat the 'Moby', a 16' runabout that I had painstakingly restored was fun and suitable for our basic boating excursions, but was just a little too small and inadequate for any offshore, or overnight fishing.

I had set my sights and dreams on a Grady White, a popular cuddy-cabin style fiberglass boat that is built and used primarily on the east coast. Drawing upon the advice and expertise of our good friends Bill Breyer and Rick Ruppert, we visited the Los Angeles Boat Show and found a floor model, twenty-two-foot Grady White Seafarer that we purchased without a motor.

Ty Ewing, manager of the Isthmus Outboard Shop informed us that he would assist me in installing a new engine on the boat, and Doug Bombard offered to let us buy a new one-hundred-fifty horse-power outboard engine with minimal markup—using the dealership cost as a base price. At the same time that we ordered the boat, we also ordered a new galvanized boat trailer for storing, hauling and launching our new boat. With Ty's help, it took me about six weeks to rig the boat, paint the bottom, and get it ready for launch. We named the boat 'NO MO', not as a reference to 'Mo' (Maureen), but more significantly that there would be 'NO MO' boats in the family! That little boat served us well for years, and we enjoyed many memorable outings, fishing trips, and other fun-filled family excursions aboard the boat.

On a sunny and calm afternoon in March of 1986, Richard Brown, captain of the Mooring Service boat *Sandpiper,* was working in the Whites Landing area rigging moorings for the upcoming season. Sometime in the early afternoon, the Harbor Department received a call that his wife Sheri, who was nine months pregnant and close to term, was on her way to the mainland to give birth. Richard stopped his rigging, steamed for the Isthmus and put his boat away for the day.

Making plans to get to the mainland quickly from the Island can often backfire, or at least become more difficult than 'the best laid plans of mice and men'. Doug Bombard knew that Richard and Sheri were expecting soon, and he had offered to fly them to the mainland when the time came. But he was not on the Island that day, having been called off-Island for one of the many things that he had to deal with as president of the company.

When Richard arrived in the Isthmus he had a couple of options available; either drive across the Island to Avalon and catch the next available boat to the mainland, or find someone to take him to the mainland in their private boat. I volunteered mine.

Crossing the channel in our new boat was not a problem. At twenty-two-foot, the *No Mo* was both seaworthy and comfortable, under 'normal' conditions. That particular afternoon the winds were light, at less than ten knots and the swell was minimal. It would be an easy crossing. Richard grabbed his bags, which were already packed, and I met him on the pier. We had a very uneventful crossing, chatting amiably about fatherhood and things in general. Richard was understandably excited, it was his second child and he felt great relief when he arrived at the hospital in time to see and be part of the delivery of his daughter Samantha Brown.

After dropping him off at the Catalina Express dock, I was about to head back to the Island when a group of four employees ran down to the dock and asked if they could ride back to the Island with me. They had planned to go into Avalon on the Catalina Express and then find a ride back to the Isthmus, but finding me on the docks and on my way back to the Island would make it a lot easier for them.

I told them to hop aboard and we cast-off and headed down the channel of Los Angeles Harbor. Ted Bauer, a bartender in the restaurant, his girlfriend Lynn, Gary Adams, and one of his snack bar employees, John Birmingham, comprised the group of four.

I had gone about half a mile, to an area near the Los Angeles Fireboat Station, when I saw the flashing blue lights of a Port Police boat bearing down on us. He was throwing a big wake and was obviously intent on something. To my surprise, he was 'chasing' me down. I shifted into neutral and drifted to a stop.

"What's up officers?" I asked innocently.

"We are performing random inspections. May we come aboard?" one of the officers asked. "Sure," I responded, reaching out to attach a line to my side cleat. I wasn't worried about anything. I had done nothing wrong and always kept the necessary safety equipment on board.

One of the officers climbed aboard and asked where we were heading. I explained that I had made an emergency run from the Island with a co-worker whose wife was having a baby and that the other passengers were fellow employees from the Island looking for a ride home. He praised me for my help in getting Richard to the hospital in time and then asked to see my lifejackets. I stepped down into the small cabin and lifted the seat under which I kept the life jackets stored. The compartments were empty.

In our hurry to get off the Island I had forgotten that Maureen and I had pulled the life jackets out during our 'spring cleanup' of the boat and hung them on a line behind the house to dry. We forgot to put them back in. I realized what had happened and explained it to the officer.

"Well, I understand your explanation, but I cannot allow you to proceed without lifejackets. You will have to follow us to the dock and then find a way to purchase or procure enough life jackets for each of you before we can let you depart. Also, I must write you a citation for not having life jackets aboard."

"Oh, come on!" I pleaded. "Didn't you hear my explanation? I fully understand your position, but please, show some consideration. I always carry more than enough safety equipment and fully recognize the need for safety and caution. But this is a special circumstance and I think I deserve a break."

"Sorry!" he told me emphatically. "The law is the law."

I thought for a moment about the situation and what I could do. "Okay. We're only a few-hundred yards from the Catalina Express Terminal. I know them well and I'm quite sure they will loan me some lifejackets. Will you follow me over there and allow me to try and resolve this issue?"

He looked over at his partner who shrugged. Turning back to me he replied, "Alright, we'll follow you to the dock."

I headed over and pulled into the dock at the Catalina Express. Tony Ross, a longtime employee with strong Island connections, walked down and spoke with me. I explained the problem and asked if I could borrow five life jackets, which I would return the following day when the afternoon Express arrived in the Isthmus. Laughing about the situation, Tony pulled out five brand new life jackets still in their plastic packages from one of the Express supply cabinets and passed them down. Satisfied, the Port Police let us go, after issuing me a ticket. I then had to deal with a boating citation for failure to have proper equipment on board.

We headed back to the Island. The following day I put the borrowed life jackets aboard the afternoon Express boat and sent them back over to Tony.

A court date was set for about a month later. I got a very nice letter from Richard and Sheri Brown, a character letter from Doug Bombard explaining my role and duties as Harbormaster and how I always adhered to marine safety requirements, and another letter from Gary Adams describing the events that led us into that predicament.

When Maureen and I arrived in court, we saw that our case was near the end of the docket. We watched with steadily growing dread as the judge handed down one severe ruling after another. One of the spectators in the courtroom whispered that he was known in the courtroom as 'The Hanging Judge'. Our turn came and I stood to address the court.

He glared down at me. "You have been charged with operating a vessel without life jackets, and five people aboard your boat. That is a serious offense. The penalty for operating without life jackets is set at five-hundred-dollars per violation. Do you have anything to say?"

"Your honor," I began, my voice quavering as I contemplated the consequences. My mind was racing. That fine would amount to twenty-five-hundred dollars. I was having trouble trying to speak.

"Well?" he blurted.

Steeling myself, I started explaining, pulling out the letters and handing them across to the bailiff as I rambled. After blurting out most of the story, the judge interrupted.

"Okay, okay. I have heard enough." He looked down at me, a slight glitter in his eyes. "I'm going to let you off. I'm happy to hear that the father made it in time to see his daughter born. But if I ever see you in my courtroom again for having violated any rules of safety, my leniency will cease."

Stunned, I looked up at him.

He instructed me, "Case dismissed. You can go."

I started to thank him, but Maureen grabbed my arm and said quietly, "Let's just get out of here before he changes his mind."

Fortunately I did not ever have to return to his courtroom.

In the winter of 1987-88', a momentous event that was destined to alter the character of the Two Harbors community began to take shape; the advent of the Isthmus' own little one-room school. For years the school-age children of Two Harbors had endured the difficult bus ride across the Island into Avalon in order to go to school.

Two people, Cliff and Marybelle Tucker, members of Channel Cruising Club and longtime Isthmus boaters, decided to do their utmost to try and establish an elementary school in the Isthmus so that the young kids would not have to endure the grueling bus ride to town.

Drawing upon the support of Doug Bombard, the Long Beach School District, most notably Superintendent Ed Eveland, Avalon Principal and District Board Member Jon Meyer, Avalon's Dr. Frank Blair, and a host of other dedicated individuals, the school slowly began to take shape.

Cliff Tucker, who owned and operated Scotsman Industries, volunteered to donate a building for the school. Eveland, Blair, Tucker, Bombard and others cut through the barriers of red-tape that usually encompass an endeavor of that nature, and during the spring of 1987, ground was broken for the little one-room school.

George McElroy, John Ermatinger, and members of the Two Harbors maintenance crew prepared the site and worked with the construction team from the mainland that shipped the building to the Island and erected it onto its foundation. Then, in September of 1988, first-year teacher Aileen Earl-Wood welcomed eighteen students into the Two Harbors Little Red Schoolhouse. The momentous occasion garnered national news coverage, it being the first one-room school to open—rather than close—in modern times.

For us it was a real blessing. Trevor was one of five first-grade students (Trevor, Nicole Latka, Paul Ermatinger, Colin Peterson and Martin Coiner) to start their education in the school, and those five would be the first graduating class that would have spent their entire elementary education in the school.

Aileen Earl-Wood did a marvelous job shuffling the curriculum of five-grades (first through fifth), giving each of the school's eighteen students the personal and grade-appropriate attention they needed. Ms. Earl-Wood stayed with the school for two years, to be followed by several other wonderful teachers, including Becky Davidson, Heidi Tiso, Lindsey Mattingly, Sea Peterson, Melanie Barney, and Trish Brown, all of whom gave our two children the guidance and educational background that helped them both to be high achievers throughout their middle and high school years, and then through college.

For the growing community of Two Harbors, having an elementary school was a true blessing for the young students and their parents, and the generosity and support of the Tucker family, Dr. Blaire, Doug Bombard and all the other giving and caring individuals that contributed to its existence will always be remembered.

The winter of 87-88' was the start of a prolonged dry period on the Island that would ultimately turn into one of the most severe droughts the Island had seen in recent times. Less than eight inches of cumulative rain fell in each of the next two years, and by the end of the second year the Island was in water restriction mode. As the drought continued, water rationing went from phase one to phase two. In phase one, water restrictions limited the hours a person could water lawns or plants, did not allow for the washing of vehicles or boats, hosing sidewalks, or otherwise wasting fresh water. In phase two, water use was extended to restrict the number of gallons per day, and per household. Any violations would result in heavy rate increases and/or fines.

During the phase two restrictions, which went into effect at the end of our fourth consecutive dry year (1989-90'), the saying 'if it's brown, flush it down, if it's yellow, let it mellow', became a popular slogan on the Island. Restaurants were told not to serve drinking water to customers—and quite frankly you would not want to drink the water anyway because it was being pumped from the bottom of the wells and reservoirs and did not look or taste very good. In our home, we learned to conserve well and effectively, although it was not much fun.

There are many little things that helped us to conserve, one of the simplest being to turn the water on slow when needed. We never ran the water while brushing teeth, turned it on only briefly when washing hands, filled one sink about a third full to wash dishes, the other about a third full to rinse, and then dipped the gray water into a bucket to be used for the few plants that we tried to keep alive. When showering, we often showered together (kind of fun) and then put the kids into the accumulated water in the bottom of the tub to bathe. Afterward I would bucket that water out for use in our sad little garden. Going through water rationing and suffering the effects of a severe drought had a long lasting influence on our entire family. To this day we continue to be water conscious.

Even though we lived in paradise, we needed to occasionally get off the Island and explore and enjoy other people, places and things. One of our most enjoyable getaways was to the Big Island of Hawaii in the fall of 1987.

During that Hawaiian vacation Maureen discovered that she was pregnant. It was a real surprise—not a mistake like our son Troy likes to tease—but a pleasant surprise. When Troy began growing in her womb, we were both elated.

For me, his birth proved to be a little easier and considerably less traumatic than Trevor's. Maureen again went to the mainland ahead of time, staying with Johnny and Elaine Vaughan awaiting delivery. As occurred with Trevor, Troy arrived at a busy time of the year for me, a few days before Memorial Day.

Elaine Vaughan served as Maureen's coach during the delivery while Trevor and I watched the Lakers and Celtics battle each other in the NBA playoffs. After my first experience in the delivery room, I really did not want to see another delivery in person. I will always be eternally grateful to Elaine Vaughan for filling in for me as coach and delivery-mate during Troy's birth. All went well, the Lakers won, and little Troy came into the world to complete our immediate family.

We returned to the Island after Maureen was released the following day, and I went back to work to prepare for the upcoming Memorial Weekend 1988—and a truly hellacious storm.

13. *Memorial Day from Hell*

I WENT BACK TO WORK on a Tuesday following Troy's birth. There was a lot to do to get ready for the upcoming 'opening weekend' of the season. Memorial Weekend is always recognized as the start of the summer boating season and historically is—or at least was—one of the busiest weekends of the year.

We still had a lot to do to be prepared for the onslaught of boats that we knew would begin arriving during the next few days. A few of the dinghy docks needed to be launched and connected. Harbor boats needed to be launched, cleaned up and readied. New staff members were still being trained. Moorings were still being rigged. Mooring reservations were being taken at a feverish pace. I jumped into the fracas with a purpose, and put in some really long hours in an effort to get everything ready. I had no idea that those long hours would pale in comparison to what was to transpire a few days later.

I always paid close attention to weather forecasts on the Island. Forecasts could often have a direct influence on the number of boats that might visit the Island on any given weekend. On Tuesday, when I returned to work, the long-range forecasts looked fine. A weak weather front was forecast to move into the Pacific Northwest on Friday, but it was predicted to go ashore well north of the Los Angeles area and make land in northern California. The forecasts remained mild on Wednesday and Thursday and the leaseholders continued to make their mooring reservations, and transient boats arrived in a steady flow to be placed onto weekend waiting lists for those unreserved moorings available. By Friday morning all coves were already nearly full and boats continued to arrive.

When I arrived at work shortly before seven a.m. on Friday, I listened to VHF Weather #1 and felt a slight bit of trepidation. The cold front moving out of the Gulf of Alaska was dropping farther south than previously predicted and the associated winds and swells were now forecast to enter the southern California bite and affect at least the outer waters. Even so, the inner-water forecasts remained moderate, with only a fifteen to eighteen knot northwest wind forecast. While fifteen to eighteen knots of wind can make for a crummy channel crossing, and make mooring and anchorage conditions a little lumpy, it was nothing to cause immediate concern.

I went onto the water and began the 'shuffle-process' of moving transient boats off of reserved moorings and onto those few moorings that did not have reservations. That process is always a challenging one and usually takes several hours. We put our senior crew to work to make the mooring moves, while the newer guys worked the fairways and stringline, checking in boats and assisting them onto moorings. The 'shuffle' process took most of the morning and it was around noon before we had everything organized and all of the boats moved around as needed. We started a lunch-break schedule, letting each patrolman go to lunch in-turn. I took a few minutes to run up to my house and check on Maureen and our five-day old son Troy, grabbed a quick sandwich and headed back down to the pier.

Upon reaching the Harbor Office, John McKay, from the Baywatch crew, pulled me aside and asked if I had received an update on the weather forecast. I told him that the last I heard was early that morning. He suggested I check it again.

Back in the Harbor Office I turned on Weather #1. The forecasts had deteriorated. There was now a forecast of northwest winds of fifteen to twenty-five knots, four-to-six-foot seas and a slight chance of rain. The cold front was dropping even further south. I thought to myself, 'Oh, great. This could become quite a mess'. It only got worse.

I discussed the forecasts with McKay and his partner Steve Troeger, and then went back out on the water to help with incoming boats. The winds were steady at about fifteen knots, with periodic gusts to around twenty. It was making it very difficult for many boats to pick up their moorings and we were all kept busy assisting boats, tossing towlines and pulling sterns around in an effort to help them moor, particularly on the more wind exposed east side of the Isthmus. Numerous boats on the east side were also calling on the radio requesting a move to the west—or more protected side of the cove—or into Fourth of July or Cherry Cove where sea conditions were much calmer. All of the empty moorings in those areas were either occupied, or reserved by boats that had not yet arrived. We could not accommodate any of the boats requesting a calmer mooring.

By three p.m., the wind and seas were becoming even lumpier and when I looked up on the end of the pier, I saw the Small Craft Advisory flag flying atop the flagpole. I advised Harbor Base that I was switching to the weather channel and listened to the afternoon update. A Small Craft Advisory had been posted, effective at three p.m. for northwest winds of fifteen to twenty-five knots and combined seas four-to-seven feet. It was not sounding good. I pulled into the docks and headed up to Doug Bombards' office to discuss the deteriorating weather.

"Hi Doug," I greeted him. He was on the phone and I waited until he was off, and then asked him, "Have you seen the weather forecasts?"

"Yes. I listened a few minutes ago after I saw the red flag go up. It's not the best, but it doesn't sound like it will get much worse," he informed me.

"Is there anything you think we should do, other than to keep an eye on the boats and try to assist the boats that are still coming in?" I asked.

He thought for a minute. "It might be a good idea to go ahead and take a good look at the boats on the east side of the cove, see if they are moored properly, and suggest they put some chafing gear on their lines. It might also be a good idea too to talk with Baywatch and make sure that they are aware of the weather and prepared to help out if needed."

"Yeah," I told him. "I already spoke to McKay and Troeger, and they are aware of the forecasts. McKay assured me that they would be ready to help if needed."

"Okay," Doug said. "I know it won't be very comfortable for some of the boats, but hopefully things will calm down overnight."

They didn't.

By six p.m. winds were gusting about thirty knots and mooring problems were starting to occur more frequently, especially on the east side of Isthmus Cove. Additionally, we had received a radio call from Bruce Wicklund at Emerald Bay that he was encountering numerous problems from the wind and seas. Emerald Bay is even more exposed than the east side of Isthmus Cove during periods of northwest winds. He had requested assistance from the Mooring Service for a boat that was wrapped-up on a mooring, but they were tied-up with several other problems in Cherry Cove. Bruce had to go into the water himself to un-wrap a couple of boats with mooring lines tangled in their propellers. His assistant, Richard Colson covered the cove while he was in the water.

I was back out on the water and helping one boat after another. Nearly every arriving boat needed help getting onto their mooring, and as the tides changed, the currents increased and numerous boats started swinging into one another. All of the available patrol boats scurried from mooring to mooring trying to help boats and prevent damage, or injuries. We had doubled-up most of the crew, putting two guys into every patrol boat to try and make the responses more effective and efficient.

When the sun dropped below the hills on the west side of the Isthmus, the temperature dropped and the gusting winds increased the wind chill factor. It was getting cold, and rougher, and it looked like we would be in for a long night.

As night fell, the winds actually seemed to back off a little bit and we released most of the day-shift crew to go home and get some food and rest. I headed home at around nine p.m., tired, cold and hungry.

Maureen was worried that I had been out on the water for so long—over fourteen hours straight, but she saw the chaos and realized that it was necessary. She was tired and stressed herself, having an infant to care for, and still recovering from his delivery. Thankfully, she had several of the local gals stop by and help her out with a few things, and drop off an already prepared casserole for our dinner. I ate ravenously, showered, and crawled into bed.

I was sleeping soundly when she shook me awake at around three a.m. I hadn't even heard the phone ring. Our graveyard guy, Mark Woolery called on the telephone requesting help. The winds had started picking up again and several boats had broken loose.

Shaking the sleep from my eyes and stretching my aching body, I brushed my teeth, dressed, grabbed my foul-weather gear and headed back down to the harbor on my bike. I could tell that the winds were getting stronger again, and the swells were starting to pound louder on the shore. A gust of wind struck me as I passed by the 'round house', nearly knocking me over. I cursed silently and continued toward the pier. I could see the pier lights illuminating the masts of sailboats rocking back and forth in the harbor and hear the clanking and rattling of the shrouds in the rigging. White, churning swaths of foam ebbed and flowed from the shoreline as the surf continued to build. At the end of the pier, in the glow from the pier and dock lighting, I could see the ruffled surface and the immediate mooring field. All of the boats moored nearby were pitching and rocking severely, and everything looked upset and disturbed. Glancing up at the flagpole, I saw two red flags flying, one above the other, indicating a gale warning. I went into the office. It was empty. Woolery was out on the water, and I could see that the Baywatch boat was gone from its usual spot at the end of the work float.

The radio went off, a frantic voice pleading, "Harbor Patrol! Harbor Patrol! We need help!"

A prolonged silence followed, and then the voice came back, "Harbor Patrol! Harbor Patrol. Do you copy?"

Another brief pause, and then Woolery responded, obviously preoccupied, "Stand by, please."

The calling person did not standby, calling out again, "Harbor Patrol. We need help, immediately!" It was a frantic call that would repeat often during the next forty-eight hours, or so.

I picked up the radio microphone and responded, "Vessel calling for help, this is Harbor Base. What is the nature of your problem and what is your location?"

The radio buzzed again and the voice came back on, "This is *Sunquest*, we are on mooring L-22 and the boat next to us is crashing into ours! We need help!"

"Okay," I responded, trying to keep as calm and cool as possible, "We will be there soon."

"Hurry! Please hurry!" the voice pleaded.

Woolery then came on the air, "Harbor Base, O.D. (my nickname), I'm glad you're there. I'm over here in Fourth of July Cove and I have a large powerboat in tow that is wrapped-up. I'm trying to hold him into the wind. Baywatch is in route, but not here yet."

"Okay, Mark. Anything else outstanding?" I inquired.

"No, that's it for now, but it's been a nightmare all night long."

"Yeah, I can imagine. I'm on my way down to hop into Harbor Unit #7. I'll head over to L-22," I informed him.

I ran down the ramp, hopped down into Harbor Unit #7—a nineteen-foot outboard and got underway. It was ugly. The swells were rolling into the normally placid harbor at about two-to-four-feet with occasional larger sets. The winds were steady at about twenty-knots from the north, gusting to above thirty. The simple act of untying the dock lines from the patrol boat was a bit of a challenge in the swell—I had to be careful not to let the surge yank the line tight and snag my hands or fingers.

As I pulled away from the dock I could see chaos throughout the nearby mooring field. It was dark, but many boats had their deck-lights on and I could see bodies moving about on board, obviously trying to cope with the situation and adjust lines. With my spotlight pointed down into the water, I headed out toward L-22. Running between the fairway separating the K and L rows, I had to dodge several boats whose moorings had drug out of place. Several moorings that should have been in a relatively straight line on the L-row were drug back into the K-row, with the boats on those moorings hazardously close together. A bright flashlight beam struck me in the eyes and I flew my hand up to shield the glare. A desperate voice rang out in the cold, dark air, "Harbor Patrol! Harbor Patrol, we need help!"

"Get the light out of my eyes, please!" I called out, trying to let my vision refocus. I looked over to my portside and saw a large powerboat with its transom almost in contact with the bow of a sailboat. The powerboat had obviously dragged its mooring from the M or N-row and drug down onto the other boat. Considering the circumstances, I altered my heading to see what I could do to help. L-22 would have to wait.

I pulled adjacent to the two boats. People were on the decks of both boats, with flashlights. I could see one man standing on the bow of the sailboat with a boathook, ready to try and fend off the powerboat that was close by. I looked the situation over, realizing that the two boats had already made contact and had some damage. The stainless steel pulpit of the sailboat was bent and crooked. Assessing a possible solution, I saw that there was considerable space at the stern end of the sailboat. Repositioning my boat so that I could 'talk' with the sailboat crew, I called out, "Do you have a good, strong dock line?"

"Yes," a voice responded. "We have plenty of lines."

"Good," I instructed him, "Take a dock-line, loop it through the bow hawser on your boat, then unhook the bow hawser and let it play out about fifteen feet."

After a brief pause while he mulled over my suggestion, he responded, "Got it! But it looks like he is still dragging and will probably drift down on us again!" We were both shouting to be heard, the din of the wind carrying our voices away on its insistent howl.

"It's the best you can do for now," I called out. "Watch your hands and fingers, but get that line attached and let it out, now!" I watched for a couple of minutes as a crewman, probably the owner, ran back to the stern and pulled out a heavy dock line. He scurried back to the bow and leaned over to run the line through the bow hawser.

"Double it up if you can," I called out to him, seeing that the line he was using was at least fifty-feet long. He ran it through twice, and then after instructing one of his crewmen on how to help him adjust the lines, I watched as he lifted the hawser off the cleat and began playing the dock line out. His boat slowly drifted back and away from the immediate danger. He had done the task well and it would at least provide a temporary solution. Satisfied with the steps taken to resolve that particular problem I told the captain of the sailboat, "I'm on another call and I'll be back. Call me on channel 9 if things get worse."

I headed over to L-22. As I got farther over on the east side of the cove, the conditions worsened. The swells were more steep and closer together. I grimaced as I saw the boats in the area pitching and rocking and swaying on their moorings. When the steepest swells rolled through, I watched the bows of the moored boats rear-up and point upward, lifting eight or ten feet into the air, pulling the mooring lines taught and exposing nearly half of the keel. Several mooring buoys were lifted clear of the water. When the swell passed by, the bows plunged into the next trough, pitching the sterns into the air so that I could see the rudders and props on the sailboats and dipping the transoms of the smaller powerboats frighteningly close to their rail cap. It was not a comforting sight.

Arriving on scene, I could see that the boat moored next to it, on L-21 was swinging wildly, its stern line unattached. Looking over the chaos, I again saw people out on decks, trying to figure out what to do. A strong gust of wind struck, blowing the stern of the boat on L-21 rapidly toward the boat on L-22. I heard a piercing female scream, "Here it comes again!" I watched helplessly as the loose boat swung into the starboard quarter of the boat next to it, rendering a sickeningly loud crunching of fiberglass when the boats made contact.

The swells were steep and rolling and I was broadside to the swell. When a big set rolled through, my boat was lifted and surged sideways away from the other boats. I readjusted my heading and turned the bow of my boat into the wind and swell, trying to get into position to talk with the people aboard the loose boat. Using the forces of the wind and swell to my advantage, I slid slowly closer to the boat. When I was within shouting distance, I called out, "Do you have a stern anchor available?"

"We have one in the aft locker," a weak voice responded.

"Good. Get it out and I'll try to come alongside and set it out behind you."

Holding my boat in position to the best of my ability, I waited while they pulled out the stern anchor. All around me I could see the chaotic mess that continued to worsen. Twice, powerful gusts of wind struck the area, associated with sheets of spindrift and howling blasts of cold air. I saw loose sails flapping on a few nearby boats, the thick white canvas snapping loudly as the sails billowed out around the masts. People were crawling about frantically trying to tie things down. Dinghies were swamped, floating upside down; some with their outboard engines canted crookedly, others with the propellers on the overturned skiff spinning around slowly in the frigid air. On one boat, an inflatable dinghy lifted into the air several feet above the deck, spinning around as a powerful gust sent it airborne, and only its painter (dock line) kept it from flying away.

When the people aboard the sailboat called out to me that they had the anchor ready, I maneuvered carefully toward them. I knew that I could not pull alongside and stay there, but had to make the transaction of passing the anchor from their boat to mine as swift and expedient as possible. The swells were steep and short, rolling into the mooring field every few seconds, and all of the boats in the area pitched and bucked radically in the rough seas. I cautiously drifted closer, keeping my bow into the wind and letting my starboard side slide toward the portside of their boat. When I was close enough to call out, I instructed them to have the anchor and chain ready to toss, and when I gave the signal, to swing it out over the rail and drop it into my foredeck. I also instructed them to keep the anchor rope on board their boat so that it would be ready to secure when I set the anchor. I pulled out several lifejackets and laid them out on the deck to cushion the impact of the anchor landing on the deck of my boat. I watched the people get the anchor and chain ready, advising them to be careful and not get the lines caught on their arms or legs, or on the safety rail of their boat. Satisfied that they seemed to be prepared, I looked out to sea and tried to time my final approach with a relatively small swell. Drifting into position, I cried out, "Now! Toss it in!"

I watched as the man on the port rail stood and lifted the anchor, swung it into the air and heaved it over the side toward my boat. It banged on the rail cap of my boat, titled precariously toward the water, but with the assist of a lurching swell, my boat dipped to starboard and the anchor and chain fell into the my boat and crashed onto the deck. I knew that it had likely caused some cosmetic damage to the inside of the boat, but that was a minor concern. I swung the helm to port, pushed down on the throttle and held my breath momentarily as my starboard stern swung toward the port side of the sailboat. With inches to spare, my boat cleared its side and I throttled back, trying to hold position again. Satisfied with the move, I let the patrol boat start drifting backward into the gap between the boats moored directly astern. Twice more the sailboat swung into the boat moored next to it, until I was far enough back to drop the anchor over the side. Releasing it with the flukes pointing backwards, I watched it sink into the black, turbulent water.

My voice could not be heard above the howl of the wind, and so I pulled forward again and hollered for the captain to take up tension and then secure his anchor line to the starboard cleat on his boat. It was a bit of an ordeal for them to get their anchor line around the cockpit of their boat and over to the other side, but they managed to perform the task. Gradually they tightened the anchor line until it held, holding the boat in an adequate position to keep the two boats apart. I waved and headed off for my next emergency.

That scene, and others very similar, continued into the early morning hours of daylight. We went from 'fire' to 'fire', helping as many boats as possible adjusting lines, setting anchors, adding scope and whatever we could do to try and resolve one problem after another.

At daybreak the chaos and havoc became even more evident.

As the sun cast its streaked rays into the eastern sky, illuminating the tops of billowing cumulonimbus clouds built-up along the distant ranges of the San Gabriel, Tehachapi and San Gorgonio mountains, the full impact of the storm could clearly be seen.

Everywhere I looked there were boats where they should not have been. The Isthmus Stringline—a row of mooring spaces for forty small boats strung along the shallow waters on the east side of the pier, was in ruins—broken apart in at least three places. Several boats rolled broadside in the surf line, two small powerboats lay high and dry on the beach, several other boats swung around loosely on the snapped main line of the mooring system, and one small powerboat floated bottom-up wallowing back and forth in the storm surge. Farther out in the mooring field, boats pitched and bucked on the swell, some canted at odd angles, several lay broadside to the swell and at least a couple swung stern-to the weather, swinging backwards on the mooring. On the west side of the pier the dinghy docks bobbed crookedly in the surf line, broken apart in several sections with large chunks of faded orange foam blocks dangling loosely beneath them and other chunks tumbling in the surf. It was complete and utter bedlam.

About the only places in any of the Isthmus area that provided a semblance of protection from the wind and seas were the westernmost areas of the Isthmus, Fourth of July and Cherry Cove. The boats moored in those locations benefitted from the shelter of the western walls of the mooring fields, tucked in behind the protective points at the outer edge of each cove. Those mooring areas were rocking and rolling to a certain extent, but nowhere near as severely as the outer rows and the east side of all coves. Many of the boats tucked under the west walls set out big fenders and allowed boats that had broken loose or dragged moorings to side-tie alongside. That helped resolve a few problems, but also created others when powerful wind gusts caused the additional strain of having two boats on a mooring either break lines or drag moorings. Every available mooring was in use. Many moorings had been cut and/or drug and were useless. Other moorings, which were broken, were used as secondary backup moorings for nearby boats. It helped to resolve several issues. It also helped that no more boats were heading across the channel. There were dozens of 'Saturday arrivals' due into the coves according to the reservation books, but no boats were heading out to the Island on this Saturday morning. A few boats that had broken loose during the night had put to sea, despite Coast Guard warnings. That served to make available a handful of moorings that could then be used to accommodate some of the boats in dire distress.

I returned to the pier. Doug Bombard was there, talking with John McKay and Steve Troeger and Richard Bates from the Baywatch team. They had just returned from Cherry Cove where a couple of large power boats had broken loose and sustained damage.

"Boy, it's a mess!" I commented as I reached the top of the pier.

Doug looked at me and asked, "How long have you been out here?"

"Since about three a.m.," I told him, and then asked, "How's the forecast? Any better?"

"No. In fact it might get worse. They just posted a storm advisory and the wind and swell is supposed to increase."

"Great," I replied forlornly, "That's just what we need. What are they calling for?"

"They are now predicting winds sustained at forty-to-fifty mph this afternoon with gusts up to seventy," Doug Bombard explained. "Seas in the Catalina Channel are due to build to upward of twenty-feet. The Coast Guard has issued an advisory for all small craft to remain in port, and for those already at the Island to remain at the Island. They stated that they already have all of their available boats and resources tied-up with ongoing distress calls and they cannot respond to any more. That in itself is a very unusual announcement, I've only heard of it being done once before, during the Labor Day Hurricane of 1935."

I watched as one of the crew hauled down the twin red Gale Warning flags and attached the Storm flag to the flagpole. A Storm flag is a red, rectangular flag with a large black square in the middle. It goes into effect with winds between fifty-five and seventy-three miles per hour, (forty-eight and sixty-three knots).

Doug Bombard then asked me, "Are you okay to continue? I'm going to go out onto the water and do whatever I can to help. I could use a deckhand."

"I'm fine. What boat do you want to use?" I asked.

"We'll take the Jeffries. It has more power than all the others."

The Jeffries, Harbor Unit #1 is an older (circa 1960's), twenty-one-foot plywood and fiberglass boat powered with an inline six cylinder Chrysler engine. Built for pulling rather than easy maneuvering, the Jeffries was not a favorite boat for many of the patrolmen because of its handling characteristics, but I loved it. It was one of those boats that could be used for almost anything, provided you did not try to make it perform like an outboard. The key was to learn what the boat 'would not do', and then you could do almost anything. I went up to the Harbor Office and grabbed a quick cup of coffee and a roll and headed back down to the pier to climb aboard with Doug.

For the following six or eight hours, Doug Bombard operated the Jeffries and I served as his deckhand. We towed dozens of boats out of hazardous situations, set out anchors, attached safety lines to other moorings and other boats, and rendered advice. Working with Doug was physically challenging, but also enriching and educational. He applied a few techniques to resolve problems that I would not have thought of doing, and he operated the boat smoothly and efficiently. I added my skills and experience to his expertise and tried to anticipate ahead of time the techniques we would apply to any given situation. We worked well together and resolved or minimized as many problems as we could. In the early afternoon, a brief lull in the weather conditions helped ease things a little bit, and Doug had to go ashore and deal with other issues. Harbor Patrolman Bob Carman hopped onto the boat with me.

During the brief lull in the weather conditions, Bob Carman and I made a run up to Emerald Bay and Howlands Landing to give Bruce Wicklund and his partner Richard Carlson a break. Just getting out around the point at Lion Head was treacherous. Steep, wind-tossed seas approaching ten to twelve feet in height rolled across the front of the point, lifting our little twenty-one foot boat clear out of the water as we climbed the face and then dropped down into the trough. When the strong gusts of wind hit, the turbulence increased even more, pitching the boat onto its beam and threatening to capsize us. It was all we could do to keep the bow headed into the impending swells and keep from pitch poling or broaching. It took us nearly an hour to make the three-mile run to Emerald Bay and tuck behind Indian Rock and the broken reef that 'protects' the cove.

Emerald Bay was a mess. Moorings were dragged all over the cove. Lines were stretched out across the fairways to moorings ahead, behind, and alongside of other boats. Bruce and Richard had done a marvelous job of keeping boats as safe as possible and assisting them with their various problems. Bruce was exhausted, having made multiple dives on wrapped propellers and trying to recover several cut mooring lines.

The Corsair Yacht Club members that utilized the majority of the moorings in Emerald Bay are known as a hearty and experienced group and they pitched-in and helped both Bruce and Richard with other boats in trouble. Fortunately, quite a few Corsair members were due to arrive in the cove on Saturday but had aborted the trip, so there were a few empty moorings that could be used when other moorings broke. Carman and I stayed in Emerald Bay for about three hours, helping where needed and giving Bruce and Richard a highly needed break.

Around four p.m., the winds and seas had eased a bit and we informed the Emerald Bay Patrolmen that we were returning to the Isthmus. The run back was not any easier than getting there, we had to be extremely careful not to 'fly-down' the face of a swell too fast and have the following seas swallow our boat into its maw. Rounding the point at Lion Head took every ounce of skill that I had to keep the Jeffries from being 'eaten-up' by the combing seas.

I had been out on the water since three a.m., nonstop for thirteen straight hours and desperately needed a break. When we got back into the Harbor, Bob dropped me at the pier and I headed up to the Harbor Office.

Gary Adams and his restaurant crew had put together plates of food and cold drinks for the guys on the water. I sat and wolfed down a hot roast beef sandwich and two cold sodas. Feeling better, I phoned my house to see how Maureen was doing. She told me that all was well, and that six-year old Trevor was being a really big help in entertaining our infant son Troy. That allowed her to relax and get a little rest. She wanted me to go home, and I told her that I would try to get up to the house shortly.

No sooner had I got off the phone with Maureen than another powerful gust of wind hit. It was followed soon after by several more strong gusts and within the hour, all hell had broken loose again. Just before sunset, the worst of the storm hit.

Bob Carman called on the radio and informed me that he really needed help. Dozens of distress calls had erupted and boats were tearing loose, dragging moorings and pleading for assistance. I called him into the dock. Patrolmen Dave Coiner, Lee Mott, Steve Slaughterback, Curt Craig, Jay Anderson, Dave Erwitt, and Chris Scholles were all out on the water, each backed up by a deckhand and helping boats in turn.

Bob Carman picked me up at the dock and we headed out for the next response. For the ensuing six hours, until around midnight, we endured the most extreme winds and rough seas that any of us had ever encountered. Although I was to witness and be out in stronger winds a few times later in my career, they paled by comparison. For one thing, those storms did not last as long and the seas did not therefore build as heavily. More significantly, we did not have upwards of seven or eight-hundred boats to deal with.

Mayday calls, distress calls, cry after cry, plea after plea shouted out over the radio. Every patrolman, the Baywatch team, the Mooring Service crew, other residents from various departments in the operation were all either on the water or supplying support wherever they could. Every available anchor in the entire town was pulled out of storage spaces and brought down to the patrol boats to try and help boats in distress. Dozens of moorings had been damaged or destroyed and there were no more anchors to be had. Several boats that had broken loose began a slow, steady circle in the Isthmus fairway—one of the calmer areas, but still a tumbled, wind-tossed mess.

One sailboat of about forty-five feet had grabbed the Coast Guard Buoy between Fourth of July and Cherry Cove. It ran a heavy dock line through the ring atop the buoy and, although pitching and rocking severely, was secure. When another sailboat—a friend of his—broke their mooring lines, the sailboat suggested they tie to their stern. Before long, several more boats tied to the stern cleat of the lead boat until seven boats were strung-out end-to-end behind the first boat. They were pitching and rolling terribly, but at least they were secured.

Numerous boats had been abandoned; the people on board taking their dinghies ashore and not caring what happened to their boats. Several dinghies swamped in the surf line and required assistance. We picked up a few people in our patrol boats that had begged and pleaded for a Shoreboat ride—even though the Shoreboats had discontinued operation the previous day due to the storm. Those pleading individuals, many of them deathly seasick and desperate, we managed to haul aboard our patrol boats and drop off on the main floats. Others on shore then helped them with blankets, food, and dry clothes.

As an example of the extreme duress it caused for many boaters, one of my very good friends, Ralph Liebman and his charming wife Maureen were moored on F-9 in the Isthmus. His mooring started dragging in the powerful winds and he called for help. He was moored in one of the more sheltered areas, tucked just inside of the west wall of the Isthmus. Earlier he had loaned his primary anchor to another boating friend whose anchor had failed and had no mooring available. When we arrived at his mooring, Ralph had his boat in gear, in slow forward, holding the mooring in place by maintaining slow and steady forward propulsion. He explained that he had lent his anchor to a friend and asked if there was any chance that we could locate another. We explained that we thought all available anchors were in use, but one of the Mooring Service guys overheard the call and said that he might be able to help. A few minutes later, the Mooring boat arrived with a two-hundred pound Navy anchor. They deployed it on a length of heavy braided line—no chain was available—and set it off his bow. Manhandling that two-hundred-pound anchor was an ordeal in itself, but they managed to drop it over and put some strain onto the anchor line. They suggested, however that Ralph remain at the helm, with the boat in gear at low idle until the winds eased. Ralph, who was around seventy years old at the time, stayed at the helm from around eight p.m. until nearly three a.m. holding the boat in gear in an effort to keep it safe and secure.

Literally hundreds of other boaters performed similar feats, all trying desperately to keep their families, crew, and boats safe.

Around midnight on Sunday, the worst of the winds began to ease. Mayday and distress calls slowed. We continued to respond to calls, but they were less hectic. Bob and I actually found the time to tie our bow to a broken mooring near the west wall and rest for a short while. At around three a.m., I told him I needed to get some sleep and he dropped me at the pier. I had been going nonstop for twenty straight hours. I went home and fell into a deep sleep. By daybreak on Sunday the worst was over.

There were several boats sunk and destroyed, but all of the people aboard those boats managed to get off safely. One powerboat of about forty-feet in length dragged anchor and was destroyed on the rocks in front of Big Fisherman's Cove. Several small powerboats were severely damaged when they broke loose on the Isthmus Stringline and washed ashore. In Goat Harbor, a dozen boats from Bahia Corinthian Yacht

Club had gathered at anchor for a Memorial Weekend cruise. Three of their large boats (between thirty-foot and forty-five-foot) were sunk and destroyed in the storm, but all crewmen were pulled to safety, several from the raging surf. Eight other smaller powerboats were sunk. One gentleman aboard a sailboat named the *Gosling*, anchored in Big Geiger Cove lost a finger in his anchor line, put it into a Baggie and transported it into the Isthmus where Baywatch helped him get into Avalon to try and have the finger reattached.

Amazingly only one life was lost. A small catamaran with two men on board attempted to sail back to the mainland during the height of the storm. They capsized off the Long Point area and Captain John Stonier and Kevin Marble responded to the scene from Avalon. They rescued one of the two men, the other was never found. In addition, one man disappeared in his dinghy during the storm on Friday night, but was found, cold, hypothermic and exhausted four days later by a commercial fishing boat about forty miles east of the Island. He reported that his dinghy (rather aptly named *Ta-Ta for Now*) had rolled over at least ten times during the first two days adrift. The man was dehydrated and bruised, but alive.

The Memorial Day Storm of 1988 would become recognized and remembered as one of the most severe storms in the history of Catalina Island. It was called 'A Hundred-Year Storm', and left an indelible mark on the entire southern California boating community.

Ironically, Avalon Bay did not suffer much from the storm. The direction of the wind and seas, and the confluences of the Island shoreline, notably the headland at Long Point, provided some shelter for both Whites Landing and Avalon Bay. There were a few wind related problems, some minimal damage, but by and large, those coves fared rather well. So did Cat Harbor, where the winds gusted strongly, and a few boats were dragged around, but the 'Cat Harbor

Millpond', as patrolman Bruce Wicklund later dubbed it, was left basically unscathed.

In the aftermath of the storm, the Two Harbors community rallied together to try and put things back together. The dinghy docks were fixed, patrol boats hauled out and repaired, and the crew was able to get some well-deserved rest. It took longer to reset and repair all of the moorings that were damaged, but most were ready and usable by Fourth of July weekend.

Los Angeles County Supervisor Dean Dana issued a proclamation praising the Harbor and Baywatch teams for their heroic efforts. Numerous television and newspaper stories were aired describing some of the harrowing ordeals that boaters endured.

Quite a few people quit boating following that storm. They simply put their boats up for sale and never returned. Many others avoided Memorial Day in future years, vowing to wait until later in the season to start their summer boating schedules.

For me, it was by far the worst storm that I ever dealt with. I saw some more powerful storms, but they did not last as long and they occurred when the coves were empty—not full of boats. For the sake of the Island and all boaters, I hope nothing like it ever occurs again.

14. Career Changes

HAVING ANOTHER INFANT IN THE family produced another big change in our lives. Maureen took several months off work before deciding to go back into the Accounting Office. The accounting office really appreciated her knowledge and expertise and Doug Bombard persuaded her to return to the department.

We found childcare with good friends Laura Peterson and Debbie Latka, rearranging our days off so that we needed the childcare only three days per week. I also found another friend in Avalon, Jody Vickers, who watched Troy while I played golf with my buddies. Maureen might not have been too thrilled by the influence that four or five golfing buddies had on Troy during the long ride to and from Avalon, but she seemed to accept it okay. It gave me the chance to continue pursuing my passion for golf, and hang out with my buddies. Except for an occasional swear word, or two, the overall influence on our young son was probably minimal.

Trevor, at seven-years old, was in school during the spring, winter and fall, and played with his buddies, Nicholas, James, Justin, Paul, Nicole, Colin and Martin during the summer months. Trevor spent a lot of time on the beaches and in the water, swimming, fishing, tide-pooling and snorkeling. He learned to swim before he was five and was a true water-boy.

Trevor also adored his baby brother and as Troy grew older, he too developed a great adoration of his big brother. Unlike most siblings, and likely due to their age difference (six years), they almost never fought or argued. Trevor was also a terrific 'built-in' baby sitter, always willing to help watch his little brother and in fact enjoyed spending one-on-one time with him. They both immersed themselves in a wide variety of outdoor and indoor activities and were very good at entertaining themselves. They both loved to play out in the hills with their buddies and there are still the remnants of a couple of the 'forts' they built in various locations around the Isthmus.

In July of 1989, Donald Root Haney, publisher of the Catalina Islander, persuaded me to begin a regular column in his weekly newspaper. Don, a wiry man in his mid-fifties had purchased the newspaper from his parents, Gene and Margaret Haney in 1955. Originally published in 1914 by Judge Ernest Windle, the Catalina Islander was the second oldest regularly published newspaper in California, second only to the Los Angeles Times. When Haney approached me about writing a weekly column, I was at first reluctant, not sure I wanted to commit to having to make a weekly deadline, and not comfortable that I could come up with enough information to be able to produce a weekly column, particularly in the winter months. But Don was persistent. He stayed a couple of days in the Isthmus aboard his little Cal 25 sailboat, which He co-owned with good friend and fellow Avalon resident Rudy Piltch. They both loved to spend time sailing around Island waters. While staying in the Isthmus, Don persisted in attempting to convince me to begin writing for him. He took me to lunch, rode around with me on the Harbor Patrol boats, bought me a beer or two after work, and really tried to talk me into making the commitment. After several meetings with him, I finally agreed to give it a try. For the subsequent twenty-one years, or around eleven-hundred weeks, I wrote and submitted my weekly column, *Between Two Harbors*, for the Catalina Islander.

In the beginning, I hand wrote the column on lined paper and Maureen typed it for me. After a few years she told me that either I needed to learn to type or quit writing for the paper. She was too busy and too occupied with other things to have to replicate my hand written documents. She bought me a used electric typewriter, and I slowly and methodically learned to type. I went through cartridges of erase-it tape, and in the beginning I hand wrote the articles and then typed them because I simply was not comfortable enough to think and type simultaneously. After a while my typing skills improved and I was eventually able to think and type at the same time. After several years of writing in that manner, we bought an IBM computer with a DOS system and I entered the computer age. It was a ponderously slow process, but eventually I became skilled enough to compose the column, print it out and fax the copy into the Islander. DOS was by far the user-friendliest system I ever used, and I would still be using it today if it was available.

Several years later we purchased another computer with Word and Windows and I gradually reached the point where I could copy, paste and e-mail. I had really moved into the computer era.

For me, writing for the newspaper became a ritual that I began to enjoy and looked forward to each week, although there were times that having to meet the Monday morning deadline was not very convenient or easy to fit into my schedule. However I never missed a week in all the years I wrote for the paper. When the Haney's sold the Islander to an east coast syndicate—a very unpopular act for many Avalon residents—I thought about quitting. But the new publisher, Lindsay Lewis persuaded me to continue.

After Haney retired, and following Lindsay Lewis, a succession of publishers and editors including Chris Abel, Sheri Walker, current publisher Dan Teckinoff and a few others served at the helm of the newspaper, and I continued to submit my weekly column. Except for a few weeks when I went on vacation, the Islander knew they could count on my article every Monday morning. And on those few occasions when I was going to be gone, I called upon my good friends Doug Owen (in the early years) and later Steve Whittington to fill-in for me. I enjoyed my years as a contributing writer and know that the experience I gained helped prompt me to write these memoirs.

Marketing and promoting Catalina Island is important to sustaining a viable tourism base for the Island community. From the early days of the Wrigley ownership, Island entities have worked hard to develop new and desirable attractions for Island visitors. From the building of the fabled Avalon Casino, to the establishment of enticing events in both Avalon and Two Harbors, the effort to enhance tourism on the Island is an ongoing pursuit.

In 1989, the Bombard family decided to put together a new event for Two Harbors, drawing upon a similar event that had originated in Avalon several years previously; Buccaneer Days.

Avalon's Buccaneer Days was actually a huge attraction for Island visitors, but it became so raucous that the City of Avalon decided to do away with the event because it simply became too big and too risqué for the small town. Thinking that the event might have a better chance of succeeding in the rustic village of Two Harbors, where alcohol consumption and ribald behavior was not as susceptible to the scrutiny and rigidity of local law enforcement, the Bombards decided to give the event a try.

Kathy King, director of Visitor Services and Wendy Adams, worked together with other managers at Two Harbors to develop and devise a Buccaneer Days format that everyone thought might work well. Little did they know at the time that the event was destined to become the single biggest attraction of the year in Two Harbors, with crowds surpassing even those on Fourth of July and Labor Day weekends.

Buccaneer Days is just what it sounds like, a gathering of pirates.

In the first year of its inception, the event drew a good turnout, with a large percentage of the people that showed up dressing as pirates and wenches and really getting into the spirit of the day. Not really knowing what to expect from the event, many of the attendees on that first year did not come prepared to dress the part, but when they saw some of the costumes and the infectious enthusiasm of the partygoers, those that were not attired in pirate garb went back out to their boats and found old clothing that they could tear-up and wear in an effort to blend into the festivities.

The event was planned for the first weekend in October, traditionally a slow time of the year but also some of the most idyllic weather. In setting that time for the event, it was hoped that the attraction might extend the boating season and enhance the overall business enterprise. It did that and then some. As the event continued to grow and attract more and more people, it soon became apparent that a phenomenon of sorts was beginning, and a regular cult following developed.

By the early nineties, Buccaneer Days had turned into such a huge event that it became necessary to begin preparations weeks ahead of time. Maintenance crews designed and built removable structures that could be setup and erected solely for that weekend. A Hoosegow where marauding pirates could be 'locked up' was constructed—with a goal of providing financial support to the Two Harbors Little Red Schoolhouse. A set of booths was designed, including; Pirate Grog, Pirate Victuals, Pirate Attire, a Tattoo Parlor, and even a Palm Reading booth, to add to the festivities. Treasure Hunts for both adults and children were established, with valuable treasure chests hidden or buried in the sand. A Customs Booth was setup on the pier to issue free Boarding Passes for visiting pirates. Costume Contests for both adults and children were initiated and some of the costumes proved to be really eye opening. From the raggedy cotton pants and ripped shirts of the deck sailors to the elaborately decorated and pompous Captain's attire worn by some of the men, the buccaneer spirit spread throughout town. The women dressed even more ostentatiously, slithering into the skimpy rags of the shipwrecked, or donning the bawdry finery of the 'ladies of the night.' There were tight corsets, flaring hips, and more visible cleavage than one can imagine. And all of the hoopla and festivities culminated with the big event of the weekend, the Buccaneer Ball, on Saturday night.

As the event grew, it soon became evident that added security was needed. Private security was brought in from the mainland to try and keep things under control and prevent any serious problems from developing. With a vast array of real muskets, swords and other vintage pirate weapons adorning many of the nattily dressed pirates, it was feared that someone might be seriously injured or killed, especially with the abundance of liquor that was consumed. After a few years of completely unrestricted displays of original pirate weapons, it became necessary to restrict the use of real swords, pistols, muskets, knives, and such. Only plastic or rubber weapons were allowed onto the premises. It did not slow things down.

For the locals, the event was a two-sided sword (pun intended). It was fun to see the outrageous behavior and attire of the marauding pirates, but it also meant long hours and hard work. In every department, from the Harbor to the Store, to the Restaurant and the Campground, crowds were huge and sometimes a touch unruly. Every individual that worked, or works at the Isthmus since the inception of the event has their own bizarre stories of things they saw and dealt with on Buccaneer Days. I know I saw my share of drunken tomfoolery, naked bosoms, unbelievable stunts, and outrageous activities, both on the water and on shore. It was really quite astonishing how some of the 'normal' people—from all walks of life—behaved when they dressed up like pirates and partied all day and night.

I can't count the number of pirates that I discovered early Sunday morning, following the Buccaneer Ball, passed out on the beach, in skiffs on the dinghy docks, in the bushes all over town, and more than once, in my own backyard.

For the bouncers at the bar, the Harbor Patrol crew, the shoreboat drivers, the local sheriff and everyone else working into the wee hours of the morning, the focus was always to try and prevent anything bad from happening and to try and get all of the drunken pirates and wenches safely back to their boats, campground site, or at least to somewhere that they could 'sleep it off'.

It is truly quite an amazing event and I am glad to have had the opportunity to participate in it, but I'm also glad that I do not have to do it anymore.

In the fall of 1989, my close friends Johnny 'Pop' Vaughan, Rich Kempster, Jeff Magnal and Bruno Williams convinced me to join them for my first of many consecutive Church Mouse Marlin Tournaments in Avalon. The Church Mouse originated when its founders Bob and Carole Butte decided that it would be fun and enjoyable to put together a small, locals only, marlin tournament as an alternative to the big money tournaments that were popular on the Island.

Beginning with a small number of boats, the tournament rapidly attracted the attention of local fishermen that appreciated the small town flavor of the event, and the fact that it was a fun loving, community fund-raising event as opposed to a competitive money event. As the Church Mouse grew, the Butte's were discussing the event with Avalon's esteemed residents Dr. Frank and his son Bob Blair, and decided to use the proceeds from the tournament to help support local charities and youth groups and organizations. Local interest and support continued to grow. Before long, participation had grown to around one-hundred boats, and the Butte's altered the guidelines to make it an invitational tournament, thereby limiting the number of boats.

The Church Mouse Tournament turned into one of my favorite fishing pursuits, fishing at different times with Johnny, Jeff, Rich, Bruno, Kevin Cloud, Keith Boutillier, Bob Siemer (aboard his boat *Reel Crazy*) and a fun loving couple from Marina Del Rey named Richard 'Dick' and Pat Ebner.

That first year, a blossoming El Nino condition portended the possibility of excellent fishing. We were fishing aboard Johnny Vaughan's thirty-foot Chris Craft *Reel Gambit*.

Johnny had a history of fishing close to the Island, earning the reputation of "Johnny Inside', in reference to his tendency to fish in the relatively calm waters close to shore. But with the prolific numbers of marlin and 'exotics' showing in the outer waters near San Clemente Island and the outer banks toward San Diego, we decided to try our luck a little farther offshore than Johnny normally fished. We plotted a tentative route that would take us to the Mackerel Bank, near San Clemente Island, and then southward perhaps as far as the 43 Fathom Bank, depending on our fishing success, or failure.

We were loaded with a bait tank full of perfect-sized greenback mackerel for marlin, augmented by a good supply of smaller Spanish mackerel for the 'exotics'—tuna, dorado, or yellowtail.

After attending the skippers meeting at the Metropole Marketplace, and then spending the night aboard Johnny's boat on a mooring in Avalon, we awoke before dawn, gulped down a cup of coffee and a Danish pastry, and headed out of the harbor. It was a beautiful morning, with the dark hills above Avalon shrouded in a light marine layer and the sea surface shimmering like a sheet of tinted opaque glass from the reflected glow of the city lights. Cruising out of the harbor entrance, the faint glow of the rising sun sent a thin veil of pink into the lightening skies.

As we rounded the east end of the Island and headed southwest, the fiery sun illuminated the sky and ocean with a surrealistic imagery of glistening sapphire and a mesmerizing panorama of ethereal splendor that captivated each of us. It was the beginning of what would turn into a wonderful day.

Rich, Jeff, Bruno and I were seated on the aft deck watching the morning unfold when Johnny called down from the bridge and disrupted our spellbound reverie, "Okay, guys. Let's set out some lures."

Each of us stood and picked up a fishing rod, checked the lure, dropped the butt end into a rod holder and started playing out line, careful to drop the lines back in a 'V' pattern that would maximize the trolling zone and help prevent the lures from tangling. Two lines were dropped back on the outriggers, farther back than the two inner lures, with one short marlin clone set back into the center of the wake. Once the lines were out, we went back to our morning routines, more coffee, using the head, splashing on sunscreen, and then climbing back onto the upper deck to keep an eye out for any sign of fish, bird activity, or anything that might indicate the presence of a marlin or any other fish. We were only about two miles from the Island, about a mile southeast of the Farnsworth Bank in an area that we considered a 'dead zone' (probably void of any fish), when suddenly the port outrigger snapped.

Jeff Magnal was in the main salon, closest to the rod, and he jumped up and grabbed it quickly, reared back and set the hook. Line screamed from the reel. "Hookup!" he yelled loudly.

Pandemonium broke out as Johnny pulled back on the throttles to slow the forward motion of the boat. Bruno, Rich and I rapidly jumped down from the upper deck and grabbed a rod, cranking the lines into the boat to get them out of the way. When the boat came to a stop, Jeff was standing with his knees pinned against the cushion of the aft rail, his rod arched severely as the hooked fish peeled line. There was no sign of any surface activity and the fish was heading steadily downward, into deep water and making us all think that it was probably not a marlin.

After peeling off about two hundred-yards of line, the fish slowed and Jeff began pumping it back toward the boat. It was a strong fish, but did not appear strong enough to be a marlin. To have any other species of fish attack a lure in that particular area of the ocean was very unusual and baffling for all of us. We wondered what it might be.

After about fifteen minutes, the fish was pulled close to the boat, and was sulking directly below the swim step. We leaned over and looked down into the purple/blue depths watching for the fish to come into view. "Color!" Bruno and I shouted together as we saw the silvery flash of a fish circling upward in the briny depths.

Looking down, we recognized the oval shaped, silver/blue outline of a member of the tuna family, but could not yet recognize the specific species. I stepped back and pulled the gaff from the rod rack. Back at the rail I leaned over and watched the tiring fish slowly but steadily circling up toward the surface. "Looks like it might be a bluefin!" I exclaimed, amazed that a tuna would be cruising around in these waters. Tensing in anticipation of sticking the gaff into the fish, I braced myself and leaned outward as it circled toward the surface. "Holy shit!" I blurted, "It's an albacore!" I reached out and swept upward, sinking the gaff into the gut of the fish. The gaff struck deeply and I leaned back and lifted the gaff upward to fling it over the rail and onto the deck. At that precise moment, I looked behind me and saw that the gaff handle was about to strike Rich in the forehead, as he leaned out to get a view of the fish. I hesitated for a moment, the fish twisted spasmodically, jerking and flapping wildly, and the gaff flew out of my grip into the water.

Stunned, I watched horrified as the gaff dropped onto the ocean surface, slipped out of the fish's belly and floated momentarily on the top of the water. Then it began to sink, ultimately disappearing into the cobalt blue depths beneath the shadow of the boat.

At the same time, the stunned fish dropped back below the surface, hesitated momentarily, and then flicked its powerful tail and caudal fins and once again started peeling line from the reel. Fortunately, Jeff had the good sense, or good luck, to have the reel in free-spool and somehow kept the line clear of all other obstructions that it might have snagged onto. The fish ran off about thirty yards of line and then slowed.

Dumbfounded, I looked at the other guys and stated lamely, "Boy, I guess I blew that one."

"Yeah," Johnny grinned down from the bridge, "You sure did."

Looking around, I asked him, "Do you have another gaff?"

He shook his head, "No, Just the flying gaff." That gaff, a very large gaff used for gaffing marlin or other really big fish, has a 'flyaway' handle that allows the person tending the gaff to release the handle and allow a heavy line tied to a cleat to contain a big fish. It's 'hook' measures nearly a foot in length and width, and the girth is roughly a half-inch in diameter. It was way overkill for an albacore, but the fish was a good sized one and probably too heavy to bounce over the rail without snapping the fishing line.

"Well, I guess we'll just have to give the flying gaff a try," I suggested.

It took a minute to pull it down from the rack in the main salon and get it ready for use. In the meantime, Jeff had hauled the fish back to the stern of the boat and was ready to give it another try. I positioned myself near his side, leaned out with the big gaff and waited for the fish to get close enough to make another effort. When it came near, I leaned out and aimed the point of the gaff into the center of the fish's body. I struck upward and the tip of the gaff penetrated the flesh of the big albacore. I lifted it upward, swung it into the air, over the rail and onto the deck. It flopped once and then lay still. We all looked down in surprised astonishment. We had landed a thirty-five pound albacore! What made the catch even more unusual was not only the location where we caught it, but the fact that nobody had seen any albacore anywhere in the southern California area for several months.

With the big albacore lying on the deck, and despite the fact that its body was ripped open across the belly and another gaping wound oozed blood in the center of its football shaped torso, we all let out a loud cheer, realizing that the fish had a very good chance of qualifying for the side-bet category of the tournament. That side bet (an optional fifty-dollars per boat entry fee), went to the boat catching the largest 'exotic' species—tuna, dorado, or yellowtail, on each day of the two-day tourney.

It was a great start to the day, but unfortunately turned out to be the only fish that we boated on day one. We did bait and hook into one marlin, and had another strike one of the trolling lures, but both billfish slipped the hooks.

When we returned to Avalon for the weigh-in, Rosy Cadman (the delightfully cheery and charismatic owner of Rosy's Fish Market, and official weigh-master for Avalon), informed us that it was the largest fish of the day—so far. Several yellowtail, a couple of dorado and a few yellowfin tuna had already been weighed, but our albacore was thus far the heaviest fish. We had about forty-five minutes to wait, and we were a little concerned when we heard that a nice yellowfin tuna was on its way to the scale. When it arrived, it was announced as weighing thirty-two pounds, and we wound up winning the day-one jackpot of fifteen-hundred dollars. We celebrated by buying a new gaff at Jay Guion's Bait Shop and had a few extra beers with our steak dinners.

Numerous marlin were caught that first day, most taken in the area to the east of Pyramid Head, San Clemente Island and out toward the 180 Fathom Bank. The tournament was shaping up to be a very good one, with lots of fish being caught and perfect fishing weather.

Early the following morning we headed out again to see what day-two might bring. Of course we tried the same area where the albacore was caught, but to no avail. Afterward, we headed out for the Mackerel Bank, about twenty-miles to the southwest.

It was another great morning at sea, with only a slight southerly swell and calm winds. Arriving in the general area of the bank, we trolled lures and feathers in a zigzag pattern for about two-hours without any action. Deciding to head a little farther south and then circle out toward the east end of San Clemente Island, we were about two miles north of the Mackerel Bank when I spotted the first marlin of the day. "Fin!" I blurted out, pointing toward the distinctive scepter-like dorsal fin and knife shaped tail of a tailing striped marlin, cutting a small wake across the glassy smooth surface as it roamed the ocean depths.

Johnny was at the helm and he altered our heading toward the tailing fish. Bruno and I jumped down to the lower deck and grabbed a bait rod. Selecting lively greenback mackerel, we each dropped back live bait while Jeff and Rich hauled in the trolling lines.

When Johnny idled back on the throttles as we slid into the area where the fish was spotted, Bruno and I kept our lines in free spool, slowly letting the baits back in the creamy looking boat wake. About thirty seconds went by when suddenly Bruno's line started peeling rapidly from the reel and he cried out, "I'm bit!"

Letting the line run for about ten seconds, Bruno tensed and lowered the rod tip in anticipation of setting the hook. At that moment, the fish burst from the surface, its shimmering body illuminated with the silvery/blue incandescence and glowing radiance of a freshly hooked marlin. But just as quickly, his line went slack and the fish was gone. It had spit the bait. We drifted for a few more minutes and then cranked in the baits. It was a good opportunity, but unfortunately it just didn't work out. We started trolling again.

After another hour of fruitless trolling, we decided to head out toward the 180. When we reached its vicinity, we came across several large kelp paddies floating lazily on one of the surface currents. One of those paddies was loaded with yellowtail and a few dorado. I hooked and landed three fish and each of the others caught at least one each. Johnny hooked and landed a nice twenty-two pound dorado.

When we got back into Avalon, the largest yellowtail that I caught weighed in at thirty-six pounds and won us another fifteen-hundred dollars for the biggest exotic on the second and final day of the tournament. At the post-tournament awards dinner, we donated half of the winnings back to the tournament, keeping enough to cover our expenses. We didn't catch any marlin in that tournament, but we did in a couple of others, including one when we fished with Bob Siemer on his boat *Reel Crazy*.

Those Church Mouse Tournaments were a real highlight of my fishing experiences on the Island, even though marlin fishing is not my favorite type of fishing. What always made them so much fun was the camaraderie of my fishing partners, the excitement of being a part of the tournament, and most of all, the wonderful people involved, from the organizers to the participants. It is a really special event.

15. Death of a Queen

AT AROUND SIX-FORTY-FIVE A.M. ON the morning of February 27, 1990, my home phone rang. I was already up, sitting in my easy chair drinking my morning cup of coffee. On the first ring, I hopped up to grab the phone in the hope that it would not wake Maureen and the kids.

"Hello?" I offered.

A frantic voice cried out, "Doug. It's John. Dipley. My boat is sinking!"

John Dipley was a renowned sport boat captain from Redondo Beach, California. I had known 'Big John' for years, having gone fishing on several of the boats that he operated out of King Harbor in Redondo Beach before I moved to the Island, and we continued to keep in touch through the years. Our friendship went way back, and he called me on my home phone because he knew that I was probably his best contact to try and respond to his boat in the quickest manner possible.

Big John is a mountain of a man, standing at least six-feet-five-inches and weighing in excess of three-hundred pounds. He always kept his head shaved completely smooth and it glowed like the dome of a large round lamp globe. He resembled a large, cheerful looking version of Mr. Clean.

"Where are you John?" I asked him, setting my coffee cup onto the table and reaching out for my shoes. I was already dressed for work.

"No. I'm not on the boat. I'm at home. The boat is at the Island, out near Ben Weston. My crew took it out to go white seabass fishing and they struck a rock. They're on the boat but it's starting to break apart!"

It was obvious that he was frantic. His boat, the sixty-five-foot commercial sports fisher *Queen of the Sea,* was a fixture in the sport fishing fleet and his pride and joy. "Okay, John, you said they are near Ben Weston Beach. How many people are on board?" I asked.

"Just two, my crew took it out last night."

"Anything more specific on their location?"

"No. They called me on the marine operator channel and just told me they're off of Ben Weston Beach and that the boat is starting to break apart. Can you go out there and do whatever you can?"

I'll head out right away," I assured him. "I'll have Maureen call the Coast Guard and Baywatch. I'll get back to you as soon as I know anything." I hung up, hurriedly dressed, and told Maureen what Dipley told me. I asked her to call Baywatch and the Coast Guard.

Ironically, the true location of Ben Weston Beach is not where most people think it is. The beach that most Islanders know as Ben Weston is actually Mills Landing on NOAA charts, and the actual Ben Weston Beach is a smaller beach about half a mile south of there. I wasn't sure which site Dipley was referring to, but they are not far apart and once we were underway, I presumed the boat would be easy to locate.

Grabbing my foul weather gear and a coat, I picked up the VHF radio and called Ray Smith in Cat Harbor. Ray always monitored channel #19 during off-duty hours, a relatively little used frequency that allowed him to remain in touch but not have to listen to all of the chatter on channel #9, the Harbor Department's standard operating channel. I told him what was happening and he said he would meet me at the dock. I ran out to my pickup truck and headed out to Cat Harbor.

It was a cold and blustery February morning. When I reached the dock, Ray was already there, waiting for me. It was close to seven a.m. He was usually out on the water around that time. I ran down the pier and hopped aboard the patrol boat. Ray knew Dipley too, having met him when we went out to pick up live squid from his boat during the squid-spawning season. I briefed him about all that John had told me as we headed out of Cat Harbor.

Rounding out around Pin Rock, a jagged little outcropping that delineates the southernmost point at the entrance to Catalina Harbor, I cursed silently. It was going to be rough. There was a westerly wind blowing steadily at about twelve knots, along with an ugly swell pattern—typical for late February along the southern California coast. The winds had remained steady through the night, and combined with a prevailing southwest swell of around five to seven feet, it had turned the waters along the backside of the Island into a grumpy mess. It was not going to be fun. I put on my foul weather gear and then took over the helm so that Ray could do the same. We started taking spray over the starboard rail as soon as we had cleared Cat Harbor and before long, both of us were soaked.

Slogging along at about twelve knots, the seas worsened as we got farther out. Soon we had to slow the boat down and try to dodge some of the 'holes' that formed when the confluence of the southwest swells mingled with the westerly wind chop. Those 'holes' on the sea surface caused the Patrol boat to drop from the crest of a swell into the empty void created by the turbulent seas. The boat thumped heavily as it dropped off the back of the swells, rattling the hull and crunching our lower backs. We slowed to about eight knots. Visibility was good. We could see the dark outline of San Clemente Island about twenty miles away, so we knew it should not be difficult to spot the boat when we reached the area of Ben Weston Beach.

It took us about thirty minutes to travel the approximate five mile distance to the site. As we neared the rocky outcroppings at the western proximity of Ben Weston Beach, we saw the *Queen of the Sea* lodged amidst the rocks, an incongruous white hulk nestled between the jumbled boulders that form the ragged spur just west of the beach. It did not look good.

We rounded the point of the rocky headland, steering even more cautiously as the swells converged more steeply and closer together.

After we passed around the outermost rock and turned in toward the beach, we were able to view the situation more clearly. It was ugly.

The *Queen of the Sea* was lying broadside between a pair of huge boulders that were roughly the size of a house. Somehow the boat had managed to become grounded amongst the jumbled mass of huge rocks in a spot that looked virtually inaccessible. We could see the two men on board frantically waving their arms and apparently shouting, although from where we were, we could not hear their pleas.

"Oh, boy," I said to Ray, "That does not look good. I don't think we can get to them and it doesn't look like they have much of a chance to make it ashore."

He looked at me and nodded. "I'm going to try and get a little closer," he told me. "Help me try to keep an eye out for submerged rocks."

The rocky point leading into Ben Weston protrudes out from land about a quarter-mile. It is strewn with massive boulders and jagged pinnacles. At the outer boundary, there is a large rounded boulder that delineates the outermost edge of the point and just inside of that is a tall sentinel-type rock that stands alone in a phallic-like pose. Just inside of that rock, several other, large boulders bulge from the sea, their barnacle-encrusted masses presenting a formidable hazard for all boats. Behind those two rocks, a small pocket of relatively calm water, perhaps forty-yards in diameter was visible. Ray pointed toward that semi-sheltered opening and said he was going to try and maneuver into the area.

Numerous other rocks jutted from the surface in the vicinity, and the big swells, rolling and crashing onto the rocks, exposed even more hazards. There was not much room for error. In addition, the larger swells lifted and tossed our little boat like a cork in a washing machine, making it nearly impossible to hold a steady course. I moved up to the bow and held onto the bowline to stabilize my stance as Ray began to weave his way between rocks toward the small clearing. It was nerve wracking and intense, and twice I thought the swells might toss our boat onto a nearby rock, but Ray somehow managed to steer us safely between the hazards and into the small pocket of relatively calm water.

I heard a cry for help and turned to look back at the *Queen*.

The sixty-five-foot boat was leaning on her starboard side, impaled between the two large boulders. A big swell rolled under our keel and when it reached the *Queen*, it lifted her upward, exposing a huge gaping hole in the bottom of the boat. I could see right through the hole in the hull and out of the big live bait tanks constructed into her aft deck. When the swell lifted the boat, I saw the two men clutch frantically onto the rail, clinging tightly to keep from being tossed against the cabin wall. When the surge passed by, the hull fell back into the passing trough and a plaintiff wail rang out in the early morning air.

That cry was the death throes of the hull. The wooden planking twisted and wrenched as the boat rose and fell in the heavy seas, and the sounds emanating from the timbers cast a woeful scream over the water. I had heard about the 'death wail' of wooden ships, but this was the first time I had seen or heard the mournful tragedy in person. It was very human sounding. At about the same time, I heard another piercing cry, this one undeniably human, coming from one of the men stranded on board.

Those two men, thirty-seven year-old Michael Bowen and forty year-old Donald Gish, worked for Dipley as deckhands aboard the *Queen of the Sea*. When they heard about a wide-open white seabass bite in the area of Ben Weston Beach, they persuaded Dipley to let them take the boat out and fish commercially for the seabass—which brought a good price at the local fish markets. Dipley usually did not 'lend' his boat out, but both men had been with him for several years, knew how to run the boat, and the opportunity for a nice cash influx was too tempting to pass up.

Unfortunately, on that fateful morning, they made a gross error in judgment when they neared the point at Ben Weston and struck the outermost rocks. They told me afterward that they lost steerage when it struck—the rudder was probably bent and rendered useless on impact—and the boat swung around the tall sentinel rock and was then pushed by the swells into its deathbed.

I looked the situation over. It was obvious that the boat was totaled and that the men had little, if any, chance of making it to shore safely. The boat was pinned about one-hundred yards offshore in pounding, five-to-eight-foot breakers with jagged rocks between them and shore. I doubted if anybody, even an expert swimmer could reach shore safety. We could not get much closer because of the swells, rocks and surge. I estimated that we were about forty-yards from their location. We could probably creep in a little closer, but not easily. Several clusters of heavy kelp beds floated on the surface between our boat and them, and the swells were cresting and breaking onto their hull.

"Help us!" one of the men cried out, "Help! Get us out of here!"

One thing I noticed was that they were not wearing life jackets. I yelled out to them, needing to raise my voice in order to be heard above the noise and din of the pounding waves and wrenching squeals of the dying boat, "Can you get to some life jackets?"

They looked around frantically. "I think so," the second man called back. He appeared to be a little more under control than the one who had yelled for help.

He had to wait while another big swell rocked the boat upward, with both of them clutching and holding tightly to the rail as the hull lifted up and then plunged back onto the rocks. Seeing the chance to let go and try two grab life jackets, he timed his effort, yanked open the cabin door to the wheelhouse and disappeared inside. He was in there for a few minutes, during which another swell slammed into the boat and rocked it back and forth. Ray and I looked at each other, hoping that he had not been injured. With a sense of relief we saw the cabin door reopen and he lurched out onto the deck holding two life jackets. They were putting them on when another swell struck the hull, knocking one of the men over and into the cabin wall. He slumped below the level of the rail cap and disappeared from our view. As the boat thumped back onto the rocks, the second man leaned down and pulled the other back to his feet. He looked shaken and was holding his shoulder as if it was hurt, but he moved back to the rail. Helping the injured man in securing his life jacket, they stood at the rail as another big swell loomed. When that one struck, the boat twisted and rose even more dramatically and we watched in amazement as the wheelhouse walls began to collapse. Broken shards of glass flew out from the windows and the radio masts and antennas tumbled from the top of the cabin.

"Hurry!" we heard the injured man cry out. "Get us out of here!"

I turned to Ray, "Do you think you can get any closer?"

"I think so. There's a lot of kelp and some debris floating around, but I think I can back her in at least a short distance. But there's no way we can reach the side of the boat."

"Yeah, I know." I looked around the small opening where we bobbed and rocked. "It looks like the best approach will be over there," I said, pointing between two dark brown blotches of kelp. "If you keep the bow pointed out to sea, you might be able to back her in and get about halfway closer."

"I'll give it my best shot," Ray responded.

We were both wearing life jackets. We both hoped that we would not need to use them.

While Ray maneuvered the patrol boat, I moved to the aft deck and called out, "You're going to need to swim out to us! We cannot get all the way to you."

"I can't swim!" The shorter of the two men cried out.

Frustrated, I gritted my teeth. "You have no choice!" I yelled back to him. "You have a life jacket on. When you jump, just start swimming toward us. I'll try to toss you a line." I paused and waited when another swell rose in the opening where we were trying to back down. That swell lifted our patrol boat precariously close to its crest, threatening to roll our boat over. I sighed a deep breath of relief when the swell passed by and we dropped back into its trough.

Ray was watching the swells closely, looking well out to sea to try and anticipate the right timing to get in as close as possible. "Okay," Ray called out to me, "Here goes!"

I snatched the towline from the tow post as I felt the patrol boat surge into reverse. Looking back at the *Queen*, I called out loudly, "Climb over the rail and stand on the outer combing. Time your jump with the swell! Jump in when the swell is at its peak and then swim toward us!"

A gray cushion floated directly behind our boat. I reached down and grabbed the boathook from the deck, and then leaned out and dragged the cushion away from our engine. There was a strong odor of diesel fuel in the air, and when I looked out over the murky black waters, a rainbow-looking sheen of diesel fuel spread all around us. That floating fuel actually helped to calm the sea surface, its oily mix spreading out to blanket the sea with a thin layer of fuel. When I looked back up, both men had climbed over the short wall of the deck combing and were perched on the outer rail ready to jump. When the next swell rocked the boat upward, the smaller of the two men (the one who could not swim) started to jump, but then panicked and re-clutched the rail. In the process, his foot slipped from the combing and he fell against the side of the boat, his arms still draped over the rail. He was hanging on the side of the boat, his feet kicking out frantically where they dangled. The surge slapped against the fractured hull, lifted it upward and then plummeted back down toward the rocks. He lost his grip and fell into the churning water. Fortunately the backwash created from the surge lifted the man outward a few yards and away from the looming hull and barnacle covered rocks. He bobbed up and outward, his arms flailing frantically in the air.

We were about forty-feet away, and could not get any closer. I reached out, and with all my might and energy, heaved the polypropylene towline. I watched it fly through the air, arching high in the wind and unwinding as it flew. Somehow, miraculously, the loop on the end of the towline dropped from the misty air and landed directly on his hand! He closed his fingers around the line and I started pulling.

In the meantime, I saw the second man time his jump with the rise of the next swell and enter the water. He popped back to the surface and started swimming toward our boat. I continued to pull on the towline, hauling the frantic fisherman toward our patrol boat.

When I got him to the stern of the boat, I called out to Ray, "Neutral, Ray! Take it out of gear!" Ray responded immediately and the boat drifted.

I had the man to the boat. I looked down into his eyes. They were bulging almost out of their sockets. It was the most terrified face I had ever seen and I knew that he was completely panic-stricken. "Poison!" I yelled at him, as loudly and forcibly as I could yell. I felt that he needed a jolt to his senses. My nonsensical comment worked.

He turned and looked up at me. "Grab the rail and help me get you into the boat!" He looked around, seemingly unsure of what to do. I reached down and tapped the transom rail cap, "Here. Put your hand here."

He reached up and grabbed the rail. I knew I could not pull him over the side without his help. "Okay," I told him, "Now put your foot on the lower unit of the motor and climb in. I'll help."

He did as instructed and I leaned over and grabbed the lower edge of his life jacket. Trying to get as much leverage as possible, I knelt down and lifted with all my might. He slid over the transom and fell into a pile on the aft deck. Breathing heavily from the exertion, I looked out and saw the second man swimming steadily and about ten yards from our boat. I took a few deep breaths and waited for him to reach the stern, then leaned over and helped him crawl aboard. Given the circumstances, he was much more composed than the first guy and quickly stood on his feet.

"Thanks," he stated calmly, "You saved our lives."

I looked over at Ray. As I glanced over at him, I could see another large set of swells building from seaward. It had taken us several minutes to accomplish the rescue, and we had drifted inward dangerously close to the rocks and rolling breakers. "Hang on!" Ray cried out, slamming the shift lever into forward and simultaneously pushing forward on the throttle.

Both the man standing and I were almost thrust off the back of the boat by the sudden forward motion, but we both managed to grab hold of something. I grabbed the tow post and he reached down and clutched the rail cap.

We looked toward the bow and gulped as we saw the looming wall of a steep and foreboding swell. The bow of the patrol boat rose, lifting skyward as the massive surge of water curled upward and threatened to spill us over. 'Oh, no!' I thought to myself. 'Not now!'

We had somehow managed to rescue the two men, avoided being dashed onto the rocks, and now it looked as if we were going to be engulfed, capsized and probably die from the power of this wave. I held my breath and waited for the inevitable.

But at the last possible moment, the patrol boat flew from the top of the wave, hung suspended in space at a perpendicular angle to the surface, and then crashed down onto the backside of the swell. The transom of the boat plunged in first, filling the aft deck with hundreds of gallons of seawater. I was knee-deep in green foaming suds, expecting to go completely under. But somehow, the little nineteen-foot Seaway righted herself, leveled-off into the trough and the deck full of water began to rapidly pour over the transom and out of the deck scuppers.

We had avoided that first threat, but another big swell loomed ahead of us. Pouring more throttle to the engine, Ray held the boat steady as we climbed its crest and then plunged again into its trough. Either we were getting accustomed to the insanity of the moment, or that swell was not quite as precarious. We cleared it and settled into the slightly more tranquil waters where we had started. I looked over at Ray, nodded my head in admiration, and breathed deeply. We had made it out safely.

After maneuvering back out of the rocky morass and into the nearby waters of Ben Weston Cove, we drifted silently for several minutes watching the final death-throes of the *Queen*. After watching the cabin walls collapse, it was only a matter of time before the entire hull would be completely destroyed. With sadness and a sense of great loss, the four of us watched the hull begin to tear apart, the screaming, moaning cries of the ship's timbers wafting out over the turbulent waters of Ben Weston Cove as the planks and ribs were ripped asunder. Within a few minutes of our having pulled the two men from her decks, the stately craft that had carried many a fisherman and plied the waters of southern California on hundreds of fishing excursions, was no more.

As we left the scene, heading back toward Cat Harbor, the Baywatch Rescue Boat approached us from the west. They had had to travel around the west end of the Island to reach our location. At about the same time, a Coast Guard Rescue helicopter flew over, circled a few times and made radio contact with Baywatch. After ascertaining that both men from the wrecked boat were safely aboard our boat, and that nobody else remained on board, both Baywatch and the Coast Guard proceeded to the site to look over the situation and see if any mitigating measures could be taken to minimize the environmental impact of the doomed vessel. Recognizing right away that nothing further could be done, they returned to their respective stations to file reports and perform all associated follow-up documentation.

The destruction of the *Queen of the Sea* and associated rescue was by far the most intense and dramatic search and rescue operation of my career. If it had been dark, we would never have managed to perform the rescue. It was a small miracle that the towline toss worked as it did. There were so many things that might have happened to thwart our efforts, and the outcome could have turned out so differently. But it worked, and my good friend Ray Smith (who sadly passed away in 2010), proved to me that cold, blustery morning that he was a true master of the seas.

About a month later, a group of friends and fellow sport fishing captains held a fund-raising dinner on the mainland to try and help Dipley get back on his feet and back into fishing. Ray Smith and I were invited to the affair. They held a raffle and raised a nice chunk of money to help Big John start over. At the dinner, Dipley and his two deckhands went to the podium and retold their version of the rescue story, emotionally praising both Ray and me for our heroics and skills in saving their lives. We were given plaques commemorating the rescue, and Big John Dipley had tears in his eyes when he thanked us for saving his crew. It's a shame we could not have saved his boat.

16. Boys Will Be Boys

PARENTHOOD IS A REMARKABLE TIME in an adult's life, not so much for what happens to the parents, but more what the children do that cause the parents to regard it as such a life-altering experience. Having our children grow up on an Island gave us the opportunity to be closely and actively involved in both of our son's daily lives.

We were very fortunate in the fact that both of our kids grew up to be solidly grounded young men with strong character, great personalities, a vision for the future and a respect for their fellow man—along with all the other attributes that a parent hopes for.

Oh, they both had their moments—those little (sometimes big) things that we needed to deal with along the way. Our oldest son, Trevor, tends to be somewhat more reserved and private than Troy, revealing his innermost feelings only fleetingly. Troy, on the other hand, is more gregarious, outgoing and carefree, 'letting it all hang out', so to speak, and living life very spontaneously. Both love the great outdoors and always preferred to be out in the hills or on the water, as opposed to being involved in any social media type of entertainment.

A couple of the 'little things' they each did during their adolescent years have evolved into some of those inevitable family memories that we all cherish and tend to bring up (often over and over again, Trevor points out to me) during family gatherings.

One of those memories occurred when Trevor was around five or six-years old, and involved one or more of his 'buddies,' Nicholas, Justin, David, and/or James.

Those five boys loved to fish, even at an early age. Trevor, and one or more of those boys mentioned above, were out fishing on the Isthmus Pier one Friday evening, catching mackerel. It's very possible that they were catching bait for one or more of their dads. As they prepared to leave the pier for home, Trevor, and/or one or more of the others, decided that it would be a fun idea to deposit a bagful of the mackerel into the drop-box in the Accounting Department.

That drop-box—built into the outer wall of the accounting office— serves as a nighttime cash drop for employees working later than normal office hours. The steel door on the drop has a handle and an inner box that then drops down into a safe. During the off-season, the Accounting Department is closed on weekends, and so the bag of mackerel that the boys 'deposited' in the drop box on Friday night remained in the safe until Monday morning. When the office girls opened the doors on Monday morning they were greeted by the pungent odor of decaying fish. For a while, as they began their daily tasks, nobody could identify where the odor was coming from. It was not uncommon to smell the lingering odors of decayed fish around the Isthmus—many people tossed their fish carcasses into trashcans rather than throwing them back in the ocean after filleting their catch. The girls thought that the smell might be emanating from nearby trash containers.

Later, when Kitty McElroy knelt down to enter the combination numbers of the safe, the pungent smell became stronger. When she opened the safe door, the smell hit her powerfully and she let out a loud and disgusted, 'Whew!"

Inside the safe, the brown-bagged mackerel had festered and decomposed, dripping the secreted juices of the decaying flesh down onto several cash bags and onto the bed of the safe.

She looked immediately over at Maureen and commented, "I think our boys have played a dirty trick on us!" Kitty was not one of the 'boys' mother's, but as an aunt and part of the 'Isthmus family' of mothers, she had a pretty good idea who had performed the prank.

The office girls (Kitty, Maureen and Nancy Delehant) cleaned up the mess and went about their day. The boys were all in school, but when Trevor arrived home, we questioned him about the incident. Both of our boys were taught not to lie, and if they tried to, Maureen could detect the deceit immediately. Trevor admitted to the prank and was given some extra chores to do around the house as 'punishment'. I thought the whole thing was hilarious, and couldn't help from showing my amusement to Trevor, which didn't set well with Maureen. But it did become a favorite family story through the years.

On another occasion, Maureen and I were preparing to go out on New Year's Eve to celebrate. We had arranged a baby-sitter for Trevor, who was about four-years old. A few minutes before we were ready to walk out the door, Trevor walked up to us, pointed at his nose and said, "It's stuck."

Maureen looked down at him, kneeled and asked, "What's stuck?"

"The shell," Trevor told her.

She reached out and tilted his head back, looking into his right nostril. Sure enough, deep inside his nasal cavity she could see the lower edge of a purple Olivelli shell. She glanced up at me and stated, "He's got a purple olive stuck in his nose."

I looked for myself. Sure enough, the small oval shaped shell was deep inside of his nose.

"So, what do we do?" I asked her.

"I'm not sure, but go get me the pair of rounded tweezers from the medicine cabinet and I'll try to pull it out."

I did as she instructed, returning shortly with the tweezers. We laid him down on the couch. I got a flashlight from the kitchen drawer and shined it into his nose while Maureen tried to reach up and grab hold of the shell. Trevor jerked his head away when the tweezers rubbed against his nasal cavity. I tried to hold his head still while she tried again. After a few frustrating attempts, during which he began to cry softly, she gave up.

"It's no use; I can't get a grip on it," she stood and looked at me, shrugging her shoulders.

"So, now what?" I asked her.

"Let's try calling Baywatch. Maybe they have an idea how it can be removed."

We made a phone call and Baywatch members John McKay and Richard Bates arrived at our house about ten minutes later. They were trying not to laugh, but it was obvious that they saw some humor in the situation. After assessing the dilemma, they each tried to reach up into his nose with the tweezers to pull the shell out—to no avail. Pondering the problem, McKay suggested that we get a Kleenex and have Trevor try to blow his nose. Maureen brought out a few sheets of Kleenex, and after about four fruitless efforts and some encouragement from all of us to try and convince him to blow harder, he expelled a deeper blow and the shell popped loose. It dangled from the opening in his nose and Maureen reached out and pulled it free.

After calming Trevor and telling him not to put anything else into his nose, we thanked the Baywatch guys and went out to celebrate New Year's Eve.

Not to be outdone, when Troy was about two-and-a-half years old, he was playing on the living room rug one evening when he sat down and displayed a silly little boy frown. Looking sheepishly up at his mother, Troy said, "I fwollowed it."

Maureen cocked her head and asked him, 'What, Troy?"

He curled his lips downward and replied, "I fwollowed it."

Smiling at his speech she asked him, "You swallowed what?"

"Da penny," he told her.

"You swallowed a penny?" she responded somewhat alarmed. He nodded his head in affirmation. She looked over at me.

I was seated by our front window and overheard their interaction. I stood and moved over to where they were in the middle of the room. Looking down at Troy, I could see nothing wrong and I wasn't quite sure how to react. "Now what?" I asked her.

"Well, I'm not really sure," she responded. "But I don't think it's a good thing to have a penny in your stomach."

I thought about that, agreeing that it was probably not a good thing to have a copper coin in your intestines. The concept of lead poisoning popped into my head and I thought that it was very likely that copper poisoning could also be a concern. I expressed that thought to her and she agreed. After giving the situation a little thought, she decided to call our family doctor, Alan Mosley, a general practitioner and regular Island visitor who, along with his wife Patsy, had become good friends. She called him at home.

When she told him about the situation, and after he was done laughing, Mosley told her that there was not a lot to worry about unless the penny did not work its way out of his system. After she got off the phone with him, she explained the solution to me.

"We need to watch for it to come out. If we don't find it within a week, they may need to go into his intestines and have it removed."

Thankfully, Maureen did the 'watching'. At the end of the second day of searching she found the penny.

For me, working in the Harbor Department steadily developed into a real passion. I loved being on the water every day, operating boats, being on the ocean, using my boating skills and helping people with all of the little things that we did every day that helped to make the Catalina boating experience pleasurable for Island visitors.

During the summer season, my routine day consisted of checking boats in and out of the coves, operating shoreboats (transporting visitors from their boats to the dock, and transporting kids and parents to the various Island camps), responding to calls for assistance, helping on the fuel dock, meeting and greeting the Catalina Express boats and other cross-channel boats, performing training exercises with both new and experienced harbor personnel, and whatever might take place on the water.

The harbor operation had a lot to cover in addition to managing the mooring areas. We ran the shoreboat operation, the fuel dock, the Salad Bowl (trash boat), the boat shop, piers and floats, and contracts administration.

On shore, I worked with the office girls, answering phones, logging mooring reservations, working on Mooring Contract administration, scheduling work coverage, maintaining records, and always interfacing and interacting with our customers in an effort to provide and improve service.

It was gratifying work. I always felt great pleasure when I was able to do some little thing to help our visiting boaters—whether it was assisting them onto a mooring or simply assigning them to a mooring in their preferred location. I can't even guess at how many boats I attached towlines to through the years, towing a stern around when they were trying to moor and the winds or currents caused them problems. Sometimes, I watched boats attempting to pick up a mooring—particularly on the east side of the Isthmus where the moorings face bow to seaward—and encounter problems because of the wind. Anticipating their need for help, I would maneuver my patrol boat into position where I could attach my towline and pull their boat out of danger without them even being aware of the fact that I had attached a line and towed their stern around, until after they secured.

I also felt really good on busy weekends when the coves were full and I was able to call a boat in for a mooring off of the 'daily waiting list' and give them a mooring assignment because of a mooring cancelation or some other action that made a mooring become unexpectedly available. Most boaters do not want to anchor, and some don't know how. If I was able to find a mooring for a boat when the coves were 'sold out', and prevent them from having to anchor, it really made their day, and made me feel good being able to help them.

I also enjoyed the growing relationships that I formed with the regular boaters. As my years working in the harbor expanded, so did my friendships within the boating community. When the boating season started each spring, especially after a long off-season, it was a real pleasure to welcome back to the Island the regular boaters that I had gotten to know. There were many regulars that fit into that category, and it would be nice to acknowledge all of them, but I would literally have to list hundreds of individuals belonging to dozens of clubs and involved with numerous fishing, sailing or cruising organizations. Suffice it to say that all of those individuals that I met and befriended over the years meant a lot to me and helped to make my career on the Island memorable.

Among the most popular sailing events that occurred for many years at Two Harbors was the annual Fireman's Race from Long Beach. That event featured a sailboat race that peaked at over one-hundred boats during the heyday of its existence, and there was one race, the early August race of 1990, when a dramatic boating mishap occurred.

Race organizers Randy and Lois Sarver from the Long Beach Fire Department, put together the August 1990 Catalina Fireman's Race, an event that attracted one-hundred-fifteen boats. The race left the starting point at the Los Angeles Harbor Light at twelve p.m. and was nearing the finishing line at Ship Rock at around three-thirty p.m. when we heard a Mayday call broadcast by the eighty-five-foot schooner *Diosa Del Mar* (Goddess of the Sea). The *Diosa*, running in third place at the time, transmitted the Mayday call after striking the southerly portion of the reef at Ship Rock. That reef, a rocky extension of the landmark rock that juts majestically as a lonely sentinel about one mile from the Isthmus, extends mostly submerged about two-hundred feet southeast of Ship Rock, dropping steeply into approximately one-hundred-foot depths on both sides.

Sailing at around fourteen knots, the man at the helm of the *Diosa*, Captain Eddie Weinberg, reported that he was nearing the finish line and suddenly noticed a small fishing skiff bobbing in the water just ahead of his port bow. Realizing that he could not avoid striking the skiff unless he turned sharply to starboard, Captain Eddie believed there was enough distance between his position and the outer edge of the reef to avoid making contact. He was wrong. The last submerged rock at the edge of the reef was lurking about four-feet underwater and the starboard bow drove directly over the sharp pinnacle, ripping a gaping hole in the bow and side of the hull. Water began flooding into the boat and within minutes the stately ship sank below the surface.

Fortunately, all of the people on board, twelve passengers, plus a crew of five, escaped unharmed, climbing into their own tender and into several other small boats that arrived on scene almost immediately.

That sinking was particularly dramatic because of the *Diosa Del Mar's* preeminent visibility in the boating community, and the proximity of all the other boats in the race, many of which had a first-hand, eyewitness view of the spectacle.

But sunken and destroyed boats were a relatively common occurrence in Island waters. An average of at least two or three boats met their final destiny in Island waters each year, sinking or destroyed by various factors; groundings, fires, mechanical failures, or unknown causes. For those of us working in the Harbor Department, the report of a sinking boat became an almost routine response.

We kept and maintained salvage pumps aboard all of our larger patrol boats, provided training for all crewmen, and made sure that all of our patrolmen had both First Aid and CPR training. Of all the boats that were lost through the years, many more were saved from sinking, from burning, or from being destroyed because of the response from our harbor crew, and Baywatch. For me it became a matter of pride and accomplishment to respond to an emergency call and provide the assistance required to prevent a boat from being lost, severely damaged, or even more importantly, to avoid personal injury.

The winter of 1991 brought another El Nino weather pattern to the Island. El Nino weather always brings some unique and unusual sea life into Island waters. Pelagic red-crabs are plentiful, sometimes washing ashore and covering Island beaches with wide piles of crabs chased ashore by predatory fish and then stranded to die and decay on local beaches. My son Troy, and Laura Peterson's son Mike, graced the cover of the Catalina Islander Newspaper holding a mass of red-crabs in their hands and arms that they had scooped off the sand.

Sightings of green turtles became commonplace, and include a few reports of the endangered leatherback turtles that can grow to a length of eight-feet or more. Killer Whales show in offshore waters, along with the earth's largest animal, the massive Blue Whale. Tropical fishes like Triggerfish and other tropical reef fishes are seen and caught, on occasion. Reports of large hammerhead sharks, including a couple that were caught by local anglers occur, as do reports of Great White Sharks around the Island. It is a fascinating time for fishermen, divers, and everyone who spends time on, and around the ocean.

The following summer was exceptionally nice on the Island. Sea temperatures climbed into the high seventies in July and August, and remained in the seventies well into the fall. During one fishing trip off the Island's west end, I hooked and landed a thirty-two pound dorado less than a mile from the tip of the Island, a very unusual catch for Catalina waters and the largest dorado I have ever landed. For visiting boaters, the warm water and splendid sunshine made the summer of 1992 one to remember.

As fall melted into winter, the storms of 92' began to arrive. Generated from the subtropics, the Island started feeling the impacts of the 'Pineapple Express', a series of storms that roared eastward from the Hawaiian Islands and brought torrential rains and powerful winds to the west coast of the United States. Catalina Island lay directly in the path of a series of low-pressure systems that inundated the Island with copious amounts of rainfall. Those storms generated more than twenty-inches of rainfall during the winters of both 1992 and 1993.

For those of us working in the Harbor Department, the storms meant increased workload to try and protect facilities and equipment and protect personal property. The storms also took a toll on families and individuals that suffered the effects of the storms; from power outages to being isolated, and from suffering damaged homes to losing fences or other personal property.

The storms also gave a few of the more adventurous Islanders the opportunity to attempt some fun and exciting water sports. Surfers benefitted from the consistent south swells that accompanied the southerly storm track, finding the rare occasion to surf Ballast Point in Catalina Harbor, and/or the high spot on Isthmus Reef.

Getting awakened in the middle of the night to respond to some sort of harbor emergency became a common facet of my work.

At least once or twice a month the phone would ring sometime during the night with the Coast Guard calling to try and locate a missing or overdue boat. Inevitably, the call would awaken Maureen and she would then awaken me to follow up on the call. On a few rare occasions I could answer their questions and provide the information they were looking for because I knew the boats in the harbor. But usually I would need to go down to the Harbor Office, look through the mooring records and then call the Coast Guard back with the results of my efforts. A few times the response required making contact with an individual—usually to pass along sad information about a family matter—or at least to give them a phone number to call. Those calls out at night took their toll on our family life, but it was all part of the job.

Usually my nighttime responses were storm related. During the winter months, I estimate that I responded to storm situations on an average of six to ten times per season. Often during Santa Ana conditions the winds blow strongly through the mountain and canyon passes but dissipate before reaching the Island. And those winds usually develop after dark as the land on the mainland cools. Identifying and knowing when or where the Santa Ana winds will strike, became a mission of mine to try and learn, understand and recognize. I became rather good at it, often outguessing the marine forecasters and even becoming a 'go-to' guy for some of my boating friends. It also helped me to be prepared for severe weather and minimized the need to be called out onto the water to react and respond to adverse weather conditions.

Even though I became somewhat of an 'expert' on predicting foul weather, there were times when I was taken by surprise and consequently had to go out in the middle of the night to respond to deteriorating conditions. During rough and stormy weather, it was always best to respond with another person—or more, if possible. We tried to establish a response system that was considerate of the harbor crew, attempting to avoid having to call an employee on their days off, or when they had already pulled a full shift.

One night I awakened around two a.m. to the distinct sound of northeast winds whistling through my bedroom window. Tuning in to the sound, I realized that the winds were increasing and the surf was beginning to build. I climbed out of bed and looked out onto the water. The winds were blowing steadily at around twelve knots, with gusts closer to twenty. I had not anticipated the winds would reach the Island that night, and consequently the dinghy docks and main float were still in place and connected. Anytime we expected severe winds, we disconnected the docks and floats, secured all the boats in the harbor, and setup a response plan prior to calling it a night. On that particular day, we had not made any of those preparations. But listening to the wind and surf, I could see that steps needed to be taken to avoid problems or damages. I dressed and headed down to the Harbor Office.

Arriving at the pier, the winds and swells had worsened. The winds were steady at around twenty, with gusts closer to thirty. The single dinghy dock was slamming against the pilings and the main float at the end of the pier was pitching and rocking in the building swell. I looked at the work schedule to see which patrolman I might be able to call in to help. I tried two phone numbers but got no response. The dinghy dock was really starting to pound against the pilings, reverberating through the floor of the office as I made phone calls. I often removed the docks without assistance when it was calm, but it was much more of a challenge when it started getting rough. Unable to contact any backup, I decided to give it a go by myself.

I started by connecting the lifting straps to the dinghy dock ramp, hoisted it a few feet above deck level and jumped down from the ramp onto the float. The work skiff was tied to the dock, as it should have been, and there was only one other small dinghy tied alongside. I climbed into the work skiff to make certain it would start, moved it to the outer post on the dock, left it running, and then stepped back up onto the dinghy dock to untie the lines from the pilings. The tide was low and the dock was lifting and rising on the swell, periodically dipping into the incoming swells and going awash. I timed the release of the last line with a passing swell, cast it off and jumped into the skiff.

I revved the little six-horsepower Evinrude engine and shifted into reverse. Looking out to seaward, I saw the approach of a large swell and realized that it was probably going to swamp the stern of the skiff as I ploughed backwards, but there wasn't much I could do. I needed to back out of the surf line as quickly as possible to avoid having both the dock and the work skiff tossed onto the beach. The engine howled and I gritted my teeth as a surge of green water rushed over the transom, sloshing a large volume of water into the bilge and soaking my pants and feet. I watched the seaward edge of the dock lift high onto the face of the swell and I thought for a moment that it was going to roll over, but at the last second, before the swell crested, the dock dropped back down and began to move slowly away from the beach. As soon as I was far enough out to spin around and push, rather than pull the dock, I made the maneuver. It was a little tricky, but once I had managed to bump the bow of the skiff onto the side of the dock, I was able to slowly push it out toward the B-row and try to secure it to a mooring.

After climbing back into the skiff, I picked up the empty gallon milk jug that is used for bailing, and emptied the seawater that had shipped over the transom when I was backing down.

I headed back to the main float. The main float was now bucking and pitching in the swell, putting considerable strain on the lines connecting the dock to the pier pilings. The lines needed to be disconnected. I climbed out of the skiff and headed up the ramp to the top of the pier to hook the chain-fall to the lifting eyes on the ramp. That completed,

I hoisted the ramp by applying the hand-over-hand method of cranking up the ramp chains, until the dock was about three-feet above the deck of the main float. When the larger swells rolled in, the three-foot height was just enough to prevent the ramp wheels from slamming down onto the deck of the float.

Using the same technique that I used on the dinghy dock, I began to disconnect the one-and-a-quarter-inch braided polypropylene lines that secure the main float to the pier. The winds were now steady at around twenty-five knots with gusts that were closer to thirty-five. As I undid each line, I swung the loose end up onto the ramp to secure it after I was done. There were two primary lines tied to each corner of the main float, with two spring-lines running in a crisscross pattern. I untied the spring-lines first, then moved to the western corner and loosened the primary line. Looking over my shoulder to ensure that everything was going as planned, I neglected to cinch-down on the line and a large swell yanked the line out of my grip. I reached down to try and grab it, but it dropped into the water. I stood and started to turn just as the ramp slammed into my head. I was knocked unconscious.

Sometime after that, I'm not sure if it was a brief moment, a few minutes, or perhaps longer, I came to. I was lying on the deck of the main float and my head was pounding. I opened my eyes and looked around. From that position, lying prone on the float, everything looked distorted and bizarre. The pier pilings were undulating before my gaze and the dark, brooding surface of the ocean flashed swarthy black shadows, as the dock rolled in the swell.

Moaning, I reached up and felt the back of my head. It was wet and I could feel a large lump. I pulled my hand down and looked at my palm. It was covered in blood. I reached up again and gently touched the knot on my head. It felt about the size of a golf ball and there was more warm sticky blood on my hand. I felt like I was going to throw up.

I lay there for a few more moments, closing my eyes because things were spinning crazily when they were open. I tried to think. It took me a few moments to realize and remember where I was and what I was doing. Slowly, I recalled what had happened.

Gathering my thoughts, I looked around again. The dock was still bucking and pitching wildly and the ramp was dangling down very close to the top of the dock as it fell and rose. The float was also swinging back and forth in the gusty winds and swells, attached by only one line. Overhead, the ramp was coming very close to where I was lying, as the float bucked up and down on the swells. I rolled away from the edge, out toward the middle of the float.

Sitting up, I looked over the situation. The winds were actually beginning to ease, but the swells continued to roll in, putting enormous strain on the single line still connected to the main float. Balancing myself with my hands, I tentatively stood up. Other than a dull ache on the back of my head, and a chilling cold penetrating my wet pants and feet, I felt all right. I took a cautious step toward the end of the float and ramp, stopping before I reached the zone where the ramp could make contact with my body. I contemplated the process it would take to disconnect the final line from the dock, realizing that it would be much easier if there were another person to hold onto the ramp and hold the dock steady. But nobody else was there. I needed to do it by myself. Timing it with an outward swing of the float, I rushed to the corner of the dock and undid the top half hitch on the dock cleat. The top hitch came loose easily, but the underlying hitch was jammed tightly from the tension caused by the swell. I tugged and pulled, and it was beginning to loosen, but when I glanced up, the dock was swinging back toward me and I had to step back away from the overhanging ramp to avoid being struck again.

It was odd to see the whole thing transpire. It seemed as if the ramp was swinging into me, but in fact it was stationary, hanging from the chain fall on the overhead beam, and it was the dock swinging back and forth that actually created the illusion. I waited until the wind moved the dock toward the west again, stepped forward, and began tugging on the lines to try and loosen the hitch. With one final yank, and just before the dock swung toward me again, I pried it loose. The line dropped into the inky black water. I jumped away and breathed a heavy sigh of relief.

Gazing over the entire scene, I was satisfied with the results. I had one more task to complete, securing the work skiff to the offshore line. Looking around, I realized that both the wind and the swell seemed to be diminishing, but it was still gusty and lumpy. I jumped down into the work skiff and retied it to the offshore line, pulled the skiff back into the dock and secured the long, trailing stern line onto the side of the main float. Satisfied that all was completed, I hopped back up onto the ramp, chain-lifted the ramp to a parallel position with the deck of the pier, and headed home on my bike.

As I neared my house, I realized that the winds and swell were dropping even further. It appeared that the northeaster was diminishing. Sure enough, during the next couple of hours before daylight broke, the winds quit completely and at daybreak the cove was flat calm.

I went into the bathroom and cleaned the blood from the back of my head and neck, tossed my bloody jacket, shirt, wet pants and socks into the laundry, put on my robe and sat down in my recliner with a bag of ice on the lump on my head. Fortunately the cut was minor and the swelling decreased after about thirty-minutes of icing. At around daybreak I crawled into bed.

When I climbed into bed it woke Maureen up. She turned to me and asked, "Is everything all right?"

"Yeah," I replied tiredly, "I'll tell you about it in the morning."

That particular Santa Ana lasted only about three hours, and the docks and floats would probably have survived without any action being taken. But it was a rare Santa Ana that built and then quit as quickly as that one, and if it had continued, the docks and pier could have sustained considerable damages if I had not cut them loose.

When I told her what had happened and she inspected the back of my head, she became quite angry, berating me for doing what I did without help. I fully understood her concerns, and in the future, I rarely did any similar responses without assistance.

17. Boating Mayhem

THERE WERE TIMES AS A first responder, trained in first aid and CPR, when I dealt with injuries and even death. Fortunately, most of the responses that I dealt with while I was working on the island were minor in nature; scrapes and bruises, bee stings and sculpin stings, and minor contusions. Treating minor cuts and/or bruises was relatively painless, both for me and for the victim.

Bee and sculpin stings could be problematic if the person suffering the sting was allergic to the offending critter. Both animals carry toxic venoms that, for some people, have the potential for serious allergic reactions and even death. On a few occasions I saw victims react adversely to both bees and sculpin, but our Baywatch team was very good at recognizing the symptoms of allergies and initiated the proper steps to treat and minimize potential problems.

There were numerous times that I responded to fishhooks imbedded in fingers or hands, puncture wounds caused by the sharp end of a gaff, fingers or other appendages cut or slashed by fish or live sharks hauled aboard a boat, fingers or hands mauled and mangled by the crushing jaws of a Moray Eel on careless scuba divers, and bodily burns from hot exhaust manifolds. Those types of injuries were fairly common and relatively easy to fix; we simply called Baywatch and they performed the necessary action to treat the victim or transport them to the hospital for further care.

Only once in all my years did I find myself first on scene to a death. On that occasion, I was working on a patrol boat when I witnessed a group on the beach at Little Fisherman's Cove waving and shouting for help. I headed over to their location and heard several voices calling out, "Help! Help! A man has drowned!"

Standing in waist deep water, about a half-dozen individuals, some wearing a wetsuit, were standing and holding up a partially submerged body. Maneuvering my boat nearby, I grabbed the radio and called out for assistance, stating that I was leaving my boat adrift and entering the water.

I shut off the engine, took off my shoes, yanked off my hat and sunglasses and jumped over the side of the boat. The water was about five-feet deep and I reached out and shoved the patrol boat away, out into a little deeper water where it could drift safely until another patrolman could arrive on scene and secure it to a mooring, or hold it in place while I dealt with the emergency. The people that were holding the body afloat all seemed unsure of what action to take. I moved into position between a couple of men that were holding the victim in place, and suggesting we get him to shore. Together, with about a dozen hands assisting, we waded out of the surf and laid the man on the sand.

He did not look good. He was of Asian descent and his skin had turned a purple/yellowish color. His eyes were open and opaquely glazed over.

I kneeled at his side and placed my two right forefingers on the side of his neck, feeling for a pulse. At the same time, I leaned over and put my ear next to his lips, listening and feeling for breath and looking at his chest for any sign of lung expansion. There was nothing. I shouted, "I'm going to start CPR. Does anyone else know CPR?"

Several voices started talking all at once. I looked around and noticed one man that appeared to be calmer than the others standing next to me. He nodded and said, "Yes, I do."

"Okay, that's great. I'm going to start with a couple of chest compressions to see if it expels any saltwater. I don't have a breathing mask. (There was one on my Patrol Boat but I forgot to get it out before jumping off the boat). As I placed my left palm onto the center of his chest and my right palm on top, I asked the man helping me, "Any idea how long he's been in the water?"

"No" he told me, "I heard the yelling and ran out to help. He was floating face down when I got there and we rolled him over and held his head above the surface."

I thrust twice, a gush of bilious greenish/gray water burst from his partially opened mouth and spilled over his chin and cheeks.

I called out to nobody in particular, "Does anyone have a towel or a rag, and can someone call out to the patrolman out there to get me a breathing mask?"

Almost immediately I was handed a towel and I saw and heard a man standing nearby call out to the waiting harbor patrolman to get a breathing mask. I leaned down and made two more chest thrusts, realizing that rescue breaths were needed, but trying to dislodge as much seawater as possible from his system before I started rescue breathing. Another gush of bile burst from his lips. I reached down with the towel and wiped off as much as possible and then cupped my hands over his mouth to try and form a sealed opening that I could blow into. Holding his nose closed with my left hand, I blew two deep breathes into his lungs. I wasn't sure how much air I might have transferred into his system, but it was all I could do without having to place my mouth directly onto his, and in his condition, that was just not a pleasant prospect.

I did two more chest thrusts, glanced up to see if there was any progress on getting a breathing mask, and saw that it would be at least a couple of more minutes. I cupped his mouth again and tried two more breaths.

The man working with me had kneeled on the opposite side of the inert body and he told me he would begin the chest thrusts. I lifted up and watched as he performed the maneuver very adeptly. Twice more I tried rescue breaths while the other gentleman performed chest thrusts. After the second effort, the rescue breathing apparatus was thrust into my hands and I placed it in position to apply breaths more comfortably. For about four or five minutes we continued CPR, thinking the entire time that it was likely a wasted effort—the man appeared dead—but knowing that as a first responder performing CPR, we must continue the process until professional medical personnel took over, or you were physically unable to continue.

After about five minutes, or more, Baywatch Isthmus arrived on scene, pulling up in their rescue van. They had been at the nearby campground on a response for a bee sting and received the emergency call on their radio.

Baywatch members John McKay and Steve Troeger immediately took control of the situation, asking me and the other CPR giver if we could continue for a few more minutes while they hooked up their equipment and contacted a mainland care facility. We continued applying CPR. After a few more minutes, Baywatch established a mechanical breathing apparatus, connected their electronic monitoring device and took over the CPR. They worked on the man for about thirty additional minutes and then, after conferring with a medical doctor on their emergency phone system, pronounced the man dead.

Nobody knows how it happened. He was scuba diving with a group of friends and had just entered the water a short time before he was seen floating face down without his mouthpiece or regulator in use. He was floating in water that was only about four-feet deep, so it was suspected that he suffered either a heart attack or another form of debilitating physical disorder.

For me, it was a traumatic ordeal that left me feeling badly for a long time. I thought about my response and questioned whether I could have done anything differently. Baywatch assured me that I did everything that I could do, but it still troubled me.

That wasn't the only death that occurred during my time in the harbor, but it was the only one where I was so personally affected. It is one thing to see a person being pulled from a boat after suffering a heart attack or carted away by others after being pulled from the ocean, but it is not a pleasant experience to be the one trying unsuccessfully to save a life.

On another rather harrowing occasion, I was standing on the dock of the main float when a twenty-five-foot Bayliner pulled in to offload supplies for the campground. There were four people in the boat, two adults and two youngsters, and it was piled high with camping gear. I was about to climb aboard one of the shoreboats when the Bayliner approached. There was nobody waiting for a shoreboat ride, so I paused to help the approaching boat secure to the dock. The operator, a rather heavy-set man in his mid-thirties, did not appear to have much experience. He stopped several yards from the side of the float, shifted into reverse and turned the wheel the wrong direction and the boat backed farther away. I thought to myself, 'Okay, this guy's definitely going to need some help'.

After backing away from the float, the man shifted into forward again, turning the steering wheel rather frantically and applying too much throttle. The boat surged forward, bow pointed toward the side of the dock. The woman aboard the boat, who was also rather large, stood up to prepare for the docking, and was tossed back onto her seat by the sudden burst of speed.

Seeing that his boat could ram into the dock, the man slammed the shift lever back into reverse and the boat lurched quickly backwards, whirring loudly as the propeller lost its bite, lifted up out of the water and cavitated loudly. Flustered, he then shoved the throttles back into forward and the boat propelled forward once again. I wanted to help, but standing on the dock, there was not much I could do. Seeing that he was quite a distance from the dock, the man shifted into neutral and looked around, apparently trying to figure out what he needed to do. I heard his wife make a loud comment, but her head was turned away from me, so I could not understand what she was saying. I assumed it had something to do with his operating skills. He tossed his hands into the air and I heard him say, "I'm trying to get to the damned dock!"

Watching the drama unfold, I stood waiting patiently while the man turned the boat around and began another approach. This time he appeared to be doing things correctly and the boat slid toward the dock. I watched the woman stand and lean over the rail in order to reach out and grab hold of one of the dock cleats, or the side of the dock. At that moment, the man at the helm suddenly shoved forward again on the throttle controls and the boat surged rapidly forward. It was slightly parallel to the dock, its starboard side about two-feet away. The boat was moving way too fast and I think the man realized that he needed to do something, but instead of slowing, he gave it more throttle. In horror, I tried to call out to the woman to get her arm out of the way, but it was too late. The boat struck the dock hard, pinning her right arm between the boat and the dock. I heard a sickeningly loud snap and saw her arm twist backward at an angle that the human arm should not make. She screamed.

Desperately the man at the helm rammed the throttle into reverse, again spinning the prop out of the air and causing the boat to slam into reverse. "Turn off the key!" I cried out, hoping that he understood. He heard me, reached down and turned the key switch off and the boat stalled to a gradual stop about four-feet away from the side of the dock.

The woman on board had slumped into the passenger seat and was holding onto her right arm, eliciting a piercing, guttural wail. Her forearm was twisted backwards and there was blood oozing from the opening in her long-sleeved shirt where the bone from the compound fracture was protruding out of the fabric. I yelled out to one of the Fuel Dock employees to call Baywatch and knelt down to grab a line from the side of the boat and get it secured to the main float. At the same time, the man operating the boat stepped over to where the woman was half-lying on the passenger seat, moaning loudly and in obvious pain. I watched in horror as I saw the man look down at the injury, turn a ghastly pale hue, and faint. He fell directly onto the woman's injured arm.

She let out the most blood-curdling scream I have ever heard, and continued to scream in agony. The two children began to scream and the sound reverberated through the harbor. People ran toward us from every direction. I had managed to pull the boat to the side of the float and secure it to the dock cleat. I jumped down into the boat and grabbed the back of the man's jacket, trying to pull him off of the hysterical woman. He was big and heavy, and I wasn't able to pull him away without assistance. Glancing up on the float, I saw several people standing there. "Help me!" I called out. Two men jumped down into the boat and we managed to roll the man off of the woman and lean him down against the inner rail of the boat. Gradually the woman's screams melted into gut-wrenching sobs, and the two children began to quiet down.

Moments later Baywatch arrived on scene. One attended to the man lying unconscious in the cockpit of the boat, the other knelt beside the woman with the fractured arm. Several more harbor personnel were on scene.

The man recovered consciousness within a minute or two, and seemed to regain control of his senses. He reached over and pulled his two children into his arms and started reassuring them. Baywatch continued to administer to the injured woman, and after stabilizing her, they lifted her onto a gurney and, aided by several patrolmen, transferred her to their Baywatch Boat for transport to the hospital in Avalon.

We helped the man and his two children gather some of their belongings, made arrangements for them to catch a shuttle bus into Avalon, secured the belongings in their boat, and towed it to a mooring where it stayed for about a week until the man and another friend could get to the Island to run it back home.

That episode was one of the most dramatic injuries I was involved with, and I shall never forget the sickening sound of that snapping bone.

Among the many shipwrecks that I dealt with, the sinking of a fifty-five-foot Spoiler powerboat one New Year's morning will always remain one of the most bizarre.

I was on a routine patrol to Whites Landing to check-in and collect mooring fees from any boats that may have pulled into the cove to pick up a mooring the previous afternoon. We patrolled those outlying coves only once or twice a day during the winter months. Cruising along the beautiful green shoreline near Empire Landing, I was a little surprised to see the silhouette of a large yacht powering toward the center of the Island. The sight was unusual because there was not a cove or mooring area near the apparent destination, and it did not look like a fishing boat. Additionally, it was New Year's morning, around eight a.m., and it just didn't seem logical that somebody would be heading to the Island at that time, or to that place. Shortly after spotting the boat, it disappeared from my view behind the sheer, rocky cliffs that start at the eastern edge of Lava Wall, a camping area on the eastern boundary of Rippers Cove. My guess was that the powerboat was probably on a fishing trip. I shrugged and didn't give it any more attention.

Continuing to cruise along, I neared the location where I had seen the boat disappear. I fully expected to see the boat either at anchor, or maybe drifting and fishing somewhere along the shoreline. Instead, I blinked in amazement when I saw it aground on the face of the cliff, its aft section mostly submerged. I quickly altered course and approached the half-sunken vessel. When I arrived on scene, I wasn't sure what to expect, but it certainly wasn't to encounter only one person on board.

Slowing as I approached, I looked the situation over. The bow of the boat was lodged into a small crevice, the anchor and pulpit wedged tightly into an approximately three-foot wide naturally formed gash on the face of the sheer stone cliff. The top of the main cabin and flying bridge were above water, most of the hull submerged. As I eased alongside, I looked down into the depths and could see that the water under the submerged stern section of the boat was deep, and it appeared that only the anchor and pulpit were keeping the boat from sinking completely. I eased to a stop along the starboard side of the boat and looked around.

Kneeling on the canted deck of the fly bridge was a man reaching around trying to disconnect wiring from the array of electronic equipment built into the helm station. He glanced over toward me and I recognized him.

Mike Porter, brother of Steve Porter, whose house we had moved into when we arrived on the Island, was crawling around trying to disconnect the electronics.

"Mike!" I called out. "What the hell happened? And what are you doing?"

He looked over at me and shrugged, "I hit the Island. I'm trying to salvage some of the electronics."

Dumbfounded, I stared at him. The boat was hanging precariously from a rocky crag and it appeared to me that it would soon break loose and sink into deeper water. It was New Year's morning and here was a boat with apparently just one guy on board trying to pull gear out of the boat before it sank. Shaking my head, I asked, "Is anyone else on board?"

"No. Just me," he told me. He was still on his knees, holding onto what appeared to be a VHF radio. He was crawling, using one hand to move toward me, and holding the radio out as if he wanted me to take it from him.

I reached out and took the radio and he turned as if to go back for more.

"Mike!" I cried out to him. "What are you doing? You need to get off the boat! It's going to sink!"

He turned and looked up at me, still on his knees.

"Are you okay?" I asked.

He looked down at his legs, "I'm not sure. My feet hurt, but I think I'm okay."

"Mike, you need to get off the boat, it's going to go down," I told him.

He looked around, seemingly reluctant to leave. After a long moment, he nodded, crawled over to the side of the bridge, and reached out for the rail of my boat.

I leaned over and helped him into my boat. I looked down at his feet. He was wearing tennis shoes and everything looked normal. "Are your feet okay?" I asked.

He moved them gingerly. "I don't know. They hurt when I try to move them. They might be broken."

"What happened? What are you doing out here?" I asked him.

"I am delivering the boat from Long Beach to Marina Del Rey. I must have fallen asleep."

I shook my head unbelievingly. How could he possibly have wound up on the rocks at Catalina if he was on his way from Long Beach to Marina Del Rey? It didn't make any sense. But he appeared to be serious and sounded sincere.

We were drifting alongside the Spoiler about ten-feet away when suddenly we heard a wrenching creak and the boat shifted slightly. Looking over to where it was impaled, we watched in fascination as the boat twisted to its side and the pulpit and anchor broke loose from the crack where they were wedged. Slowly, but steadily the hull of the boat slid backwards, gradually sinking lower and lower into the clear blue water until, with an odd swooshing sound, it slid completely below the surface and came to rest about ten-feet below. We looked over the side and stared at the submerged boat. It looked very odd. The visibility was very good and it was almost like looking down into a swimming pool. To see a big, beautiful powerboat sunken in the depths was truly a strange sight. I looked over at Mike. He smiled wanly and shrugged.

"Let's get you to Avalon and have them check you out," I said to him.

He nodded and I shifted the boat into gear and headed into town. On the way, I tried to get as much information as I could from him, but without much success. He stuck to the story about the delivery from Long Beach and that he had fallen asleep. When we got into town, the Avalon Baywatch guys took him into the hospital and I heard afterward that both of his ankles were indeed broken. Apparently, he had been sitting at the helm station with his feet up on the dash and when he struck the Island, his feet crunched against the console, breaking both ankles.

The boat was later salvaged, refloated and towed back to the mainland. For many years the scars of the anchor, pulpit and chunks of fiberglass remained visible in the little crack on the face of the rock wall. I was about the only person—except perhaps the salvage crew—who might recognize the fragments of the boat glittering on the rock wall, and realize their origin.

18. *Wildlife*

IN THE SPRING OF 1991, the Catalina Conservancy completed their 'Animal Control Fence' project, the initial step of a long-term process of eliminating most of the non-native animals from the Island. For us, it was a sad day, the beginning stages of the eradication of all the Island's wild goats and pigs. Prior to that time, we thoroughly enjoyed the pleasure of seeing, photographing, and eating the animals—particularly the wild boar. I have always applauded the Conservancy for their conservation efforts, but I do not agree with their handling of the Island's animals.

Through the years, our son Trevor and his good buddies Nicholas and James McElroy caught numerous baby pigs, and then raised them in pens near the McElroy's house, feeding them table scraps from the restaurant and other resident's homes, and growing them until they were plump, healthy and tasty. Compared to the boar that roamed wild, the pen-raised pigs were delectable table fare.

The fence that was constructed to begin the animal removal process spanned the Island terrain from a point behind the USC Marine Science Center and across the hills and valleys to another point above the hills behind Cat Harbor. Following its erection, the Conservancy began a systematic eradication program that included capturing pigs in traps, using hunting dogs, shooting the animals from helicopters, and hiring paid hunters to kill off and remove the pigs and goats from the Island's west end. After ridding the west end of all goats and pigs, the program expanded to the remainder of the Island.

The techniques they applied were merciless, especially the helicopter killings. Using skilled marksmen, the helicopter pilots flew low over the canyons and hillsides, sometimes herding the goats onto ridge tops and then driving them over the edges of the cliffs where they plunged to their deaths on the rocks below. Or they merely mowed them down with their automatic weapons. Similarly, they herded the pigs into clearings or dead-end terrain and then mowed them down with machine gun style high-powered rifles. I saw some of the carnage while out on hikes and viewed video footage that one of my good friends and co-workers shot with his camera. It was a very controversial and contentious undertaking, but perfectly within their rights as 'landowners' of the animals that were considered 'domestic' game by the California Department of Fish and Game. It was a sad day for most residents of Two Harbors, and many Avalon residents, when all of the goats and pigs on the Island were eliminated. It also tainted the reputation of the Conservancy for many people.

Among the many surprises of nature that we encountered during our Isthmus years was the treasure of finding Paper Nautilus shells (Argonauts) on Island beaches.

The Paper Nautilus, *Argonauta argo Linne*, is often found in tropical and temperate seas, but is quite rare in southern California. As the name implies, the shells of the Paper Nautilus are thin, paper like, and quite delicate. In some areas of the tropics, nautilus shells can reach lengths of more than a foot, but in Island waters, a four or five-inch nautilus is a real find. The Argonaut, which is a distant relative to the octopus, normally swims in open ocean waters, but occasionally washes ashore on Island beaches during storms.

On the Island, most commonly during El Nino conditions, the lovely and highly prized shells might wash ashore during the winter months, usually December and January. On those years when they do show up, it is a contest between local residents to walk the beaches at the right time (usually low tide) and locate the occasional shell.

During our thirty-two years on the Island, our family probably found a total of about two hundred nautilus shells, the largest measuring about four inches in length. I made a small, glass-faced oak case to display our finest shells.

We also gathered and saved other Island shells, the most abundant being the Olive shell, *Olivella pedroana Conrad*, or San Pedro Olivella. We found that purple-hued shell in far greater numbers than the paper nautilus, filling several ornate jars with the half-inch to three-quarter-inch long specimens that we called Purple Olives. Another 'treasure' we sought was the semi-delicate coffee bean, or California Trivia shell. Those small brown-hued shells also look like the name implies—a small brown coffee bean. Also found most frequently during El Nino conditions, we found perhaps one-hundred of the small shells during our thirty-two years, half filling an oval shaped pint-size tequila bottle.

We also found a few Indian artifacts through the years. By far my most 'prized' artifact is a perfectly shaped Indian pestle, a stone used for grinding maize by the original inhabitants of Catalina Island, the Chumash, or Tongva Indians. That pestle I found on the beach right in front of our house at low tide one afternoon. It measures about one-foot in length, is about seven inches in diameter at its narrow end, and about nine inches at its thickest end. It is proudly displayed on a stand that I made out of a block of exotic Purple Heart wood.

In addition to the pestle, we also have a few Indian beads, pieces of broken soapstone bowls and carvings, and one small soapstone bowl. Most of those items we found very near our house, which is built upon a small knoll that is a recognized Indian midden site.

Closer to the beach is an Indian burial ground. During extremely wet years, when rain erosion cut furrows across the low hill leading down towards the seashore below our house, it was quite common to see the yellowed bones of the long buried natives become exposed. On one occasion, the full skull of an Indian was uncovered, but usually it was only a fragment of an arm, leg, hand or foot. Whenever those bones appeared, either I, or a neighbor would go out with a shovel and bury the exposed bones.

Other treasures that we accumulated through the years were animal bones. Our favorite bones were the perfectly arched rib bones of a large blue whale that washed up onto a small beach near Salta Verde Canyon one year. When it was discovered, Trevor and a couple of his friends went out to the site in a boat and swam ashore to try and collect bones.

Trevor told us about the effort to gather the bones, and it sounded quite difficult. The whale was in a messy state of decomposition and the smell was powerful. Parts of the carcass were exposed, but thick layers of crusted blubber and whale skin still clung to the bones. They took machetes and large knives ashore when they swam in, and used those to try and cut the loose skin and blubber away from the bones. I can imagine how nauseating and disgusting the process must have been because I have seen dead mammal carcasses quite regularly on Island shores. The stench and gooey mass of the rotten skin of a dead marine mammal is very unpleasant. But Trevor managed to remove and drag two rib bones, the vertebrae from its spine, and two lesser rib bones down to the beach, tie them to a surfboard and float them out to their waiting boat.

We tied the rib bones to our fence, forming a large, approximately eight-foot tall arch that spanned the perimeter of the fishpond in our yard. We displayed the vertebrae on the edge of the pond, using its twenty-inch diameter core as a display table.

In the yard we also had a buffalo skull, goat horns, deer antlers, wild boar skulls, and other assorted animal bones and antlers that we either found in the hills, or from animals that had been shot and subsequently eaten. For our boys, the opportunity to grow up in a place where those types of things were considered commonplace was a uniquely rare experience, and one that we felt very blessed to be able to watch them live and enjoy.

In 1992, General Foreman George McElroy retired after thirty-four years of dedicated service to the Two Harbors community. His retirement party was a touching event attended by hundreds of good friends and current and former co-workers. Longtime resident and accomplished 'Jack-of-all-trades', John Ermatinger replaced George as General Manager. John and his wife Ann Marie, an employee of the

USC Marine Science Center, and their two children, Paul and Elysa, had been key members of the Isthmus community for many years.

Ermatinger, his right hand man Chris King, and the entire maintenance crew (as well as the Harbor Department) had their hands full the first winter following George's retirement. It proved to be another very wet and stormy year, with torrential rains damaging roads, homes, boats and docks. There was also a succession of storm related power outages that compounded the challenges of keeping the little village of Two Harbors in operation. Ermatinger, Chris King, Paul Wintler, David McElroy, Chris Peterson, Kevin Inkster and several others did a stellar job of keeping the roads serviceable, the store and restaurant running, repairing damaged homes and doing all the things needed to avoid a shutdown of the community.

In the Harbor Department, I worked closely with Harbor Director Tim Bombard in pursuing the challenging job of keeping the harbor's fleet of boats running, the docks and floats safe and secure, responding to water related emergencies, and providing the services needed for water activities. We worked with the maintenance crew and other departments to ensure that whatever needed to be done was done as a team.

The winter storms of 92'-93' destroyed the Middle Ranch Road, washing out a big section of the road near the old Stagecoach structure. It would take Conservancy road crews two full years to affect repairs to the damaged section of road. The storms also destroyed the one-hundred-twenty-five year-old windmill that stood as a historical landmark of the Isthmus Yacht Club—the former Civil War Barracks. Longtime Isthmus Yacht Club member John Nelson took on the dubious task of trying to restore the old windmill, and his talent and perseverance resulted in its complete restoration later that summer.

That winter also brought about one of the most unique water-sport adventures to ever occurr in the Island's interior, a white water rafting adventure along 'Little Harbor River'.

Chris Peterson and Louie Latka took their sons, Christian, Mike, Little Louie, Chris and David, into the interior during one of the torrential rainstorms and launched an inflatable raft into a normally dry wash that had turned into a raging river. On the heels of more than seven inches of rain in a three-day period, the runoff and flooding had created a river that was running about twenty-feet wide and four-feet deep in the normally dry wash that runs along the Isthmus Road to the northeast of Little Harbor. The flooding washed out much of the main road, but with their four-wheel drive and a high profile pickup truck, the guys managed to drive out to the area with a rubber raft in the back of the truck.

Donning life jackets and extra paddles, the Peterson's and Latka's then proceeded to run a white-water rafting excursion from about a mile inland all the way to the beach in Little Harbor. After riding the rapids onto the beach, they piled the raft back into the pickup truck and repeated the adventure several times. The video footage of the rafting trip is an epic reminder of the power of those winter storms. We also have video footage of the local kids, including our sons on bicycles, towing each other through knee-deep water in the Isthmus Plaza on surfboards when flooding inundated the 'downtown' section of the Isthmus.

Although we did not get it on film, another unforgettable event took place one stormy afternoon with the Two Harbors kids and the school bus.

On that day, another wet storm was predicted to arrive late in the afternoon. With the interior roads already a muddy mess from previous rains, the bus driver, Dave Bryan, questioned the wisdom of driving the kids to school. His concern was that the storm would arrive during the day and washout the roads. After closely monitoring the morning newscasts, with prognosticators calling for the heaviest rains to hold off until early evening, it was decided that the bus trip should be able to proceed without worry. It did not.

Strong southeast winds started blowing early in the morning, the first harbinger of a strong storm system. By around noon the skies over the Island turned into a low-hanging mass of heavy cumulonimbus black/gray clouds and rain seemed imminent. Around one p.m. thunder and lightning erupted and the menacing clouds burst forth with a torrent of heavy rain. For the next three hours, torrential rains inundated the

Island's interior with more than two inches of rainfall. Already saturated gullies and washes quickly filled with the runoff and began rushing inexorably toward the ocean. The normally dry wash leading into Little Harbor, where only a few days before the Petersons and Latka's had river rafted, turned once again into a raging river.

When school was let out in Avalon at around three p.m., Dave Bryan realized that the drive back into the Isthmus would be a difficult one. There were about twelve kids on the bus and it was his responsibility to get them all home safely.

He headed out of Avalon in a pounding rain. Road conditions as far as the Airport in the Sky were not too bad. That section of the road was paved with an asphalt/slurry type of coating and he encountered no difficulties. Upon making the turn onto the dirt portion of the road, which started immediately beyond the airport, the road became a muddy mess. His bus was equipped with four-wheel drive, and he needed that extra gripping power in order to keep the bus on the road. Applying all of his considerable driving skills to the task, Bryan managed to reach the Little Harbor Campground. The water in the first culvert was running strong and about two-feet deep. When the bus crossed the ravine, the water rose up into the first entry step into the bus.

After he cleared the first of the two concrete culverts that cross the road where it intersects with the main road, the second one was really rushing. He stopped the bus and climbed out to look it over. It appeared to be running about three to four-feet deep and was at least twenty-feet wide. It would be too risky to drive through with all the kids in the bus. He walked back to the public payphones at the campground and phoned the Isthmus, explaining his dilemma. After speaking with the front office, he was told to wait by the phone and they would call back.

It was still pouring rain and when some of the parents heard the news about the problem, Chris Peterson and Louie Latka suggested they take the inflatable raft they used to do their white water rafting trip and try to use it to transport the kids across the river. They called Bryan back and explained the plan. He was reluctant, but agreed to look the situation over when they arrived.

Several of the kid's fathers and mothers, including Maureen and I, piled into vehicles and drove out to Little Harbor. After assessing the plan and discussing it with Bryan, it was decided to give it a try. David McElroy and John Ermatinger helped Peterson and Latka heave a length of mooring line across the river and secure it to the front end of the bus and the rear end of one of the other vehicles on the other side. The raft was then launched and hand-pulled across. Reaching the other side without any difficulties, three of the kids climbed into the raft and were safely hauled across to the other side. After doing that twice more, the last raft trip took bus driver Dave Bryan along, and all the people from the bus were safely on the other side. The bus remained parked where it was until the water level dropped the following day and Bryan hitched a ride out to retrieve it. Of course, the kids loved the raft adventure—what a fun way to get home from school!

During another rather violent storm that winter, we listened to the lamentable story from one of the former mechanics who was new to the Island and tried to drive into Avalon one night when flooding was imminent. He proceeded to watch his car get washed out into the ocean at Little Harbor while attempting to drive across the flooded road near the Little Harbor Campground. His brand new pickup truck was destroyed.

Yet another casualty of that winter's storms was the loss of the *Kingfisher II.* That venerable old boat had served in the Mooring Service for many years, rigging moorings, salvaging boats, servicing docks and floats, and providing dive and rigging service to local camps all over the Island. It was secured to a mooring in Isthmus Cove when a moderate northwester blew into the harbor late one winter night. Everything was in order and secure when the harbor shutdown for the night, but in the morning the *Kingfisher* was gone—sunk on the mooring in about sixty-feet of water.

Divers from the mooring crew donned their scuba gear and went under to try and determine the cause of the sinking. They discovered two popped planks at the stem of the old wooden boat. The wind and swells had put enough strain on the planking to cause it to pop loose. The *Kingfisher* was a real fixture on the Island, having been in operation when Doug Bombard assumed control in the mid-fifties. It was a Monterey hull, constructed in 1916, with solid oak ribs and fir planking. She had faithfully serviced the mooring service for at least thirty-years, and retained a sense of pride and dependability despite her age. After divers inspected the plank damage, it was decided that the boat was not salvageable. Early the following morning, the mooring crew attached float bags and lifted her off the bottom so that the maintenance department could drag her up onto the beach and crush the remains with the D-8 Caterpillar. It was truly the end of an era.

Later that year, the *Kingfisher II* was replaced with the *Kingfisher III*, an old steel Navy LCM that the mooring and maintenance departments converted to a mooring service vessel.

In June of 1993, Doug Bombard announced a restructuring of the management of Doug Bombard Enterprises. Both he and Audrey had worked tirelessly for years, forsaking personal time in an effort to provide a viable business for their families, friends and Island visitors. They needed to take some personal time for themselves. Not only was Doug running the Isthmus operation, he was also actively involved with managing the Catalina Channel Express service.

While announcing that he was stepping down as acting manager of both operations, Doug appointed his son Greg as President of the Catalina Express, and named General Manager John Ermatinger as Vice President of Operations for Doug Bombard Enterprises. At the same time, he appointed Randy Bombard as Vice President of Marketing and Public Relations for Two Harbors. Coinciding with those changes, Tim Bombard resigned his position as Harbor Director to pursue other interests in the marine industry, and Chuck Silvers, who was serving as the leader of shoreboat operations, was announced as the new Harbor Director. Those administrative changes came as quite a surprise to the entire community, but to all of their credit, business proceeded as usual and the transition went relatively smoothly.

Later that summer, another icon in the community announced his retirement, Ty Ewing. Ty, a very accomplished marine mechanic, had served as the Outboard Shop manager and chief mechanic for Two Harbors for nearly forty years. He and his wife Patty and their son Ricky were moving from one island to another, from Catalina to Kauai. Ty was replaced by Jim Morrow, an accomplished mechanic that had worked with Ty and served as Captain of the *Island Supplier*—the freight-hauling vessel for Two Harbors for several years.

Another rather significant change that occurred that same year was the departure of Charlene D'Amore from her position as Office Manager and Contracts Administrator for the Harbor Department. Chuck Silver's wife Ann moved into Char's position in the harbor. Michelle Hiniker also moved to the Isthmus from Avalon, married Purchasing Agent Randy Phelps, and joined the Harbor Office staff that year. Michelle quickly learned the intricacies of the mooring operation, the Master Lease, and the oversight of the harbor operation, and would ultimately assume the top position in the office. Her addition to the harbor team led to a long-term professional relationship with me that lasted until my retirement in 2010.

With all the changes that took place in the company that year, I questioned whether it might be time for me to make a career move. I had a close friend that worked as one of the top organizers of the Longshoreman's Union in Los Angeles Harbor, Don Robertson. Don had spoken to me several times about considering going to work in the Longshoreman's industry, pointing out the advantages of much better pay, less strenuous work and exceptional benefits. Maureen and I discussed the option at great length, but we really loved the Island and most aspects of our jobs. The deciding factor was our two sons. We realized that the lifestyle they were living was truly exceptional and something that could not be matched—especially anywhere in southern California. We decided that for us, the ability to give our sons the chance to continue growing up on the Island, outweighed all of the other factors, and we decided to stay. It was a 'quality of life' decision, and for us, a good choice.

On the heels of the wild winter of 1993, the entire community pitched in to get things ready for summer. There was a lot of cleanup work and repairs to be made, in all areas of the operation. For me, the task of having all of the boats and docks ready for Memorial weekend brought about more work than usual. Not only had some of the boats sustained significant damage from the storms, but the maintenance department was 'buried' in a long list of repairs and much needed maintenance in order to have all support facilities and services ready for summer. As a consequence, they could not provide their customary assistance in getting the dinghy docks and main floats ready for use.

I worked with Chuck Silvers and Dave Coiner to allocate manpower from our harbor crew to service the dinghy docks, fuel dock and main floats. Grinding, sanding and painting docks and floats, as well as performing the routine harbor patrol duties, boat and shoreboat maintenance and repairs, made for long days and sore and aching muscles. Regardless, when Memorial Weekend arrived, everything was in order and ready for the season to start.

That summer was a busy one, but was made particularly memorable because of a rash of fires that broke out and created considerable consternation. Fires on the Island are always a major concern because of the dry and widespread shrubbery and grasses that cover Island terrain, and also because of the remoteness and limited resources available to fight them once they are started.

The first of those three fires broke out on Fourth of July Weekend on the point above Pin Rock in Catalina Harbor. That fire, reportedly started by kids playing with fireworks, burned around three hundred acres and seriously threatened the Banning House Lodge, as well as the entire Two Harbors community. Fanned by winds gusting to more than twenty knots, the fire spread rapidly over the hills adjacent to the Banning House, seriously threatening that century-old structure. Hundreds of residents and visiting boaters responded to the fire, grabbing hoes, shovels, rakes and any other implements they could find to try and help hold back the flames. Some of the responders ran up into the hills wearing only swimsuits and flip-flops to help fight the fire.

David McElroy climbed aboard the D-8 Caterpillar and blazed a firebreak straight up the hill adjacent to the Banning House, rumbling through dense smoke and nearby flames in his quest to cut an adequate firebreak. Brad Foote, leader of the firefighting team, praised McElroy's effort, combined with the response from all the local residents and visiting boaters from helping to divert the flames around the lodge, and ultimately save both the lodge and probably the entire community.

A month later another brush fire broke out near Big Fisherman's Cove, ultimately burning about thirty acres. That fire was also identified as having been started by youngsters playing with fireworks.

The third fire of the summer started in the hills above Two Harbors and the cause was never determined. Fortunately that fire started on a Tuesday morning following the annual Fireman's Catalina Sailboat Race and party, and several dozen firefighters from the various mainland fire teams that were participating in the race were still on the Island. They teamed-up to fight the fire with the local members of Isthmus Station 55 (Five-guys, One Truck, No Phone—according to their popular T-shirt), and extinguished the fire after it burned only about twenty acres.

19. White Seabass

FOR ME, THE BEST FISH in the ocean is the white seabass. Those magnificent fish (*Atractoscion nobilis*) were once abundant in southern

California waters, but after years of intense commercial fishing, loss of habitat, and particularly the advent of the gillnet fishery, the white seabass was very close to going onto the endangered species list.

Catalina Island is one of the most prolific fishing grounds for white seabass, and living on the Island gave me the opportunity to fish for them on a regular basis. My successes were good and I learned the fishing techniques that helped to increase the numbers of fish that I began to catch. But the fishery was in danger, and in the winter of 1994 I became acquainted with Don Kent, director of the recently established Carl J. Hubbard fish hatchery in Carlsbad, California. Kent, a marine biologist and director of Hubbs/Sea World Research Institute in San Diego, was working with the California Department of Fish and Game in an experimental program to artificially reproduce and raise juvenile white seabass in captivity. Under the auspices of OREHP, the Ocean Resource Enhancement and Hatchery Program, Kent and his team had established a 'growout' station in Newport Bay where they were nurturing juvenile white seabass that had been spawned from seabass broodstock in the Carlsbad Hatchery. Kent came to the Island and talked with me about trying to establish a growout facility on Catalina Island.

I took a trip to Carlsbad and saw the hatchery, and then went to Newport Beach where I met Jock Albright, the site manager for the fledgling growout pens that were the first of a dozen sites developed in southern California expressly for raising white seabass. I was impressed, and believed that the program could really be a boon in the effort to try and restore white seabass populations.

When I returned to the Island, I discussed the concept of having a growout program in Two Harbors with Doug Bombard and he promised to support the idea, provided that it did not infringe on any part of the Two Harbors operation or the marine environment. He also made it clear that he could not provide financial support and that the project could not affect my regular duties. I assured him that there would be no conflict and initiated the steps to try and establish a growout station.

After sharing that information with Don Kent, I proceeded to try and identify a method of getting the project started. By chance, I was talking about the proposed project one afternoon with Stephen McElroy, who had left Two Harbors Enterprises to become facilities manager for the USC Wrigley Marine Science Center. He told me about an old, unused fiberglass raceway, a heavy-duty three-thousand gallon elongated tank that had been used on a research project and was abandoned in their 'bone yard'. Following Steve's suggestion, I spoke with facilities director William 'Mack' McFarland, and he told me that we could use the raceway if we found outside funding to support the project.

Knowing that we had one of the most philanthropic supporters of marine enhancement seated at the top of the administrative hierarchy of the Santa Catalina Island Company, Mr. Paxson 'Packy' Offield, I made an appointment to meet with Packy and discussed the idea of establishing a growout facility with him.

Packy was completely supportive and made the commitment to provide the necessary funds to back the project through the Offield Foundation, provided that all necessary permits and paperwork was in order and approved. I worked with Don Kent, the Department of Fish and Game (DFG) and Mack McFarland to ensure that everything was in order. I then worked with McElroy, McFarland and a few others at the Marine Science Center to setup the tank and plumb the saltwater hoses that would keep the tank running smoothly. Later that summer we received our first delivery of one-thousand-seven baby three-inch long white seabass.

Caring for the baby fish was relatively easy in the beginning when they were young and tiny, but as they grew and matured, the demands increased. Not only did they eat more (ground and processed pellet food), but they also pooped more. The tank cleaning process increased proportionately.

For me it was a time consuming affair. I went over to the Marine Science Center every afternoon after work to feed the fish. Stephen helped me put together a vacuum system for cleaning, and design an oxygenator made with a fifty-gallon drum filled with PVC scraps. The feeding process took about two hours a day. Once a week on my days off I spent an additional two-to-three hours vacuuming out the detritus from the bottom of the tanks and scrubbed the scum off the walls. Initially I tried to do the work reaching over the side of the tank, but eventually discovered that it was easiest to just climb into the tank and clean it from within. The water was about four-feet deep and the sea temperature around sixty-five degrees, so it was not too uncomfortable.

Everything was going along just fine until one day when the fish were about six-inches long. I decided to feed them an extra helping of tiny live anchovies and sardines that one of the mainland based sport boats offered. I had fed the growing fish a few live anchovies before and they gobbled them readily. When the captain of the *Sport King* out of Long Beach Harbor offered us five scoops of live bait, I jumped at the opportunity. I figured that those five scoops would keep the seabass fed and happy for at least a couple of days. I dumped all five scoops into the pen. I had no idea of the consequences.

About five-hours after dumping the bait into the raceway I received a phone call from Stephen McElroy. "Hey, buddy," he stated rather somberly, "You'd better get over here fast. Your fish are all dying and floating to the surface."

I stopped whatever it was that I was doing, hopped into a patrol boat and raced over to the Science Center. On scene, I rushed up to the tank and looked inside. Hundreds of dead anchovies and baby seabass were floating upside-down on the surface. An odd smell permeated the air.

Stephen was standing nearby. "Shit, Stephen!" I blurted, "What the hell is happening?"

One of his associates, Dr. Kathy Ann Miller, a USC professor and marine biologist intervened, "I think the tank has ammoniated from an excessive amount of dying fish."

"What does that mean?" I asked.

"The anchovies and sardines are dying and in the process they secrete abnormal amounts of ammonia. The young seabass are unable to cope with the increases in toxicity and they too start to secrete additional amounts. More than likely all of the fish will die," she replied, stoically.

I looked back into the tanks, mortified by what was happening. "Is there anything we can do?"

"Well," she told me, "You can try to remove the dead fish and pump more water into the tank to try and flush it out. If you are lucky, some of the fish that are near the bottom where the toxicity levels are not as high might survive."

"Okay, thanks." I turned to Stephen, "Can you help?"

"Sure," he responded immediately, "I'll get some nets and empty trash barrels; you turn up the volume of the salt water flow and open the drain a little wider."

We started working. After increasing the input flow, I grabbed a net and began scooping out dead fish. It was about half anchovies and sardines and half baby white seabass. After three months of nurturing and caring for the fish, to be scooping them out dead was a painful ordeal. Together, and with the help of a few other volunteers, we scooped out all of the dead fish that were floating. More fish were lying on the bottom, and we reached down and netted those out as well. By the time we were finished, it was nearly dark and we were arm weary and tired. But there were still a few hundred baby seabass swimming around in the bottom of the tank, congregated in the widest end where the saltwater intake valve was pumping a steady stream of fresh water into the pen. We were not sure if the remaining fish would survive, but we had done all that we could. We turned the intake volume back to normal and went home.

Early the next morning, at first light, I hopped into a patrol boat and headed back over to see what had happened overnight. With great relief, I found that all but three of the remaining small seabass were still swimming around, appearing to be healthy and strong. I scooped out the three dead ones and tossed them into the buckets. Later that same day I made a count of the dead fish before heading out about a mile from shore to dump the dead carcasses into the ocean. I counted four-hundred-fifty-six dead fish. It was a tough lessen to learn, but we all learn from our mistakes. I never dumped huge quantities of bait into the pens again.

A few months later, in October, we loaded the surviving fish into a saltwater tank on the back of a truck and drove them out to Cat Harbor for release. The fish measured about eight-to-nine-inches in length and Michael Domier, marine biologist for the Carlsbad Hatchery pronounced them healthy and strong. We released a total of five-hundred-seven fish that day, a momentous occasion for the fledgling program.

All of the fish released into the wild are tagged in their cheekbones with a tiny bar-coded wire tag that biologists can identify and link with the growout site and determine the progeny of the released fish.

For the following two years, using the onshore raceway, we raised and released a total of about two-thousand juvenile seabass into Island waters.

As the Catalina Island Seabass Program (CISP) continued to find success, Catalina became one of the key entities of the OREHP program. With the help of dozens of volunteers, notably Pete Fielding and Jerry and Alex Barber, we built a new, floating pen system capable of holding upward of ten-thousand juvenile seabass. Stefan Luithi, a former employee of mine served as the pen coordinator.

About a year later, the administrators of the Hatchery decided to build and construct a larger pen system of their own for Cat Harbor, a large eighty-by-eighty-foot net pen that could hold large numbers of juvenile seabass and also be utilized as a backup broodstock pen capable of holding around fifty-to-seventy-five mature seabass.

Scott 'Scootch' Aalbers became site manager and he set to the task of catching and caring for several dozen legal size white seabass that were eventually transferred to Carlsbad to be used for egg harvesting and enhancing the capacity in the growout project. I worked with Scootch, Don Kent and others to help get that secondary pen system up and running.

About the time it was completed, Posh Gardiner, an Islander and former commercial fisherman and close personal friend of Packy Offield, was brought into the program to replace Scootch, who was relocating to San Diego with his future wife KC, to further pursue his career in the marine industry. Posh quickly and insightfully inserted improvements to the pens, replacing the cumbersome fiberglass raceways with a much more efficient and improved net-pen system. He worked with Hubbs and their crew to coordinate and improve the logistical challenges of fish deliveries, tagging procedures and daily operations. He also worked with Packy and Packy's personal assistant Gail Hodge, to restructure the administrative oversight of the program, establishing the Catalina Island Seabass Fund Inc., (CISF) a non-profit 503-C foundation that replaced the Catalina Island Seabass Program.

I personally feel very good about my involvement in the program and am extremely grateful to Packy Offield for his support and contributions. Because of his philanthropy and dedication to the cause, and because of the countless hours of volunteer work performed by many Island people, with dozens of other individuals that donated time and energy to the project, the future of white seabass fishing in southern California appears bright and promising.

In January of 1995, the Island was once again slammed with a series of powerful Pacific storms that dumped copious amounts of rain and ravaged Island homes and roads. During one particularly powerful storm, the primary road into and out of Avalon—the Summit Road—suffered serious damage. Runoff from that storm undermined the road above Whites Landing, effectively cutting off all interior transportation.

Interior school kids were left stranded and missed school for three consecutive days until the weather settled and Baywatch Isthmus stepped-in to transport the kids by boat into town. When it was determined that the roads were 'unsafe' for normal traffic, a school transportation plan eventually was developed that utilized the dive boat *Garibaldi*— backed-up once again by Baywatch Isthmus—to provide transportation to and from school for the dozen, or so, interior students. The 'school boat' service would continue for approximately three months.

In the early stages of the road closure, all access into Avalon for groceries, business, and other daily needs of interior residents was also halted. Doug Bombard generously provided several weeks of free boat excursions aboard the *Garibaldi* so residents could get into town for groceries and other essentials. Fortunately, after about three weeks, the roads were patched-up enough for four-wheel drive vehicles to make the journey, but all drivers were advised that the roads were still 'considered unsafe' and use of the roads was done 'at your own risk'. The school bus and all other commercial vehicular transportation were not allowed access. It made it difficult for interior residents, but by car-pooling and collaborating to purchase essential supplies, the partial road access was at least manageable.

Those storms also knocked out power on several occasions, leaving the Isthmus without any reliable source of electricity. During those power outages, the maintenance department hooked-up two large portable generators to provide power to the sewage treatment plant, and the General Store and restaurant. Those local residents fortunate to have personal portable generators used them to keep freezers and refrigeration operating.

Along with the personal inconveniences, numerous homes suffered storm damages. At our house, the fence was blown over and severely damaged, part of the roofing was torn loose and rainwater flooded part of our living room. Other homes suffered blown out windows, roof damage, trees toppling onto them, and downed tree limbs damaged a couple of vehicles.

It was the start of a wild winter and another El Nino weather pattern.

As accustomed as I was to responding to storms, that winter seemed to generate an unusually high number of late night emergency calls. It seemed like at least once a week, and sometimes more, I was called out in the middle of the night to respond to storm related situations. North and northeast winds were commonplace, although they lasted only for a day or two and then quickly turned around and struck again from the south and southeast.

One evening we were sitting at home listening to the rain drum on the rooftop and the phone rang. It was around ten p.m. I was surprised to hear Doug Bombards' voice on the other end.

"Hi, Doug," he said to me rather humbly. "I'm really sorry to call you at this time of night, but my car got stuck out here at Shark Harbor and I tried to call Randy or Tim (his sons) but couldn't get hold of either one. Do you suppose you could try to drive out here and pick me up?"

I didn't hesitate, "Sure, Doug. You're at Shark Harbor?"

"Well, I'm actually at the phones at Little Harbor. I hiked over here from Shark."

"No problem," I told him. "I'll be out there as soon as I can." I dressed, hopped into my pickup truck and headed out for Little Harbor. It was sloppy and messy on the roads. A couple of times I had to really floor the gas pedal in order to make it through the mud and up the steep grades above the USC cutoff, and near Deer Valley, but I spun and slid my way up and over each of the treacherous areas.

When I arrived at Little Harbor, Doug was standing under the minimal covering of the small outdoor phone booth. He was soaked, and I could see that his pant legs were covered in mud almost to his knees. He was wearing light brown loafers, and they squished and sloshed as he climbed up into my pickup truck. He explained to me that he was returning from a City Council meeting in Avalon, and when he tried to cross the ravine at the bottom of Shark Harbor, his car lost traction and slid into the ditch on the shoulder of the dirt road. He tried for quite a while to drive out of the quagmire but only managed to become more stuck. Finally he gave up and hiked over to Little Harbor to call for help. I drove him home, wet, muddy and tired.

Another unseasonable northerly storm struck in mid-May, creating havoc in all of the coves between the Isthmus and Emerald Bay. During that blow, which hit on a Friday night with winds gusting close to forty knots and combined seas of six-to-eight-foot, the entire harbor crew was kept busy assisting and responding to boats in distress. Patrolmen Jerry Barber and Rob Foland teamed together to pull a couple of sailboats off the rocks at Little Fisherman's Cove. They also pulled an unconscious woman from the water after a Jet Ski that she was riding on crashed broadside into the hull of an anchored sailboat. My Assistant Harbormaster Dave Coiner worked with patrolman Matt Delehant to save several boats from serious damage. Mark Woolery, Doug Owen, Bruce Glass, and the entire Isthmus team worked together to save dozens of boats, and prevent injuries. In Emerald Bay, Bruce Wicklund and Shirley Daley teamed-up to minimize problems for the boaters in both Emerald and Howlands Landing. It was another difficult storm to deal with, but the resiliency and dedication of the crew kept problems to a minimum.

20. A Memorable Marlin

WHEN TREVOR TURNED THIRTEEN, I promised him a fishing trip to Baja, Mexico.

His birthday is August 30th, not a good time to be in Mexico because of the heat and the possibility of hurricanes, so we planned the trip for late October. It meant that he would miss a few days from school, but we spoke with his teachers and they organized a set of study plans for him, including the compilation of a daily log, or diary.

At the end of October, Trevor and I, along with my brother Dave, flew to Cabo San Lucas where we joined our good friends Ralph and Betsy Woodhouse on their boat *Baja Bandit*. It was the first time in Cabo for Trevor and he didn't waste any time in wetting a line. Shortly after arriving in the marina and saying hello to Ralph and Betsy, Trevor grabbed a fishing pole and a chunk of squid and dropped a line off the side of the dock. Within a few seconds he hooked into a fish and cranked up a feisty jack creville. For the next hour, Trevor caught fish after fish, most of them less than a pound in weight, but a few were a little larger.

He laughed and laughed when he caught a rather large puffer fish and watched it inflate to the size of a basketball, and then roll onto its back and float belly up on the surface. He entertained himself that way for the remainder of the afternoon, taking time only to eat a quick dinner before going back to his fishing. Ralph kidded him by saying, "Hey, Trevor, you might want to save a little of your energy for tomorrow when we go out to try and catch something bigger." Trevor just grinned and kept on fishing.

Early the following morning we headed out to pursue some serious fishing. The local fleet had found good success in recent days with dorado and small tuna to the south and up toward the Buena Vista area, but the marlin fishing was a little slow. Ralph was hoping that we might find a marlin for Trevor, so we headed onto the Pacific side of the peninsula.

We trolled for several hours without any luck, testing the waters out near the Jaime Bank. It was a perfect day for fishing, with calm seas and mild winds, but the fish were not cooperating. By midday, Ralph decided to head back in closer to shore in the hopes that we might find at least some dorado to catch. He put us back onto a course toward the little fishing village of Cristobal, located about fifteen miles northwest of Cabo.

As we neared the fishing grounds near Cristobal, we found a floating steel drum about a mile-and-a-half from shore. That rusted old drum had attracted a large number of medium sized dorado. We pulled in the trolling lines and Trevor, Dave and I tossed out live baits. Instantly, all three of us were hooked up. For the next half-hour, we took turns hooking and landing about twenty dorado, keeping six and releasing the others. For Trevor, it was his first experience in catching dorado and he was really pumped with excitement. After catching all that we wanted, Ralph suggested we head out and search for something a little bigger and more impressive.

We put the bait sticks away and set out a series of marlin clones and tuna feathers. Ralph put the *Bandit* on a course of southwest, straight out from the shoreline. We had gone less than a mile when suddenly the starboard outrigger snapped and line started peeling from the reel. Trevor, Dave and I were all standing in the cockpit, having just completed the setting of trolling lines, and we told Trevor to grab the rod that was bit.

Trevor reached out and pulled the rod from the rod holder. Line was peeling from the reel, the clicker screaming loudly.

Dave hollered loudly, "Hit it!"

Trevor lowered the rod tip a little and then reared back and set the hook.

"Again!" Dave called out. "Hit it again!"

Once more, Trevor reared back and put all one-hundred-ten pounds of his thirteen year-old body into the swing, trying to sink the large hook into the fish. At that moment, an explosion of white water erupted about sixty-yards off our stern as a majestic marlin burst from the sea, leaped upward and then crashed back down into the shimmering blue water. Twice more it jumped, twisting and shaking its massive head as it tried to spit the hook. "It's a blue!" Ralph hollered down from the bridge. "And it's a nice one!"

The big fish dove back below the surface and really took off. Line sped from the reel at an alarming rate. Trevor held on tightly, reaching down with his left hand to disengage the clicker. The noise from the reel lessened, but the line continued to run from the spool, which was emptying rapidly.

"I'm going to start backing down!" Ralph called out. "Try to recover line as I chase it!" he instructed Trevor.

Dave and I stood alongside giving encouragement and shouting out advice. Trevor, despite his youth, was already an experienced fisherman, and although he had never hooked into anything that big, he knew instinctively what to do and how to do it. He cranked as fast as he could, sometimes gaining a little line, sometimes needing to just hold tight and wait while the fish made rapid bursts of speed away from the boat.

It soon became a struggle of power and will. The mighty marlin stayed just below the surface, continuing to swim out away from the boat. Trevor put all of his energy into the fight, keeping a constant pressure on the rod and gaining line whenever he could. After about thirty minutes, the fish surfaced again, leaping and twisting from the water in a spectacular display of brute power and natural beauty. It was obvious that it was starting to tire a little as the leaps were not quite as high and the ensuing bursts of speed were slowing slightly.

Watching Trevor fight the fish, I was impressed with his focus and his dogged determination. At thirteen, he was just starting to develop the physical characteristics that turn a boy into a man, but by most standards he still looked like a thin, wiry young boy. But, even though he was thin, he had the vigor and stamina of youth and the resolute perseverance of a maturing adult. Sweat poured from his skin and the narrow, taut muscles on his forearms and biceps rippled with the strain that he was putting into the battle. He was putting all of his energy and concentration into the fight, and I looked at him with a new respect and admiration.

Meanwhile, Ralph continued to operate the boat, backing down whenever possible and always trying to keep the fish off the stern. He shouted down encouragement occasionally, letting us know when he was shifting in and out of gear.

Finally the fish neared the boat and Dave and I prepared to try and get ready for its release. We had all agreed to release the fish, wanting only to get it to leader and get a few good pictures. Betsy was filming the battle with a video recorder, and also had a camera ready for snapping photos when the fish got closer to the boat. Dave and I both wore gloves, knowing that a marlin's bill could be really abrasive and dangerous.

Trevor made a final aggressive pull and Dave reached down over the side of the boat and grabbed the leader, made a single wrap around the palm of his hand, and started to pull the massive fish closer to the side of the boat. All of a sudden the marlin flicked its powerful tail, made a small leap and burst out of the water, leaping forward about ten-feet. Stunned, Dave stepped backward, releasing the leader as the fish flopped back to the surface, drenching us all with a splash of saltwater and swimming rapidly away from the boat. It was a short burst of speed, but it peeled out about thirty yards of line.

Twice more Trevor fought the fish to the side of the boat, and twice more we could not hold onto the leader. Each time, the marlin seemed to sense that it could avoid our effort to get it alongside by jumping from the water, and each time it twisted and jumped, we lost our grip and watched it swim away.

After nearly three hours the fish was at leader again and I had a brief grasp on its massive bill, when suddenly it rolled, turned rapidly and plunged under the boat. I lost my grip and it sped down into the boat's shadow. Trevor lowered the rod tip down into the water, but the fish continued to head down and peel line from the reel. When it finally slowed, we saw that the line was snagged on something under the boat and Trevor could not pull it free. We expected the line to break at any moment.

Suddenly Betsy cried out, "It's behind us!'

We were all focused on the line going under the boat, looking down into the briny depths while Trevor leaned outward and held the rod tip as far away from the rail as possible in an effort to let the line slide freely on whatever it was snagged upon.

We looked off the stern of the boat, into the bright rays of that sweltering Baja sun, and saw the big marlin sluggishly lifting up out of the water, obviously too tired to jump high. It had surfaced at an angle about ninety degrees away from where Trevor's rod went under the boat. Ralph came down from the bridge and stood near Trevor, assessing the situation.

"Well, Trevor," Ralph observed, "Your line is obviously caught on something under the boat. I don't think there's any way we can get the fish back to the boat unless we cut the line and try to splice it back together."

"Sure," He replied softly, obviously exhausted.

After Ralph explained the strategy Dave and I worked together to reach down with a gaff and slip the crook of the hook under the line and lift it up to rail level. When the line came within reach, I grasped it tightly and pulled in about ten-feet, dragging the marlin toward me. It was swimming sluggishly on the surface, flicking its massive tail slowly.

Ralph reached over with a pair of fisherman's pliers and cut the line. "Okay, Trevor, reel it in!"

At that point, if the fish had decided to make a run, there was no way I could hold onto the line.

Trevor did as instructed. When the cut end of the line was reeled back onto the spool, Ralph looked it over carefully and commented, "Surprisingly, it doesn't look too frayed." He looked over at Trevor and said, "You did a great job Trevor! Now let's see if we can get this thing tied back together." Luckily, the marlin was staying almost stationary, and I gradually gained a little more line as I tightly gripped the cut off section.

Working rapidly, but carefully, Ralph tied a double fisherman's hitch between the severed ends and then instructed Trevor to reel it onto the spool. He did as instructed and the line was reconnected to the rod and ready to go again.

At that instant, the marlin came back to life. The time it spent lurking off the stern without any rod pressure must have invigorated it, because suddenly it leaped twice and then started peeling out line once again. Had it happened ten seconds earlier, it most certainly would have pulled out of my grip and swam away. Trevor steadied the rod, holding the tip high while the mighty fish spun off about a hundred yards of line. Then it started to sound. Plunging downward, into the purple/blue depths, the marlin reached a point directly beneath the swim step and began a slow circle.

"Darn!" Ralph blurted out, "I'm afraid it's doing the death circle."

A marlin that is hooked and fought for long periods of time sometimes tends to dive deeply and then sulks in the depths. The radical pressure changes from shallow to deep water can put too much strain on their internal organs and they die. After several minutes of watching the fish slowly circle below the stern of the *Bandit,* the circles growing constantly tighter, Ralph recognized that had likely occurred.

We weren't sure how heavy the marlin was, but it was a big one, definitely in excess of three-hundred pounds. To try and drag it up from the depths using the fulcrum of the rod was nearly impossible. "We're going to have to hand line it up," Ralph stated.

He turned and looked over at Trevor. "Okay, Trev, you step back and reel the loose line back onto the spool while we try to pull it up. It's very possible that the line will break, but we'll give it a try"

Donning a pair of gloves, Ralph, Dave and I took turns hauling up the fish. It was difficult work. The line was slippery and the fish was heavy. We were all sweating profusely, drinking water and pouring it over our heads as we worked. After about twenty minutes, Dave called out, "Color". The fish was about thirty-feet below the boat and floating on its side. When we reached the one-hundred-eighty-pound leader, we breathed a little easier and pulled a little harder. Gradually the big fish rose from the depths, floated to the surface and lay belly up alongside the boat.

Ralph picked up the flying gaff, leaned over the side and stuck it into the middle of the marlin. "Let's try and pull it through the transom door," he said to Dave and I.

We both stepped out onto the swim step and got a grip on the fins, Dave clutched the tall dorsal fin and I grabbed the left caudal fin. The three of us then put our backs into the effort and dragged it through the open gate. It barely fit. Exhausted, we all sat back on the rail and stared down at the huge marlin. It was by far the biggest I had ever seen while fishing. I had seen larger at the weigh-in scales, but not on a boat that I was fishing on.

I walked over to Trevor and put my arm around his shoulder. "Good job, son," I said to him. He looked up at me and smiled sheepishly, exhibiting the little impish grin that his mother and I always thought was so adorable.

I was impressed. Trevor had shown a determination and willpower beyond anything I had ever seen in him. I realized that he was growing up. It gave me a sense of deep parental pride and he had definitely made a 'rite of passage' that day. But that would not be the end of the story.

———— ∞∞∞ ————

The big blue marlin lay across the aft deck, its broad bill touching one side of the cockpit sole and its wide tail touching the other. If I remember correctly, it measured eleven-feet, eight-inches and had a girth of fifty-three inches. It 'taped out' at three-hundred-eighty-six pounds! Not bad for a boy's first marlin.

It was getting late in the afternoon and the late October sun would set shortly after five p.m. Wanting to get back into the dock before dark so that we could take pictures and find a local family to take the marlin home for food, Ralph decided to 'highball' it back to the dock.

We had gone about a-quarter-mile, the exhaust ports just starting to rid themselves of the thick black smoke of accumulated blowby that is typical when a diesel powered boat throttles up, when suddenly a thunderous, hull shaking roar erupted and the boat lurched to about half speed.

Stunned, I looked around, thinking that we must have run onto a reef. But that didn't make any sense. We were miles from any underwater hazards, about six miles from shore in an area where we all knew there were no submerged reefs or rocky outcroppings. I looked up onto the bridge, where Ralph stood at the helm looking down toward the stern.

"Ralph," I called out. "What the hell happened?"

"The damn anchor fell off the bow. It must have caught in the running gear."

Looking back toward the stern, I tried to comprehend what had happened. Dave came up to me and also looked around, seemingly confused. "Jesus Christ!" he exclaimed. "That felt like we struck solid ground."

"I'm going up onto the foredeck to see what happened with the anchor," I told him, stepping up onto the side deck and working my way toward the bow. When I got there, I looked down at the roller guide and chain locker. A length of the half-inch galvanized chain was hanging loosely over the rail of the bow pulpit, drooping downward. I stepped onto the pulpit and looked down. The chain dropped about a foot below the gunwale, and then ran tautly down under the bottom of the boat, looped over the keel, and then continued back toward the stern of the boat. I kneeled down, reached over the side and gave it a pull. It was immovable, stretched as tightly as chain can be stretched.

When I turned and went back to the aft deck, Ralph was standing there waiting. He had lifted the aft deck hatch and inspected the bilge. At least it was dry. Dave was at his side, as was Trevor. "What the heck happened?" Dave asked Ralph.

"The anchor clip must have come undone," Ralph responded. "I think the anchor and chain are wrapped around the starboard propeller."

Ralph's ground tackle consisted of a heavy-duty stainless steel anchor weighing sixty pounds, along with four-hundred-feet of hot-dipped galvanized steel anchor chain. It rested on a stainless roller guide with an attached anchor windlass that fed into a fiberglass chain locker. Both anchor and chain were secured to the chain plate with a quarter-inch cable that snapped onto the chain to keep them securely attached to the bow. For some reason, the small attachment cable had popped loose and the anchor plunged off the roller housing and into the water, dragging the chain with it and, because of the high speed of the boat, got sucked under the keel and ultimately wrapped on the prop.

"I'll get my mask and snorkel and take a look," I told him, moving unhesitatingly toward the small cabin that Trevor and I were sharing. I pulled my mask and snorkel from my bag and went back out on deck. I was already wearing swim trunks, as I usually did when we were fishing in Baja. Stepping over the huge marlin lying on the deck, I climbed out onto the swim step and slid my mask over my forehead, adjusted the snorkel and dropped into the water. Surfacing briefly to adjust the mask, I took a deep breath and then dived down under the boat.

As I dove, the fathomless depth of the ocean was overwhelmingly beautiful. The sun was lowering in the sky and the water had turned darker, a brilliant aquamarine blue at the surface, fading to a richer cobalt as I gazed down into the deep. It was momentarily mesmerizing, but I snapped back into focus and looked upward toward the boat's running gear. Dangling under the starboard propeller, the shining sixty-pound plow anchor swung slowly back and forth as the boat rocked on the gentle southerly swell. A tightly wound mass of anchor chain was wrapped around the shaft, with the chain forming a cone shaped knot that looked a lot like a silvery beehive. I took a few moments to check the propeller and rudder, before turning and swimming out from under the boat. Reaching out to hold onto the edge of the swim step, I pulled the mask from my face and spoke to Ralph and the others.

"Yeah, the anchor is dangling from the starboard prop. But it's hanging loosely, swinging about four-feet below the shaft and it doesn't appear to have damaged the propeller. The chain is wrapped around the shaft, in a big knot, but there doesn't appear to be any damage to the rudder, or shaft, either."

"Okay," Ralph commented. "Do you think there's any chance of un-wrapping the chain and releasing the anchor?"

"I doubt it," I replied. "But I'll go back under and take a look"

On the next dive, I reached up and tried to tug on the leading edge of the chain where it fed back from the bow. It was rock solid and immovable, the chain overlapping itself and locking it tightly into the knot that wrapped around the shaft. When I resurfaced, I told Ralph, "I can't budge the chain. But if I take a length of line down and wrap it around the anchor flukes, I think we can pull it up against the rudder strut and secure it so that it won't swing around or slap against the hull."

"That sounds good," Ralph concurred, "I'll get you a dock line."

Together we worked on the problem until we felt it was satisfactorily secured.

"Okay," Ralph commented, "Lets' fire up and head for the barn."

Ralph climbed back up onto the bridge and started the port engine. He shifted into gear, idling slowly in forward for a few minutes in order to keep a close eye on the effect the movement might have on the wrapped anchor gear. There was no noticeable influence under the boat and he gradually increased speed. Running on one engine, he was not able to reach full cruising speed, so we chugged along at about eight knots. It took us about three hours to reach port, pulling into the slip at the Cabo Marina about an hour after dark.

Because we had arrived so late, it was impractical to try and do much with the marlin, and so we tied it onto a line and dropped it into the water behind the boat to keep it as fresh as possible. Early the following morning, we hauled the marlin out of the water, hoisted it up from its massive tail with the dinghy davit that was mounted on the foredeck. After taking several photos with Trevor standing proudly alongside, we dropped it to the dock and waited for a group of local fishermen to haul the fish away

It had been quite the fishing experience. We were all extremely pleased that Trevor had caught such an impressive fish, but the anchor problem still loomed over our heads. We really hoped that it had not done major damage to any of the running gear, starboard transmission, or engine. We would not know that answer until Ralph found a diver to untangle the mess and then test the engine.

Later that day, a diver from the marina arrived to try and resolve the problem. He brought along three air tanks, tools, and an assistant. After donning his dive gear, he slipped off the dock and went under the boat. He worked quickly, first disconnecting the anchor from the chain, tying it to a line, and dropping it down to the ocean floor. He then worked with the loose end, unwrapping the chain from the shaft and letting it fall to the bottom (we pulled the gear up later). Other than a couple of small dings in the prop, he could not see anything that looked problematic. When he reported his findings to Ralph, we all breathed a sigh of relief—at least for the moment. Ralph thanked him profusely, paid his fee—with a nice bonus—and bid him farewell.

He started both engines, relieved when the affected starboard engine fired right up and sounded fine. We remained tied to the dock to perform the test.

Rather amazingly, when Ralph shifted into gear, the deformed damper plate twisted back into its normal shape, reversing the deformity that it had undergone when the wrap-up happened. Relieved and surprised to hear that news, Ralph said he wanted to cast off and try a test run. We cast off the dock lines and headed out of the harbor. After we were out of the marina, and everything sounded and looked okay, Ralph throttled up and reached cruising speed. I took over the helm while Ralph and Dave went below to visibly inspect the situation. Returning to the bridge, they reported that everything looked okay. By nearly every imaginable standard, the boat had survived almost unscathed. We were very lucky.

Trevor and I had to fly back to L.A. the following morning, and so we had lost the second day of our planned fishing trip. But that was okay. Trevor had caught his marlin, and it was truly an impressive fish. We had an ice chest full of dorado to take home. All in all, Trevor's thirteenth birthday trip had turned into a fishing trip that we will never forget.

21. End of an Era

FOR MAUREEN AND ME, OUR lives were closely intertwined with our work. Working as the Harbormaster, my interaction with the accounting department—which Maureen managed—was an everyday occurrence. For most married couples it is probably not best to work with your spouse, regardless of your compatibility levels. We worked okay together, but there were moments in both our personal and professional lives when we did not see eye to eye. As a married couple there is a tendency to 'take things home'. It was therefore a very positive move when Maureen applied for, and subsequently accepted a position with the USC Wrigley Marine Science Center as their financial administrator and office manager.

While it was a positive move for Maureen and me, it was a rough pill for Doug Bombard to swallow. As he told Maureen several times in following years, "It was really tough losing you in the accounting department."

Doug had really come to depend upon Maureen for her bookkeeping and administrative skills, and having her resign her position with the company was something he regretted to see happen. He was, however very gracious, telling her, "I'm sad to see you go, but I also understand that it is a good professional move for you to make, and I wish you the very best." Doug's magnanimity and genuine support and recognition of his 'extended family', were qualities that make him such a special man.

It was in the summer of 1995 and the Science Center was in the initial stages of what would prove to be the beginning of a prolific growth period for the USC department. When it was established as a marine science center in 1976, the institute operated with a goal of providing a working marine environment for the marine studies program at USC. Having an Island based facility for researchers and professional development served the University well. It was somewhat underutilized from what was originally envisioned, and about a year after Maureen went to work there, the University hired a new director, Dr. Anthony 'Tony' Michaels to join the program with a goal of expanding the facility. It proved to be a very good move for the University, the Science Center, and for both Tony Michaels and Maureen.

Within a couple of years the Science Center grew exponentially, expanding all of its programs and developing plans for a physical expansion of the facilities. Drawing upon a large endowment from the Wrigley and Offield families, the newly named Phillip K. Wrigley Institute for Environmental Studies soon became one of the premier marine science centers in existence, drawing scientists, professors, and marine specialists from all over the world.

Dr. Michaels proved to be a very dynamic character and an astute businessman. His energy and infectious personality was ideally suited to take over the program. Taking full advantage of the resources made available to him, Dr. Michaels wasted no time in initiating the steps needed to begin an overhaul of the Marine Science Center.

Maureen found herself at the heart of the expansion and her extensive business and office acumen quickly solidified her position with the Institute. She and Tony Michaels, along with her close friend and business associate Ann Close, worked tirelessly to keep the burgeoning Science Center on its goal of becoming a world-renowned marine institute.

In 1996, General Foreman John Ermatinger made the surprise announcement that he was vacating his position to move to Montana with his family. Mike Blackmore, a longtime Catalina boater and Island supporter, replaced Ermatinger as Vice President of operations for Doug Bombard Enterprises. Mike's connection with the Isthmus included his role in establishing the Little Red Schoolhouse, his affiliation with both Channel Cruising Club and Fourth of July Yacht Club, and long standing support of the Island. His role with the company lasted for only a short time because of a totally unexpected and disturbing announcement that happened in early January of 1997.

On Monday morning, January 20, 1997, the entire staff of Doug Bombard Enterprises was called together to attend a special meeting. As usually occurs whenever anything out of the ordinary happens in the workplace, speculation about the impending meeting was rampant. It was widely known that the overall business was suffering financially. Peripheral costs of operating a private business on the Island were soaring, particularly the 'hidden costs' like insurance, taxes, health care costs, permitting and compliance expenses. There was concern about possible layoffs, cutbacks, or reduced benefits. Nobody was quite sure what to expect, but when the reason for the meeting became known, every individual who lived and worked in Two Harbors was shocked.

Doug Bombard announced that he was terminating his lease with the Santa Catalina Island Company. After thirty-nine years of dedicated stewardship, he and his family were leaving Two Harbors and turning the operation back over to the Santa Catalina Island Company.

His termination announcement was very emotional, for his entire family and for every person attending the meeting. Under his stewardship, the community of Two Harbors was a tightly bonded entity that formed more of a family atmosphere than a business enterprise. For me, and for every other person living and working in Two Harbors, his stunning announcement not only came as a surprise, but it cast a heavy cloud over our lives. Everyone living in Two Harbors assumed that the Bombard kids would take over the operation when Doug stepped down. Nobody expected to hear the news that they all would be leaving.

As we all sat together in the main dining room of Doug's Harbor Reef Restaurant and listened to his emotional explanation of why he was terminating his lease, we couldn't help but wonder what it would mean to us personally and professionally. Would employees be able to remain on the Island? Would we still have jobs? Who would assume leadership of the operation? When would it all play out?

There was a lot of anxiety, uncertainty and confusion for all employees following Bombards' announcement, however it was made abundantly clear that the Isthmus operation would continue to exist. There would be a transition period while the Island Company and Bombard Enterprises worked out the details of the turnover, which was to take place at the end of December. The big question was, who would assume control and how would that affect all of us that lived and worked in Two Harbors? It would prove to be a difficult transition for everyone involved.

In the following months, while the Bombards negotiated the terms of their termination and the disposition of all the improvements and physical properties that existed, the employees of the company, including myself, prepared for the upcoming summer season.

On the heels of another rather wet and stormy winter, there was a lot to be done. Everyone in the company set their wheels in motion to get ready for summer. It proved to be another challenging endeavor because the spring months arrived with an unusually high number of blustery storms. March was particularly windy and rough and the winds and turbulent seas caused numerous problems for the Harbor and Mooring Service crews. Dinghy docks were damaged, one of the company work skiffs was destroyed, moorings were drug and damaged. It was a tough beginning to the year and the shadowy pall of uncertainty surrounding the future of the Isthmus loomed over everyone's head like a big dark shroud.

However, when summer arrived, the feverish pace that coincides with the arrival of the busy season pushed the unsettled speculation about the future of the company onto the backburners. There was work to be done and the entire Two Harbors team banded together to make sure that the business ran smoothly and Island visitors received good service.

In mid-August, the announcement was made that Doug Bombard and the Santa Catalina Island Company had reached an agreement of separation that would pave the way for a new entity to be formed and take over the management of the Isthmus operation. Two Harbors Enterprises (THE), a wholly owned subsidiary of the Santa Catalina Island Company, would be established to assume administrative control of Two Harbors. That company would also take over the existing Master Lease with the California State Lands Commission to oversee all water operations. Included in the changeover, Two Harbors Enterprises would assume control of all land based operations in the Isthmus as well as oversight of existing leases with affiliated yacht clubs, management of the campgrounds, and all associated business operations.

Additionally, it was announced that a Human Resources team would be established that would begin a process of interviewing and hiring employees for the new company, and that all current employees would be given the opportunity to apply and be considered for employment. That was a big relief for everyone working for the company, but it still left a lingering question in the back of everyone's mind, whether or not they would be accepted by the new company.

When the season began to wind down, the interview process began. A team from the Santa Catalina Island Company arrived in Two Harbors to begin the onerous task of selecting which employees would remain with the company.

Doug Bombard Enterprises, as operating agent for the Island Company, had always retained an undefined autonomy from the Island Company, managing and operating the Isthmus as a separate entity, except for the necessary interaction of lease arrangements and associated professional oversight that occurred between the Bombard family and the Island Company. As a consequence, most residents of Two Harbors, and employees of Doug Bombard Enterprises, had seldom experienced any direct involvement with the Catalina Island Company. It soon became quite evident that many things would change.

While the Human Resources Department from Avalon worked to perform and finalize the employment interviews, Doug Bombard and his family toiled through the formalities of agreeing upon financial compensation for the improvements and physical properties of the operation. There were a lot of details to agree upon, from machinery and equipment, to existing inventories and structural additions and improvements. Those negotiations were not easy, with each side endeavoring to maximize their position at the bargaining table. As an employee, I saw the negotiations from the sidelines, but the intensity and difficulty of the process was palpable.

In the middle of December, I was scheduled for an appointment to submit my application and discuss continued employment with the new company. Ironically, a rather severe Pacific storm hit the Island on the night preceding my scheduled interview. That storm impacted the interior roads and the Island Company administrators were delayed in their arrival. It was just as well because I was on the water responding to storm related problems. The storm that blew in brought some considerable rain, nearly two-inches over a twenty-four hour period, and had sustained winds above thirty knots with gusts higher than fifty. It created numerous problems on the water and kept the entire crew and me busy during most of the night and into the early morning hours. When the storm began to abate around nine a.m., I headed home to try and get a little rest before the Island Company officials arrived.

The storm left behind quite a mess. Despite the efforts of the Harbor, Baywatch, and Mooring Service crews, one section of the dinghy docks, one small powerboat, and several dinghies were damaged. In addition, the main float sustained damage when heavy swells slammed the float into the pier pilings and ripped a large hole in the dock's outer framework. My assistant Dave Coiner, aided by Harbor Patrolmen John Rosenfeld, Eric Sommer, Carrie Dunlop, Bruce Glass, and Ryan Kerr-Bombard, teamed together to put the harbor back together while I went home to try and get a little rest. I was able to sleep for about two-hours, and was then notified that my appointment for an interview was ready to take place.

Because of my position as Harbormaster and a department manager, I met with several leaders of the Island Company, CEO Ron Doutt, CFO Sharon Johnston, Corporate Secretary Cheryl Allison, and transition facilitator Lynn Davidson. Even though I was confident of my abilities and believed that the new company would benefit from my knowledge and experience, I was tired and a little nervous.

The interview went very well and I was informed that I would retain my position as Harbormaster, but that I should also be prepared to expect a significant modification of my duties. It was the beginning of a professional relationship that would prove to be challenging, rewarding, and quite different than it was during the Bombard years.

At the end of December, the annual Two Harbors Christmas Party took place. Always a joyous and memorable affair, the final Christmas Party with the Bombard family was nostalgic and emotional. It truly was the end of an era, and for those of us who had worked with the

Bombards through the years, the party was bittersweet. There was an overwhelming sense of impending loss, of friendships, and levels of professional comfort. The family atmosphere that had prevailed for so many years would inevitably alter, if not disappear entirely. There was an underlying feeling that big changes would be happening, and change is often difficult. At the same time, there was the awareness that the impending transition would give Doug and Audrey Bombard the time and the opportunity to unburden themselves of the strain and stress of trying to hold things together in a faltering company. It would also allow them to pursue some of their own personal dreams and desires. For the other family members, the windows to the future were a little less clear, but for each of them, Randy, Wendy, Greg, Tim, and their families, they went out with the knowledge that they were all leaving behind a legacy that would never be forgotten.

On January 1, 1998, the new operating entity, Two Harbors Enterprises (THE), replaced Doug Bombard Enterprises and the beginning of another era was underway. Bold and immediate changes occurred. First and foremost on the agenda was the announcement that John Phelps, former Harbormaster in Avalon, had been appointed as General Manager of Two Harbors Enterprises.

Phelps appointment to the helm of the new company gave everyone in the organization a sense of relief. Rather than seeing an 'outsider' without ties to the Island community taking over the leadership of the Isthmus, John Phelps arrived with a deep-rooted connection to the Island and a reputation of having strong management skills, a friendly and personable character, and a history and awareness of the Isthmus operation. His appointment was well received by all.

Soon after assuming control, Two Harbors Enterprises announced a significant pay increase for all employees. Under the Bombard realm, wages were considerably lower than comparable wage scales on the mainland; however, employees of the company did not pay rent. All housing expenses, including rent and utilities, were part of the job. When Two Harbors Enterprises assumed control, wages rose considerably for most employees, but monthly rent schedules were also established and the net income level very closely balanced out.

The new company offered a very good benefit plan, similar to the one that had existed for employees with Doug Bombard Enterprises. The new company also 'grandfathered' vacation accruals for all employees, honoring accruals based upon original date of hire. It was a very generous agreement by all standards.

For me, the biggest changes in my work came in the administrative area. Under the Bombard realm, I was in charge of the daily operations of the Harbor Department, but the Bombard family administered the operating budget and all related administrative duties. I worked with the Contracts Office in the oversight of Mooring Subleases and renewals, but the financial responsibilities fell solely under the jurisdiction of the Bombards. That was destined to change.

In early January, all of the department managers were called into a series of meetings with the officials of the Catalina Island Company to develop a strategy for moving forward. Ron Doutt, as Chief Executive Officer for the Island Company, chaired the meetings, laying out an outline that detailed managerial duties and expectations for all departments. Quickly it became apparent that all of the managers would be held too much higher standards in the administrative responsibilities of each department. We were all charged with developing operating budgets as well as building and designing departmental plans and objectives.

I immediately immersed myself in trying to learn the basics of budget development, working with other managers and with Avalon administrators to formulate an approach for the upcoming summer season that would allow me to try and improve operations and increase both revenues and gross margins. Operating budgets, gross margins, and financial statements were all new to me and I called upon Maureen's expertise to help me begin to understand their nuances. I also worked with Harbor Office manager Michelle Phelps and her assistant Stacy Straub to build a viable format for administering all aspects of the Mooring Contract process. All of that started during the already hectic months of preparing the harbor for the rapidly approaching summer season. I could see that my job would require a whole new level of commitment and responsibility. I felt that I was up for the challenge.

The appointment of John Phelps as the new leader of the operation was very quickly recognized as a good move. He immediately immersed himself in the daily operations, taking the time and initiative to become acquainted with his managers and employees. Even though the family spirit that had existed under the Bombard realm was tainted, Phelps brought his bold personality and methods of managing to the table, introducing a spirit of camaraderie and fun to the workplace. His jovial personality extended to workers at all levels of the organization, and his willingness to work alongside his employees helped demonstrate his commitment to making the transition as smooth and seamless as possible.

Phelps became a visible and active part of the daily workplace; at times driving buses, running heavy equipment, operating boats, and regularly cruising around the community on his ATV to check on the progress of various projects and let everyone know that he was directly involved in all aspects of the operation. He also took the initiative to host several social gatherings at his home, or on the beach, inviting all of his employees. His self-engineered gas-powered cocktail blender was the hit of many parties. At the same time, Phelps demonstrated a desire to strive for and initiate numerous improvements to the operation. His connections in the marine industry and his influences in the hierarchy of the Catalina Island Company helped pave the way for the purchase of new equipment for nearly all departments; new machinery for the maintenance department, outboard motors for the harbor boats, new fixtures for the store and restaurant. He also worked with landscaper Steve Whittington to formulate a plan and design for a new lawn—a first for the Isthmus—between the restaurant and the public restrooms. That lawn addition, along with new pavers in the plaza, fresh paint on all the facilities, and other aesthetic improvements really enhanced the look of the community, and John Phelps was instrumental in making the improvements happen.

For me, working for John Phelps was a new and different experience. His background of twenty-five-years as Avalon Harbormaster gave him considerable insight into the workings of the harbor. On the other hand, Avalon and Two Harbors operated on a distinctly different set of rules and regulations, particularly with regards to the Master Lease. Because Avalon was an independent city with a grant of the Tidelands, they operated under their own City-developed guidelines. Two Harbors operated under the blanket of a very complicated and closely regulated set of policies and procedures that fell under the close scrutiny of the California State Lands Commission. As a consequence, Phelps and I sometimes butted heads when it came to administering the harbor.

I felt compelled and obliged to adhere to the guidelines of our Master Lease, but Phelps sometimes suggested we modify our policies to reflect those that he was familiar with in Avalon. It was not always easy to resolve our differences, but we found a way to compromise and make the differences in our managerial techniques work for the good of the company.

Soon after Phelps assumed the leadership role in the company, a series of strong winter storms impacted the Island. Catalina Harbor was hit particularly hard by one storm, damaging the Cat Harbor Pier and dinghy docks. Making repairs to the damaged pier and docks would normally have taken considerable time, but Phelps redirected all available resources to make the repairs, drawing upon the Maintenance

Department, Mooring Service, and the Harbor Department to work together to get the job done. Materials to build new docks were ordered, the pier was repaired, and Cat Harbor was back in full operation within weeks. It was the first of many such decisive actions that Phelps would take during his tenure that expedited a quick resolution to a problem. It helped that the Catalina Island Company saw the need and was willing to provide the necessary funding, but it was Phelps perseverance that paved the way. It was soon very obvious that life in the Isthmus was changing, and for the most part, the changes were positive and progressive.

The Catalina Island Company also instituted a series of professional development programs for all Two Harbors employees. 'Charm Schools' became a regular part of the workplace, a whole new concept for most employees. Classes for nearly all full-time employees began to take place, offering training in interpersonal skills, customer relations, and job-specific training. For most of us, it was our first experience with professional development training, and the results and benefits of the training soon became obvious.

As Harbormaster, it was evident to me that the transformation from a 'mom and pop' operation to more of a corporate environment had its pluses and minuses. I missed the casual and personal approach that served the Bombards well for so many years, but I also recognized that the world—and even Catalina's secluded little domain—was gradually moving into a new era. Methods of running businesses were changing and things like Worker Rights, Environmental Health and Safety, and Governmental Compliance were areas that all managers needed to know. The training sessions that I attended went a long way toward helping me understand how to be a better manager.

Another item in the Harbor Department that was still unresolved was the issue of mooring ownership. Originally scheduled for resolution at the end of 1997, the Submerged Lands Master Lease was put into a 'holdover clause' with the State Lands Commission because of the ownership issue. Ongoing since 1982, the debate over ownership continued.

My involvement in finding a resolution to the fifteen-year dispute became more active. I worked closely with Ron Doutt and Alan Scott, the State Lands agent in charge of the Catalina Master Lease, to try and bring the matter to closure. Legal maneuvering by a coalition of mooring owners disputing the elimination of ownership had prevented the approved long-term Master Lease from going into effect. Several court dates and negotiating sessions took place between the State Lands Commission and the 'Mooring Coalition', without reaching a resolution.

Throughout the legal proceedings, I interacted closely with several of the representatives of the mooring owners, including Cherry Cove Yacht Club members Richard 'Dick' Wilden, Phillip Stein, Lance Kluger, Don Briscoe, William 'Bill' Davidson from Fourth of July Yacht Club as well as several members of Newport Harbor and Los Angeles Yacht Club. All were very involved in the in the mooring owner's efforts to try and convince the State Lands Commissioners to change the Master Lease in favor of continued mooring ownership.

During those interactions with the representatives of the 'Mooring Coalition', I forged some good friendships. Even though I represented the Harbor Department, I believe that the individuals that I worked with and got to know on a personal level recognized that I was not 'in the enemy camp', so to speak, but merely was trying to do my job and remain neutral during the prolonged negotiations with the State Lands Commission. It would be several more years before the issue finally came to a resolution.

22. Yacht Clubs and New Responsibilities

EASTER WEEKEND ON CATALINA ISLAND is always a special affair, thanks in part to the dedicated efforts of one particular southern California Yacht Club; the Corsair Yacht Club of Emerald Bay.

In their early years, the Corsairs discovered the beauty and tranquility of Emerald Bay, Catalina Island, and eventually secured a land lease with the Santa Catalina Island Company in a small canyon near the Boy Scout Camp. In the early 1950's, a group of Corsairs decided to put together an Easter Cruise to the Isthmus, where they could share the joys of Easter with their families and with Island youngsters. As the years progressed, the Isthmus Easter Cruise became a tradition that the Corsairs continued, and it became one of the most eagerly anticipated events for the Island community.

Each member of the Corsairs brought a minimum of one-dozen brightly colored hard-boiled Easter eggs (in later years the eggs turned to plastic), to hide on the beaches for local youngsters to gather on Easter morning. The Easter bunny (the effervescent Tony Baldwin served as the bunny for many years) provided every child in attendance with their own Easter basket stuffed with colorful shredded paper to cushion the eggs. In addition to the Easter egg hunt, the Corsairs also put together a hat decorating contest, an Easter punch bowl for the adults (emphasis on the punch), and a hors d' oeuvres party on the beach. Both of our sons attended every Easter egg hunt from the time they could walk until they turned thirteen. It was, and still remains, one of the most special weekends of the year for the Isthmus community.

Their Easter cruises were not always idyllic, and the cruise of 1997 turned into one that some members would probably like to forget. Late March and early April can sometimes bring contrary weather. Such was the case that year.

The weekend began gloriously enough, with fair winds and calm seas on Thursday and Friday, when the majority of Corsair members arrived in the cove. Approximately forty Corsair boats made the cruise, along with another one hundred-plus visiting boats.

Saturday morning dawned bright and fair, a robin egg blue sky hovering over the silvery ocean. But when I listened to the marine forecast, I felt a sense of foreboding. A weak weather front was passing to the north and forecasters predicted the possibility of moderate northwest winds to develop behind the frontal passage. I checked weather forecasts and recent updates. Most forecast models showed the strongest winds staying to the north of the Island, but one of the models showed the winds dropping southward and encompassing Island waters. It could get blustery.

Everything went well throughout the day. The winds and seas remained calm and mild, and several dozen more boats arrived in the Isthmus to celebrate Easter.

Usually I worked until around five p.m. on Saturdays, but with an invite to the Corsair punch bowl and hat decorating party, I headed home at around four o'clock and changed clothes. Maureen and I then headed down to the beach to join in the Corsair festivities.

I still had an uneasy feeling about the weather, and so I elected not to partake in the punch bowl offering. In years past, I had accepted a glass or two of the tasty punch, a tropical concoction that the Corsairs (notably Roger Civalleri) mixed in a Sabot sailboat and that contained considerably more alcohol than fruit mixes. It had 'knocked the socks off' many an imbiber.

The party was just getting into full swing—the hat-decorating contest was over—and guests and members of the Corsairs were mixing and mingling around the hors d' oeuvres table. The sun dropped below the western summit of the adjacent hills and the air temperature dropped rapidly. I looked out over the harbor and noticed a few dark ripples on the distant sea surface, which up to that point had remained peaceful and placid. A moment later, a brief but powerful gust of wind whipped across the beach, ruffling the table coverings and blowing a few plastic cups and paper plates onto the sand. I looked out again at the water and saw the sight of a distinct and darkening wind line moving noticeably from west to east. I felt a brief and peculiar calmness settle over the beach and the ambient air temperature rose significantly for a few minutes. Then suddenly everything changed.

A powerful blast of cold air whipped across the beach, stirring a cloud of dust and sand that prompted nearly everyone on the beach to turn their faces and heads away from the onslaught. I looked out over the water again and grimaced at what I saw.

The darkening wind line that had formed outside of the cove had rapidly become a bubbling boil of whitecaps. On the outer rows of moorings, the moored boats were rocking back and forth and being pushed toward the east by the stiff wind that had suddenly developed. I walked over to Maureen and said, "This doesn't look good. I'm going to head out to the Harbor Office and check in with the crew."

She was shivering, pulling her lightweight jacket tightly around her neck and shoulders in an effort to ward off the chilling wind. "Okay, I think I'll head back to the house," she informed me. "Do you think you'll be long?"

"I hope not," I told her. "But the wind is really starting to kick up and we've got a lot of boats in the Harbor. I'll be home when I can."

I was really glad that I had not consumed any alcohol. From the looks of things on the water, it could get really crummy. I said a quick farewell to Corsair Commodore Rowland Noriega, thanking him for the hospitality, and telling him that I had to go out and check on the harbor. He told me that he completely understood and thanked me for joining them. Other Corsairs were beginning to pack things up as the cold and blustery wind continued to whip across the beach, stinging exposed skin with sand.

When I reached the pier, I looked out and saw one of the Harbor Patrol boats under tow on the west side of the harbor. A large powerboat, about sixty-foot in length, was broadside against a similar sized sailboat with several people out on deck attempting to fend off. Almost immediately the radio erupted with the voices of frantic boaters calling for assistance. In addition to the gusty winds that had begun, a strong tidal current developed, adding to the tumult. That tidal current was typical when neap or spring tides formed and resulted in tidal swings of six-to-eight-feet. On those occasions, sailboats with a deep, full displacement keel caught the brunt of the currents, while the powerboats were prone to the effects of the wind. The combined forces of the contrary wind and current resulted in moored boats 'drafting' together. It was a phenomenon that occurred semi-regularly, but was amplified by stronger than normal winds. The tidal effect usually lasted for about one-to-two hours during peak ebb and flow.

Recognizing that numerous problems were occurring, I hopped into a patrol boat and headed out onto the water to lend assistance. For the next two hours I worked with Patrolmen John Rosenfeld, Eric Sommer, Ryan Kerr-Bombard, Richie McIntyre, Dave Coiner, Bruce Glass, Carrie Dunlop and Shirley Daley to assist dozens of moored and anchored boats in various states of distress. It was one of those cold and blustery nights that required strong boating skills and equally focused personal fortitude to cope with the penetrating winds and turbulent seas.

Fortunately, at around midnight, the winds quit almost as abruptly as they began. When the winds stopped, the seas moderated considerably and the crew, other than graveyard patrolman Mark Woolery went home for some well-deserved rest.

For the Corsairs it was also a difficult evening. Not only did many of them require assistance during the worst of the stormy weather, the overall mooring conditions were not comfortable. On the other hand, the Corsairs were somewhat used to lumpier than normal conditions at Emerald Bay, which is a beautiful cove and mooring area, but is subject to considerably more turbulence than the coves in the Isthmus. For most of them it was just another rocky and rolling night on their boats.

Even though I had been out on the water until after midnight, I awoke early in order to be back at work at seven the next morning. Sunday was normally my day off, but on nearly all holidays, I worked at least part of the day because of staffing limitations. Sitting in my easy chair looking out our picture windows at the harbor, I could see that even though the winds had abated considerably during the night, there was still a lump in the harbor. Boats were rocking back and forth and the telltale sound of loose rigging, clanging in the shrouds, was evident. I finished my coffee, wolfed down a bowl of Cheerios and headed down to the pier on my bike to begin my day. Maureen would be following soon, taking Troy down to the beach to participate in the Easter egg hunt.

When I arrived at the Harbor Office I could see that even though the harbor was relatively calm, a noticeable wind line existed outside of the mooring fields. Gazing out at the horizon, I could also see the distinctive 'shark-tooth' outline of the swell pattern; a ribbed horizontal line that indicated a steep and short ocean swell. It would likely be a lumpy channel crossing for the boats returning to their mainland ports.

Air temperatures were also unusually cool. A quick check of the temperature showed the ambient air temp at forty-four degrees. It would be a chilly Easter egg hunt for the kids.

Everything was in order in the Harbor. Mark Woolery reported that everything had stayed relatively calm and under control during the night. The normal Sunday morning crew arrived on time at seven o'clock, and when I saw Maureen walk down the beach with our sons, I headed down the pier to join her and watch the egg hunt.

As the kids gathered on the beach to await the arrival of the 'Easter Bunny', the winds began to blow a little stronger. Originating from a westerly direction, the typical 'Isthmus fan' amplified the force of the wind and the resulting fifteen-to-twenty knot breeze and cool air temperature caused many to try and seek shelter behind the walls of the restaurant. The resulting egg hunt was much shorter than usual, with many of the children spending only a few minutes searching for eggs before giving up and telling their parents they were cold.

As the morning progressed, the winds continued at a steady fifteen-to-twenty knots and temperatures remained at least ten degrees below normal. Seas in the Catalina Channel grew progressively worse and by early afternoon a Small Craft Advisory was in effect for hazardous seas.

For the Corsairs, as well as all other boats that were on the Island for the weekend, it was a rough and tumble return crossing, but the vast majority of boats needed to return home regardless of the sea conditions in order to be at home for work—and school—the following day. It was one of those things that Catalina boaters sometimes encounter, and one of many such disruptive influences of nature that took place through my years in the Harbor Department.

On Maureen's fortieth birthday, the four of us, Maureen, Trevor, Troy and I drove into Avalon for a birthday dinner, a movie, and then home. On the way back from Avalon, my vehicle—we had an Isuzu Trooper at the time—started wobbling oddly. I stopped in the center of the road, since traffic on the Island is not an issue, and stepped out to look at the wheels. I walked around the front of the vehicle first, saw nothing wrong, and moved around back. The right side looked fine, but when I looked at the left rear wheel, the wheel was extended about fifteen inches out from the wheel well, suspended on the round iron bar of the rear axle. My eyes popped in surprise, amazed that the wheel could be that far away from the side of the car without collapsing. I walked up to the driver door and leaned into the cab. "We've got a problem," I told Maureen and the boys. "I think we're going to have to take a walk."

When Maureen and the boys climbed out and looked at the wheel, they started to laugh. It did look rather funny. I told her I was going to climb in and start the car and try to pull it over to the side of the road. I was almost certain that the wheel would collapse in doing that, but it was directly in the middle of the road and it would be difficult for anyone to drive around, especially one of the Island Company busses or trucks. I started the car and rolled slowly to the left. Somehow the axle remained where it should be but the wheel stuck out more than a foot.

Pulled off to the side, we all gathered an armload of groceries (we had shopped at Safeway while in town) and headed down the road toward Little Harbor where we could make a phone call. We hadn't gone far when it started to lightly rain. Troy was just a little guy, around four-years old and he started crying. He just wasn't sure what to make of the whole thing. I had Maureen help me lift him up onto my shoulders and we continued on. Troy still seemed upset, so to lighten the mood we began singing. Trudging along in the dark, on the rocky dirt road on the downgrade between El Rancho Escondido and Shark Harbor, we sang songs ('Follow the Yellow Brick Road' and others) and giggled. Neither Maureen nor I can carry a tune in a bucket, but the boys seemed oblivious to our inadequacies and sang along with us. When we finally arrived in Little Harbor at the pay phones, sometime after ten o'clock, Maureen called her boss Dr. Tony Michaels and he graciously drove out and picked us up. We were soaked to the gills, muddy and cold, but otherwise in good spirits. It would prove to be one of Maureen's most memorable, if not forgettable birthdays.

As the year of transition progressed, changes continued to unfold. Yeoung Yu, the Korean Master Chef who had worked for many years at Doug's Harbor Reef Restaurant, retired. Randy and Brenda Bombard and their family departed for Costa Rica, and Gary and Wendy (Bombard) Adams and their son Russell left the Island for their new home in the State of Maine. Tim Bombard went to work with Greg Bombard at the Catalina Express. Nineteen-year employee Michelle Mileski and her partner Dan McGowan left the Island for a lengthy sailing odyssey. Bob Carman, a fixture in the harbor operation for many years, transferred to the camping department as its new manager. Sean Hammond took over the management of the restaurant from Gary Adams, to be replaced a few months later by Bill Horner. Dave Long was appointed as manager of the Dive and Recreation Department.

It was an interesting time for all, and I just tried to roll with the flow. It soon became evident that the Santa Catalina Island Company was determined to make improvements in both the physical grounds in Two Harbors, and the methods of operation.

As the summer season wound down, a directive for all managers to assume control of their individual operating budgets and business plans really began to take shape. Immediately following the busy Labor Day weekend, the Island Company instructed all managers to submit operating budgets for the following year.

For me, and for most other managers, it would be a first. We had received a basic, general outline of what was expected from each of us, and how to develop the plans, and were given a due-date for submittal. I worked for about two-weeks on the harbor operations budget, assembling information and outlining tentative proposals. When the big day arrived, several managers headed into corporate headquarters in Avalon to present plans to the Island Company, including John Phelps, Ann Luchau, Pam Cadman, Laura McElroy, Louie Latka, and Bob Carman. We rode into town together in John Phelps' sports utility vehicle, discussing thoughts and ideas along the way.

We were scheduled to meet with CFO Sharon Johnston, corporate secretary Cheryl Allison, and CEO Ron Doutt. When we gathered in the meeting room at the Island Company corporate office on Metropole Avenue, Ron Doutt's presence was noticeably absent. There was some small talk while everyone awaited his arrival, but we were not at all prepared for what took place when he walked in the door.

Ron Doutt had already proven that he was a very astute and formidable businessman. His background and experience with the Island Company and prior to that, the Wilmington Transportation Company (another of Wrigley's holdings), was well known and highly regarded. In the few company presentations he made during the corporate transition, he had impressed all with his knowledge and professionalism. We were not sure what to expect on this first day of budget preparations, but it certainly was not what occurred.

A large, burly man with an impressive thick black mustache and a nearly bald head, Ron Doutt was an imposing presence. His countenance, although somewhat cherubic by nature, did retain an underlying intensity.

He walked into the room but remained standing. The fact that he did not take a seat seemed particularly disconcerting. Holding a thick folder in his large hands, he looked slowly around the room, pausing momentarily as he looked into each of our eager faces. After conveying the distinct message that he was directing his comments to each of us individually, and holding out our budget packets, he stated firmly and without qualm, "This is a bunch of crap!"

Stunned by his comment, we all looked furtively at one another, unsure of how to react to his statement. He looked around at us again, standing stoically at the head of the large, rectangular shaped mahogany table, holding the thick folder of paperwork at chest height, and commented, "I expected a viable operating budget. These submittals provide me with almost nothing to work with. I expect each of you to work with Sharon Johnston, Ann Luchau, and John Phelps and come back to me one week from today with a budget submittal that makes sense." With that he dropped the packet onto the table, turned on his heels and walked out.

Silence filled the room. I looked around sheepishly and saw that all of the other managers from the Isthmus felt similarly timid and dumfounded.

Sharon Johnston broke the awkward silence that engulfed us all. "Okay," she commented almost cheerily. "It looks like we've all got some work to do!"

For the next several hours, excluding a short half-hour lunch break, we sat together in the Island Company meeting room listening to, and interacting with Sharon Johnston and her staff while they outlined and explained the expectations that Ron Doutt had for a budget submittal. For each of us from the Isthmus, there was a good understanding of the basics of how each of our various departments operated, what revenues and expenditures were, and what it took to make each department operate efficiently. We just did not know how to put it together into a professional business plan. Sharon and her staff helped us to understand those expectations.

The long ride back to the Isthmus was tempered with the knowledge that Ron Doutt's unequivocal rejection of our original submittals was not personal, but simply that he expected things to be done a certain way. We discussed the need to work as a team to put together a new set of plans that adhered to the outline that Sharon Johnston had presented to us.

During the following seven days, forsaking nearly everything that we would have normally put at the top of our priority lists, the Two Harbors management team worked together to design and develop a revised budget submittal that we all hoped would satisfy Ron Doutt. For me it was a time of learning, and I began to realize that I found real pleasure in the professional growth. I always had a solid underlying grasp of the fundamentals of managing the business side of the harbor operation, but to learn the basics from the financial and administrative sides, gave me a whole new sense of pride and empowerment. I worked hard, interacting with Ann Luchau and John Phelps, to develop a revised set of proposals and felt hopeful, if not confident that our next meeting with Mr. Doutt would go a little better.

A week later we returned to Avalon. When Ron Doutt walked into the meeting room the following Monday morning, each of us held our collective breaths when he stood for a moment at the head of the table, and for emphasis, looked around at each of us as he had done the week previously. I felt myself gulp as he stood there, doubting my earlier confidence.

But as he looked around the room, a smile spread slowly across his stalwart features and he quietly commented, "Okay. This is better. We've got a start. Now let's get to work and put these individual budgets together into a set of comprehensive business plans that all of us can live with."

At that point he actually rolled up the sleeves of his white dress shirt, and sat down at the head of the table to begin the revision process.

The remainder of that day impressed me on a professional level more than any day of my life. Ron Doutt delved deeply into the budget submittals with a phenomenal amount of astuteness and clarity. His insight and knowledge of business and financial strategizing was astounding. I listened and absorbed his wisdom like a sponge, and by the end of the day I had a better fundamental understanding of how the true professional world of business operates, than I had ever known.

Throughout the ensuing ten years, until he retired from the head of the Island Company, I continued to learn from, and appreciate the wisdom and talent of Mr. Doutt. Between Ron and Packy Offield, who sat in on business meetings only occasionally, I began to fully appreciate what constitutes a true professional in the business world. For me, both men served not only as mentors and inspirational leaders, but also helped me to understand and recognize the influence that a great leader can have on an organization.

I also discovered that Ann Luchau, Director of Human Relations and Vice President of Administration, possessed a very solid understanding of budget development and finances. Her involvement in the budget process was to interact with all department managers in the creation and submittal of budgets, and the development of pricing schedules, expenditures, and wages. John Phelps financial acumen was not as strong as Ann's, and he generally deferred to her for budget oversight. Phelps strengths were in the fields of motivation and inter-personal relations, as well as project oversight and planning. He helped to bring the process of budget development together by working individually with all department managers to map out strategies for repairs, maintenance and physical improvements for the various operations. In addition, his connections in the marine and construction industries often helped to identify, locate and procure parts and equipment at reduced prices. With the support and assistance John and Ann provided in the budget development process, all of us managed to get through that first year successfully.

In following years, I always felt good about the successes of the harbor operation. For each of the next ten-years, the gross margin of the Harbor Department showed improvement. I will admit that I tended to understate revenue projections to a certain degree so that my budget would not only be met, but show improvement. Ron Doutt recognized my 'lowball' techniques on a couple of the budget submittals and suggested alterations, but even with those adjustments, I still managed to exceed projections every year. I always felt a certain amount of professional accomplishment in my understanding and success in running the harbor operation.

As Harbormaster under the new Two Harbors Enterprises regime, I also became more and more involved in the marketing and public relations program. During the Bombard reign, Doug and Audrey served as 'ambassadors' of the Island for nearly all of the social gatherings, both on the Island and on the mainland. When they moved off the Island and John Phelps took over at the helm, the role of 'ambassador' fell into my lap. Phelps was very active and enjoyed being the 'formal' representative for the company in the majority of the inter-company social activities, but he preferred to stay on the sidelines for most yacht club and other organizational gatherings. Representing the company in those social endeavors became one of my new duties.

Club and organizational cruises are always a huge part of the Catalina experience. As Harbormaster, my interaction with the many clubs that frequent Island shores (the Yacht Club Directory of southern California lists more than eighty southland based clubs) grew exponentially as my career blossomed. Every weekend from around early May until late October, club cruises took place in West End coves. The more I got to know regular visitors, invitations to yacht club parties became commonplace. During the summer months, it was a rare weekend that I did not receive at least one invitation to attend a club function—usually Friday or Saturday night dinners—because those were the only functions that took place when I was not working. I made it a point to attend all that I could.

It was good to have a respected member of the Harbor Department representing the company, and Maureen was very gracious to accompany me to the vast majority of the events. Most of the socializing we did was in the local coves, Isthmus, Fourth of July, Cherry Cove, and Cat Harbor, but we also attended functions in Emerald Bay, Howlands Landing, and the Whites Landing area. There were many wonderful people that we got to know through the years attending yacht club dinners and the club members made us feel welcome and appreciated.

In addition to the Island-based clubs, dozens of mainland yacht clubs, boat dealerships, and other marine organizations also held cruises to the Island, usually hosting their parties on Isthmus Beach and utilizing the bandstands for their club and organizational functions. Dozens of organized cruise events occurred each summer, many of them annual events with years of tradition and history in their makeup. There is a very long list of those cruise events, and I would love to name and acknowledge all of the wonderful people that organized and were involved in their group's Island experiences, but that truly would entail several hundred pages. Suffice it to say that both Maureen and I really enjoyed the friendships and great times that we had representing the Island at the various functions, and greatly appreciate the hospitality and friendships that we made as a result of those events.

Another promotional undertaking that I started as a member of the marketing program, was to host a series of boating seminars on the mainland. Those seminars, which I entitled *Discover Two Harbors,* were initiated with the help of good friend Jeff Stress, who served at the time as the advertising representative for the San Diego Log Newspaper.

The Log is recognized as the preeminent bi-weekly newspaper for the southern California boating industry. Jeff is an avid Catalina Island supporter and visitor, and his connections with Isthmus residents eventually led to his pro-bono involvement with the Two Harbors marketing and promotion program.

Jeff's connections and respect in the marine industry spread to nearly every nook and cranny in the boating community, and before long, he convinced me to expand my writing career from the weekly column I did for the Catalina Islander, to include a bi-monthly column for the Log Newspaper. I wrote that column, under the byline of 'The Catalina Connection', for about two years, discontinuing my involvement when management changes at the Log did not fit well with my perception of what we were trying to accomplish.

But my friendship with Jeff continued, and he helped me connect with Jay Carson, who worked in a variety of capacities with West Marine Stores, the primary leader of recreational boating supplies and equipment on the West Coast.

Jay Carson convinced me to begin the boating seminars, initially putting them on at various West Marine Stores in southern California.

Intended to introduce new boaters to the Island—particularly the Two Harbors venues—the seminars offered a slide show, details about what the Island has to offer, a mooring demonstration, anchoring and mooring information, and personal insight and suggestions about boating and visiting Catalina Island. In the beginning, Kathy King worked with me to co-host the seminars, and her involvement added to the success of the program and helped make my job easier.

After a few years working with Jay Carson, numerous yacht clubs and boating organizations also requested that I offer seminars to their members, and I expanded the presentations to several other southern California venues.

Another 'duty' that I assumed soon after T.H.E. was formed, was to represent Two Harbors at various yacht club openings on the mainland. Each spring, dozens of yacht clubs in the southern California area hold their opening day ceremonies, officially dedicating the opening of the yachting season and introducing their commodores and new officials to their members and assembled guests. Those openings are traditionally sober and ostentatious affairs, featuring the pomp and circumstance of yacht club rites and rituals, and require specific adherence to time-honored yacht club traditions. As a 'distinguished guest' at the club openings, I did my best to adhere to the customs and formalities, wearing the customary beige slacks with tie and dark blazer, and meeting and greeting the club officials with grace and charm. Maureen would usually accompany me and was very gracious and enchanting. I always felt proud having her at my side.

The 'openings' always took place on weekends in early spring, and we attended as many as possible, sometimes three or four per day. The company did pay for our basic expenses, but the time and energy required to attend the events placed another burden on our personal lives. I will always remain grateful for Maureen's support. Without her at my side, I know I would not have made it through the rituals.

In my position as Harbormaster, I was called upon to handle administrative duties and problems that popped up from time to time. Foremost in the 'problem solving' areas were the various mooring related issues. Individuals that lease moorings on the Island are very passionate about their boating activities, and quite often conflicts would develop that required my intervention. When someone changed boats (usually moving up in size), the issue of mooring compatibility arose. In an effort to avoid singular, arbitrary rulings that could lead to accusations of 'favoritism', I formed a mooring committee to oversee all mooring related issues. That committee, consisting of the Harbormaster, the leader of the Mooring Service, the Office Manager, and the Assistant Harbormaster, would then review all pending mooring issues and make rulings and decisions based upon 'fair and reasonable' evaluations. The formation of that committee helped me to maintain a non-biased and impersonal ruling on mooring related issues.

My involvement with the State Lands Commission, on matters ranging from the issue of mooring ownership, adding new moorings to come into compliance with the terms of the Master Lease, building and installing new dinghy docks for Cat Harbor, and resolving disputes over policies and procedures in both our operation and the Island camps that overlapped our areas of jurisdiction, required a lot of my time. I felt very fortunate to have such good support from the rest of the harbor team, especially because the spring months of 1999 once again proved to be particularly rough and windy.

23. USC Bound

ENTERING HIS SENIOR YEAR IN high school, our son Trevor applied for college. He applied to the Cal State system and USC. His first acceptance was from Cal State San Marcos, a gratifying accomplishment. But we were keeping our fingers crossed that he might be accepted to USC.

When Trevor's official looking envelope from the University of Southern California arrived in the mail, we waited anxiously for him to get home from school to open it and see if he had been accepted. We sat down together on the couch as he opened the envelope and pulled out the top, nine-by-eleven-inch sheet of engraved USC stationary that had the following two words boldly imprinted onto the page; YOU'RE IN! It was a special moment for our family and Maureen and I could not have been more proud.

Because of her employment with USC, Maureen qualified for free tuition from the University—a huge benefit. Without it, there is no way we could have afforded his tuition. Room, board, and personal expenses would be taxing enough, but he did earn some scholarship money from Avalon High, which has a remarkable scholarship program, and those funds, along with cash that he had earned working summers in Two Harbors, helped us get him through all five years at USC. When he graduated in 2005, with a Bachelors Degree in International Relations, we were very proud parents.

Troy, our youngest son was in middle school, in Avalon. His daily ritual of riding the bus to and from Avalon was not always easy. For both of our sons, their middle and high school years always made me think about the classic stories that our parents, grandparents, or other relatives used to tell about their challenges when they were in school—trekking long distances, waking early, suffering through the elements of nature; rain, wind and snow.

For our boys, snow was never a factor, but attending school was much more difficult than it is for most youngsters in southern California.

I always woke early, usually around daybreak. My morning routine was to boil water for coffee, perform my morning ablutions, make an initial wakeup call for the boys, pour a cup of instant coffee, make a second wakeup call, prepare a bowl of cereal, toasted bagel, pancakes, or oatmeal for the boys, and then give the final wakeup call. If they didn't respond right away, I sang them a little song; '*Summertime, and the living is easy, fish are jumping out of the sea, my mama's rich and my daddy's good looking, so hush little baby, don't you cry*'. Rarely did I get through the first verse because my voice is terrible and it made the boys cringe, so I seldom had to sing a second verse.

The bus arrived on the road near our house at six-twenty a.m. It arrived in Avalon at about seven-forty-five a.m., fifteen minutes before classes began. The bus departed Avalon at three-thirty p.m. and arrived back at the Isthmus at around four-forty-five p.m. It was a long day. In addition, the steep, winding and bumpy roads made it nearly impossible to study, sleep or do anything productive along the way. The kids usually just sat quietly staring out the windows, or talking amongst themselves. It was definitely a toilsome ritual, but to their credit, our sons and the entire list of Isthmus children who endured (and still endure) the long journey to school, should feel a sense of pride and accomplishment for making it through the grueling routine.

Similarly, the school bus drivers, notably Dave Bryan and Dezi Jones deserve recognition, if not an award, for having the patience, fortitude, and professional composure to perform the duty day after day without 'killing' any of the kids. I can only imagine some of the arguments, comments, or incidents that must have taken place aboard the bus during their years of service.

In the fall of 1999, another series of blustery northwest storms materialized in Island waters. During one of those storms, in late November, an incident occurred that ultimately left me feeling baffled and confused.

November is typically a month when boating activities slow down significantly. With shortened hours of daylight, cooler weather, and the chance of stormy seas, few boaters venture out onto the ocean during the month of November. When boats do visit West End coves that time of year, the Harbor Department always takes preventive measures to try and minimize the potential for boating incidents to take place, but unfortunately the best laid plans don't always work.

It was a quiet Sunday in the third week of November. A weak weather system was passing through the southern California bight, bringing a slight chance of showers. Winds and seas were forecast to be moderate. There were about two-dozen boats scattered around the various coves, with several of those scheduled for departure. One of the boats, a forty-eight-foot powerboat moored in Fourth of July Cove was among the boats scheduled to depart.

As the day progressed, and we went about our daily work routines, there was not much thought given to potential problems. About half of the moored boats had already departed for the mainland and no new boats were arriving. By late afternoon, as the day shift completed work, I got together with our swing-shift patrolman Mark Woolery and discussed the current weather forecasts. The Coastal Marine Forecast remained relatively mild, although projected wind velocities had increased to include gusts to twenty-knots, somewhat higher than usual, but still well below advisory levels. At around five p.m., I headed for home.

Later that evening we were sitting around watching a movie when I felt a sudden gust of cool breeze on the nape of my neck. Our front windows were open and when I looked over, the drapes were billowing into the room. Maureen shuddered slightly and asked me to close the front windows. Even in the gloaming, I could see the emergence of whitecaps on the inky sea surface, and the black outline of the eucalyptus tree limbs danced lazily from the force of the gusting winds. I grimaced and realized that I should probably make a phone call down to the Harbor Office to initiate a storm response—if it was not already in progress.

A few moments later my concerns were verified when Mark Woolery called on the telephone and informed me that a Small Craft Advisory was now in effect with winds expected to increase to twenty-five-to-thirty knots out of the northwest with occasional stronger gusts. It was already blowing at those velocities in the harbor, along with an increasing two-to-three-foot swell rolling into the cove. I informed him that I would be down to the pier within a few minutes to take the necessary steps needed to prevent problems. I then instructed him to make a couple of phone calls to other patrolmen requesting more assistance. I told Maureen and the boys that I needed to go down to the harbor and help out, hoping that it would not take too long. That wish did not come true.

When I arrived at the pier, the dinghy dock was already slamming into the pilings. Only one dinghy dock was in place. Mark met me at the ramp that leads down onto the dock and we began the process of disconnecting it from the pier. Mark worked the hoist while I went down and began untying lines and relocating several small dinghy's that were tied alongside. Dave Coiner was already out on a patrol boat, assisting with other problems. Woolery and I worked together to remove the dock and move it out onto a mooring.

Having completed that task, we returned to the pier and met with Ryan Kerr-Bombard and John Rosenfeld, agreeing to head out onto the water and make sure everything was in order. I hopped into a patrol boat and headed for Fourth of July and Cherry Cove, while the others teamed together to check on the west and east side mooring areas.

It was growing increasingly rough in the cove, with the northwest winds gusting to around thirty-knots and the swells growing to two-to-four-foot. With the night sky completely obscured by a thick blanket of silvery gray clouds, no moon or stars were visible. The pervasive darkness hung heavily in the chill air. As I rounded the point leading into Fourth of July Cove, I cursed when I saw the vague outline of the vessel *Gils Toy*, a forty-eight-foot California powerboat, bobbing on its mooring along the northern wall of the cove. It was not a safe mooring to be on during adverse weather, and I was disappointed to see it still there, despite the fact that, according to our records, it was scheduled to depart that day.

Approaching the boat in the darkness, I turned on the spotlight. Flashing the light briefly across the windows of the boat to get the owners attention, I floated nearby waiting for someone to come out on deck. Gil Fuller, the lessee of the mooring and owner of the boat, opened the cabin door and poked his head out.

"Hey, Gil," I called out to him, raising my voice to be heard above the din of the wind. "In case you haven't noticed, it's getting pretty rough. This mooring is not a good place to be in these conditions. I suggest you drop the mooring and move to a better location, away from the cliffs."

His boat was rocking and pitching heavily, the bow lifting high on the face of the swells and then dropping down into the trough, with the hull swaying and rolling back and forth from the combined wind and seas. His mooring, D-9 in Fourth of July Cove, is located on the northern facing wall of the cove. It is a lovely spot when the weather is mild, but when storms develop, it is one of the worst places to be. Situated about ten-feet from the cliffs, the stern mooring weight is set into the rocks at the foot of the cliff in about eight-feet of water. The bow weight is in deeper water, about eighty-feet from the cliff, but if anything should happen to the bow line or ground tackle, the boat would swing around and immediately go aground on sharp, jagged rocks.

Gil Fuller is a regular visitor to the cove, a member of Fourth of July Yacht Club and a real nice guy. He looked down at me in my small patrol boat and stated, "I know it's getting rough, but I can't move the boat. I have my girlfriend on board, but she doesn't know how to do anything."

"Are you the only ones on board?" I asked.

"Yes. Just the two of us, and she doesn't know anything at all about boating," he told me.

That was one of the things I never quite understood about some boaters. A forty-eight-foot boat is a big responsibility and requires a certain amount of skill, knowledge and experience to operate, and generally requires more than one capable person to ensure safety. That concept applies even more during the off-season when sea conditions can change rapidly.

"Okay," I hollered out to him. "If we can get somebody to help, and then put someone onboard with you, can you move the boat to deeper water?"

"Sure, I think so, if you have someone that can help me."

"It will take a few minutes," I told him, 'But I'll be back as soon as I can. Go ahead and start your engines and have everything ready to go when I get back."

I checked in with the other patrolmen. Mark Woolery and Ryan Kerr-Bombard were still working on the water, checking on a couple of boats moored on the east side and helping them relocate to calmer waters in the shelter of the west wall. I asked for an ETA back to the dock and was told it would be about fifteen minutes. I then heard Dave Coiner call *Gils Toy* on the radio and inform him that he would be there soon to offer a hand.

A few minutes later the work skiff broke loose from the dinghy dock and I responded to try and pull it out from between the pilings before it was destroyed. In the distance I heard a frantic radio transmission. "Mayday! Mayday! We're going on the rocks!"

I recognized Gil Fuller's voice. "Can you operate the boat?" I heard Dave Coiner call back.

"No, I wrapped the mooring line in my propellers," Fuller responded frantically. The situation was obviously deteriorating rapidly, but I was involved in another response and I needed to concentrate all of my energy into saving the work skiff.

It took me about ten minutes to pull the skiff out from under the pier and get it re-secured onto a mooring. Once that was finished, I climbed back into a patrol boat and headed back out on the water, anxious to see how things were going with Fuller's boat. When I rounded the point and headed into Fourth of July Cove, I looked out and saw *Gils Toy* aground on the northern wall of the cliff. In the darkness, the boat looked incongruously out of place, seemingly resting comfortably on the rocks and appearing as if it was positioned there intentionally.

'*Oh, boy,*' I thought to myself, '*That doesn't look good.*' The winds were howling, lashing my exposed skin with salt spray and the seas churned and swirled under the keel of the patrol boat, tossing it around like a cork.

Dave Coiner was on scene in unit #1, with John Rosenfeld on board as a deckhand. I knew that the boat had only been on the rocks for a few minutes, but the rocks below the hull were bold and jagged, and it was very likely that the hull was holed. If the boat was pulled off the rocks, there was a good possibility that it would sink. On the other hand, if immediate action to pull it off was not taken quickly, the boat would undoubtedly break apart and be a total loss anyway.

Gil Fuller helped make the decision. "Help! Tow us out of here!" he bellowed. "Hurry! Please hurry! My boat is being torn apart!" We could hear the boat's hull moaning and groaning on the rocks as the wind and swell rolled it back and forth. The crunching noise of the fiberglass screeched and wailed in the darkness.

"Okay, Gil," I heard Dave Coiner call out. "But the hull might be holed already. If I can pull you off, the boat might sink once it is pulled free."

"That's okay," he called back. "At least it's better than breaking to pieces here on the rocks!"

"Alright. Go up to the bow and we'll throw you a line. Run it through the hawse pipe and drop the loop over the cleat," I heard Coiner tell him as he maneuvered around to position the boat as close as possible to the bow, while Rosenfeld prepared to heave the towline.

John Rosenfeld threw the towline out and it landed cleanly over the bow rail, a perfectly executed maneuver. Fuller reached down and picked up the towing eye, ran it through the hawse pipe and draped it over the bow cleat. "Okay!" he hollered, "It's on!"

I watched Coiner shift into gear, pulling forward until the line straightened. When the line become taught, Coiner briefly shifted into neutral to avoid an abrupt yank on the line, and then immediately shifted back into forward and put a slow, steady strain on the towline. The boat heeled slightly onto its starboard side and I watched and waited until a swell rolled under the keel. Seeing the boat lifting upward, I thought it was going to pull free, but it remained stuck.

The patrol boat—one of the Crestliner, diesel-powered units with a Volvo outdrive—surged forward and revved loudly under the strain. The stern dug into the black water and began throwing a deep furrow of bubbling white foam as the propeller spun and cavitated. The bow of *Gil's Toy* swung away from the wall about forty-five degrees, but remained stuck. Seeing that the hull was still pinned hard aground, I saw Coiner ease back on the throttle when the surge flowed back out away from the wall and the boat settled back down on the rocks. He waited until another surge began lifting the hull upward, and then applied heavy throttle once again. With that effort, the boat swung out nearly ninety degrees and slid a few feet out to seaward, but the surge dropped again and the boat stuck fast once more. On the third effort, the boat floated free and Coiner maintained a steady throttle and headed out into deeper water. There was another row of moorings directly ahead of the D-row, with extra heavy ground tackle designed to hold larger boats. I headed for one of those moorings, to stand by.

At about that time, another call for help burst out over the radio and I diverted to assist a boat on the west side of the Isthmus. Coiner and Rosenfeld continued with the rescue of *Gil's Toy.*

While I was assisting with the other boat, Coiner encountered a problem while attempting to tow the *Gil's Toy* onto the other mooring, wrapping his own propeller into a floating line. Baywatch arrive on scene and assisted. Somehow during the effort, John Rosenfeld fell from the deck of the patrol boat into the water. I overheard the situation, but was unable to respond. A couple of minutes later, I heard Coiner announce that he had cleared the line from his prop, pulled Rosenfeld back into the patrol unit and was heading for the dock to drop Rosenfeld off and pickup another deckhand.

I completed my assist with the other boat and returned to the site where Baywatch was assisting *Gil's Toy.* We could see that the bilge pumps were working constantly, and Baywatch was aboard checking the bilges. They discovered that the bilge pumps were not keeping up with the flow of water into the hull. Obviously there was hull damage and unless more aggressive steps were taken, the boat was destined to sink.

Coiner arrived back on scene with Ryan Kerr-Bombard and pulled out the salvage pump from the bow of the patrol boat and readied it to go aboard *Gil's Toy.* The patrol boat's salvage pump is a five horse-power gas-powered Briggs and Stratton with a twelve-thousand gallon per hour centrifugal pump. It is equipped with about twenty-feet of suction hose and a slightly larger length of discharge hose. They managed to get it onboard and operating, and it quickly de-watered the boat, but within a few minutes, water was once again filling the bilge and overwhelming the boat's bilge pumps.

Baywatch asked if another pump was needed. Coiner advised them that the pump placed onboard was adequate to dewater the boat, but that it would need to be run periodically unless the flow of water could be stemmed. A call was made to the mooring service crew, requesting a diver, and a short while later the dive service arrived and, despite the rough seas, dove under the hull and made an inspection.

Meanwhile, as predicted, the wind and seas were easing, and by midnight the wind and swell were back to almost normal. With no further complications in the harbor, I went home to get some sleep.

For the next several hours, the mooring service and Baywatch teamed together to make a temporary patch under the boat and stem the flow of seawater. Ryan remained on board through the night in case the pump was needed again.

Fortunately, the skilled patch-job accomplished between Baywatch and the mooring crew held through the night and by morning the boat was still afloat. With daylight and calm seas, a secondary dive and temporary hull patch was made. Later that same afternoon Vessel Assist towed the stricken boat back to the mainland where it was hauled out of the water and inspected by a marine surveyor. I realized that there would be a full investigation and a lot of paperwork and reports to complete and submit. I fully expected that the insurance investigation would rule the incident and damages an 'act of God' and that Fuller's insurance would cover the salvage costs.

It caught me totally unexpected when a few weeks later I was contacted by attorneys representing Gil Fuller's insurance company, with a lawsuit blaming us for the grounding.

For nearly a year I was involved with the legal battle between Fuller's insurance company and the insurance company for the Catalina Island Company and Two Harbors Enterprises. I was astounded that it was even being contested, considering the circumstances that led to the incident. After all, there was an unexpected storm, an 'act of God' that materialized unannounced. Then, when the storm hit, we did everything we possibly could to help get the boat out of danger. To think that his insurance company was attempting to hold us responsible for the accident was absurd.

After about a year of litigation, the insurance company for Two Harbors paid off a full claim to repair the boat. I was flabbergasted. I felt no animosity or resentment toward Gil Fuller. In fact, he had been appreciative and a true gentleman throughout the entire situation. My angst was generated from the results of the litigation, which in effect, placed blame for the incident and subsequent damages on our department. It seemed outrageous to me that the legal system could twist the facts of the incident around to place the blame for the grounding and resulting damages anywhere other than the owner of the boat. From this particular case, I can see why the aberrations that exist in the culture of our country's legal system are so widely criticized.

24. Bird Rock

IN LATE 1999, I RECEIVED a series of phone calls from a man inquiring about making a visit to Bird Rock to film a television documentary. At first I was very skeptical, but polite and cordial with the gentleman, listening to his explanation of his interest in making a film feature about the tiny little island. I knew that Bird Rock was a privately owned island—owned by a family that lives in Glendora, California—and the family had retained ownership of the Island following a court ruling that excluded it from the Wrigley purchase of Catalina.

That family, headed by Bill Chaffey and his wife Ann, and a couple of other investors, had purchased Bird Rock in 1920 for one-hundred-forty dollars.

After I had received about three phone calls from the purported filmmaker, I began to think that perhaps he was legitimate, and so I brought the subject up with Maureen. I had written his name down, and when I told her it was a man named Huell Howser, she informed me that he was indeed a legitimate filmmaker who aired a featured series known as *California's Gold*—a sequence of documentary films that focus on the 'hidden treasures' of California. I had never seen or heard of his show, but after Maureen convinced me of his credibility, I resolved to take more interest in his intent to make the film, and help him bring it to fruition.

The next time he called, we discussed details and made arrangements to work with staff members from the USC Wrigley Marine Science Center to make a physical visit to the little offshore island.

Bird Rock, White Rock, or Bird Island as it is sometimes called, is slightly more than one-point-three acres in size. Located about half a mile from the Isthmus Pier and about three hundred yards from the nearest point of land near Big Fisherman's Cove (where the Marine Science Center is located), the island is virtually barren. Volcanic in nature, the tiny island sports one small area of rocky soil that supports a patch of cactus and a cluster of the rare and endemic Malva Rosa plant (*Lavatera assurgentiflera*).

For the film shoot, Huell Howser brought five members of the Chaffey family and his cameraman, Luis Fuerte, to the Island for filming. His itinerary was to gather together at the USC facility, climb aboard a small Boston Whaler, disembark on the 'Rock' and film his documentary. Maureen went with me on a shoreboat with Huell and his group to USC, where we met with USC staff members. Following introductions, we all headed out to climb ashore onto the tiny little island.

Howser proved to be a real character. His country drawl and infectious personality quickly set the tone for a fun and interesting afternoon.

I had never set foot upon Bird Rock, despite the fact that it was only half a mile from my front door. There was never a reason, need, or desire to visit the foul smelling and desolate little domain. Home to thousands of seagulls, cormorants, pelicans, and other less prolific seabirds, along with hordes of sea lions and harbors seals, the small island is covered in guano, layer upon layer of bird droppings. Especially when the air is moist, the aroma of the guano is potent and often pungently overwhelming, and we expected to find it quite offensive. However, because it was late October and the prevailing weather exhibited the dry, low humidity conditions of fall, the guano smell was surprisingly minimal.

We were aboard two small skiffs. Maureen, Huell's cameraman and I were in one skiff, and Huell and the Chaffey family were in the other. USC staff members, Diving Safety Officer Cyd Yonkers and one of her associates operated the skiffs. As we approached the easterly lee of the little island, the skiff operators nosed the bow of the Whaler's into a small carved out enclave between submerged rocks and we all stepped ashore. All of us made it onto the rocks without mishap.

After stepping onto the slippery contours of the guano covered rocks, we carefully made our way up the steep slope onto its low, flat surface. Reaching the pinnacle, we stopped and looked around. There was not much to see, but Huell seemed to find it fascinating.

"Well" He drawled, "Would you look at that!"

Looking around, I wasn't quite sure what he was referring to, and so I said nothing. He moved a few feet, motioning Louie to follow him with the camera, and stopped before the cluster of cactus and scrawny Malva Rosa plants. "Now, what do you suppose those things are?"

I looked around at the others, and nobody offered a response, so I took the initiative. "Well, Huell, it's mostly cactus, with a small cluster of Malva Rosa."

Cyd Yonkers, who is a biology specialist from the Marine Science Center, then proceeded to explain to Huell about the unique existence of the spindly little plant clusters. "The Malva Rosa is an endemic flowering plant that is very rare and at one time was thought to exist here on Bird Rock and no other place on earth," she told him. "After finding it here, we have taken cuttings and the Catalina Island Conservancy is now culturing it back to prominence here on the Island. When it flowers, it exhibits a profusion of beautiful pink flowers, tinged with a light purple or pale crimson that are truly lovely."

"Well, can you imagine that?" said Huell as he waved Louie closer and for the effect of the camera, pointed directly at the stringy limbs of the water-starved plants. "So, these plants are found nowhere else on earth except for this tiny little Island? Don't you find that fascinating?" he asked nobody in particular. We all nodded, smiling at his enthusiasm.

For the next two hours, our little group 'explored' the island. It took about three minutes to walk the entire length of Bird Rock, but somehow, Huell Howser found dozens of fascinating little features to point out and, for the sake of the camera, identify and expound upon.

He seemed to appreciate my participation in his film making and called upon me to comment and discuss the 'incredible profusion' of fascinating findings and observations on the barren little rock. How he could consider a few clusters of cactus and scrawny plants, or an old rotting and abandoned plywood blind so fascinating was baffling to me. But Huell was obviously enraptured and his enthusiasm was contagious.

One of his plans for the filmmaking was for all of us to have lunch on the island, and so we had brought along brown bags with sandwiches, chips and drinks. About an hour into our adventure, we took time to eat lunch. There was no place to sit, without plopping down on dried bird droppings, so we all stood around munching on our lunches. Because it was dry and the aroma was minimal, the lunches were not tainted too badly by the smell, and we all managed to finish our meals.

At the end of about two hours, we waved the Whaler's back over to the loading zone and climbed back aboard the skiffs. Huell directed us to make a circumnavigation around Bird Rock so that he could film it from all sides. His running dialogue kept us all entertained.

It proved to be a fun and entertaining afternoon, and the featured special entitled 'Bird Rock' California's Gold #2004, has aired dozens of times on Huell's primary channel KCET, Los Angeles. It is also syndicated in other areas, and can be found on the internet. According to Huell, who spoke with me several times on the phone after the film was edited and aired, "The Bird Rock special was one of my favorite works of all time!"

One evening in February of 2001, assistant harbormaster Dave Coiner, who also served as captain of the dive boat *Garibaldi,* and the small semi-submersible underwater viewing boat the *Looking Glass*, got together with me to try and coordinate a nighttime viewing of spawning squid.

The *Looking Glass*, a twenty-foot long, ten-passenger semi-submersible boat was a new offering by Two Harbors Enterprises, a venture aimed toward enhancing the visitor experience and bolstering business for the company. The boat was built with a deep hull, filled with nearly a ton of concrete in the keel to hold her deep in the water, and outfitted with two large, four-by-twelve foot viewing windows that remained about six-feet below the ocean surface when underway. Two rows of bench seating ran lengthwise along the windows, affording the occupants a complete view of the underwater world. It offered people that are uncomfortable with snorkeling or diving the opportunity to experience the joys and beauty of underwater sea life without having to get wet.

Unfortunately, the operation of the *Looking Glass* was short-lived, partly because it was just too small and carried too few passengers to make a profit, and partly because the market for that type of venture just didn't seem to fit in with the overall scope of business in the Isthmus. But on that one remarkable night, the *Looking Glass* provided an experience that many residents of Two Harbors will never forget.

There was a prolific squid spawn occurring in the Isthmus at the time. Dozens of commercial squid boats had been harvesting the squid. Dave Coiner and I teamed up to prepare a set of squid lights that we suspended from the rail of the *Looking Glass*. After getting everything setup, we cruised out to the outside row of moorings shortly after dark and picked up a mooring. Turning the lights on, we sat back to wait. It didn't take long. Within minutes, darting squid appeared all around the boat. Soon after, the squid increased in numbers and volume, their presence filling the viewing windows with the spectacular display of a full-blown squid spawn. Before long, tens of thousands of spawning squid milled around the *Looking Glass*, darting around in search of a mating partner.

When the 'market squid' of Catalina spawn, the males are attracted to the females pulsating mantle, the fibrous tissue that forms the body of the small, six-to-ten-inch long cephalopod mollusks. A squid is truly a fascinating creature with three hearts, a jet propulsion system for movement, and in the males, an extraordinary reproductive organ. Endowed with a relatively enormous penis (the male squid has a penis that can be as long as the mantle and head combined—or nearly the length of their entire body) the male squid uses its gigantic organ to mate with the females. In their mating frenzy, both creatures exhibit an amazing tendency to pulsate fluctuating color patterns, changing in a chameleon like manner from a rusty brown to bright shades of reddish ochre, vibrant russet and several shades of silvery white, speckled with undulating dots and oscillating blotches of the darker shades.

Seeing the male squid darting around in frenzied eagerness to find a female, and then connecting with her (sometimes three or four males mate simultaneously with one female) was truly a fascinating and mesmerizing sight to witness. At times the squid were so abundant outside of the windows of the little sub that they filled the view with a moving, pulsating mass that was so thick that it obscured the brightness of the squid light, casting the interior of the *Looking Glass* into a spectral yellowy glow.

Adding to the hypnotic spell of the scene that was occurring just inches from our eyes, Dave was playing a taped recording of 'Through The Looking Glass', a magnificent piano arrangement by Paul Cardall that fully enraptured the viewers and was absolutely perfect music for the spawning rites.

After seeing the beginning stages of the spawn, I hopped aboard a Shoreboat and ran a shuttle service for local residents between the dock and the *Looking Glass*. Maureen and our kids were among the first to see the squid spawn, accompanied by their buddies James, Jeffrey, Justin and Nicholas. Each viewing session lasted about fifteen to twenty minutes, and it took us until nearly midnight to give everyone a chance to observe the enchanting event. We made another attempt to put together a viewing the following weekend, but as is their nature, the squid had disappeared from the cove, more than likely relocating to another less intrusive place where they could reproduce without being watched.

For us, opportunities such as that one were the types of events and real life experiences that added to our storied fascination with the Island.

The winter of 2001 proved to be another wet and stormy time. As is commonplace during an El Nino weather condition in southern California, Catalina Island was once again battered by southerly storms. I vividly recall the harrowing experience of battling near hurricane force winds and seas in the normally protected waters of Catalina Harbor on another stormy night.

On that occasion, a low pressure system spawned from the subtropics—an event that local forecasters like to refer to as the 'Pineapple Express' because of its development in the vicinity of the Hawaiian Islands—bore down on Catalina Island with a vengeance.

In its early stages, the storm built from the southeast, creating strong gusty winds that roared into Isthmus Cove and created havoc for a brief time in the anchorage and mooring fields on the 'frontside' of the Island. The harbor crew worked feverishly to minimize problems or damages to docks and floats, and for the few visiting yachtsmen moored in the cove.

Not unexpectedly, the onslaught of the storm from the southeast did not last too long, about six hours, before switching to a more southerly direction. When that change in direction occurred, Catalina Harbor began to bear the brunt of the storm. Catalina Harbor usually provides the safest and most secure mooring and anchorage areas on the entire Island. But when powerful southerlies develop, even the protected confines of that cozy little harbor can feel the vengeance of Mother Nature.

It was near dark when the effects of the storm really began to develop. Winds, which had been gusting to around thirty-knots suddenly increased to fifty-to-sixty knots. Along with the winds, a southerly wind chop of about four-feet began rolling into the narrow gap that serves as the entrance to the harbor. Along with the winds, a lashing rain began. The heavy rain, bolstered by the powerful wind, whipped into the cove, rapidly drenching everything and everyone in its path. Spawned as they were from the southern latitudes the heavy squalls began to cause problems.

When the first distress call went out, I was at home finishing an early dinner after spending several hours dealing with problems in the Isthmus. Around six-thirty p.m., I received a radio call from Cat Harbor Patrolman Ray Smith. A forty-six-foot sailboat was dragging her mooring and endangering other boats.

"I'll be out there in about ten-minutes, Ray," I informed him. "Meet me at the dock." Donning my foul weather gear, I slipped on my mud boots and hopped into my pickup truck to head out and assist.

When I passed by the old Civil War Barracks (now the Isthmus Yacht Club) and headed down the roughly quarter mile stretch of dirt road that leads to the Cat Harbor pier, it was all I could do to keep my little Datsun pickup truck on the road. Already the rains had created a quagmire of slippery mud on the red-clay road, and my pickup slid and spun erratically. Somehow I managed to keep the truck from sliding off into the adjoining fields, and when I arrived at the Cat Harbor Pier, Ray was there to meet me.

Immediately we heard another distress call. "Harbor Patrol! Harbor Patrol! Help! There's a sailboat banging into us!"

The forty-six-foot sailboat had dragged its mooring about eighty-feet and was banging into another vessel.

"We're on the way!" Ray hollered out on the radio. "Put fenders out if you can," he instructed.

Ray was at the helm and I cast off the dock lines. It was a challenge just getting off the dock; the gusting winds were so strong that the patrol boat was pinned firmly against the side of the float. I put out my right leg and pushed off as hard as I could and Ray poured the power to the engine. We just managed to clear the end of the dock and headed out into the storm.

Spindrift pummeled the boat. The raindrops were large and intense, and combined with the wind, stung our faces. We both tried to duck under the top of the console as much as possible to avoid the strongest wind gusts, but we also needed to keep a close eye out for floating debris and the numerous buoys and moorings in the back basin of the harbor.

We arrived on scene and assessed the situation. The forty-six-foot sailboat had drug its bow mooring weight and was nearly broadside along the port rail of a thirty-four-foot Catalina Sailboat. It bucked and pitched in the short, steep seas, crunching into the port-bow area of the other boat. We could see that some rail and stanchion damage had already occurred. We spoke briefly to each other, actually yelling in order to hear ourselves over the din of the storm, and concurring that we could alleviate the immediate problem if we could get a line from the bow of the sailboat to another mooring ahead of us and to our own port side.

While Ray carefully maneuvered into position along the port side of the larger boat, I hollered out to the crew of the sailboat, asking for a heavy dock line. Fortunately the crew seemed competent and one of them managed to heave me the loose end of a length of braided five-eighth rigging line. Grabbing the line just before it splashed into the water I informed Ray that I had it secured. He slowly steered toward the upwind mooring as I played-out the tailing end. I was beginning to think that the line was not long enough, when a brief lull developed and Ray left the helm to grab the pickup pole on the adjacent mooring. He walked it back to me, I secured it with a bowline to the bow hawser and we drifted back toward the sailboat until we could converse with them once again.

"Okay!" I called out. "The line is secure. Pull yourselves forward if you can."

They tried desperately to haul in the tendered line, but could not overcome the force of the persistent winds. Ray and I consulted again and agreed that we needed to try and get a towline onto the stricken vessel and pull them forward. That act required another exploit of adept maneuvering on Ray's part, and fortuitously he managed to get into position without mishap and I heaved a towing line to the crew. Pouring all of the power of the small six-cylinder engine into use, Ray slowly towed the sailboat forward until they were clear of the other boat, and secured to the second mooring. Both parties would deal with the consequences of the damage at a later date.

We were only just cleared from that incident when another distress call went out. Another boat was dragging its mooring. Applying similar techniques, we resolved that situation as well.

For the subsequent four-hours, Ray and I responded to one distress call after another as the relentless winds continued to create havoc. One of the sailboats that we were assisting wrapped its propeller in the mooring lines and requested assistance to get it cleared. In the existing conditions, diving on a wrapped prop was next to impossible, but Dave Coiner, who had joined in the response effort in Cat Harbor, informed us that he would attempt to dive on the boat and try to get it clear.

Donning his dive-gear, we picked Coiner up from his personal boat—a twenty-eight-foot trimaran—and took him to the boat in distress. As we stood by, Dave went over the side and dove beneath the stricken vessel.

It is often difficult in calm conditions to unwrap fouled mooring lines, but in the gnarly sea conditions that existed, we thought it nearly impossible. The boat was bucking and rocking up and down so severely that the rudder and prop were periodically visible. Attempting to get under a boat pitching so erratically was extremely dangerous, yet very cautiously and carefully, Coiner somehow managed to cut the boat free and we managed to secure it to another mooring. We took Coiner back to his boat to dry off, and hopefully get some rest.

A short while later we heard another distress call. "Mayday! Mayday! A boat has flipped over!"

That harrowing call came from a small powerboat moored in the back of the harbor, and when we responded and heard the details, we realized that it was Dave Coiner's boat that was in trouble. Ray turned around and headed to the shallow anchorage area.

Arriving on scene, we were shocked to see the blue bottom paint of Coiner's trimaran floating upside-down in the anchorage area. It was only about five-feet deep where the boat was capsized, a shallow-water area where vessels with shallow drafts could safely anchor. Frantically we looked around. About ten-feet forward of the capsized boat, we saw Dave Coiner in the water, dog-paddling toward us. We coasted alongside and pulled him up into our patrol boat.

Seemingly unshaken, Coiner informed us that a strong gust of wind had caught under the aumans of the boat and lifted it about thirty-feet into the air, flipping it upside down in the process. The mast snapped when it struck the muddy bottom and the boat settled back onto its anchor line, upside down. When we asked him how he had gotten out, Coiner calmly replied, "Well, I was a little confused because everything was upside-down. But I realized the easiest method of escape was the forward hatch, so I just crawled along the inside of the cabin top until I reached the forward hatch and then I swam out." Fortunately his family was not on board the boat when it flipped over.

Shortly after Coiner's incident the storm began to abate. We had a couple of other minor responses, but somewhere around two o'clock in the morning we were able to put the boat away and call it a night. The following morning the mooring crew helped 'right' the boat and Coiner began the tedious process of putting her back into shape.

In addition to the chaos on the water, the powerful storm also caused some problems onshore, breaking windows, knocking down fences, and felling several trees. That storm was one of many that left indelible marks on our memories, but it also left a lasting monument of sorts that always tends to trigger the vividness of that particular night.

One of those trees, a young eucalyptus tree near the Isthmus Yacht Club was completely uprooted and blown down. It was in an isolated location, so it was just left there lying on its side to rot away. But surprisingly, that tree managed to re-root, and send up a secondary trunk about ten-feet from the original root system. That tree is still there today, with its original trunk on the ground and a new root-ball implanted in the soil.

Life in a resort community, on an island renowned for its romantic allure, rarely has any negative connotations. Therefore, it seems to strike close to home on those rare occasions when sad things happen.

The entire Island community was shocked and saddened when the venerable James 'The Admiral' Walker passed away on August 1, 2001. Jimmy Walker left behind a legacy that is unparalleled. He was a true icon and a wonderful personality, whose influence on the Isthmus community affected every individual that knew, and admired him for who and what he was.

For some strange reason, Jim Walker decided to wear his full black leather riding attire on a motorcycle trip to Sturgis, Montana—the wildly popular annual bike ride that attracts thousands of motorcycle enthusiasts to the tiny little hamlet of Sturgis each year. While riding through Nevada, with the temperature index hovering at about one-hundred-ten degrees, Walker basically cooked himself alive.

A witness reported seeing him pull off to the shoulder of the road, lay his bike down on its side, and lie down. The witness called 911 immediately and paramedics arrived on scene within minutes. They discovered his body temperature was above one-hundred-six degrees when they found him, and although he was still breathing, all of his internal organs were in shock. They tried desperately to initiate cooling measures on his body, and transported him to the nearest hospital, but he died in route.

A week later, his Island friends put together the biggest and most impressive memorial service that has ever taken place at the Isthmus. Approximately fifty boats participated in a sea burial near Emerald Bay, followed by a touching and emotional memorial gathering at the Harbor Reef Restaurant. It was a fitting tribute to the man whose vibrant personality and admirable character left a lasting impression on every single individual that he met.

The year 2001 was also significant for one of the most sobering disasters in the history of the United States, the horrific tragedy of 9/11.

Islanders, like Americans everywhere, were shocked, saddened and bewildered by the unfolding story of the horrific attack on the World Trade Center, the Pentagon, and United Airlines Flight 93.

I was sitting at the kitchen table early that morning sipping on my ritualistic cup of Instant Folgers coffee and half-heartedly watching Channel 7 news when the first plane struck one of the Twin Towers. Hearing a sense of incredulity and concern in the announcer's voice, I focused more intently on the report. Watching the first plane approaching the Tower, it appeared to me to be a small private plane as it headed directly for the upper section of the building and crashed. I shook my head in a state of confusion, wondering how a small plane could strike a skyscraper. But as the shocking reality of the news report grew, I realized that there was much more to the event than I originally perceived. I rushed into the bedroom and gave Maureen, who was still asleep, a gentle shake.

"Hey," I said to her quietly but urgently, "You'd better come out here. There's something horrible happening in New York City."

She jumped out of bed, grabbed her robe and hurried with me out to the living room. We arrived back in front of the television set just as the second plane banked around and then took direct aim at the second Tower. When it struck and burst into flames, she blurted out an audible "Oh, my God!"

We turned and looked at each other, shock and disbelief infusing our souls. Without taking our eyes from the television screen, we moved together and held tightly onto one another. In horror we listened to the reports, and then gasped again when the streaming video footage of the Pentagon attack came on the screen. Like the rest of the nation, we could not believe what was happening. Somehow, we managed to get things together to send the kids off to school, remaining tuned in to the news coverage.

Like Americans everywhere, the remainder of that fateful day and the events that unfolded, left us feeling hollow, confused and angry. It set the stage for a gradual change in our perceptions of life. Sadly, our new perceptions instilled an awareness that there are evil forces in the world that have the sole purpose of engaging acts of terrorism without regard for human life or the sanctity of man. Realizing that there are regions in the world where heinous acts of that type are commonplace brings little solace. In the aftermath of the tragedy, we can only hope that the forces of good will outlast and overcome the forces of evil.

25. Mother Nature Unleashed

AFTER NINETEEN EMBATTLED YEARS OF discussions, negotiations and public hearings, the long term Master Lease for State tideland waters at Catalina Island was finally approved and went into effect in November of 2001. As anticipated, private ownership of State Submerged Lands (moorings) was ruled impermissible and all moorings previously considered privately owned reverted to a Sublease basis. In effect, those individuals that purchased moorings through the years were 'grandfathered' into the newly enacted twenty-year Master Lease with the Santa Catalina Island Company and Catalina Island Conservancy, to retain the use of their mooring site on a one-year renewable sublease arrangement.

For individuals that owned the moorings under the provisions of the previous State Lands Lease, it was a bittersweet and somewhat uneventful occasion. The battle over ownership during the previous nineteen years had diminished to a whisper as the previous mooring owners resigned themselves to the realization that the State Lands Commission was not going to alter their decision, and except for an ongoing silent resentment for a few of the owners, the transition from ownership to Sublease rights was nothing more than a paperwork change in their annual mooring renewal forms.

For me, the whole process had been an interesting, challenging, and eye-opening experience. The interactions with the myriad of players involved in the process left me with an array of friendships that would continue on the Island. I feel good to have developed solid relationships with some of the key players in the coalition of 'mooring owners' that fought the battle with State Lands to retain ownership. Their passion for the Island never ceased to amaze me, and getting to know the individuals involved with the 'ownership' issue through the years gave me an appreciation for all that they brought to the Island community.

Additionally, my involvement, with California State Lands officials, particularly Submerged Lands Managers Alan Scott and Jane Smith, Doug Bombard, Ron Doutt, and other Island Company officials, Doug Probst, Rose Ellen Gardiner, Ann Muscat and other representatives of the Catalina Conservancy, and various members of the many public agencies involved in the long and drawn-out process, helped me grow as a businessman and a professional. I learned a lot along the way and also gained insight into how complicated and frustrating working with governmental agencies and other public entities can be.

Through it all, I also appreciated the assistance and support of several key employees of Doug Bombard Enterprises and later, Two Harbors Enterprises; notably Michelle Phelps, John Phelps, Ann Luchau, Char D'Amore, Wendy Adams, Megan Poulsen, Linda Buchanan, Stacy

Straub, Doug and Jamie Owen, Kathleen Mitchell, Dave Coiner, Doug Millard, Steve Mercadante, and others who helped me to keep things running smoothly and work through the mountainous volumes of paperwork and internal processing throughout the nearly two-decades of dealing with the Submerged Lands issues. Without all of their help and support, I know that my involvement in the process would have been even more difficult and problematic.

It was a relief to finally put the issues of our State Lands Lease to rest, although on a personal level, I still believe that the whole concept of mooring ownership is not necessarily a bad thing, and that all of the previous mooring owners truly did get screwed over by the State. When the decision to eliminate private ownership went into effect, I sympathized with the mooring owners, but was glad to finally be able to move forward without the shadow of an unresolved Master Lease hanging over our heads.

While boating is generally considered a relatively safe and passive recreational pursuit, there are times when inherent dangers can result in unexpected damages or injuries. During my years on the Island there were numerous incidents that occurred, and like any other form of activity, they usually occur when least expected.

An example of things that can, and did happen, transpired on a stormy day in the late winter of 2003. During that moderate weather occurrence, I was at work and dealing with the effects of a mild northeaster that blew in during the night on a Friday.

There were about forty boats in the harbor on that particular Friday, despite the forecasted northeast condition. The winds began at around midnight, gusting into Isthmus Cove at about twenty knots. We had anticipated the potential for winds, and so the dinghy docks had been removed, the ramp on the main float lifted, and all boats moored bow to seaward as a precaution. By around two a.m. the winds had increased to around twenty-five knots, accompanied by short, steep seas of about two-to-four-feet. It was lumpy and grumpy in the cove, but not really dangerous.

I awoke around five-thirty a.m. as usual, and immediately looked out my front window into the cove. In the muted glare of early morning, I could see that white caps were covering the entire bay and a two-to-three-foot northeast swell was thumping onto the beach. I looked around searching for problems, but all appeared to be in order. I went about fixing a cup of coffee and a bowl of cereal before heading to work.

When I arrived at the Harbor Office at around six-fifteen, there were two people sleeping on the Harbor Office floor. They stirred when I opened the door and looked up at me sleepily.

"Good morning," I greeted them, with a questioning tone.

"Oh, Hi," the male responded. He was a man in his early twenties bundled into a sleeping bag and lying alongside a female, who appeared to be even younger.

I waited for an explanation.

The man sat up, rubbing sleep from his eyes. "Oh, we're sorry. We were ashore last night and when we got back here to the pier, our friends that we came to the Island with had already returned to their boat. There was nobody around to get a ride from, and so we decided to wait here until somebody showed up."

I smiled and nodded my head. "That's okay," I told him. "Sorry to have woken you up so early, but I do need to get to work and check things out. Feel free to stay here for a while longer, but I'll need a little space cleared to be able to reach the radio and my desk."

The young lady sat up as well, bundling her sleeping bag tightly around her shoulders. "Oh, we're sorry," she apologized, "We'll get out of here and out of your way."

"No, seriously," I told them. "You're certainly welcome to stay. I just need a little space to get started with my morning routine."

They both stood, looking around the interior of the small building.

"Please," I offered them, "Feel comfortable to sit, or even lie down again if you'd like. I just need this area by the phones and radio. Go ahead and make yourselves comfortable."

It was quite obvious that they were both awake by then, so I asked them what boat they were on, and in which cove. They informed me that their friend's boat was moored in Cherry Cove and that they had all gone in to the Harbor Reef Restaurant for dinner and cocktails the night before. Their friends decided to go back to the boat early, and the two of them stayed and closed the bar. After that they went for a walk to Cat Harbor, and when they returned, everything on shore was buttoned up and nobody was around. They checked the office door, finding it unlocked (which it usually was), and so they settled down to wait for someone to show up and simply fell asleep.

About that time a slightly stronger gust of wind rattled the windows and shook the walls of the office. They looked out, surprised to see the choppy conditions in the cove.

"Wow!" he blurted. "It's really rough! When did that happen?"

Chuckling, I replied, "It started blowing in around midnight. It's lumpy, but not too bad. It can get a lot worse than this."

"It must have started blowing right around the time we got here," he informed me. "I think it was right around midnight when we came into the office."

At that moment, the radio hummed loudly, a prolonged burst of static filling the quiet room, and then a voice boomed out, "Isthmus Harbor Patrol!"

I reached for the radio, turning the volume down before keying the microphone. "This is the Isthmus Harbor Patrol. How can we help you?"

A pause filled the air and then the radio boomed out again, "Isthmus Harbor Patrol. We're on a mooring here in the Isthmus and it's really rough. We want to drop the mooring and find a calmer place to moor."

"Okay," I replied, "Do you plan to head around to Cat Harbor?"

"We don't know," the caller responded. "Is there any other place to go that might be calmer, like Cherry Cove or Avalon?"

"No," I informed him. "Cherry Cove will definitely not be any better. I'm not sure about Avalon. We have not heard from them yet this morning, but it's more than likely just as rough, if not rougher there. The only real protected cove in this type of condition is Catalina Harbor, on the backside of the Island."

It was quiet for a few moments and then he asked, "How far is it to Cat Harbor?

"Fourteen miles," I informed him. "Seven miles to the West End, and then seven miles back."

Another longer pause developed, and then the voice came back on the air, "Okay. We're going to head around to Cat Harbor. Can you or someone come out and standby while we drop the mooring? I'm not sure we can get loose from here without help."

"Sure," I informed him. "But you'll have to give me a few minutes. I'm in the office and I'll need to go out and get a Patrol Boat."

"That's okay," he answered. "It will take us about fifteen minutes to get everything ready here on the boat."

"Alright," I advised him. "Give me a call on the radio when you're ready."

The young couple stepped out of their sleeping bags and rolled them into a ball. "Sorry to be keeping you from your duties," the man told me. "We're going to go see if we can get a cup of coffee."

"It's really not a problem," I told them. "Besides, I don't think the restaurant is open yet."

"That's okay," the young woman spoke quietly. "We need to use the bathroom anyway. Can we bring you a cup back when the restaurant does open up?"

"Oh, thanks, but I've already had my coffee this morning. But if you'd like, I can take you out to your boat when you return, if you're ready to head out."

"No, thanks," she responded. I think we'd rather stay ashore and wait until our friends come in. It looks pretty rough out there."

They departed and I flipped the radio over to Weather-1 to listen to the morning update. It was very similar to the existing forecast, and by experience, I figured that the winds would die-down sometime right around noon, if not before. At about that time, Cari Dunlop opened the office door and entered.

Cari was one of our patrol crew. She had started out working in the restaurant and Visitor Services office, but transferred into the harbor after a year or two on the Island. Cari was in her early twenties and showed a great interest in learning a career working on the water. When I tested her, both with written questions and on a boat to demonstrate her operational skills, she showed great promise and we gave her the opportunity to join the crew. Her upbeat personality and eagerness to learn quickly made her one of the crew favorites.

"Good morning, Cari," I greeted her.

"Hi, O.D."

O.D. was my nickname in the harbor. Kathy King had stamped the nickname on me one year when she was working in the Harbor Department and there were five other Doug's working for the company; Doug Bombard, Doug Owen, Doug Gould, Doug Houghton, and Doug Baca. Kathy decided that she would use my initials to create an easy moniker, but she also decided that D.O. (Doug Oudin) didn't have a very nice ring to it, and so she reversed the letters to make it O.D. Of course, someone else interjected that the initials O.D. actually stood for overdose. Whichever the choice, the nickname stuck, and stayed with me through the years.

With Cari in the office, we formulated a plan to get out on the water and get started with our morning. The work skiff was tethered on its offshore line on the side of the main float, so we lowered the ramp and hopped down into the skiff. I dropped her at a Patrol Boat, returned to the dock and waited for her to come pick me up.

Almost immediately, the radio rang out and the gentleman who had called earlier informed us that he was ready to drop his mooring. With Cari at the helm, we headed over and stood by while they dropped the mooring, advising them to drop the line 'away from the wind' first. The boat was a thirty-six-foot Catalina sailboat, and the crew appeared to be competent. They cast off without any problem and motored slowly out of the mooring area, their boat pitching and bucking in the short, steep swells. Watching them motor away, Cari began cruising up and down the mooring rows, looking for any problems on the moored boats. All seemed in order, so we cruised over into Fourth of July and Cherry Cove to look things over there as well. Everything seemed to be holding together in all coves, so we headed back to the dock.

At the dock, we discovered Cari's good friend Jack Laisure standing on the end of the pier. I dropped Cari off so that she could go up and talk with him. At about that time, another boat, a twenty-eight-foot sailboat, was cruising slowly down the fairway, heading toward the pier. I motored out toward them and asked if they needed any help. They informed me that they were just going to drop a couple of passengers off at the dock.

I told them that would be fine, but to be very careful because it was quite rough alongside the dock. As they motored slowly forward, I watched their boat rolling and pitching in the swells.

When the boat neared the dock, Cari and Jack walked down the ramp and stood-by in case they required any assistance. I was standing off in the patrol boat watching the boat make its approach when a radio call was transmitted requesting a shoreboat ride. Since the boat requesting a ride was on a nearby mooring, I headed in its direction to transport the passengers to the dock.

After cautiously picking up two people from their boat, I headed back to drop them off. About fifty-yards from the float I heard a loud yell, followed by a scream. Looking toward the main float, I saw Jack and Cari merge together rather frantically and the sailboat that was bobbing nearby began spinning wildly away from the dock. From my vantage point I could not tell what was happening, but judging from the movements and reactions of Jack and Cari, it appeared that there was a problem of some sort. I slid into the main float and helped the two passengers climb off the boat and onto the dock.

At the same time, the sailboat continued to move erratically, seemingly out of control and heading beyond the end of the main float and dangerously close to the surf line.

Cari was standing with Jack, intently focused on wrapping a white cloth around his bloody hand, which he held stiffly in front of him. I hesitated briefly, recognizing that there was a problem but also seeing the sailboat continuing forward into dangerously shallow water. At that moment a slightly larger swell rolled under my keel and I watched helplessly as the swell lifted the sailboat, broached it sideways, and propelled it toward the beach.

I could hear voices yelling and saw frantic movement along its decks. I was torn between a choice of heading for the dock or trying to assist the sailboat heading toward the beach. At that moment a second large swell rolled under my keel, lifted the sailboat onto its crest and pushed it rapidly forward and into the breaking surf. I heard yelling come from the boat and several people jumped up onto the deck as the boat rolled onto the beach, her keel stuck fast to the sandy bottom. Recognizing the potential for a worsening situation, I quickly maneuvered into position to try and get a towline onto the boat.

Several swells crested and crashed onto the hull of the stricken sailboat, the spray sending sheets of foamy white water over the decks. Keeping the bow of my patrol boat pointed into the incoming swells, I allowed the winds to push me back toward the surf line. When I was within shouting distance, I called out, "Get someone onto the bow and I'll try to heave you a towline!"

I watched as a male individual crawled forward toward the bow of the sailboat, using the safety rails and mast for support. When he was at the bow, I instructed him, "I'll throw you a line. Try and put the loop onto your bow cleat."

He nodded and I reared back to heave the line toward him. It was a tricky act, trying to keep the bow of my boat into the wind and swell, and at the same time leaving the helm in order to throw them a towline. I timed my heave with the surge of a cresting wave and threw the line. My towline fell short. Frustrated, I rapidly curled the towline back onto my boat and prepared for another toss. Again it fell short.

Recognizing that it would be extremely difficult to throw the line onto the boat without risking my patrol boat getting caught by a breaking wave, I called out to the man again, "Do you have a boathook?"

He looked back toward the stern. "Yes!" he hollered back. Then turning to one of the other passengers that were clinging to the rails, he yelled to nobody in particular, "Get me the boathook!"

I waited while the aluminum pole with a plastic, hook-shaped tip was passed up to the man kneeling on the bow. Once he had it in his hands, I instructed him, "I'll throw you my towline. The line floats and I'll try to get it close enough so that you can reach it with your boathook."

Another larger swell broke just beyond the keel of my boat and knocked the man off his feet as the wave crashed onto the port side of the grounded sailboat. "You okay?" I hollered out.

Shaking the saltwater from his drenched body, he shook his head up and down as he climbed back up onto his hands and knees, still clutching the boathook in one hand.

I repositioned the patrol boat and prepared for another toss of the line. Backing as close as I could to the breaking surf, I heaved the line as high and far as possible. It almost reached the bow of the boat, but fell short. Moving back to the helm, I put the boat into slow forward and held it in position and allowed the wind and swells to push me slowly toward shore. Keeping one eye on the incoming swells and the other on the sailboat, I drifted back until the towline floated close to the bow of the beached boat. Seeing another larger swell developing, I was just ready to throttle forward to avoid being caught in the break of the wave, when I saw the man reach the loop on the end of my towline with the boathook. Taking a deep breath as the patrol boat rose to the top of the crest, I was certain that my boat was going to get tossed into the breaking surf, but the swell rolled under my keel and broke just a few feet behind my stern. I breathed a big sigh of relief and watched as the man dropped the line onto a cleat just before the breaking wave struck his boat.

I throttled forward, trying to get the line taught but not allowing it to yank too severely. When I looked back again at the sailboat, I saw that the man on the bow was once again knocked to the deck and this time he was not climbing back up as quickly. Also, I noticed that the other three people on board the boat had jumped into the surf and waded ashore. They were calling out to the man on the bow and he was waving to them as if saying, 'I'm okay'.

When my towline became taught, I eased forward on the throttle, keeping a steady strain on the beached vessel. The boat had flopped over onto its starboard side with the keel and rudder exposed to the cool morning air. Realizing that it was not about to budge while it lay on its starboard side, I waited and watched for another incoming swell to roll it back to port. Three waves later, the boat rocked back to port and I poured on the power, attempting to pull the boat free. It moved a little, the bow swinging a few feet outward, but the swell rolled back out under its keel and the boat stuck fast once again. Twice more I timed the incoming swell while applying power, dragging the boat into slightly deeper water each time, and then on the third effort, the bow swung rapidly into the swell, the boat righted itself and, as I held a steady pull, the sailboat knifed through the next incoming wave and bobbed up and down as it floated behind me into deeper water.

After successfully pulling the boat off the beach without any visible damages (other than a little scraped-off bottom paint), I towed it slowly to a mooring. The man on the bow handled the mooring lines adroitly and we had it secured. I then informed him to go below and check the bilges. After a few minutes he returned to the deck and told me the bilges were dry.

Pulling alongside, I asked if he was okay.

"Yeah," he informed me a little hesitantly. "I think I'm fine. A little shook-up, but other than being soaking wet and cold, I think I'm alright."

"Do you want to go ashore?" I asked him.

"No. Not yet," he responded. "I think I'll change clothes first, if I have dry clothes, and check things out down below. But if you could come back in about twenty-minutes, I would like to go ashore then and see how everyone else is."

I assured him I would return in a while and headed for the dock to see what had happened with Cari and Jack.

Upon reaching the dock I was met by harbor patrolmen Ryan Kerr-Bombard and Doug Millard, who had arrived while I was dealing with the beached sailboat. They informed me that Cari was in the Harbor Office waiting for Baywatch to arrive and attend to Jack's injury. Turning the boat over to Millard and Kerr, I went up to the Harbor Office. Cari and Jack were seated, a concerned expression on Cari's face.

"So what happened?" I asked, as I looked down at a blood-soaked white t-shirt that was wrapped around Jack's hand.

"When the boat approached the dock, it got caught in a swell and surged forward. Jack tried to reach out and fend-off and his hand got caught between the bowsprit and the landing post on the main float. It tore off his finger. I have it here in a baggy," Cari told me, holding up the bloody stump of a finger inside of a clear plastic bag.

At about that moment, Baywatch entered the office and looked down at Jack's hand. I can't recall which Baywatch guys responded, but I think it was Matt Lutton and Kevin Marble. They immediately took over the first aid treatment, un-wrapped the t-shirt and then re-wrapped it with gauze and ice. They then made the necessary phone calls and arranged for transportation to Avalon Hospital and then a mainland trauma center. Unfortunately, doctors on the mainland were unable to re-attach the finger and Jack wound up with a stump where his finger used to be.

Not long after that incident, and while Baywatch was transporting Jack to the hospital, another distress call came in from Cherry Cove. A man was reportedly injured in a dinghy. Patrolmen Millard and Kerr responded and discovered a man lying prone and apparently unresponsive in an inflatable dinghy.

The dinghy was tethered to the stern of a sailboat moored in the cove and there was a woman on deck who informed them that the man had slipped and fallen from the deck of their boat while trying to secure the dinghy to the stern.

Assessing the situation, the two patrolmen discovered that the man was cut and bruised, with multiple minor contusions to arms, leg and shoulders, but otherwise seemed to be okay. They assisted him into their patrol boat, picked his wife up from their boat, and transported both back to the Isthmus dock to await medical aid.

Yet a third injury occurred that same morning when a visiting boater stepped down into an open deck hatch, breaking a bone in his leg. He too received medical treatment from Baywatch Isthmus and was later transported to Avalon Hospital, about twelve miles away by boat.

Having three injuries of varying levels of severity occur during one relatively mild storm was somewhat unusual, but it was one of those episodes that just go to show how strangely fickle the nautical tendrils of fate can be, regardless of the severity of storms.

26. A Big Birthday

WHILE 2003 WAS A SOMEWHAT uneventful year in some respects it was a rather momentous occasion for my darling little wife. Maureen turned fifty that year, and as she often likes to do, she turned her half-century celebration into a month-long event.

For starters, my family initiated the extended birthday celebration with a spirited party on the mainland at the home of good friends Ralph and Betsey Woodhouse. My sisters Sheri and Vicki and my brothers Dave, Mark and John all pitched-in to help make the birthday bash a rousing success. Using a theme of 'Back to the Fifties', we all thoroughly enjoyed the first of her celebrations, drinking, dancing and laughing away a long and memorable weekend.

A few days later, after returning to the Island, we surprised the 'birthday girl' with another birthday party, this one for Island friends, and a surprise visit from her sister Barbara, from Grants Pass, Oregon, and brother James, from Milton Washington.

To add even more flare and hoopla to the 'turning of the half-century mark', I helped to organize a two-week vacation getaway with Maureen's brother Kevin Ash and his bride-to-be, Janet, to the exotic paradise of Costa Rica.

In Costa Rica, we enjoyed the hospitality of Randy and Brenda Bombard at their beachside resort in Nosara, visited the tropical rainforest of Monte Verde, experienced a Zip Line tour at the top of a jungle canopy near the continental divide, toured the countryside in our rented car, and shared a million laughs and great times. I'm not sure if that was the first year that Maureen turned her birthday observance into a month long event, but it certainly wasn't the last. It seems to be a habit now just about every March.

Whenever I left the Island for more than a couple of days, I always needed to find someone to cover my commitment to submitting a weekly article for the Catalina Islander Newspaper.

Since the day I started writing the weekly column 'Between Two Harbors', in the summer of 1989, I did my very best to never miss a deadline. The deadline for the article was Monday mornings (with a little leeway if necessary). It wasn't always easy to find the time, the material, and the self-discipline to put together a seven-hundred to seven-hundred-fifty word article about the happenings and events in Two Harbors, but I committed to original publisher Don Haney to 'meet the deadline', and then followed through with at least another half-dozen other publishers and editors of the weekly Island newspaper for more than twenty years.

During those times when I was gone from the Island on vacations, I called upon the writing expertise of good friends Doug Owen, Steve Whittington, Scott Panzer, and on at least one occasion, my wife Maureen, to fill-in for me. Steve Whittington was by far the most consistent 'ghost writer' that I called upon, filling in for me on dozens of occasions through the years. It was he that sat in for me during our Costa Rica trip.

One afternoon in early September of 2003, an incident occurred with a boat picking up a mooring that merits a brief recounting. It involves a shark.

It was a Saturday afternoon and a glorious day on the water. The sun was shining brightly and a faint whisper of afternoon breeze rippled the calm surface of Isthmus Cove. It was an active weekend for Island boaters with most coves near mooring capacity.

A late arriving sailboat called in on the radio requesting a mooring in Fourth of July or Cherry Cove, but both of those coves were full. The boat was offered a mooring on the H-Row, the outer row in Isthmus Cove, and although it was not their first choice, the visitors were pleased to learn that at least there was still a mooring available.

Patrolman Steve Mercadante, who was working the west side of the Isthmus, responded to the mooring request and gave the arriving sailboat the mooring assignment over the radio. He was preoccupied assisting another vessel and advised the boat to go ahead and pick up the mooring, and he would get with them shortly.

A few minutes later a rather frantic call rang out on the radio, "Isthmus Harbor Patrol, Isthmus Harbor Patrol, there's a shark on our mooring!"

I was operating a shoreboat at the time and I shook my head quizzically when I heard the radio transmission. One of my passengers was talking with me as we motored toward his boat and I was not sure if I heard the call clearly. Glancing down at the radio, I waited for a response.

Steve called back on the radio, trying to clarify what was heard, "Vessel calling, can you repeat your transmission?"

"Yes, Isthmus Harbor. You assigned us a mooring, H-5, and there's a shark on our mooring."

A long pause ensued, and then Steve responded. "I'll be right there."

Curious and baffled by the connotations of the radio call, I turned to the man riding on the shoreboat with me and asked if he had heard the call. When he concurred, I informed him that I was going to head over to the mooring in question and see what was going on. He readily agreed to go check it out with me.

I diverted the shoreboat toward the H-Row and arrived at about the same time that Steve Mercadante arrived in his patrol boat. The sailboat that had been assigned to the mooring was standing off about thirty yards to seaward of the mooring with all of its passengers standing on deck.

Mercadante cruised slowly over to the mooring, looking down into the water as he made the approach. When he reached the floating pickup pole, he stepped up onto the bow of his boat and looked deeper into the water. He reached up and scratched his head, then turned toward me and lifted both hands upward, the universal gesture of 'what's up?'

I tilted my head to the side, questioning his reaction. We were close enough to communicate verbally, although I could not see anything from my vantage point.

"So, what's going on?" I asked him.

There's a shark on the pickup pole," he informed me rather nonchalantly.

Befuddled by his comment, I maneuvered closer to the mooring wand and looked down into the water. Sure enough, I could see the white underside and the dark blue/gray back of what appeared to be a five-to-six-foot blue shark, seemingly clinging to the submerged end of the pickup pole.

About that time, the *Sandpiper*, one of the mooring service boats arrived on scene. Captain Dan Deinlein and his deckhand Jamie Nelson had also heard the radio call and responded to the scene. Recognizing that the situation was mooring related, Mercadante called out to Deinlein, "Dan, do you guys want to deal with this one?"

"Sure," Dan told him, while maneuvering the *Sandpiper* into position so that he could back his low aft deck close enough to reach the mooring wand. Once he was close enough to reach the pole, Jamie reached out with gloved hands and slowly pulled the wand up out of the water. When the approximately six-foot long pickup pole line cleared the water, the shimmering sides of the shark broke through the surface.

It was definitely alive, squirming eel-like as Jamie pulled it up over the stern and onto the deck of the mooring boat.

A small flotilla of other boats had arrived nearby, all having heard the radio call or seen the commotion from nearby boats.

Dan jumped down from the helm and went aft to assist Jamie in dealing with the writhing shark. Fascinated, we all watched as Jamie and Dan untangled the shark from the mooring line, cut away some strands of monofilament fishing line, and then rather ceremoniously picked the shark up by the tail and tossed it back into the water. Momentarily stunned, the shark floated atop the surface for a moment or two, and then flipped its long tail fin and slowly swam away. A muted cheer went out on the warm afternoon air from the numerous people watching. Dan turned toward the waiting sailboat and gave them a 'thumbs up' signal, indicating that they were all clear to go ahead and pickup the mooring.

More than likely the shark had been hooked by a fisherman on a nearby boat and became entangle while the angler was fighting the fish, or it may have been hooked somewhere else and the fishing line just tangled in the mooring lines as it swam near. Whatever the cause, that little episode was a first for me, and for all others involved.

As odd as that episode was, yet another incident involving a live animal caused quite a stir for a group of folks aboard a powerboat moored near Little Fisherman's Cove that same afternoon.

That boat, a thirty-six-foot power vessel called in on the VHF radio to report that a rattlesnake had swam out to their boat and climbed inside one of their aft deck cabinets. I was in a patrol boat at the time and closest to the vessel in question, so I cruised over to their location to look into the matter.

Upon arrival, I tied my patrol boat alongside their boat and climbed aboard. They explained how they had watched the snake swim out toward their boat, slither up onto the swim step and then snake its way across the deck and into a small side compartment on the port side of their cockpit. I asked them for a boathook so that I could take a look.

Handing me the boathook, I cautiously reached out and used the end of the hook to slide open the compartment. At first I could not see anything, but on closer inspection, coiled tightly in the back corner of the storage compartment, I could see the diamond-patterned skin of a medium sized rattlesnake pulsating its scaly reptilian torso and shaking the six or seven 'buttons' at the tip of its tail.

I turned to the people standing on the other side of the cockpit and commented, "You're right, it is a rattlesnake. As a precaution, you all might want to go into the main cabin and close the door."

Having said that, all except one man who appeared to be the owner of the vessel, went into the cabin, and I climbed back over the rail and reached down to my VHF radio. Keying the microphone, I called for Steve Mercadante to see if he was available to help. A short time later, as I sat on the rail cap and kept a close eye on the snake, Steve pulled alongside and climbed aboard.

Looking the situation over, he asked the captain of the boat if he had a Gunnysack, or some similar bag or container. Unable to provide a sack of any sort, the owner of the boat asked if a five-gallon bucket would be of any help. Conferring briefly with Steve, we devised a possible plan of attack to remove the snake from its hiding place.

While Steve coaxed the snake gently with the tip of the boathook, I gingerly placed the five-gallon bucket in position at the edge of the small fiberglass compartment. After a few moments of prodding and coaxing, the snake uncoiled slightly and slithered onto the opening edge of the bucket. However, it seemed to recognize the trap that was awaiting and rapidly curled back up into the corner. Twice it lashed out with its bared fangs, striking the metallic end of the boathook. Quite obviously the snake was in an aggressive, defensive posturing mode. Again, Steve prodded and coaxed, and on his second effort, the snake unfolded and curled into the sides of the bucket.

Adroitly, Steve then reached out with the end of the boathook, slid the hook portion into the handle of the bucket and carefully lifted the bucket a foot or two off the ground and swung it toward the stern of the boat. Once it was clear of the aft combing and swung out over the sweep of the swim step, Steve lowered the bucket into the water and tilted it sideways.

With a sigh of relief from all those inside of the main cabin, and from Steve and I as well, we watched as the snake swam rather rapidly (almost glided) across the surface of the water until it reached the edge of the rocky shoreline and disappeared between the dark lava rocks that form the topography of the reef at Little Fisherman's Cove.

In the spring of 2004, the Catalina White Seabass Program that we had started about ten-years prior really began to show results. By the end of that year, we had released more than seventy-five-thousand juvenile fish back into the wild, a significant milestone for the program.

Additionally, scientists and marine biologists involved with the restoration effort reported the successful recovery of several adult hatchery-raised fish. Working with Hubbs/Sea World President Don Kent, marine biologists Mark Drawbridge, Dr. Michael Domier and other staff members from the Carl J. Hubbard Hatchery in Carlsbad, California, the Catalina program had moved into a preeminent position in the restoration effort.

To bring further support and awareness to the recovery program, I worked with officials from Hubbs/Sea World, Western Outdoor Newspapers (WON), United Anglers (UA), and others involved in the restoration effort to organize the first annual Catalina Island White Seabass Tournament in May of 2004. WON editor Pat McDonnell brought tournament organizer Kit McNear and United Anglers President Tom Raftigan to the Island for preliminary meetings to design and develop the tournament, and their efforts, along with the support of corporate sponsors and employees of Two Harbors Enterprises, helped make the tournament a huge success.

Not only did the tournament bring increased visibility and awareness to the program, but it also helped the scientific research aspect of the restoration effort by spreading the word to anglers about their ability to help support the project by donating the heads of legal-sized white seabass in order to gather data for the program.

In that first tournament, several dozen white seabass were landed and earned prize monies of over thirty-thousand-dollars for participating anglers. Island fishermen Bob Butte, Mark 'Pooey' Bray, Al Berry, and Chris Spiros had the distinction of being the second-place winners, weighing-in a twenty-seven pound white seabass that earned them a nice cash award plus several valuable prizes.

Later that same year, renowned artist and sportsman Guy Harvey visited Two Harbors to put together a featured television series on the Outdoor Life Network (OLN) channel, entitled *Portraits From the Deep; The Catalina Island White Seabass Program.*

Catalina program manager Posh Gardiner and I worked with Harvey and his film crew for a full day in Catalina Harbor, assisting his team in underwater filming of the release of approximately seven-thousand juvenile white seabass, as well as taking video footage of the thirty or more mature white seabass that were being held in the Cat Harbor pens as broodstock for the Carlsbad Hatchery. It was a real pleasure to work with Guy Harvey and his crew, and the film series went a long way toward furthering awareness of and support for the restoration effort.

During the ensuing years, until my retirement in 2010, the Catalina Seabass Fund successfully raised and released more than one-hundred-thirty-thousand juvenile seabass into Island waters. Current analysis of the seabass fishery shows a marked improvement since the program began in 1995, and white seabass fishing around the Island is better than it's been since the early sixties.

With an El Nino condition in evidence along the coast of California during the summer of 2004, Island fishing excelled. The early summer saw an outstanding white seabass bite develop, with Island anglers reaping the benefits.

For me it was a really great summer of fishing, not only because I landed several hefty white seabass, yellowtail, and even a few tuna later in the season, but also because I was able to fish with my 'three' sons and watch each of them catch some impressive fish. Both Trevor and Troy, and my 'third son', Logan Gardiner, (Troy's best friend), fished with me on numerous occasions that spring and we all landed some impressive white seabass ranging from twenty-five to forty-five pounds. Later in the summer, when the yellowtail action improved, we hooked and landed dozens of feisty 'tail's, ranging from fifteen to over thirty pounds. One of our fishing trips was particularly inspiring for me as a father.

Troy and I were out fishing for yellowtail at Eagle Reef, near Emerald Bay. We were slow trolling live mackerel on a bright, sunshiny afternoon. Action was a little slow, with only a couple of calico bass and medium sized barracuda hooked and released. At about the time we ran out of bait and were ready to head for home, we made a final pass near the red navigational buoy that marks the northeastern boundary of the reef.

Gazing down into the shimmering blue water near the buoy, Troy called out to me and pointed. "Dad! There's a big school of yellowtail!"

Looking in the direction he was pointing, I did not see anything. I told him so.

"They are about ten-feet down, and it's a big school. There must be fifty or more!" he told me excitedly.

I turned the wheel and made a wide circle, passing over the edge of the kelp line that marks the eastern boundary of the reef. Troy climbed up onto the bow and stood atop the forward cabin, gazing intently into the depths with his left hand raised to his brow to try and shield the glow from the sun and glare.

"There!" he shouted, pointing a few degrees to starboard. "There's the school!"

I looked in the direction he was pointing, not seeing anything at first, but then spotting the distinctive bright yellow fin of a tailing yellowtail. I maintained the course I was on, so as not to run directly over the top of the schooling fish, but close enough that I could allow our baits to drag over the slowly swimming fish.

Eagerly we watched our lines glide directly across the surface where we had seen the fish, but nothing happened. I swung the bow around and made another circle over the school. We saw them teeming again but there was no action.

For the next half-hour, or so, we tried to entice the fish to take our bait, to no avail. The fish simply did not seem interested in feeding. As frustrating as it can be, there are times when fish just will not go after a fisherman's offering.

"Let's go get Trevor and have him bring his spear gun!" Troy suggested.

"Do you know where he is?" I asked.

"Yeah, he's at USC" (referring to the Marine Science Center), he told me. "I'll give him a call." Troy pulled out his cell phone and Trevor answered right away. Excitedly explaining what we had seen, Troy spoke with Trevor for a few minutes and then turned to me and said, "He said he'd meet us at the dock in ten-minutes."

We cranked in the trolling lines and headed for the dock at Big Fisherman's Cove. Trevor met us there with his wetsuit and spear gun in hand. We loaded his gear into the boat and headed back for the reef.

Arriving in the general area where we had seen the yellowtail, we began a slow circle, peering intently into the clear blue water. At first, we thought the fish had moved on. However, as I turned the *No Mo* around for another pass, Troy called out, "Over there!"

The school had moved a few hundred yards from where we had first spotted them, but the distinctive yellow flashes just below the surface revealed their presence once again. I slowed our forward motion and shifted into neutral. "How close do you want me to get?" I asked Trevor.

"Let's just wait here until I get my gear on, and then stop the boat about fifty-feet from the edge of the school," Trevor responded.

It took him only a couple of minutes to don his wet suit, fins and snorkeling gear, and when he indicated that he was ready, I shifted into gear and eased forward until we saw the leading edge of the school, and then I shifted into neutral and shut off the motor.

Slipping quietly into the water off the stern of our boat, Troy and I watched eagerly as Trevor glided away from the boat, kicking stealthily with his long diving fins so that they would not splash on the surface and alert the fish. About twenty yards from the boat, Trevor deftly curled and slipped smoothly underwater.

Troy and I intently stared at the ripples where Trevor had submerged, waiting anxiously for him to surface. After about thirty-seconds, we saw his head pop out of the water and hold up his left arm to wave us over.

I started the engine and headed slowly in his direction. Nearing his location, I shifted into neutral. We could see that he was struggling somewhat, kicking steadily with his fins and holding both arms below the surface. When the boat drifted close enough, Trevor reached up with his right arm and called out to Troy, "Here! Grab this while I climb into the boat!"

Passing the butt end of his spear gun up to Troy, Trevor flicked his fins and reached the swim step. He then reached up and grabbed the handle at the top of the transom and pulled himself over the low-cut stern. After removing his fins and jumping rapidly to his feet, Trevor stepped quickly to Troy's side and reached over to take the spear gun handle. He then began pulling the trailing line that led out of the reel of the gun and started a slow and steady, hand over hand pull. A few moments later he told Troy, "Get the gaff, just in case we need it."

Troy reached down and pulled the gaff from its bracket under the gunwale and waited.

A moment later, Trevor stated, "It's okay, Troy. I won't need the gaff." At the same time, Trevor leaned over the side of the rail and hauled a brightly glowing yellowtail over the side of the boat, its silvery sides sparkling in the sunshine and its golden tail and dorsal fins outlining the greenish/blue coloration of its broad head and shoulders. Bright red blood flowed steadily from the dark hole in the center of its body where the spear had entered, and as it flapped in the air, the blood splattered all over the cockpit of the boat.

I reached out and gave Trevor a 'high five', and Troy did the same. We all talked animatedly for a few minutes, guessing the weight of the fish at close to thirty-pounds. After a few minutes, Trevor suggested that Troy should jump in and try to spear his own fish.

At first, Troy declined. His diving experience to that point was minimal, limited to primarily diving and spearing a few halibut and several small fish in the shallow water near shore. He had speared one small yellowtail (about two pounds) under the fuel dock in the Isthmus, but he had never tried diving in the open ocean, nor tried to spear any big yellowtail. But Trevor was convincing and encouraging, and after a few persuasive comments, he convinced Troy to give it a try. Trevor removed his wetsuit and other gear and then assisted Troy in putting it on. They were basically the same height and weight, and the suit fit him perfectly. Once he was suited up, I re-started the engine and cruised slowly back toward the area where we hoped the fish were still lurking. Sure enough, not far from where Trevor had shot his yellow, we saw the school cruising around lazily, seemingly undisturbed by the shooting that had occurred a short time earlier.

I eased the boat into the vicinity of the fish and shut down the engine. Trevor was speaking calmly with Troy, explaining the technique of entering the water, kicking the fins cautiously, and loading the spear gun by leaning back with the butt of the gun placed firmly into his lower abdomen. Troy had never loaded the powerful rubber coils of Trevor's spear gun and he was not certain he had the strength or ability to perform the maneuver. But, like a real trooper, he was at least willing to give it a try. After entering the water and easing himself over to the side of the boat, Troy tried unsuccessfully to load the gun on his first attempt. With some advice and encouragement from Trevor, he did manage to cock and load it on the second effort. Having done that, Troy began moving slowly away from the side of our boat.

Watching him swim away, I felt a little trepidation. This was a rather daunting undertaking for a relatively inexperienced fifteen-year old, and I could feel my pulse racing. I realized that Troy was diving in waters approximately one-hundred-fifty-feet deep, more than a half-mile from shore in an area where sharks were not uncommon.

Escalating my concerns even further was the fact that Trevor had speared a yellowtail just a short time before, and it had bled profusely on the end of his spear. I kept a wary eye on the surrounding sea surface, watching intently for the telltale sign of any fins.

When he was not more than ten-yards from the boat, even closer than Trevor had been, I watched anxiously as Troy flipped slightly upward and then slipped below the surface. Not more than ten-seconds later (although to me it seemed much longer), Troy popped back up to the surface and waved rather frantically.

"I think he got one!" Trevor shouted excitedly. "Let's go help!"

I started the engine and slipped it into gear. Keeping an eye on Troy, I eased in his direction, pulling the gearshift into neutral when I neared his location.

He was obviously struggling to remain on the surface, straining against the forces of both the elements and the pulling power of what we assumed was another feisty yellowtail. As we neared his location, Trevor leaned over the rail and grabbed the handle of the spear gun.

As Troy swam back to the swim step and climbed into the boat, Trevor pulled on the braided, eighth-inch diameter line that led straight down under the boat. Back aboard, Troy went to Trevor's side and reached out to help him haul in the line. When it reached the surface, Trevor leaned over and grabbed the shaft of the spear, and then leaned back and hauled a wildly flapping large yellowtail over the rail.

We all yelled out whoops and hollers, high-fiving and back slapping one another. Troy's fish was even larger than Trevor's, weighing in at a whopping thirty-five pounds! I stared down on the deck of my Grady White at the two fish, and felt extreme pride and admiration for my two sons. They had accomplished a feat that was impressive by free-diving standards, and had done it with seemingly relative ease.

The boys then tried to convince me to jump in and shoot my own fish, but I declined. I felt that I had enough fatherly pride to rejoice in, and besides, I'm not sure I could have done what they had done, and my ego would probably have bruised if had I failed. We decided that two big yellowtail was enough and headed for home.

I really enjoyed the retelling of the event when Maureen got home from work later that afternoon. It was a real bonding experience for the boys and I, and a day that all of us will undoubtedly always remember.

At the start of the summer season in 2004, Dave Long resigned his position as manager of the Two Harbors Dive Shop, and his wife Gina stepped down as coordinator of marketing, and special events for Two Harbors. The Long family, including their children Jake and Jarod, relocated to Avalon. Hillary Boyce took over management of the Dive Shop.

That year was also a momentous year for our son Trevor, when he graduated from USC with a Bachelor's Degree in International Relations. Following graduation, Trevor returned to the Island for one last summer of fun before venturing off into the 'real world' to see where life would take him.

As fate would have it, he happened to meet one of the young ladies matriculating at the USC Marine Science Center in pursuit of her Master's Degree in Marine Biology, Lauren Czarnecki. The two hit it off immediately, especially when Trevor took her out to watch the squid spawn on their first date. She loved the experience, and their relationship blossomed.

Coinciding with their new relationship, Trevor realized that his true vocation in life was to remain connected with the ocean, and he subsequently redirected his ambitions of becoming an international relations expert to retaining his affinity with the sea. He began taking dive classes, gained certification in an array of diving venues, studied for and obtained his Fifty-Ton United States Coast Guard License, and stayed with the USC Marine Science Center as a waterfront technician. When Lauren was appointed as the Marine Lab Manager, the young couple settled into a comfortable life on the Island that would eventually lead to their wedding the year following my retirement.

The fall of 2004 also left another indelible mark in the annals of stormy weather.

Beginning with an early September storm, the fall of that year seemed to batter the Island with one storm after another. A northeaster hit the Island in early November, causing all sorts of problems for visitors, harbor patrolmen, and the Baywatch crews.

One boat, a thirty-six-foot powerboat, struck Johnson's Rock, near the Island's West End, at the height of the storm and one man nearly lost his life. Baywatch members responded to the stricken vessel and pulled four men from the frigid waters, including the captain of the sunken vessel, who according to Baywatch members Lance Dempsey and Matt Lutton would not have lasted much longer, had they not been able to jump in and pull him aboard their rescue boat.

Another storm struck on Thanksgiving Weekend, a rousing northwester that roared in on Saturday night and created havoc for the estimated two-hundred boats that were visiting the Isthmus area. One of those boats, a forty-eight-foot power vessel moored in Cherry Cove, popped a plank and sank on its mooring. Nine people had to be rescued from the water by Isthmus Harbor Patrol and Baywatch Isthmus.

Battered throughout the night by the strong winds and heavy seas, the forty-eight-foot powerboat began rapidly taking on water around three-thirty a.m. An immediate distress call was made, but by the time rescue personnel arrived on scene, the boat was awash, its aft decks covered in water and the entire cabin flooded. All nine passengers had jumped overboard and were hanging onto the boat's swamped dinghy or clinging to nearby mooring buoys.

My Assistant Harbormaster Doug Millard, along with Harbor Patrolmen Mark Woolery, Rob Grant, and Mooring Service member Jamie Nelson, along with Baywatch members Kurt Fredericks, Matt Lutton and Lance Dempsey were helpful in the rescuing of those individuals and with the subsequent storm responses that continued through the night and into the next morning.

In addition to the chaos for visiting boaters and response crews, the storm also forced the cancellation of all cross-channel traffic from the passenger carrying fleet.

A rather common occurrence on the Island, stormy weather is known for the overall effect it can have on both residents and visitors. As it did on that Thanksgiving Weekend, the storm forced the Catalina Express, Catalina Cruises, and Catalina Flyer to cancel their scheduled runs from the mainland, stranding hundreds of people on the Island, including several hundred kids at Island camps.

Longtime Island residents are accustomed to the inconveniences associated with boat cancellations, including the inability to access the Island. They have also learned to cope with the onerous problem of not having groceries and other supplies available when storms prevent Catalina Freight Lines from operating the tugs and barges that supply the Island with everything from milk and bread, to fresh fruits and vegetables. Fortunately freight barges cancellations are rare and do not go on for more than a day, or two. On the occasions when cancellations occur on a busy weekend—and shelves are already empty because of high visitor counts—then the lack of available consumer goods becomes more problematic.

The problem is even more exacerbated with Island camps, whose staff members plan for the feeding of two or three-hundred kids for a set number of days, then discover that because of stormy weather, they must come up with food and other supplies for another day, or perhaps even longer. On those rare occasions, things like spaghetti, macaroni, pancakes, and other staple-type meals must get them through. It's much the same for Island families and something that we learned to cope with through the years.

27. Chaos in the Isthmus

IN EARLY MAY OF 2005, all seemed to be going smoothly until one of the cross-channel passenger boats crashed into the Isthmus Pier. That incident was destined to have a long-lasting impact on the Harbor operation and really made my job a lot more difficult.

It was a calm and otherwise 'normal' Monday afternoon. The *Catalina Countess,* a steel-hulled, one-hundred-twenty-seven-foot long, seven-hundred-ninety-three passenger boat that operated primarily for the Island based camps, was making its weekly Monday afternoon landing at the Isthmus docks. On board were approximately two-hundred kids destined for the Boy Scout Camp at Cherry Valley.

It was my day off and I had just returned from a round of golf in Avalon when I received a phone call from Michelle Phelps informing me that the *Catalina Countess* had just struck the pier and done considerable damage. Michelle was in Avalon working on a project, but she heard about the incident and phoned me. I hopped onto my bike and rapidly peddled the roughly quarter-mile distance to the pier. Upon my arrival, I could see that the *Countess* was standing-off in the fairway. There was a rather large gathering of people near the Harbor Office, milling around, pointing, and talking excitedly with each other. I parked my bike near Visitor Services and walked out toward the end of the pier.

Immediately I could see some of the damage. The ramp leading down to the docks was askew, there were planks popped incongruously out of place, a couple of pier pilings were leaning out of position, and several of the green and white painted wooden rails along the end and eastern edge of the pier were broken and splintered.

Approaching the office, I encountered Rob Grant standing outside, talking with several people. Baywatch was attending to someone near the ramp, and several other Two Harbors Enterprises employees seemed to be attending to other individuals.

"Hi Rob," I greeted him. "What happened?"

"We're not sure. I was on the dock preparing to toss the monkey fist (an intricately woven rope attached to a heaving line). I looked up and the *Countess* was heading toward the end of the dock. The boat seemed to be approaching way too fast, and when I realized that it was going to hit the dock, I yelled out for everyone to run. I grabbed hold of the loading ramp so that I had something to hang onto. Then I saw people running and when I looked back, the *Countess* crashed into the dock and then hit the pier."

"Are there people injured?" I questioned.

"I'm not sure. Baywatch seems to be treating someone over there," Rob told me, pointing toward a group of people that were shielded from my view.

"What about on the boat? Are there injuries on board?" I asked.

"I haven't heard," Rob paused, obviously shaken by the situation. He looked at me with a serious expression. "It hit really hard," he almost whispered. "I was prepared for the collision and I grabbed hold of the ramp rail for support, but I saw several people knocked over on the pier and on the dock. I don't know if any of them were hurt. It splintered the dock post (a heavy, twelve-by-twenty-four-inch laminated post that serves as a docking support on the main float). Big chunks of splintered wood flew all over the place. I was hit by one chunk, but it didn't hurt me."

Fortunately, injuries were minimal. A few people sustained minor cuts and bruises, but nothing serious. There were also a couple of kids aboard the boat that sustained bruises when they got knocked down at the point of impact, but luckily the injuries all seemed minor in nature and did not require serious medical attention.

I walked out to the end of the pier and looked down. One of the ramps leading down to the main float was dangling in the water, its wheels and the flap that normally rest on the deck of the float submerged. I turned to a camp counselor that was standing nearby, "Do you know if anyone was on the ramp when the boat hit?"

"No. There was nobody on either ramp," she informed me. "A couple of our counselors were at the top of the ramp when they saw how fast the boat was going. They turned and ran. One of them got knocked off her feet, but she's okay."

Members of the Mooring Service, along with other employees from the maintenance department and the harbor, were on the dock assessing the situation. I walked over near the end of the pier, stepping carefully over and between twisted planks and pier decking to take a closer look at the damage. Looking down, I could see that at least three pier pilings were snapped off, their splintered ends jutting uselessly into the air. Most of the rail along the east side of the pier, from the end of the Harbor Office out to the seaward corner was destroyed, as was the entire section adjacent to the ramp that dangled in the water.

I spoke with other people who had witnessed the accident. They all reported basically the same story; 'The *Countess* was going way too fast and just crashed into the end of the pier'. Whether it was pilot error, a mechanical failure, or some other factor that caused the crash was unclear, although an investigation by the Coast Guard and the Department of Transportation later reported that there was likely a mechanical problem with the shifting mechanisms on the boat that contributed to the collision.

The remainder of the afternoon was a whirlwind of activity. Because of the damage done to the pier and railings, and for safety reasons, the pier was closed to all public access. We scrambled in the Harbor Department to find a way to get people ashore, ultimately settling on tethering a small dock on the beach adjacent to the pier and near the dive shop that could be used as a drop-off point for shoreboat passengers, and for loading and offloading dinghies. We also put a couple of the young local kids to work shuttling guests from the nearby dinghy docks to the loading dock. It worked adequately, but with the rise and fall of the tides, the dock needed to be adjusted periodically and there were times when people had to step into the surf line—getting feet and shoes wet—when trying to use the small dock.

We also set up a shoreboat shuttle with the *Countess* to get the Boy Scouts off the boat and ashore in Cherry Cove. Fortunately the seas were calm and we were able to pull alongside the *Countess*, in the lee of her hull, picking up the youngsters at the side loading entryway of the boat. The shoreboats did not match up well with the height of the loading area, but by using deckhands on each shoreboat to assist the kids, we managed to get them all off the boat and ashore safely. Had the boat been occupied by less agile individuals, the process might not have succeeded.

With other cross-channel carriers scheduled to arrive later that same afternoon, we contacted our friends at the USC Wrigley Marine Science Center to see if their pier and docks could be used as an interim landing site until the engineers could get to the Island and assess the pier safety issue.

Director Tony Michaels and facilities manager Steve McElroy readily agreed to work with us to divert the *Catalina Express* and other carriers to their facility. Two Harbors General Manager John Phelps, was instrumental in arranging the logistics for the alternate dockage plan, arranging for shuttle busses to transport the passengers between Big Fisherman's Cove and the Isthmus. He ran the busses himself on several occasions.

I also got together with Phelps and maintenance manager Louie Latka to modify one of our old patrol boats to be used as a 'beach barge'. Hauling the flat-decked center console patrol unit up to the Upper Shop, we worked with Latka, David McElroy and Jimmy Ristau to design and attach a short aluminum ramp to the bow of the patrol unit. Using pulleys and heavy-duty hinges, the boat was setup so that it could pull right up onto the beach, lower the ramp onto the sand, and allow passengers access without getting their feet wet (usually). It wasn't the most perfect system, but it got us through the weekend and into the following week when engineers from Connelly Pacific arrived to assess the pier damage.

After inspecting the end of the pier, the pilings, and the deck structure, Connelly Pacific submitted an assessment that included a 'temporary fix' to the pier that would get us through the calm and benign summer season, but basically condemned the pier in anticipation of winter storms. Again, John Phelps was instrumental in negotiating the terms of the pier evaluation and subsequent repair agreement, using his knowledge and experience in the industry to expedite the process.

The following Monday, crews from Connelly Pacific arrived on the Island with replacement pilings, deck timbers, steel gussets, and all of the materials needed to make the necessary, albeit temporary repairs. By the end of the week the job was completed and the pier was reopened, although the eastern end of the pier, where the worst damages were done, was boarded off and that end, including the hoist was inaccessible.

During the next few months the wheels were set in motion to tear down and completely rebuild the pier, but at least we were able get through the busy summer season.

It was also in the summer of 2005 that the Long Beach Unified School District notified the Isthmus community, parents, and school administrators that they intended to close the Little Red Schoolhouse because of declining enrollment and financial shortfalls in the District.

An immediate outcry of complaints and indignation began. After all the hard work, effort and personal expense that had gone into the development of the Little Red Schoolhouse, to hear that it was scheduled for closure was a hard pill to swallow.

Led by staunch supporters Dr. Frank Blair, Long Beach School Board Member John Myer, and dozens of dedicated Isthmus residents involved with the school since its inception, an effort was made to convince the School District to reconsider. Following several meetings concerning the matter, Long Beach School District agreed to re-evaluate the pending closure, if alternate funding could be made available.

A concerted fund-raising effort commenced. Dozens of concerned and supportive individuals became involved with the effort to raise enough money to stave-off the closure. The Two Harbors School Foundation, established by Cliff Tucker and Doug Bombard to provide administrative support to the school, agreed to serve as the non-profit entity that would administer the financial aspects of the fund-raising effort. Mike Blackmore helped setup and establish the non-profit foundation.

Michelle and Randy Phelps took the lead role in seeking support from the boating community, and the response from the boaters was incredible. Hundreds of individuals responded to the request for support, donating generously to the cause. Yacht Clubs and other boating organizations pitched-in to help, organizing fund raising efforts of their own and making substantial contributions. The support and contributions poured in from all over the Island and by the end of the summer, nearly two-hundred-thousand dollars had been raised, enough to ensure that the doors to the school could remain open for at least a few more years—by which time it was hoped that the District funding would resume. I worked closely with Michelle Phelps in her fund-raising endeavor, writing letters and supporting her in the cause. When the fall semester started, it was a great relief to hear the sound of the school bell ringing out clearly on the still September air.

One rather significant change took place at the school that fall when teacher Sea Peterson retired from her position after nine-years of exceptional service. New teacher Sarah Perez took over the position that Sea was vacating.

Sea, daughter-in law of Pete and Dorothy Peterson, and her husband Bill, were leaving the Island to move to the mainland. Later they relocated to Hawaii in order to be near Bill's father Pete, on the Island of Kauai. A wonderful teacher who followed in the footsteps of her predecessors, Sea was instrumental in guiding students attending the one-room school to scholastic accomplishments that set the stage for their future academic success.

For the Isthmus community, the departure of Sea and her family ended nearly sixty-years of Peterson family presence. Their home, the 'Bobwhite House', as it was referred to through the years, was the home where Pete and Dottie Peterson resided prior to their retirement, and where the Peterson clan grew up. It held many memories for the family and very well could be a story all its own.

It never ceased to amaze me how things could go wrong so quickly and unexpectedly. The pier incident sent the entire community into a tailspin, but the resilience and adaptability of the Isthmus community and the people that make it up, as well as the response and resolution to the school closure, demonstrate how perseverance and willpower can overcome seemingly insurmountable obstacles. Similarly, good judgment and common sense are powerful tools that can go a long way toward resolving problems and minimizing potential calamities.

One afternoon, in the late summer of 2005, on an otherwise lazy, sunny, and laid-back type of afternoon, a near disaster occurred when an inflatable dinghy flipped over and went out of control while on a routine cruise near Cherry Cove.

That dinghy, a twelve-foot, hard-bottomed inflatable, powered by a fifty h.p Honda outboard engine, was cruising along outside of Fourth of July Cove with a fifty-year old male operator at the helm. It was traveling at a speed of about twenty-five knots, typical for that type of skiff when seas are calm and winds minimal. Perhaps the operator did not see the steep boat wake he was approaching, or maybe he just thought his dinghy would 'jump' over it without mishap, but when the dinghy encountered the boat wake, the skiff rose into the air, flipped over and tossed the man into the water. Landing upright, the dinghy continued underway at high speed with nobody at the helm.

Emerging from his dunking unharmed, the man popped to the surface and looked around. His dinghy, which had changed direction about one-hundred-eighty degrees, was bearing directly down on him. Twisting to the side just as the dingy approached, it struck a glancing blow, leaving a couple of minor contusions on his cheek and shoulder.

Shoreboat operator Cici Sayer, a veteran shoreboat operator, who lived on her sailboat and had worked in the Harbor Department for several years, saw the incident unfolding as she returned from Cherry Cove with a boatload of passengers. She put out an immediate distress call on the VHF radio. "Isthmus Harbor! Harbor Base!" she called out. "There's a flipped over dinghy running out of control and a man in the water with possible injuries in front of Fourth of July Cove. Call Baywatch and send the Harbor Patrol this way!" At the same time, Cici altered her course toward the location to assist.

As she approached the vicinity of the incident, she looked over and saw that the out of control inflatable was again bearing down on the man in the water. Realizing that it could seriously injure, if not kill the helpless victim, she made a quick decision to try and put her boat between the man in the water and the rapidly approaching inflatable.

Turning quickly to starboard, Cici put full power to the shoreboat and spun the helm. She was about twenty-feet from the man in the water, and the unmanned dinghy was on a direct course for his position. It was all happening very quickly and Cici held her breath as the gap between her boat and the inflatable boat narrowed. At the last second, the inflatable bumped the starboard bow of the shoreboat, deflecting it just enough to send it reeling a few feet to the west of the man in the water.

At about that time, Harbor Patrolman Jeff Nelson arrived on scene. Seeing that the man in the water appeared to be okay, and the Baywatch Isthmus boat was approaching the scene, Nelson diverted toward the rampaging dinghy and tossed his towline over the side, in an effort to foul the runaway skiff's propeller with his towline (an effective method of stopping an unoccupied boat by causing it to wrap-up in the propeller). While usually effective, on this occasion the maneuver was not working.

After Baywatch pulled the minimally injured man onto their boat, Baywatch member Lance Dempsey called Nelson alongside and hopped aboard his patrol boat. Dempsey instructed Nelson to try and maneuver as close to the wayward dinghy as possible. Nelson gave chase to the runaway dinghy, trying to match its speed and direction. As it drew near, Dempsey proceeded to leap from the rail of Nelson's patrol boat onto the pontoon of the inflatable and reached over to shut down the engine.

It was a potential disaster, and only the quick thinking and professional skills of the responders prevented the accident from becoming a tragedy, rather than just another boating incident.

Another oddity occurred that fall when three fires broke out on the same day, destroying two boats and killing one raven.

Boat fires are fortunately few and far between on the Island. On average, I would guess that serious boat fires occurred only once every few years in the Isthmus. Therefore, it was completely bizarre to have two major non-related boat fires and another fire on shore, occurring on the same day, within three-hours of each other.

The first fire broke out on a boat moored on A-1-Isthmus, the closest mooring to the docks and pier. There was a middle-aged couple on board the boat, cooking a late morning breakfast, when something went inexplicably wrong in their small galley. Cooking potatoes on a Butane stove, the man was adjusting the burner when suddenly the stove exploded in flames. The eruption of flames was so rapid and intense that it spewed flaming liquid onto his clothing and forearms, and into the interior cabin. On fire, the man leaped out into the cockpit, onto the rail cap and plunged into the water.

Shouting and pandemonium ensued as the flames spread quickly. The woman on the boat stepped back toward the swim step, where her husband was climbing out of the water and cried out frantically, "Are you okay? How badly are you burned?"

He looked up at her as he climbed out of the water. "I think I'm okay," he told her, looking down at his forearms. There was a slight amount of red discoloration and blistering on his hands and arms where the fluid from the stove had exploded, and his facial hair was rather severely singed; his eyebrows and eyelashes gone.

Mooring Service crewmen Dan Deinlein and Jamie Nelson were departing the dinghy dock in their work skiff when the fire erupted, and they pulled alongside and got the two people off the burning boat and into their skiff, then dropped them off at the dock to seek treatment.

Because the boat was so close to the main dock, Baywatch was on scene within moments. As soon as they pulled alongside, the Baywatch team of Lance Dempsey and Curtis Culp initiated fire suppression with their high-powered fire hose and the fire was extinguished within minutes. But the volatility of the liquid Butane and subsequent flames were so intense, that the boat burned so rapidly and severely that it was virtually a total loss.

Fortunately for the man aboard the boat, his quick thinking and immediate action of jumping into the water minimized the burn injury, but he did require medical attention, and after the initial fire response was over, he was taken into Avalon for treatment.

Not more than an hour later, another fire alarm was sounded, the piercing wail of the fire siren emanating from the alarm system at Visitor Services. The Two Harbors Fire Department responded to the alarm and discovered a small brush fire at the base of a telephone pole on the bluff above the west side of Isthmus Cove. Apparently a raven had landed on the telephone pole transformer, grounded its wing on the high-power line, and sparked an electrical jolt that immediately fried the unsuspecting bird. When it dropped to the ground it burst into a ball of flame and ignited a small brush fire. Fire crews quickly extinguished that fire. One of the firefighters quipped, 'Quoth the Raven, Nevermore'.

Amazingly, about two-hours later, another frantic fire call burst onto the airwaves. "Harbor Patrol! Harbor Patrol! There's a boat on fire at the end of the B-Row."

I was on duty on a patrol boat and I looked over toward the end of the B-Row and saw dark gray smoke billowing from a boat moored on the end mooring, B-16. I headed in that direction.

Harbor Patrolman John 'Noj' Eccles was already on scene, and I overheard him pleading with a woman standing on the deck of the boat to evacuate and get onto his boat.

"No!" she wailed, clutching desperately to a light colored Siamese cat. "Not without my babies!"

"There are babies on the boat?" I heard John call back. "How many, and where are they?"

"I don't know where they are!" she cried. "My two babies! I want my babies!"

John looked over at me and called out, "I'm going aboard to try and find the babies!"

The boat was nearly engulfed in dark smoke, turning blacker by the minute and I could see flames beginning to creep out of the open cabin door. "John! It's too dangerous!" I yelled out to him. "The smoke will kill you!"

"How old are the babies?" I yelled out to the woman standing on the deck clutching her cat in her arms.

"They're my babies, my kitties! You have to save them!"

Eccles heard her response and hesitated. There were no children aboard the burning boat; they were cats. He turned to the woman and told her, "You need to get off the boat! Baywatch is on the way! They will try to get your cats, but we need to get off this boat!"

A boater, Ron Bohanan from the nearby sailboat *Nuage* had arrived on scene a few moments before and hopped aboard the burning boat to help. Between them, they managed to pull the frantic woman off the boat and onto John's patrol boat.

Baywatch arrived on scene and began fire suppression.

There were boats all around with people standing on deck watching the fiasco. I knew how dangerous smoke from a boat fire, particularly from a fiberglass boat is, so I initiated an immediate evacuation of all people from the surrounding area. Working quickly, we cleared the immediate area of all people, taking some of them to the docks on our patrol boats, while having others start up their boats and leave the area.

After all people were clear, I returned to the scene. The boat was engulfed in flames, despite Baywatch's efforts to put it out with their powerful fire hose. Before long, the fire burnt through the mooring lines and it was endangering other boats. I called out to Baywatch and they agreed that we should try to tow it out of the congested area.

Taking out my anchor and tossing it over the stern rail of the burning boat (I knew that the chain would not burn, and fortunately the smoke was blowing away from me), I felt the anchor snag under the rail. Pulling the boat stern-too, I started a slow, steady tow along the west wall and out toward open water. When I cleared the last row of moorings, I cast off my towline and let the burning boat drift while Baywatch continued to pump water into the flaming hull. By the time the fire was extinguished, only a partially intact cabin and gutted-out hull remained.

Cautiously, Baywatch member Lance Dempsey boarded the boat, in the vain hope of finding the missing cats. Miraculously, he found one of the two cats alive, curled up under a galley sink in the back corner of a bulkhead that had not burned. It was still breathing and was taken up to the Banning House Lodge for further treatment, but the smoke inhalation was too severe and the cat succumbed during the night.

Both of the burned vessels were completely totaled and were later towed to the mainland by Vessel Assist for disposal.

Adding even more drama to the number of incidents that took place in 2005 was the crash of a small helicopter in Little Geiger Cove one October afternoon.

I was in the Harbor Office working on the budget for the following year, when I overheard a faint radio transmission broadcasting what sounded like a possible helicopter crash. Because the radio transmission was very faint and broken, I assumed that it was likely transmitted from somewhere on the mainland, but due to the potential seriousness, I moved quickly to the radio and turned up the squelch, then keyed the microphone and asked the station calling to repeat their call.

The response that I heard was static filled and faint, but I ascertained from the transmission that a boater had seen what he thought might be a small helicopter crash somewhere near Little Geiger Cove; a small cove about halfway between the Isthmus and Emerald Bay. Patrolmen John Pytlack and Jason Rose were on duty that afternoon, and the three of us jumped into our primary response vessel, Harbor Unit #4, and headed immediately for Little Geiger Cove. I instructed the office to contact Baywatch Isthmus and inform them of the situation.

When we rounded the steep rocky point that forms the eastern boundary of Little Geiger and looked around there was nothing immediately visible. But as we moved closer to shore, a bright reflection revealed the telltale remains of a small helicopter mangled and crumpled into a small pile and slightly concealed behind a large boulder.

"Christ. It is a helicopter!" Pytlak shouted.

I immediately picked up the microphone and called the office. "Harbor Base. Harbor Base," I announced. "Advise Baywatch Isthmus that there is a helicopter down at Little Geiger. We cannot see anybody from where we are, but I am going to put John and Jason ashore to check it out."

Little Geiger Cove is a tiny little bay that is home to the Offshore Cruising Club of southern California. It is located about one mile west of the Isthmus, about halfway to Emerald Bay. The club leases the isolated little cove from the Catalina Island Company and has a small yacht club structure built onto the hillside where the narrow canyon funnels into the ocean. The shoreline is not more than fifty-yards in width, and is covered in small rocks and boulders that drop off steeply into a sandy area where yacht club members anchor. What remained of the helicopter was twisted into a jumbled pile almost directly in the center of the small rock strewn beach.

Carefully, I eased the patrol boat into the surf zone. There was a light afternoon breeze and an associated wind chop that left little wavelets breaking gently onto the pebbled shore. Pytlak and Rose climbed up onto the bow of the patrol unit and hopped into the water when the bow neared the beach. They dropped into water about waist deep and waded ashore.

From the patrol boat I watched anxiously as they approached the downed aircraft. I glanced around to see if there was any sign of Baywatch, but they were not yet in sight. Gazing around the cove, I caught a glimpse of a black streak draped across several of the prevalent sugar-bush plants and scrub oak trees that cover the steep canyon walls. Looking up higher, I realized that there was a telephone pole on each side of the steep canyon and that the black line draped over the trees and bushes was part of a power line. It appeared to be very close, if not tangled into the downed craft. Alarmed, I rushed up to the bow to cry out the danger to Pytlak and Rose. At the same time, they emerged from behind the crushed shell of the helicopter carrying an inert body.

Pytlack cried out, "There's two men! Both are badly hurt! Get Baywatch here quickly!"

"Okay! I've already called Baywatch! Be careful! There is a power line down! It might be live! Keep away from the power line!"

The two patrolmen carefully laid the injured man down on the rocks. "The power line is tangled in the blades and around the tail. We're going to get the other guy out!" Rose shouted.

Before I could respond, Pytlak and Rose ran back to the scene and disappeared behind the tangled wreckage. Dave Coiner arrived on scene with Rudy Smits, and Dave jumped in and waded ashore. A few moments later they pulled another man from behind the twisted metal and carried him to the rocky beach, laying him carefully alongside the other man.

At about the same time I heard the roar of another boat and turned around to see the Baywatch boat rounding the point at high speed, the flared bow of the response unit casting a wide sheet of spray outward. As it neared, the roar of its twin engines dropped suddenly as the boat squatted and came to a stop just a few feet astern of my patrol unit. Baywatch members Lance Dempsey and Curtis Culp immediately took over the rescue effort. I will say that I have never seen a more competent, efficient, and professional rescue than the one I witnessed that afternoon.

Within minutes, Baywatch had called for additional backup, placed the two men onto gurneys and with help from Coiner, Pytlak, Smits and Rose placed them aboard their response boat. To expedite treatment, I turned the helm of my patrol boat over to Pytlak and hopped aboard the Baywatch boat to take over its operation so that the Baywatch team could concentrate on treating the victims. All of our crew did occasional training exercises with Baywatch in the event of this type of emergency. I took the helm and ran the Baywatch boat to the dock at Big Fisherman's Cove where a Coast Guard Life Flight helicopter was preparing to land.

Dozens of other individuals were on scene, ready to assist with the medical response. With the help of personnel from the USC Wrigley Marine Science Center, the two men were loaded onto the Medevac helicopter and transported to the mainland.

According to immediate medical reports, both men were in critical condition with major internal and external injuries. Later, I heard that both men survived, although at least one of them suffered long-term after effects.

I also learned that the helicopter was reportedly on a pleasure flight, checking out the scenic beauty of the Island and had dropped down into the canyon for a closer look when the blades made contact with the power line, thus causing it to crash. It was fortunate that the sailboat that had originally called in the emergency had seen the helicopter go down, otherwise the accident and the victims could have gone undiscovered for days.

In retrospect, the response and heroism of patrolmen Rose, Pytlak, Smits and Coiner, along with that of the Baywatch Isthmus team of Lance Dempsey and Curtis Culp, almost assuredly saved the lives of the two men.

Additionally, we used the incident as a training exercise for possible future responses, giving particular attention to systematically assessing the scene before initiating a first response. Had the power line been live the consequences could have been much worse. Fortunately it was not, and we later learned the lines have a built-in automatic shutdown in the event of this type of accident.

28. Sea Serpent

In December of 2005, the maintenance department began the dismantling of the Harbor Office, preparing the pier for demolition and the eventual construction of a new pier.

For me, the loss of an office to work from would haunt me for the rest of my career. The original plan was to construct a new Harbormaster's Office immediately upon completion of the pier project, but one stumbling block after another occurred. All that actually took place was the addition of a small 'temporary' rented building, about half the size of the previous office.

Following the removal of the office, all of the administrative functions for the Harbor Department were moved from the end of the pier to a small office at the back of Visitor Services. During the winter months while the pier was under construction, the temporary location sufficed, although not having sight of the harbor was somewhat problematic.

As the month of December rolled on, Connelly Pacific began shipping construction materials, pilings, deck timbers, and all of the lumber and supplies needed to build a new pier. Utilizing the Isthmus Beach as a staging area, construction crews created quite a pile of machinery, building materials, and equipment for the job.

Work was scheduled to begin in early January of 06', but 'Murphy's Law' intervened. Between bouts of bad weather, cancelled barges, late shipments of materials, and housing logistics issues, it was late January before workers arrived and began tearing down the old pier. However, once the work started, the project rapidly moved forward. Tearing out the old pilings, decks and planking went really quickly, with large sections removed in a relatively short time span. Installing new pilings was the most time-consuming aspect of the new construction, since each pile needed to be sunk deeply into the submerged sand and substrate with a pile driver.

Once the work started, the pier was closed completely for the duration of construction. Crews started on the land end of the pier and worked toward the seaward end, tearing out the old and installing the new as they moved outward.

To facilitate getting passengers and guests on and off the Island, I got together with John Phelps and the maintenance crew to help design and construct new dinghy docks that could withstand the rise and fall of the tides, and remain intact whether floating or settling onto the beach. Utilizing the same basic design concept that was incorporated into the construction of the Catalina Seabass Pens, the new docks were built using twenty-foot lengths of solid construction PVC tubing, linked together with side chambers and then attached with heavy-duty galvanized steel hinges. We built a total of seven of the docks, enough to run from the high-water line to the shoreward end of the main float, which remained moored at the end of the inaccessible pier. The docks actually worked out even better than expected, thanks partially to a mild winter, but also because they were considerably more flexible, stronger, and more practical than the previous docks with their fragile, foam flotation.

To ensure safety, Phelps suggested a handrail be added to one side of the docks, using aluminum 'speed-rail' construction. That addition really proved to be a good one since the docks had a tendency to rock and roll in the surf area, and would have undoubtedly resulted in a lot of people falling off into the water without something to hold onto.

As it was, the dock system got us through the winter with minimal problems or mishaps. It was very fortunate that it was such a mild winter and spring, with only three separate occasions when the docks had to be pulled out completely because of rough seas. Indeed we experienced a mild 'off-season'.

There were a few close calls, like the weekend of the Catalina Marathon, when six-hundred-fifty marathon runners arrived at around five-thirty a.m. to compete in the long distance run, and choppy seas were in evidence. We called nearly the entire crew in to help get everyone ashore safely, positioning dockhands every few feet along the rail of the dinghy docks to assist the runners in traversing the rocking and rolling platform without being tossed into the water. That event, along with a few others when the weather got sloppy but not severe, really put the docks to the test, and they held up remarkably well.

Connelly Pacific completed the majority of the pier project by mid-May, just before the start of the busy summer season. For the Harbor Department, it was a huge relief to have a usable pier back in service, a fueling system back in place, and a small office at the end of the pier to work in once again.

The summer of 2006 brought a couple of more fish-related events that I feel compelled to share. One of those was the 'Halibut Olympics' that took place in Catalina Harbor at the start of the summer season.

All winter and spring, an unusually heavy biomass of bait (squid, sardines, and anchovies) congregated in Island waters. Those heavy spawns resulted in some outstanding fishing for both local and visiting anglers. White seabass catches were good all spring, followed by prolific runs of barracuda, bonito, and calico bass. But by far the most rewarding and unusual fish spectacle was the halibut bonanza that took place in Cat Harbor during late spring.

As they often did, the young fishermen of the Isthmus, notably James and Jeffrey McElroy, Logan Gardiner, and Troy Oudin, were the first to get into the action.

For several consecutive days, the boys arrived home after school and went out to Cat Harbor on fishing excursions, returning with impressive catches of fresh halibut. In the beginning, most of the halibut they were catching were of the smaller size, from legal lengths of twenty-two-inches, up to about thirty-inches (ten-to-twelve pounds). Our freezers at home were quickly filled and the boys began passing out filets to neighbors. After the first few days of fishing, the boys began to tell us about an unusual aspect of their fishing expeditions.

It seems that the halibut in Cat Harbor were behaving somewhat oddly, leaping out of the water and creating an aerial show that was rarely seen. While halibut are known to jump from the water on occasion, the halibut in Cat Harbor were jumping and leaping profusely, putting on a show that the McElroy boys dubbed the 'Halibut Olympics'.

Intrigued by their story, Maureen and I walked out to Cat Harbor the following afternoon to see what was going on. We walked out the Cat Harbor road and as soon as the back harbor came into view, we saw multiple splashes rippling the calm surface of the bay. As we got closer, there was no doubt that we were watching halibut flipping up into the air and splashing back down into the water. It was an almost nonstop show, with halibut ranging in size from tiny little fish of less than a pound, to a few good-sized fish, probably close to twenty-pounds, or more. I couldn't believe what I was seeing. In all my years of halibut fishing (I started catching halibut at five-years of age while fishing with my dad) I had seen perhaps half a dozen halibut jump. That afternoon I think I might have seen two-hundred!

The halibut were feeding on schools of 'pinhead' anchovies that were visible in the shallow water in the back harbor. With an abundance of anchovies shoaling on the surface, the halibut were lying in wait on the bottom, and then charging up to the surface and becoming airborne as the anchovies passed over and the aggressive halibut leaped into the air as they fed on the hapless anchovies.

Troy and Logan were fishing on the Cat Harbor dinghy docks and had already landed two legal-sized fish. When I arrived, I couldn't help but ask them if I could give it a try. They were 'casting plastic', small fish-shaped rubber lures attached to a small lead-head hook. Troy handed me his rod, and on my second cast I hooked a small halibut, releasing it at the dock.

I was amazed at the spectacle of so many jumping halibut. At any given moment, at least one halibut seemed to be in the air, their numbers were truly prolific. That fishing spectacle went on for nearly a month. After a while, we told the boys not to bring any more fish home, we were simply inundated with halibut. I went out several more times with the boys, catching several legal-sized fish of my own, most of which I released.

One afternoon toward the end of the bonanza, we went out in Troy's small skiff to try and catch live bait and see if they might entice larger fish than the plastics were producing. After catching a few dozen small anchovies in their throw-net, we started a drift behind the Cat Harbor stringline. We hooked several halibut, including one about ten pounds that Logan decided to keep. We were about ready to call it quits when Troy caught a small herring, measuring about ten inches in length. I said to him, "Those are really good halibut bait. We used to use those while halibut fishing on the mainland."

"Okay" he said. "I'll give it a try." He hooked the herring in its back, just behind the dorsal fin and flipped it out away from the boat. It had just landed in the water when suddenly his line started to peel from the reel. I watched with a grin on my face as he waited a few seconds and then leaned back to set the hook. The line suddenly screamed from his reel and he looked over at me with wide eyes and huge smile. "Wow!" he blurted out. "This one feels really big!"

For the next few minutes Logan and I watched Troy fight the fish. It was pulling our little ten-foot skiff toward the western shoreline of the bay. The fish would make a short run, Troy gained line back, and then the fish peeled off another run. That happened about six times, and then Troy had the fish near the boat. It was only about five-feet deep, but the water was typical Cat Harbor murk, with visibility less than three-feet. Even though the fish was right under the boat, we could not see it.

Troy pulled upward with the rod tip, eliciting another short burst from the hooked fish. It created a dark swirl of sandy mud around the boat as it swam away, into shallower water. As the fish settled down, Troy hauled in again until the fish was alongside. In water that was only about three-feet deep, we looked down and saw the broad back of a halibut that we estimated to weigh over thirty-pounds.

At that point, Logan commented lamely, "Troy, we don't have a gaff."

Looking around, I could see that he was right. They had taken the gaff out of the skiff and left it on the dinghy dock when they first started fishing.

We had drifted, and been pulled, about fifty yards from the end of the docks and were very close, perhaps only about thirty-feet from the beach.

"Okay!" Troy stated. "Let's beach it!"

The fish was lurking on the bottom, flicking its broad tail occasionally, but remaining basically stationary. Logan grabbed one paddle from under the forward decking of the skiff, and handed me the other. We began a slow, steady paddle toward shore, being careful not to paddle too close to the fish, or too erratically.

Twice more the fish made short, brief runs away from the boat, and both times Troy cranked it back alongside. When we were within six-feet of the beach, Logan put his paddle down and stepped out of the skiff, on the opposite side of where the halibut was lying. Slowly and deliberately he walked around the bow, positioning himself in water less than a foot deep and spread his legs out so that he had solid footing and good balance. "Okay" he told Troy. "Lead him over to me."

Troy moved toward the bow of the little skiff, swinging the rod tip toward Logan. His rod bent heavily as the big halibut sulked in the shallow water; its weight bent the rod into a half circle. Not wanting to snap the rod, Troy eased back and tried again. On the second effort the halibut moved slowly forward, toward Logan. When it was almost directly between his spread legs, Logan reached down and grabbed both sides of the big fish, gripping its slippery, nearly two-foot wide girth and heaved it onto the leading edge of the sandy beach.

The halibut exploded in a burst of sand and water, its huge tail flapping in the shallow water and throwing a wide arc of saltwater that drenched Logan and sprayed up into the skiff. Flipping up into the air again, the big halibut splashed back down into the six-inch deep water and flipped once more, twisting in a hundred-eighty-degree spin and landing back at Logan's feet.

Logan reached down to try and get another grip on the sides of the big fish, but it was slimy, slippery, and strong, and his effort resulted only in another drenching as the big halibut flapped its broad tail once more and streaked away from the shore. Troy's line snapped and the fish was gone.

Troy started laughing. I realized that I hadn't taken a breath for several moments as I looked over at Troy and then at Logan. I took a deep breath, heard Logan start to laugh, and then I joined them in their mirth.

I think I would have reacted differently if I had just lost the biggest halibut I had ever hooked, but both Troy and Logan seemed to be unfazed by the loss, high-fiving each other and still chuckling as Logan climbed back into the boat. "That was really cool!" Logan commented, "Sorry I let it get away."

"No big deal," Troy responded happily. "It was just fun to hook it and try to land it on the beach."

He was right; it was a great experience, and one that both boys will always remember. It was also a fitting end to the 'Halibut Olympics', because that afternoon turned out to be the last big display of the show. The anchovies nearly disappeared overnight, and except for a few lingering splashes, the 'Halibut Olympics' came to a close.

Later that summer, in early August, I had the unique opportunity to swim with a 'sea serpent'.

Early one Wednesday morning, I received a phone call from Maureen about a strange fish that was swimming around in the shallow waters of Big Fisherman's Cove. She suggested I head over to the cove and take a look, if I could. It was not particularly busy at that moment in the harbor, so I stopped at my boat the *No Mo*, picked up my mask and snorkel and headed over to the Marine Science Center to see what was going on.

When I arrived in the cove, several dozen people were standing around on the pier and adjacent concrete abutment staring and pointing into the small embayment on the north side of the pier jetty. I docked *No Mo* and wandered up to the top of the pier. Floundering around near the surface was a strange looking sea creature. It was big, at least twelve-feet long and radiated a metallic silver blue/ocher coloration all along its narrow, tapering body, and a brilliant reddish dorsal fin. A couple of people were snorkeling near the strange creature, which was slowly circling around the small estuary, its long body undulating snake-like as it swam.

Among those standing on the wall watching the spectacle was Kristy Holland, Maureen's assistant at the Science Center and a former employee of mine who had operated the *Salad Bowl,* the marine trash boat that picked up trash in local coves from boaters. I turned to Kristi and asked her, "Do you know what it is?"

"It's an oarfish," she told me. "It's been swimming around here for about an hour. My understanding is that they live in deep water, are extremely rare, and are almost never seen in these waters."

I decided to get into the water and take a closer look for myself. Taking off my shoes and socks, work shirt, and sunglasses, I slipped on my mask and snorkel and climbed down the rocks to the water's edge. Sliding into the water I dog-paddled over to the area where the odd creature was circling.

When I neared the fish, its coloring and luminescence were incredible. Its shimmering silvery sides radiated a pulsating flow of color changes, ranging from incandescent blue to a rainbow pink and crimson red along its full-length dorsal fin. The darker splotches along its upper sides and back glowed warmly with rich shades of light brown, yellow and copper. It seemed to pulsate color changes like a chameleon, the colors rippling slowly from tail to head, and then back, almost as if it was programmed with an internal lighting system.

I swam alongside the fascinating creature, not more than three or four-feet from its long and narrow torso. Its eyes were relatively small, about the size of a golf ball, jet-black with an opaque bluish film covering the pupil.

I stayed in the water with the fish for about half an hour, mesmerized by its beauty and strangeness. It was probably sick or injured, although there was nothing visibly wrong that I could see. Its behavior, and the fact that it had found its way into the shallow cove, indicated that something was wrong. It appeared very docile, lethargic and seemingly untroubled by the humans that were swimming around staring at it and taking underwater photos. I wished I'd had a camera, but I did not. A few days later I was able to see photos that others took.

After I got out of the water, several others took their turns swimming with the creature. I returned to work and later heard that the fish had died and washed up onto the beach.

Afterward I learned that the oarfish (*Regalecus glesne*) is a rarely seen denizen of the deep that is known to inhabit all temperate waters. Known in some cultures as the 'King of the Herring', the oarfish can grow to impressive lengths, with one specimen found washed up on a beach in Japan reportedly measuring nearly seventeen meters (fifty-six-feet) in length. It is this stupendous size and their brilliant, regal-like bright red fin coloration that probably led to its reputation as being a 'sea serpent' by ancient mariners. For me, swimming with the strange sea creature was an awesome experience.

When the fish died, biologists from the Marine Science Center contacted the curator of the Natural History Museum in Los Angeles and they were very interested in seeing the specimen. After pickling the fish in a solution of formaldehyde and brine, the fish was shipped to the mainland and later put on display by the Museum. It measured over fifteen-feet in length and weighed approximately one-hundred-eighty pounds. It reportedly is a prime attraction in the oceanographic section of the museum. It somehow seemed quite ironic that the 'sea serpent' had chosen a marine sanctuary for its demise.

29. A Terrifying Accident

MOST PARENTS HAVE MOMENTS IN their children's upbringing when they must cope with the gut-wrenching worry that accompanies accidents or injuries. Trevor's Jet Ski incident when he was very young was the most frightening accident of his childhood, but Troy had an accident when he was a senior in high school that was really terrifying.

He and his friend Jeffrey McElroy were riding All Terrain Vehicles (ATV's), a pastime that many of the older boys in the Isthmus enjoyed on a regular basis. On that particular day, the two youngsters were riding their 'quads' on the steep hills above the Banning House Lodge. They were several hundred yards apart, cruising downhill with Troy in the lead. It had rained heavily a few weeks previously and there were some rough places on the narrow dirt road that followed the ridge behind the Lodge. As Troy made a turn on the steep grade just above the horse stables near the Banning House, he didn't see a deep crevice across the road that had been caused by the rain. His front wheels dropped into the ditch and his ATV came to an abrupt stop. He was traveling at about twenty miles per hour and when his quad stopped so abruptly, he was thrown over the front end. He landed in the middle of the dirt road on his face and chest. The ATV flipped once, flew into the air and came down on top of him, crushing him into the road and then flipping over once more and landing upright on all four wheels. The engine was still running.

When Jeffrey reached his side, Troy was seated in the middle of the road holding onto his head. He was not aware at first that Troy had crashed, but when he saw him start to stand, he saw the back of his head and shoulders covered in blood. Troy turned to him and said, "I need to go see Baywatch."

Jeffrey was stunned, still unsure of what had happened. When he saw Troy climb back onto his ATV and head down the hill, Jeffrey followed him to the connecting road in front of the Little Red Schoolhouse and he turned off to go to our house and tell us about the accident. Jeffrey arrived at our house looking pale and concerned. He informed us that Troy had crashed on his ATV and was at the Baywatch station. Maureen and I were both home at the time and we quickly hopped into our Isuzu Trooper and rushed over to the station.

Troy was lying on a gurney with his head already swathed heavily in a gauze wrap. One side of his face was bloody and skinned, oozing a pinkish film through a matted layer of dirt and tiny rocks imbedded in his cheeks and forehead. His head was wrapped heavily, like a turban, and a dark stain of blood had formed on the backside of the wrap. His face was pale and his eyes unfocused. We kneeled at his side as Baywatch continued to administer to his injuries and simultaneously conversed with a mainland hospital.

Baywatch members Steve Powell and Rob Pelky were attending to his injuries. They told us that he had sustained an injury to the back of his head, multiple contusions to his face and chest, but did not appear to have any broken bones or internal damage. They advised us that he needed to be transported to a trauma center for care. I felt myself feeling faint. Looking over at Maureen, my anguish and concern palpable, she reached out and clutched my arm. "He's going to be okay," she reassured me. "We need to be calm. He needs us to be strong." Her words soothed me a little. She was right. We both needed to be calm and collected and let him know that we were at his side and standing-by to help him get through the ordeal.

Baywatch informed us that they had a Medevac helicopter in route and that it would arrive at the USC Wrigley helicopter pad within twenty minutes. When Maureen asked if we could accompany him in the helicopter, they informed her that one of us could go along. Maureen asked me to go back to the house and gather some things for both of them. I didn't want to leave him, but I realized the necessity to do whatever we could to expedite his transport, so I rushed back to the house, grabbed several personal items that Maureen told me to gather and headed back to the Marine Science Center.

Troy was conscious, but not completely focused. When I asked Baywatch about the severity of the injury to his head, they were cautious in their response, but supportive and positive. I watched helplessly when the medical crew from the Medevac Service landed and loaded the gurney into the side of the helicopter, helped Maureen aboard and lifted off. When I said goodbye to my son, he returned a wan smile and whispered quietly, "I'll be okay, dad." I prayed that was going to be true.

I asked Maureen to call me as soon as she knew anything, and told her I would be ready to hop aboard the next boat heading to the mainland. She suggested I wait until she called, just to be sure that she didn't need other things from home, and to get a diagnosis of the extent of the injuries from the doctors at the hospital. I drove home and waited.

Waiting for news in a situation like that is torture. All sorts of thoughts run through a person's head during duress of that nature. I tried to focus on the positive thoughts, but it's not an easy thing to do. Time seems to move in slow motion and minutes seem like hours.

It was about three hours after they departed for the mainland when Maureen called. The news was mixed. The doctors thought that he would recover without any permanent damage, but the head injury was rather severe. A large chunk of his skull was peeled from his cranium and there was extensive bleeding and bruising. They applied about twenty metal staples to his skull to reattach the section that was torn loose. There was also some grit and grime that was embedded in his facial skin and on his chest, but they believed that they were able to remove the majority of it without any lingering after effects. His shoulder was dislocated and his chest and upper back bruised, but x-rays revealed no broken bones. They also discovered a crack in his jawbone that could necessitate surgery and wiring the jaw together. They planned to keep him in the Intensive Care Unit for a minimum of twenty-four hours, perhaps longer depending on his progress.

When she told me those things I wasn't sure whether to feel relieved or be more concerned. But then she said this to me; "Troy is going to be just fine. After they performed the surgery on his head and cleaned-up his facial contusions, he looked up at me and said, 'Hey, mom. Get the camera and take some pictures. I want to post pictures on Facebook!' After he told me that, I knew he would be okay."

With a certain amount of relief, we discussed what else we needed to do. I gathered a few more things together and made plans to head over to the mainland on the next available Catalina Express boat later that afternoon. It was a difficult wait, but I did my best to try and remain positive and not dwell on the negatives.

The Medevac helicopter had taken him to Harbor General Hospital in Torrance. Because he was seventeen-years old, he was admitted to the trauma wing of the Children's Hospital and the entire medical staff was top notch. He did not have to go through the red tape and onerous waiting and processing that usually occurs in the adult emergency room. The attention and care that he received was exceptional and the staff even brought out a cot and blankets so that Maureen could stay with him in his room during the first two-days of his recovery.

Thankfully, he recovered completely. The back of his head retains a large, 'J'-shaped scar from the injury, but there are no other lingering complications. His jaw fracture was determined minor and resulted in only a 'soft diet' for several weeks. He was lucky, and we feel eternally blessed and relieved. We were very grateful and appreciative to our Baywatch crew, Steve Powell and Rob Pelky, the helicopter Medevac team, and to the attendants at Harbor General Hospital. After that accident, Troy began wearing a helmet whenever he climbed aboard any other ATV's, and we think he also might have developed a little caution.

On July 21, 2006 a very bizarre weather phenomenon occurred around the Island; a freak storm that was almost unworldly, and that left long lasting effects on some parts of the Island.

There was a subtropical influence in evidence, the remnants of a tropical disturbance that rolled in off the southern deserts and into the southern California basin, bringing with it a couple of days of high humidity, thunderstorms and significant amounts of rain to some areas.

I always kept a close eye on the weather, relying on local forecasts and my experience to try to be prepared for any potential weather related problems. It is extremely rare to have any negative weather activity in July in southern California. While I was aware of the tropical influence in effect, I was thinking that the Island might see a few isolated thunderstorms and perhaps even a little rain as the humidity built in the late afternoon. Keeping an eye on an area of thunderheads forming to the southeast, and moving northwest from the mainland area between Newport Beach and San Diego, I thought that the likelihood of potential thunderstorms would probably increase during the evening hours, but probably dissipate when the sun went down.

I left work at about five-thirty p.m., went for my customary late afternoon swim in front of our house, and then settled down to enjoy a cold beer. When I arrived home, I talked with Maureen about the possibility of a thunderstorm developing and she expressed her typical excitement.

Maureen loves thunderstorms and lightning. For her, because they are so infrequent in southern California, the onset of thunderstorms always gives her a real thrill. She sat with me on the front porch, sipping a glass of wine and watching the thunderheads approach. About thirty minutes after we settled down to watch the dark clouds that continued to build from the northeast, a burst of gusty wind preceded the arrival of a few heavy raindrops. We sat together enjoying the splattering of rain that began falling, the large, warm raindrops few and far between. It was what I often referred to as 'a six-inch rain'—a drop every six inches.

Suddenly a long rolling boom crashed out of the heavy skies, accompanied by a distant flash of lightning. The skies burst open with a brief torrential downpour, sending us scurrying into the house for cover. A few scattered drops were fine, but the cloudburst was a little too much for both of us, and we sought the shelter of the living room, watching the squall through the front windows. It was short-lived, lasting only about ten minutes, but the rains were heavy enough to drench everything and leave the distinct aroma of moistened soil lingering in the still, ocean air. Behind the squall, the skies opened to reveal a wide circle of bright pastel blue, surrounded by other, more distant thunderheads. It was quite a celestial sight, the puffy white-tipped cumulonimbus clouds outlined starkly against the brilliant azure blue sky and the dark terrain of the hills.

Thinking that the nature show was likely over, we went into the kitchen to prepare dinner. I was prepping a white seabass filet for the frying pan while Maureen was slicing apricots from our tree, and other fruit for a salad. She also had a couple of yams baking in the oven.

I kept glancing out the front and side windows of the house, remarking that it appeared that another line of squalls might be moving in our direction. About the time that we sat down at the dinner table to eat our meal, a dark shadow moved over the house and we looked around at the darkening gloom. There was definitely another thunderstorm approaching as we heard the distant roll of thunder and watched a black wall of storm clouds drop lower and lower toward the ocean surface, obliterating all views of the distant mainland.

We ate our food rather quickly, anxious to leave the table and watch the approaching weather front. The thunder and lightning were getting closer and we could feel the heavy stillness in the early evening air. It was about seven o'clock, and the sun had dropped below the hills outside of Cat Harbor, casting the Isthmus into the deepening shadows of approaching nightfall. We moved out onto the front porch to watch the stormy weather arrive. We had been outside for only a few minutes when a powerful, blast of warm air whipped through the surrounding eucalyptus trees, shaking their branches and sending leaves and dried eucalyptus pods flying through the air. The winds lasted only a few seconds, but we could see that their sudden onslaught brought several people on boats moored in front of our house scurrying out on deck. They looked around, scanning the dark clouds swirling overhead, but then most went back down below decks to return to their meals, or whatever else they were doing.

I had an odd feeling about the weather. It was very unusual. The sky to the northeast, beyond Bird Rock and out toward the mainland, was turning a peculiar orange color, blanketed with an almost yellowish tint that was interspersed with dark black patches riddled with frequent flashes of lightning. Another dark line, that I recognized as a wind-line was spreading rapidly across the distant horizon. Yet another low and very black cloud was moving in from the hills above Big Fisherman's Cove, its mass obliterating all traces of the sky and even the low, mountainous peak that lies beyond the bowl-shaped canyon that forms the sheltered haven of the Marine Science Center.

A bright flash of lightning lit up the skies, followed almost immediately by a booming crash of thunder, and then everything went black. The power was out. We could see bolts of lightning all around, out over the ocean and on land. Immediately, I assumed that the lightning had struck a power pole or transformer.

Looking out onto the water, I could see a sheet of whitecaps spreading rapidly into the mooring fields as boats started rocking and swaying in the winds. Boaters rushed back out onto their decks, pulling in towels that were draped over lifelines to dry, and tightening rigging lines that had begun rattling against the spars.

The fire alarm sounded at Visitor Services and we watched from our house as we saw the Isthmus Fire team head out into the hills. Lightning had reportedly sparked several small brush fires in the dry interior.

As the heavy black wall of clouds rolling toward us from the northeast arrived, another burst of heavy, torrential rains began, punctuated by flashes of lighting and peals of thunder. At the same time the winds increased, gusting to perhaps thirty knots. Those winds were hot! Outrageously hot, with ambient air temperatures increasing suddenly by perhaps twenty-degrees.

"Wow! Maureen exclaimed. "That wind feels like a blast furnace."

"It sure does," I responded. "I've never seen anything quite like this."

The air was thick and heavy, the sky coal black, but rippled with that orange/yellow tint that we had seen in the clouds while gazing out to seaward a short time earlier. Strange, billowing streaks were evident in the clouds, churning like a swirl of butterscotch stirred by a blender into a bowl of chocolate pudding. Flashes of lightning lit the undersides of the clouds, revealing wave-like folds in the low hanging masses that seemed separate, yet integrated. Every few minutes the 'blast furnace' heat returned, instantly turning the moist air thicker and heavier and causing perspiration to form on our skin. To further cast a specter of surrealism to the weird sky, strange little orbs of glowing orange spun around in the dark and menacing air, illuminating the billowing clouds with a fiery hue that came and went in whirling streaks. Whether it was a type of lightning or something else, nobody knew.

Along with the heat, the winds swirled and gusted, rattling the windows and roaring through the branches of the nearby eucalyptus trees. "I think I had better head down to the harbor," I told Maureen. "This looks like it could get really gnarly."

"Don't you have people on duty?" she asked.

"Yes. But there are only three patrolmen working and if this continues, they're going to need some help."

I went to the laundry room to pull out my foul weather gear, slipping the bright yellow rubberized jacket on as I sat down to put on my mud boots. I left the pants in the bag, relying on the coat and boots to keep me relatively dry. "I'll see you in a little while," I told Maureen. "I don't think this will last very long. You should probably stay inside, there's a lot of lightning and you'll be safer staying in-doors."

I could see that she was disappointed in my leaving, but it was my responsibility to respond whenever threats to safety or property occurred in the harbor. Fortunately, just as I started to leave, the power came back on. I suggested that it might be good to pull out the candles and check the oil lamps in the likely event that the power might go out again. I hopped on my bike and headed down to the pier. Steve Mercadante was arriving to help, along with Scott Cincotta. We jumped into action with Alex Barber, Brett Ruppert, Bruce Glass, Larry Potter, and the rest of the crew.

For the next several hours, the odd and erratic weather continued.

I hopped into one of the patrol boats and went out onto the water to help out. Several boats were calling for assistance when the gusty winds struck and several dinghies were flipped over or had broken loose and were drifting away. Boats were breaking and dragging moorings. In the anchorage at Little Fisherman's Cove several boats were dragging anchors, crashing into other boats and creating bedlam. There was no way we could respond to every call; we just did our best to respond to the most frantic and serious calls for assistance.

At around eleven p.m., almost as suddenly as it had started, the freaky weather quit. One minute it was windy, dark and wild, and the next it was still and quiet. Looking out to the east, the skies had cleared over the ocean and the sky above the mainland glowed with the yellowish sparkle of a million lights. We could see the black wall of the thunderstorms moving away toward the southwest, beyond Cat Harbor. But there was another odd, yellowish glow emanating from the east, and we were to hear later that it was the glow from the large Empire Landing fire that ended up burning thousands of acres and destroyed vast expanses of pristine environment and natural Island habitat. Fortunately, it did not cause any major damages to either the Isthmus or Empire Landing communities.

The storm that occurred on that memorable Saturday night in mid-July was by far the most bizarre and peculiar storm I have ever seen. It was similar to thunderstorms that happen in other areas of the country, particularly the Midwest and the south, but it had elements that were truly unique; the strange cloud colors and formations, the incredible heat changes, and the overall feeling of surrealism, as if we were on another planet. It was a storm I'll never forget.

30. The Love Boat

WINTERS ON THE ISLAND RUN a gamut from mild to severe, with most falling somewhere in-between. When the off-season of 2006-07 began, the early indication was that it might be a wet winter. An early rainstorm arrived in October, creating a few problems for Buccaneer Weekend, and bringing nearly an inch of rain. As winter settled in, the storms that began to arrive brought powerful winds, but little rain.

By early January, the Island was beginning to feel the impacts of limited rainfall. An early January weather system was forecast to bring copious amounts of rain to the southland, and while some areas did receive significant rainfall, Catalina had only a sprinkling of moisture, but lots of wind and rough seas.

That early January storm, packing strong winds and rough seas, was a particularly brutal system that lasted for more than forty consecutive hours and hit local coves hard. The winds created havoc, forcing the complete removal of all docks and floats, and made it impossible to get to and from shore by any means other than swimming through breaking surf. The few boaters that rode out the rough seas were forced to remain on board their boats throughout the harrowing ordeal.

Local surfers Deon Hallum and our son Trevor tested the surf on Isthmus Beach, catching several decent rides, but the shore-break proved too severe for their surfboards, and both surfers had their boards snapped in half by the powerful waves.

The stormy weather also brought a return of the giant squid, stranding numerous specimens, some as big as six-feet long, on the Isthmus shoreline. It also resulted in another good showing of Paper Nautilus shells, although the majority of the delicate shells that were found broke into fragments in the heavy surf.

It was a colder winter than usual, with temperatures dropping into the thirties on a few days, which is very rare for Southern California. We did not have any heat in our house, other than a small portable oil heater and the oven, so we just bundled-up in layers during those coldest days. As the winter progressed, numerous storms brought strong and disruptive winds to the Island, but very little rain. Based upon statistics provided by local weather statistician Paul Wintler, the winter of 2006-07 proved to be the driest winter on record, with a meager two-and-forty-five-hundredth inches recorded for the entire year. As a consequence, phase one water rationing would be imposed later that summer, and the drought continued for nearly three years before finally breaking in the winter of 2009-10.

As I've alluded to from previous years, the lack of rainfall on the Island is serious, and a real hardship for the local population. Additionally, with limited rainfall comes the threat of brushfires.

In May of 2007, the infamous KBRT fire left Catalina burning. A fire of epic proportions, the KBRT fire (so named because of its origin near the KBRT radio station) began on the summit above Toyon Bay and very nearly resulted in dire consequences for the City of Avalon. The fire burned thousands of acres, crested over the hills into Avalon Canyon, and was roaring directly toward the hapless town. Gratefully, the combination of a talented and dedicated team of firefighters, accompanied by an unexpected and fortuitous wind shift, saved the city from total devastation. As it was, the City sustained only minimal direct damages, but the fire and associated negative publicity left a blistering effect on tourism for several years.

Oddly, immediately after the fire was extinguished, the City of Avalon was back in full operation, while the West End, including Two Harbors, was just beginning to absorb the brunt of the fires impact.

Even though the fire did not get close to the Isthmus, it burned much of the infrastructure that provides utility services to the interior. Water lines were scorched, and for a short time, the community was without fresh water. Fortunately, Southern California Edison was able to hook into alternate resources and restore water within a day. Such was not the case for electrical or phone service.

All of the power lines leading out of Avalon were destroyed, including poles and electrical transformers. Phone lines melted and disintegrated. The Isthmus and all of the other small communities in the interior went into full blackout, without any discernible timeline for repairs.

General Manager John Phelps and Louie Latka and his crew (with the help of dozens of others) put an immediate plan in action to try and minimize the potential impact of the loss of power. A large portable generator was brought out of storage to provide emergency power to the sewage system and the restaurant. It could not provide enough power for other parts of the operation. With no active phone lines, or even any cell-service, communications were nearly impossible. Using the minimally effective marine radio services (operating on twelve-volt systems), a plan was developed to purchase as many portable generators as possible from Home Depot and other retailers in the San Pedro area, and have them shipped to the Island to provide temporary power for Island homes, the General Store, Banning House Lodge, Visitor Services, the Dive Shop, and all other Isthmus operations.

For the following eleven days, the constant hum of portable generators throbbing through the day and night was a constant reminder of the ongoing disruption that everyone in Two Harbors was coping with.

Perhaps the most disruptive of all was the loss of phone service. For people living on the Island the telephone is a very important tool for staying in touch with family members, friends, business associates, and all other mainland connections. When the phones go out, which happens periodically, particularly cell sites, communication with 'the real world' comes to a halt. It's one thing to have a short-term disruption, but to lose all contact for eleven consecutive days is really crummy. That is exactly what happened to those living on the west end of the Island in the aftermath of the fire.

Oddly, there was one small place, atop a short sea wall next to Visitor Services, where those with Verizon cell service could usually, but not always, get a signal. It was very strange, but that one little spot was the only place where Verizon users could stand to make and accept calls. Individuals with Verizon phones became very popular.

Most long-term Islanders are accustomed, to a certain extent, to the remoteness and inherent isolation that comes with living on an island, and are prepared for the occasional disruption when cut-off from the mainstream. But it usually happens during the winter months, when the pace is slower. To be cutoff during the middle of May, when the summer season is just blossoming, created a myriad of problems. For me, and the entire Harbor Department, the biggest problem was the inability for Mooring Lessee's to phone in their mooring reservations. Many Lessee's merely turned to the Internet, sending their mooring reservations into the office via e-mail (after an emergency generator was connected to the Harbor Office). But not all of the Mooring Lessee's were familiar with the Internet link, and so many reservations went unmade, and when the Lessee or their guest arrived, there was often another boat on their mooring. That put an extra burden on the harbor crew, but all the employees used patience and good customer service to get through the difficult period.

The fire also caused about a one-week disruption to interior travel, including driving into Avalon for groceries and other personal needs. Those of us with boats used that alternate method of travel, usually taking others along on the trip.

Pam Deinlein and Terri Bailey in the General Store, and Laura McElroy and Paul Chvostal in the Purchasing Department also did an outstanding job of finding and obtaining needed supplies and materials.

It was a very challenging and unusual time in the Isthmus, but once again the resiliency of the local population enabled them to get through it without too much stress or suffering.

By the time the immediate aftereffects of the fire were resolved, it was back to full summer mode for all Islanders, although the negative media reports and coverage of the fire did have an effect on seasonal business. Avalon was more affected than Two Harbors, but the combination of the fire, the dismal economic downturn that was happening nationwide, and the high price of fuel, made the summer less busy than 'normal'.

One of my fondest boating friends, Pat May, passed away in the summer of 2007. Pat May and her husband Bob, who preceded Pat's death by a few years, were the quintessential boating couple. They typified the embodiment of what a true lover of Catalina Island is all about, having discovered Two Harbors several decades earlier and made it their 'home away from home' for as long as their lives would allow.

Like so many other couples (and single individuals as well), who discover the magical allure that exists on Catalina, the May's truly loved the Island, its people, and all the things that helped to make it such a huge part of their lives.

Those of us who lived, or currently live on the Island, know that same feeling, and fully understand and recognize the attraction, the bond, and the love that makes Catalina so very special.

Mired in a serious drought in the fall of 2007 and on water rationing, Islanders were happy to see a wetter pattern begin to develop in November and December. Winter storms that had missed the Island for most of the previous year once again began to impact Island shores.

The drought was easing and although the winter rains helped replenish the Island's water resources, there was not enough rainfall to replenish all of the water tables and phase one water rationing remained in effect.

It was also in the fall of 2007 when our youngest son Troy transferred from Cal State Long Beach to the California Maritime Academy. His acceptance at the prestigious maritime institute was a source of great pride for Maureen and me, as it was for seven other Island families.

That was the year that seven students—an impressive number for such a tiny community—from Catalina Island applied for and were accepted into the Academy. In addition to Troy getting into the Marine Engineering Department, Avalon High School students Chaz Delehant, Nick Radde, Ray Ponce, George Foote, Tommy Gill, Devon Bray, and part-time Islander Kim Butte were all accepted to the Academy.

Following in the footsteps of recently graduated Islanders David Latka, Fletcher Canby, Piper Cameron, and Jon Cornelius, the California Maritime Academy in Vallejo, California was undoubtedly becoming a magnet for Island students, whose background of Island life and marine experiences bodes well for the future of the marine industry.

One problem that plagued me throughout my career as Harbormaster was the task of trying to keep reasonable control over the anchorages around the Island.

Within the Leased premises under our jurisdiction there was a relatively strict set of rules and regulations governing anchoring and mooring practices and procedures in all coves. Outside of the leased areas on the Island (including the tidelands outside the City of Avalon), anchoring falls under the auspices of the State of California navigational codes, which does have specific guidelines but no means of enforcement. The Coast Guard, Sheriff Department, local Harbor Police, and private operations such as Two Harbors Enterprises, tend to take a 'hands-off' approach to boats anchoring in areas outside of their 'zone of influence.'

As a consequence, in many areas around the Island, there are a number of anchorage areas that tend to attract 'unsavory elements', a 'wharf rat' class of individuals living on boats, often of a derelict nature. Cat Harbor is one of those areas.

In the spring of 2007, a large, eighty-two-foot wooden-hulled powerboat, the *Intrepid*, pulled into Cat Harbor in the hopes of finding a 'permanent home'.

After the boat dropped anchor in the designated anchorage area, the captain of the boat began making inquiries and discovered that there is a relatively safe 'unregulated' anchorage area near the harbor entrance, and outside the 'zone of influence' of our Master Lease. When the captain of that vessel discovered the opportunity to anchor without restrictions, he purchased some extra ground tackle, moved his boat and setup in the anchorage just to the south of Pin Rock, at the southern entrance to the harbor.

I met with him shortly after his arrival and discussed our anchorage policies, rules and restrictions. He was pleasant and cooperative, but he also insisted that he knew the boundaries of our lease premises and informed me that his intentions were to leave his boat at anchor in the 'open anchorage' area for an extended period of time. We discussed having it attended at all times, and he assured me that it would be, at least 'most of the time'.

When winter approached, toward the end of October, I met with him again and conveyed my concerns about the boat remaining in that location when southerly storms develop. I explained that the location was fully exposed to southerlies, and that it was not a good idea to leave the boat in that area when storms threatened. My advice seemed to fall on deaf ears, and the boat stayed where it was, riding out the first two mild southerlies that struck in late December and early January.

In late January, a stronger, more intense weather system bore down on the Island. I spoke with Harbor Patrolman Rudy Smits and asked him to go out to the boat and advise the captain of the impending storm. Rudy reported back to me that the boat was unattended.

I made several phone calls, finally making contact with the boat captain late in the afternoon, just a few hours before the storm was due to strike. He assured me that he would be back aboard his boat later that day. The rapidly developing storm system built from the southeast, forced cancellation of the scheduled Catalina Express boat that evening, and the captain did not make it back to the Island. It remained unattended.

As the storm built, the winds gradually shifted from southeast to south. The winds began to howl shortly after dark and the seas built rapidly. By midnight, winds were gusting above thirty-five knots and the swells rolling into Cat Harbor from the south built to six-to-eight-feet outside the harbor entrance. At around three a.m. I received a phone call from Rudy that the *Intrepid* had broken loose and was drifting into the mooring area, creating havoc. I dressed in my foul weather gear and drove out to Cat Harbor to help.

Patrolmen Rudy Smits, Larry Potter, Bruce Glass, and James 'Doc' Blythe were on scene, manning both patrol boats that service the cove. I was met on the dock and hopped aboard with Rudy.

Frantic distress calls had erupted on VHF channel 9. One twenty-seven-foot sailboat at anchor reported that the big powerboat had crashed into its bow, causing damage. Another twenty-eight-foot sailboat at anchor reported that the boat had tangled in its anchor rode, snapped the line and sent him adrift. Rudy and I responded to its location.

That sailboat was without power and drifting toward the mooring field. The winds continued to gust into the thirty-to-forty mile per hour range and the seas—due to the southerly influence—were rolling into the cove at about four-to-six-feet. A stinging rain added to the miserable conditions. Rudy was at the helm, and he maneuvered into position where I could get our towline onto the distressed sailboat. We were only about fifty yards from the nearest mooring, and Rudy skillfully towed the boat into position where the crew on board could reach the mooring pole and secure the boat to the mooring.

In the meantime, we could hear the other patrolmen talking on the radio with other boaters, all reporting that the big powerboat was drifting rapidly through the mooring field and threatening to crash into their boats.

After we cleared with the small sailboat, Rudy headed toward the *Intrepid*. It had drifted near three or four other boats, narrowly missing them as the winds pushed it inexorably toward shore. When we neared the menacing hulk, it was bearing down on another moored boat, a fifty-foot sailboat. The captain of that boat was on the radio, frantically crying out a Mayday call.

"Mayday! Mayday! The monster boat is going to hit us! Help! Help!"

Rudy and I arrived on scene just as the *Intrepid* crashed into the hapless sailboat. We heard the crunch of wood and fiberglass over the cacophony of the wind and rain. Broadside to the wind, the starboard stern of the *Intrepid* slammed into the sailboat, its massive hull pinned against the port bow. The screeching of metal accompanied the wail of splintering wood and fiberglass as the two boats slammed together. With nobody on board the big powerboat, it was basically impossible to get a towline onto the boat, and even if it could be done, it was unlikely that our small patrol boat could tow it against the force of the wind and seas.

After a few minutes, the force of the big powerboat pinned against the hull of the sailboat caused the bow mooring line to snap, and mercifully, when the sailboat swung in the wind, the two boats separated. Damage to the sailboat was obvious; the pulpit was ripped loose, the stanchion dangled loosely over the rail, and a large, gaping hole in the port bow was visible.

When the mooring line snapped, the *Intrepid* drifted away. It was blowing toward the point that separates Cat Harbor from Wells Beach. Following its movement in our patrol boat, we watched helplessly as the big boat blew down on the shoreline. With a resounding crunch it struck the rocky shore adjacent to the crumbling Wells Beach Pier. We could hear the grind and splintering of wood, and the wail of twisting planks and ribs. Of all the places in the inner portion of Cat Harbor, that small stretch of rocky shoreline where it went aground was by far the most treacherous. Lined with jagged rocks and boulders, we knew without a doubt that it could not survive. Already we could see holes in the bottom of the boat as it rocked back and forth in the three-to-four-foot swells breaking under its keel, and the sounds of cracking planks and timbers was mournful.

We diverted from the scene and went back to talk with the victims of the powerboat run amok. Thankfully nobody suffered any injuries, but there were extensive damages, especially to the fifty-foot sailboat. We assured all of them that we would do our best to put them in touch with the owners of the *Intrepid* and provide them with Incident Reports and insurance information.

For a few more hours we worked in Cat Harbor, assisting boats that were having mooring problems and making sure that those boats that had broken loose or suffered damages caused by the rampaging powerboat were secure and not taking on water.

By daybreak, the winds and swells began to ease. We returned to the *Intrepid*, which was now listing at about a thirty-degree angle on her starboard side, with huge, gaping holes in her hull. It was low tide and the boat was nearly high and dry, with only a portion of her keel and running gear still submerged. Waves of about two-feet slapped against the parts of the hull that were still in the water. We could see a portion of the anchor line dangling from the bow, and leading out into deeper water. At first we thought that her anchor had drug, but later discovered that the three-quarter-inch galvanized steel anchor chain had snapped under the force of the winds. It would be about three hours before the incoming tide would once again inundate the boat, submerging most of the hull and cabin structure that was currently exposed. A couple of the harbor guys, along with another fellow that claimed to be designated by the captain to 'keep an eye on the boat during his absence', initiated an effort to go aboard before the tide rose and see what they might salvage from the boat.

That is when things got very strange.

The 'salvage team' secured a tall ladder from the rocky beach onto the starboard rail cap on the *Intrepid* and used it to climb aboard. In the wheelhouse, where they first looked, there wasn't much that appeared to be of any significant value. They pulled out an older VHF radio, binoculars, the compass, and a few personal odds and ends, but the boat was not equipped with any useful navigational equipment or electronics. On the top deck they removed a portable, three-thousand-kilo-watt generator, lowering it to the sand with dock lines.

In the main cabin there were several nice deck chairs, tables, and other furniture that they pulled out, and it was at that time that they began to discover an abundance of pornographic items and materials.

Cameras, film screens, exotic props, photos of nude men and women, boxes full of explicit video tapes, sex toys, risqué women's clothing, and other sexually oriented materials and objects were found in every room and nearly every drawer and cupboard. It was obvious that the boat was being used, or at least had been used at some point in time, as a porn studio.

Focusing on practical items and boating gear, the salvage crew concentrated on trying to remove useful objects and components, leaving the sexually oriented material in place. In one of the staterooms, they pulled a large brown paper bag filled with wet paper money from a closet that had been partially underwater when the boat flooded. At first glance, the cash appeared real, but on closer inspection, they could see that the bills were 'bleeding' ink, and probably counterfeit. When that was discovered, they called in Isthmus Sheriff Bruce Strelow, turning the bag full of money over to him.

Eventually, as the morning wore on and the tide crept back up to flood the cabins and most of the superstructure, the salvage effort was aborted. By noon, the entire boat, other than the top deck, wheelhouse and upper walls of the cabin, was underwater. Things started floating away, including a lot of the sex stuff.

For several weeks, people walking the beaches in Cat Harbor stumbled upon DVD tapes with covers depicting graphic sexual content. Photographs and bags filled with unique objects that likely served as sexual props were found washed ashore. The Catalina Islander Newspaper dubbed the story 'The Love Boat' in the report that detailed its bizarre story line.

After I left the scene and reported the details of the incident to the Coast Guard, I went home to get a couple of hours of sleep. When I returned to the office, I learned that both the FBI and the Treasury Department were on scene to investigate the matter. Later that afternoon, the captain of the *Intrepid* returned to the Island aboard the Catalina Express. After several hours of interrogation by the authorities on scene, the man was transported to the mainland for further questioning. After supplying the authorities with contact information for the owners of the boat (a company registered as L.A.Sex.com), they were also questioned and investigated.

To the best of my knowledge, neither the FBI nor the Treasury Department made any official charges since there was no proof of child porn or other 'illegal' sexual activity, and the 'counterfeit' money was supposedly used only as a prop in one of the films produced aboard the boat.

A crew from the mainland was dispatched to mitigate potential environmental cleanup, removing the fuel tanks and all hazardous materials from the boat, at the owner's expense. A few days later the captain of the boat returned to the Island to recover the few items salvaged by the original 'salvage team'.

After several weeks of badgering, persistence and threats of legal action, I managed to get a check for twenty-thousand dollars issued from the owners of the boat to enact a cleanup and removal of the remains of the hulk. Using the company's D-8 Caterpillar, David McElroy and the maintenance crew bulldozed the remnants of the 'Love Boat' and shipped the debris to the mainland for disposal, putting an end to one of the most bizarre salvage incidents of my career.

About a month later, in mid-February, another storm slammed into Cat Harbor and destroyed most of the old Wells Beach Pier. It's possible that the 'Love Boat' had hit the pier when it was blown ashore, weakening it from its already rickety condition, but nobody knows for sure. The pier was already in a sad state of disrepair, having been condemned a few years previously.

That old pier had been in use since the early sixties—when the Bombards were managing the Isthmus operation—and was originally built by a consortium of oil industry companies to service an offshore oil response plan on Catalina Island. After the oil companies abandoned the oil response program, the pier was used primarily for servicing moorings in Cat Harbor and as a fishing platform for local anglers.

Fortuitously, when the storm struck, most of the pier decking and timbers collapsed in one major section, making cleanup much easier than it might have been had the pier broken into smaller fragments. As it was, it took several dump trucks full of fractured timbers, pilings and deck planking before the remains were all hauled off the beach and out of the water. Also, the quick and professional work performed by David McElroy, Louie Latka and the rest of the maintenance team helped avoid potentially dangerous and hazardous consequences had the debris drifted out to sea.

That same storm sank another boat in Cat Harbor, a twenty-eight-foot powerboat that was on a mooring in Wells Beach. Mooring crews pulled the hulk from the water and it was eventually hauled out, crushed and shipped to the mainland for disposal.

Adding to the fierceness of that storm, yet another sailboat suffered an unknown fate when it disappeared from its anchorage in the Isthmus. That boat, a twenty-five-foot sailboat that had arrived in the anchorage area in Little Fisherman's Cove about a week prior, was also left unattended. During the night, another vessel called on the radio and reported that the sailboat appeared to be dragging anchor. A patrolman responded, assessed the boat at anchor and determined that it was definitely not in the same position in the anchorage that it had been, but that it did appear to have stopped dragging and was once again anchored securely. In the morning the sailboat was gone. The owner notified the Coast Guard to report its disappearance, which was announced on Channel 16, and all ports and harbors were notified, but it was never seen again.

For me, as Harbormaster, all of those types of incidents required follow-up and volumes of paperwork. Reports for our records as well as copies and additional information for insurance companies, the Coast Guard, Sheriff's Department, and the State Lands Commission notification all needed to be completed. That work alone was enough to keep me busy, but I was also charged with overseeing the daily operation of the harbor, getting the fleet and the docks into shape for the summer, putting together a budget, performing employee reviews, giving boating seminars, working with the marketing team, and covering patrol or shoreboat shifts as needed.

The workload and my many years of long, hard hours were beginning to take their toll. I began to think about retirement, but with our son Troy still in college at the California Maritime Academy, and our commitment to him to pay for his college education, it was not yet a serious consideration.

Later that summer, another act took place that brought about a gradual change of atmosphere on the Island and with my job; Ron Doutt retired as President and CEO of the Santa Catalina Island Company, my principal employer. Soon after that, Paxson 'Packy' Offield also stepped down from his position as Chairman of the Board. Those two men represented the backbone of Catalina Island. It was their influence on the Island that had set the flavor and the tone of the Island community for many years. In their positions, both men had the respect and admiration of nearly every person living on Catalina, and replacing them would be a real challenge.

Change is often difficult, and unpredictable. When those two men stepped down from their positions with the Island Company, it set in motion a gradual change that proved to be very difficult for many Islanders to accept.

From a business standpoint, the changes that began to manifest all over the Island were perfectly understandable. The country was mired in what was to become the 'Great Recession' that began in 2007, and it not only impacted the Island, but also the entire nation for years to come. As a consequence, business decisions and actions began that created disharmony in the Island community. It was the start of a difficult time for many Island residents and as usually happens in times of duress, the 'blame' for the discord was aimed at the 'new regime'; Randall Harrell, John Dravinsky, and Geoffrey Rusack. They were Ron Doutt and Packy Offield's replacements in the Island Company.

In all fairness to those new executives, the 'circumstances of the times' played a large role in the business decisions that impacted a lot of longtime Island residents. The deep recession that engulfed the American economy was felt strongly on Catalina Island. Cutbacks and budget trimming were necessary.

At the same time, the new administrators brought in a new and different philosophy to their positions. Their techniques and business practices were more corporate and less personal. In an Island where a 'family-type' atmosphere had existed for so many years, the new corporate philosophy seemed cutthroat and impersonal. New catchphrases were being heard 'around town'; the terms, 'upscale', 'luxury market', and 'high end clients' were being bantered around. For me, and I believe for most Islanders, those phrases carried connotation's that did not fit the perspective that most Islanders have for Catalina, nor did they adhere to the philosophy that William Wrigley Jr. had expounded with his vision of making the Island a place for 'everyman' to visit and enjoy.

For some, the changes were direct and severe; many jobs were cut, families uprooted, and duties altered. It was a difficult time for nearly everyone. Even for those not directly impacted by the changes, the transition was difficult. They had friends, family members, and co-workers who were impacted by the political and economic decisions being made. It was particularly difficult for those living in Avalon and working for the Santa Catalina Island Company and its affiliates, but nearly every business in the small city felt the impact of the economic climate and the associated corporate changes.

Coinciding with inner-company cutbacks, layoffs and other changes, the Island Company also enacted a significant rate increase for nearly all of the Island based yacht clubs. Eleven clubs leased facilities from the Island Company, paying an annual fee for the privilege and opportunity to retain the use of club sites and structures in coves from Moonstone Cove all around the Island to Catalina Harbor. Historically those lease rights saw some minor increases in pricing, but beginning in 2009, clubs began seeing increases that sometimes more than tripled their existing fees. Those cost increases created considerable hardship for some of the clubs, ultimately resulting in the termination of two of the leases, and causing severe financial duress on others.

I received many phone calls and had numerous discussions with affected club officials about the situation, but as I told them, the matter was beyond my control and any attempt I made to discuss the matter with SCICO administrators was ignored. It was another corporate action that cast a deeper pall on the overall socio-economic picture of the Island community.

In Two Harbors, we faced our own difficulties and hurdles. For me, the challenges were intense, but not overwhelming. Fortunately, the harbor operation was not impacted as severely as many other Island venues. Despite the recession, boaters throughout southern California clung tenaciously to their one burning passion, to keep and use their boats, whenever and as much as possible. As a consequence, boaters and other Island visitors were cutting back on some of the peripheral pleasures associated with boating; dining out, taking tours, etc., but those who owned their own boats were determined to continue visiting the Island.

That helped me to rationalize and defend proposed cutbacks to the harbor operation because, despite the downturn in the overall business, the revenues from the harbor remained positive. I worked especially hard and long on that year's business plan, submitting a final proposal that kept most of my year-round and seasonal crew intact. Other departments in the company did not fare so well, and quite a few Two Harbors residents lost their jobs.

Yet another administrative change occurred in 2008 when Steve and Becky Mucha resigned their positions with the Harbor Reef Restaurant to open their own little restaurant in Salem, Oregon. Steve and Becky were instrumental with 'turning around' the reputation of the Harbor Reef Restaurant during their years on the Island.

A very likeable couple, Steve as restaurant manager, and Becky as coordinator of special events and catering, gave the community of Two Harbors seven years of dedicated and top-notch service. Their wit, charm and hard work brought a delightfully refreshing touch to the workplace, and their culinary experience and improvements that they brought to the restaurant made it a treat for both local residents and guests to enjoy. Their departure left a void that would be hard to fill on a personal level, but Steve's training techniques and practices were so thorough and complete that the crew left behind had sufficient talent and ability to carry the restaurant through the summer, and into future years.

That was also the year that the Two Harbors community lost one of its favorite and most highly regarded legends, the venerable Dr. Ben Massey. An icon in the community for more than half a century, Dr. Ben was a friend, a respected boater, and a true ambassador for the little hamlet of Two Harbors. Coming from an extended family that includes his charming wife Linda and their two children, Ben is one of five generations of the Massey clan that have called the Isthmus their home away from home through the years. His passing was truly a sad occasion for all those people who knew, revered, and loved him.

Another oddity of nature occurred in November of 2008 with the sudden appearance of approximately two-dozen tiny little hammerhead sharks in Catalina Harbor.

Hammerheads are another marine animal that is relatively rare around Catalina. During my thirty-two years and several thousand days of being on the water—hundreds of those while fishing—I can recall seeing only three hammerheads anywhere on the Island. I actually caught, and released one while fishing for mako sharks one year off the West End, that weighed about eighty-pounds, and I saw a much larger one—perhaps twelve-feet long—while out squid fishing one night. The only other hammerhead I've seen on the Island was an eight-footer that a couple of the local guys caught and brought back to the dock.

The point is they are not very common in Island waters. To have several dozen show-up in Catalina Harbor was indeed an oddity.

They were cute little suckers, averaging about twelve-to-eighteen-inches in total length. More than likely the tiny little sharks were Smooth Hammerheads (*Sphyrna zygaena*), of the family *Sphyrnidae*; the most likely species to be found in southern California waters.

Undoubtedly, a female hammerhead found its way into Cat Harbor and delivered her pups in the warm waters of the back harbor. They are a viparious species—one that delivers live babies—as opposed to egg laying animals. Known to abandon their young to fend for themselves soon after birth, the mother hammerhead likely swam away shortly after delivery. As is their habit, the young then stayed together for several weeks, learning to feed and survive as a group, before heading off to either join other schools, or to scour the seas as loners.

Several were caught and released during the roughly three-week period that they frequented the harbor. Having the opportunity to see them swimming around in the bay, and to actually catch and be able to inspect them closely, was quite the thrill for many local residents—most of whom had never seen a hammerhead.

Their unique head configuration, with a wide, flat head called a cephalofoil that juts out from their jaws as much as three-feet in a fully-grown specimen, is truly a strange sight to see. Their eyes sit at the outer appendage of the cephalofoil, rotating and scanning in a full one-hundred-eighty-degree range with each eye. They truly are one of the oddities of nature and their presence in Cat Harbor created a lot of excitement and enjoyment for those who saw them in the cove.

31. Helicopter Tragedy

ONE OF THE WORST ACCIDENTS to happen on the Island during our over three decades living there was the tragic helicopter crash that occurred in May of 2008 when four people lost their lives.

I was working that day, operating a shoreboat in Isthmus Cove when I heard the helicopter approaching from seaward. Even though there is no regular 'chopper' service to Two Harbors, it was not unusual to hear the beat of a helicopter in the Isthmus. Charters occur on a casual basis, and it is quite common for the Coast Guard and Sheriff's Department to fly over the Isthmus, or land for responses to a variety of situations.

I was not really paying much attention to the helicopter until I heard an unusual 'pop' break the routine thumping of the rotating blades. When that 'pop' sounded, I looked up and the helicopter was almost directly over my head. I saw a flash of what appeared to be fire bursting from the base of the blades, where they come together at the center. I cocked my head and watched curiously as the thumping sound of the blades and motor took on a different pitch. At about the same time, I noticed that the helicopter was losing altitude. I wasn't sure whether it was an intentional maneuver or if something was going wrong, so I continued to watch.

After a few moments, I realized that the helicopter was definitely not 'behaving normally'. It was making a completely different beat than usual, and I thought to myself that it sounded as if it was in reverse. I continued to watch.

It was dropping at a steady angle, faster than it should be dropping under a normal flight pattern, and I became extremely concerned. I picked up the VHF radio and called Harbor Base.

"Harbor Base. Harbor Base. This is Shoreboat #9. I'm watching a helicopter approach from seaward and it appears to be in trouble." By the time I had uttered those words; my concern grew stronger as the helicopter continued to plummet. "Harbor Base!" I called rather frantically, "I think the helicopter is going down. You'd better notify Baywatch and be prepared to launch a response."

I thought the helicopter was going to crash into the center of town, about where the public restrooms are located. I held my breath as it cleared the palm trees and eucalyptus trees that are near the restrooms, before it disappeared from my vision. I knew that it was dropping way too fast, and that something had gone terribly wrong. Suddenly a flash erupted behind the trees near the center of the Isthmus, followed by a billowing plume of black smoke.

"Harbor Base!" I transmitted, "It crashed. There's a helicopter down out near Cat Harbor.

I heard the siren at Visitor Services cry out and could see people running on the pier and on shore. The cloud of black smoke grew and spread on the moderate Isthmus breeze. I was about two-hundred yards from the pier when the crash happened. When I reached the dock, I quickly tied the shoreboat to the dock cleats and ran up the ramp to the office. The radio was going crazy with people aboard boats trying to call-in the emergency.

I quickly learned that both Baywatch and the Isthmus Search and Rescue Team were notified and on way to the scene.

The helicopter had crashed at the edge of the baseball field in Cat Harbor. Several heroic individuals that were nearby rushed to the scene and managed to pull two of the six passengers from the flaming wreckage, but four individuals perished.

All six of the passengers aboard the helicopter, including the pilot, had deep roots on the Island and the tragedy affected many Islanders and their families. It was by far the most tragic incident to happen in the Isthmus during our tenure and our hearts went out to the victims and their families.

While helicopter and plane crashes are rare on the Island, they do happen. We happened to be driving into Avalon one afternoon a few years after moving to the Island, when a small Lear Jet carrying six passengers crashed at the Airport in the Sky. We arrived on scene shortly after rescue personnel had extinguished the flames. All six people on board that plane also perished.

Catalina's Airport in the Sky tends to have a certain amount of notoriety as having a landing strip that is difficult for planes to land. In actuality, most pilots that frequent the runway consider it to be more than adequate. The problem that most pilots unfamiliar with the landing strip encounter is recognizing the 'hump' that exists in the center of the strip. That hump throws off their perception, leading an inexperienced pilot to think that the runway ends, where in reality the hump is near the middle section of the runway. As a consequence, several plane crashes have occurred when those inexperienced pilots try to adjust to the false perception of the strip ending, and then get into trouble. Also, the overall 'newsworthiness' of a plane crashing on Catalina Island tends to make more headlines than it might at a less media visible locale. I have been on several small planes that landed at the Airport and never felt that the landing strip was anything but safe and adequate.

There was rarely a moment on the Island when I was not enchanted with the natural beauty and splendor of the special little paradise that was my home. I'd awaken early each morning to an appreciation of my surroundings and the scenic wonders of our very own Shangri-La.

Each year brought a distinctly different transformation of Island terrain, as well as the variety and uniqueness of each season. From the vibrant greenery of a wet winter to the universal brown landscapes of a hot summer, the nuances of nature on the Island always made for a fascinating panorama of spectacular vistas and inspiring scenery. It is an idyllic lifestyle, generally peaceful and stress free.

However, with the changing of the guard at the top of the corporate ladder, along with the associated downturn in the national and local economy, I was being pressured to help 'turn things around' in the overall business projections of the company.

Two Harbors Enterprises was actually holding its own financially, but the Avalon venues operated by the Santa Catalina Island Company were struggling. Overall visitor counts to the Island were down considerably, affecting hotels restaurants, cross-channel carrier counts, and all recreational venues on the Island. As a consequence, all departmental managers of SCICO and its subsidiaries (THE, IRE, and CIRS) were under the gun to trim expenses and increase revenues. Nearly every department within the corporate structure faced mandatory cutbacks to four-day workweeks during the off-season, along with a reduction of seasonal staffing and hourly allocations.

I worked closely with John Phelps and Ann Luchau to do some budget trimming and positive revenue enhancement, and managed to get approval on a budget plan for 2009 that included some cutbacks in the Harbor Department but nothing too severe.

A few bouts of rough and unseasonable weather impacted the early months of the 2009 season, with several weekends 'blown-out' in April and early May. Those storms put a damper on the early part of the season and further impacted the financial picture, but when summer arrived, visitor counts increased significantly and it looked like we would survive the year without a significant downturn.

But by far the most shocking and surprising change that took place that season was the retirement of Executive Vice President and General Manager John Phelps.

In early August, and during the height of the busy season, Phelps informed the staff that he would be departing at the end of the month. His announcement came not only as a shock to the community and his employees, but was surrounded by a certain amount of ambiguity.

I had known John for years, both when he was Harbormaster in Avalon, and working for him for eleven years at Two Harbors. He brought a lot of good things to the Isthmus, was the driving force that helped hold the community together following the departure of the Bombard family, and served the company faithfully during his tenure.

He left rather quietly, with no going-away or retirement party and his departure left a big hole in the administrative realm of Two Harbors Enterprises.

For me, the writing on the wall was getting bolder. Wholesale changes were taking place within the organization and the 'Great Recession' was digging its roots ever deeper into the overall stability of Catalina Island. Wide-reaching changes were looming all across the Island.

After a period of time, with Ann Luchau serving as Acting General Manager of Two Harbors Enterprises, the Island Company eventually appointed Oley Olsen as Executive Vice President and General Manager of Two Harbors Enterprises. Oley had served with the Island Company for many years, as Vice President of Hotel Operations and as Vice President of Two Harbors Enterprises, so he was intimately familiar with the Two Harbors operation.

As we went into the budget process at the close of the 2009 summer season, all of the managers were challenged once again with improving revenues and cutting expenses. Like with most businesses, the simplest step for increasing revenues is to increase prices. But in a struggling economy, where so many people were being affected by the economic downturn, raising prices tends to decrease sales, or in our case, lower visitor counts. Coinciding with that concept, reducing expenses especially in a service-related industry usually means reducing payroll. As manager of the harbor operation, I was reluctant to do either.

As an alternative to increasing revenues, I looked very closely at the primary sources of Harbor Department revenues, sublease rates and transient mooring fees. I found three aspects where adjustments could be made that would increase revenues without raising prices, and submitted those changes in my budget plan. All three adjustments were accepted by our corporate administrators and approved by the State Lands Commission, which oversees and must approve any and all changes in pricing or policies within the scope of the Master Lease.

I then turned to the manpower section of the budget and made a few changes that reduced both year-round and seasonal payroll expenses, leaving the core crew intact and only minimally affected. At the same time, I was undergoing employee reviews, and with the escalating cost of gas, rent increases, and overall inflationary costs for nearly all consumer products on the rise, I was hoping to implement wage increases. That further complicated my business plan and added more stress to my job. It was a difficult time in the workplace, and the pressure was further increased by the onslaught of several rather severe off-season storms.

Fortunately I had a solid crew, and with Michelle Phelps and Megan Poulson in the office, and Steve Mercadante, Bruce Glass, Larry Potter, Mark Woolery, James 'Doc' Blythe, Jason Rose, James Dollack, and Rudy Smits working together to keep the harbor running smoothly. I was able to concentrate on applying the majority of my energy into developing an acceptable budget plan, which, when completed and submitted, I believed to be solid and reasonable.

I was taken completely off-guard when I went into the budget meetings at the Island Company offices in Avalon and discovered that my budget submittals were slashed radically and only vaguely resembled the plan that I had submitted.

We were in the corporate offices on Metropole Avenue (Steve Mercadante was with me), meeting with CEO Randall Harrell, COO John Dravinski, CFO Sharon Johnson, and Two Harbor's executives Oley Olsen and Ann Luchau. When they handed me a copy of the preliminary budget plan, I was stunned. The plan showed nearly a forty-percent decrease in manpower for the harbor, with three full-time and several seasonal positions eliminated. I reacted strongly.

"You've got to be kidding!" I spoke out.

Randall Harrell looked at me curiously, a look of puzzlement on his brow. "Isn't this the budget that you submitted?" he asked me.

"No," I replied. "This budget contains cutbacks in manpower that would make it impossible for us to operate effectively."

He looked around the table, obviously perplexed. There had obviously been some miscommunication within the corporate hierarchy and it was clear that Randall Harrell was not aware of the situation.

After a few rather awkward interchanges between the executives, Steve Mercadante and I were asked to leave the room for a few minutes. We went out into the lounge and sat around waiting for about thirty minutes. When we were called back in, Randall Harrell spoke to me.

"Obviously there was some miscommunication. I would like you to look over this plan, consider the changes that were made to your original submittal, and return early next week with a revised submittal. Please work closely with Ann and Oley so that you are all in agreement with your next submittal."

I went back to the drawing board after hearing from Oley that they had been forced to make some last minute modifications to my budget submittal in order to meet the demands of the company. The whole situation was extremely frustrating. I felt as though I was getting my legs chopped out from under me as a manager and that it would be nearly impossible to avoid severe cutbacks to the department. Rather than roll over meekly and accept the proposed cutbacks, I took the initiative to put together a hastily assembled fact sheet of the harbor operations success and performance for the past ten years. In that memo, I pointed out the successes of the department, the indisputable evidence of ten consecutive years of Gross Margin improvements in the final budget statements, along with a picture of the top-notch customer service, accompanied by results of customer surveys conducted by the company regarding the Harbor operation.

With that information in hand, we returned to the corporate offices and met again with company officials. The information I provided, along with my steadfast insistence that deep cutbacks would cripple the Harbor Department, resulted in a modified budget plan that did include the loss of two full-time positions along with some minimal seasonal cutbacks.

It was not what I had hoped for, but at least it was not as severe as it could have been. When I informed the two fulltime employees that they would be losing benefits and facing a further reduction in hours, it left me sad and extremely frustrated.

I returned to the Harbor Office and sat at my desk. For the first time in my career I thought to myself; 'I don't like my job anymore'.

That thought didn't stay with me for long. I walked down the ramp to the dock, climbed into a patrol boat and headed out toward Cherry Cove. Once I was on the water, my negative thoughts faded into the deep recesses of my head. I was still living on Catalina Island, working on the Pacific Ocean in a pristine and relatively unspoiled paradise. It was a dream job, almost a fantasy, and one that I had enjoyed thoroughly for more than thirty years. What more could a man ask for?

We had a tough Buccaneer Weekend that year. An unseasonable northwester blew into southern California on the Wednesday preceding 'Buc Days', bringing a light sprinkling of rain, but more significantly, gale force winds.

Those winds gusted above forty-knots, and were accompanied by ten-to-twelve-foot seas. The storm roughed up the Catalina Channel, discouraging all but the bravest (or dumbest) pirates from venturing out to the Island early in order to secure a good mooring for the weekend. Its impact lasted through Friday night, although the rough conditions did ease to a Small Craft Advisory by Thursday afternoon. Even with the wind and rough seas, the Isthmus mooring area, including Fourth of July and Cherry Cove's, was at near capacity by Saturday morning and filled completely by the afternoon.

Driving shoreboat that weekend was particularly challenging, because the lingering northwest swell did not diminish completely until Sunday. I always drove shoreboat on Buccaneer Weekend. I was the only daytime operator; all others were needed for the ridiculously busy night shift.

Having to contend with rocky and rolling conditions in the mooring fields made it difficult. But it was also always a lot of fun to pickup boatloads of pirates, dressed to the hilts in their finest or at least most creative pirate garb. It was particularly entertaining to load and offload some of the 'wenches', dressed in their low-cut dresses, ripped and torn skirts, and assorted tantalizingly risqué garments of their choosing. For those who have experienced Buccaneer Days on Catalina Island, I'm sure they can appreciate what it is like to work the weekend. For those who have not seen it, they should. It is truly one of the most racy and risqué parties that one can imagine; perhaps similar in some respects to 'Mardis Gras' in New Orleans, or 'Carnival' in Brazil.

In November, another powerful northwester bore down on the Island, this one arriving over the Thanksgiving Weekend. That storm created havoc for several hundred boats that were on the Island to observe Thanksgiving, and made things very difficult for the entire Harbor Department.

The storm that arrived on Thanksgiving Weekend in 2009, struck late in the day on Friday after quite a few boats had already made the trip to the Island for the traditional Thanksgiving feast offered by the Harbor Reef Restaurant. Many of those boats elected to cut their visit short and return to the mainland rather than cope with the predicted gale force winds scheduled to hit the Island.

I was working on a harbor patrol boat on Friday, assisting a few arriving boats onto moorings and checking on other already moored boats to ensure that they were tied properly, had chafing gear in place, and were not too tight on their mooring.

While assisting a sailboat onto its mooring, a gust of wind at around twenty knots caught the sailboat broadside and pushed it toward another boat moored nearby. In his haste to avoid making contact, the captain of the sailboat powered into reverse, his stern bearing down on my patrol boat. Anticipating that possibility, I veered to starboard with my harbor unit, precisely at the time that an inflatable raft blew off the deck of the moored boat. The small raft floated into the air directly toward the center of my boat. Reflexively, I reached up to fend off the wayward raft—one of those inexpensive little rubberized rafts that are designed to hold two people—and felt something pull in my upper back when the raft pinned my arm against the aluminum framing of the patrol unit's sun cover.

A stabbing pain deep under my shoulder blade developed, causing me to grimace with discomfort. I managed to pull the wayward raft onto the foredeck of my patrol boat and returned it to its owner. For the remainder of the afternoon, I worked in discomfort, minimizing the use of my left side as much as possible. I didn't think too much about the muscle strain that had happened. Through the years I had dealt with numerous pulls, strains and minor injuries, working through them without too much disruption.

But that strain lingered, staying with me for a few months and caused me continual physical discomfort. It was even hard to sleep at night and the lack of sleep, combined with the chronic pain in my upper back and chest left me feeling irritable and uncomfortable.

In late January, a series of powerful winter storms slammed into the Island, once again bringing gale force winds and rough seas that lasted nearly a week. At one point, wind gusts above seventy-five miles per hour were recorded in Catalina Harbor. The entire Harbor team was kept busy day and night dealing with problems and trying to minimize damage. Numerous boats dragged moorings and anchors, two boats sank off the Island's West End while trying to get around to the relative protection of Cat Harbor. Baywatch Isthmus rescued two of the four people on board by jumping into the frigid, storm tossed seas, and pulled the other two off their boat just before both sailboats sank into the depths.

In the middle of one of the storm systems, when the wrap-around effects of a southeast gale was slamming into Isthmus Cove, I suffered another injury, pulling a groin muscle while trying to disconnect the main float from the end of the pier. That strain, combined with the lingering upper back strain that continued to bother me, knocked me out of commission for a few days.

I felt badly about not being available to help out the rest of the crew during the stormy weather, but my body was just not up to the task. Also, while sitting at home recuperating, I realized that the thrill and excitement of fighting storms, responding to emergencies, and dealing with all the associated problems of running a harbor was not all that fun anymore. The thought of retirement loomed larger in my mind.

Even though I had reached retirement age, we still had our son Troy in college at the California Maritime Academy, and we had made the promise to both of our sons that we would put them through college so that they would not be burdened with the stigma of student loans after graduation.

In February, Troy found the opportunity to return home for a few days. We had not seen him for several months and it was great to have him home. I took a couple of vacation days so that we could go fishing together and each of us caught a thirty-pound class white seabass.

After returning to work a few days later, I had a particularly rough day. Several issues had developed in the workplace requiring my immediate attention, and two of the patrolmen were out sick. I had to put in several physically exhausting hours on the water. Both my back and leg were bothering me, and when I got home later that evening I was tired, sore and physically and mentally drained.

At the dinner table, Maureen suggested that I take a few days of sick leave. I was never one for taking time off without a really good reason to do so. In my mind, a few aches and pains did not justify missing work. I balked at her suggestion, but Troy chimed in on the subject.

"Dad," he spoke to me seriously, "You should retire."

I looked at him and smiled. "Thanks, son," I responded, "You're probably right. But you have a year of college left to complete, and we're not in a solid enough financial position for me to quit working just yet."

He looked me directly in the eyes and said, "You can retire, dad. I'll take out a student loan."

Maureen and I looked at each other. We both felt an overwhelming sense of pride, recognizing the sincerity in his words and his demeanor.

I responded emotionally, "That's very thoughtful and I really appreciate your offer. But we promised both you and Trevor that we would do our best to put you through college so that you would not be burdened with paying off loans when you graduate. We intend to stick to our promise."

Troy looked at me thoughtfully, and then spoke again, "Look, dad. I only have one year of school left. When I graduate, I will be a marine engineer and the maritime industry has one of the best job markets in the country. I'll be earning really good money and I know that I'll be able to get a job right away and pay off a student loan without any trouble."

He paused and we all sat quietly for a moment, and then he continued, "You're getting worn out, dad. You've worked really hard for more than thirty-years and you need to retire."

"He's right," Maureen chimed in. "You are tired. You've pushed yourself too hard, especially in recent months. All the problems in your job are starting to take a toll and I want us to be able to enjoy our lives together when we are ready to leave the Island. You should think about his offer."

I sat there quietly for a few moments, feeling deep paternal and communal love and pride. Looking at Troy, I truly realized that he had turned the corner from childhood to adulthood, and that he was not only sensible and responsible, but also thoughtful and caring. I felt a lump growing in my throat, and when I spoke, it almost wouldn't come out. "Okay, son, your mother and I will talk about it," I managed to say. "But right now, there's a Laker game on. Let's go see if they can beat the Clippers."

A couple of days later Troy returned to school. I returned to work. We didn't talk about the subject of retirement for a few days, but then one evening Maureen brought it up. We discussed the idea in a preliminary manner, tossing out pros and cons, discussing our financial situation and deciding to put together a summary of all of our assets and try and truly analyze whether we were in a stable enough position to consider the possibility of my retirement.

We had known from the moment that we moved to the Island that the day would come when it was time to leave. For those living and working in Two Harbors, there is no option of owning a home in the Isthmus, or of staying in a home if you are not working for the company. It was that simple. We lived in a company town, and when you stopped working, you would leave.

Knowing that, we had purchased a rental property in Washington about fifteen years previously. It was an investment property, an older home that Maureen didn't really like much, but served as a good investment for our future. Several years later, we purchased a second home in Grants Pass, Oregon that Maureen also did not like but was also an investment property. We then sold the home in Washington and purchased a three-bedroom home in Grants Pass, built in 1978 that Maureen likes to say 'has good bones'. Our goal was to move into that home and upgrade it once we were there. After purchasing the home, we rented it out, knowing that it would be there for us when the time came.

For the next several weeks Maureen and I discussed the possibility of my retirement. We both contributed to saving plans and we had a few investments in mutual funds and other investment markets, but we agreed that there was not enough in our personal accounts to live comfortably if we were to both stop working. She is seven years younger than I, and she made the suggestion that if I were to retire she would continue to work, staying on with USC as long as possible and then hopefully finding work in Grants Pass. There was a lot to consider and the thought of leaving the Island was rather daunting, so we put things on hold for the time being.

We went about living our lives in a normal fashion. I was busy getting ready for the upcoming summer season. Maureen was constantly busy at the Marine Science Center, working with a wide variety of university related study programs, research entities, marine biology programs, and her primary job of administration and finance for the Institute. Thoughts about my retirement went onto the backburner for a while.

32. An Emotional Farewell

IN EARLY MARCH, THE CHILEAN earthquake created a tsunami that threatened the west coast of the Unites States and Mexico. Catalina Harbor is particularly prone to tsunami affects, and the entire Island was put on alert following the quake.

While damages were minimal on the Island, the predicted tsunami did cause a few problems for the harbor and those living, or visiting on boats.

Typically, the impact of a tsunami is most noticeable in shallow bays and low-lying coastal shores. Cat Harbor is a very shallow bay, nearly enclosed with only a narrow entrance leading into the cove. As a consequence, the ebb and flow of tidal surge is vividly evident when tsunami conditions develop. The Chilean tsunami did not create massive surge activity, but it did generate enough to create some impressive water movement. At three different times during the four-hour tidal disruption, the docks in Cat Harbor sat high and dry as a result of the surge. Currents were running at about six-to-eight knots as the water slowly rose and fell inside of the harbor. A couple of boats dragged their moorings in the tidal surge, ending up several hundred yards from their original location. A huge mudflat was exposed briefly when the water ebbed out of the bay, and then the baseball field covered with saltwater as the tide flowed back in. It was not a severe tsunami impact, but it was quite a sight to see.

I aggravated the muscle strain in my upper back while trying to re-secure one of the dinghy docks that had snapped a line during the peak of the tidal surge, and when I got home that night, Maureen informed me that she had made a decision; I needed to retire. I agreed.

After coming to that decision, we discussed the timing and possible consequences of giving notice to the company. We were not sure how they might react. Would they expect us to leave our house right away? Would they want, or consider a transition period while a replacement was found? Would there be an option of me being retained in a consultant position? We were very uncertain about the prospect, and so Maureen suggested we consult with our close friend Elaine Vaughan.

Elaine is very professionally connected and we had often sought and appreciated her input and feedback regarding work-related issues. As our kid's godparents and longtime friends, we knew we could always depend on Johnny and Elaine Vaughan for both personal and professional advice and support.

We met with Elaine and discussed the pending announcement. Her counsel was astute and forthright, and I followed her advice.

Somewhat appropriately we thought, since we had moved to the Island on April Fool's Day in 1978, I submitted a resignation notice to our company President, Oley Olsen, on April 1, 2010—thirty-two years to the day after we moved to the Island.

The following couple of months were sort of a blur. Following Elaine's advice, I gave a two-month notice, plenty of time to find a replacement. I also negotiated a minimal consulting fee that would go through the end of the year. Additionally, the company accommodated our request to be flexible with a departure date, allowing us to make a gradual transition out of our home and off the Island.

At about the same time I gave my notice, Maureen sat down with her employers and explained our plans. We did not want to try and move into USC housing. It was time to move off the Island and begin the next phase of our lives. She negotiated a six-month contract with the University, agreeing to be flexible and open-ended regarding her employment following the end of that six-month period. We both continued to work through April and May, with me choosing a targeted retirement date of Thursday, May 27, 2010—the Thursday before Memorial Weekend.

I had agreed to help with the search for a new Harbormaster. My Assistant Harbormaster for the past nine-years, Steve Mercadante, was in my opinion the logical choice as my replacement, but it became evident early in the search that the company was intent on finding someone outside of the organization. I thought it much more sensible and practical to promote Steve to take over my duties. His administrative experience was somewhat minimal, but he had a thorough knowledge of the daily operation, has excellent boating skills and knowledge, and was a good team leader and motivator.

After the search was trimmed down to three final candidates, I stepped out of the interview process, suggesting to Oley Olsen and Ann Luchau that the final decision be made between them and corporate officials in Avalon.

They selected Phillip Winters as my replacement. Because the process of selecting my replacement took nearly the entire two months, Phillip did not start work until later in the summer. Steve Mercadante filled-in as interim Harbormaster, performing my duties until Phillip Winters arrived in mid-July. I would have the opportunity to spend time with Phillip during the fall and early winter as a consultant, going over as many of the details of the job and duties as possible.

On Thursday, May 25, I walked off the pier as Harbormaster for the last time. The walk up the hill to my home was emotional. Thoughts and memories flooded my mind as I reflected on random things that I had seen and done through the years. It was very strange to be sitting at home on Friday of Memorial Weekend, rather than working. I had not had a holiday off for more than thirty-years other than Christmas, which is the one holiday of the year when boaters tend to not visit the Island. Sitting in my lounge chair, or on my front porch and gazing out at the swarm of arriving boats was very odd. Several times, I wanted to reach down and pickup the radio that I kept near the front windows of our house, to tell one of the harbor patrolmen about a situation that I could see developing out of my front window. But I refrained. I was retired. It was no longer my job to keep an eye out the window.

On Friday evening, I was the center of attention at my retirement party.

Maureen organized the party, working with Two Harbors Enterprises to put together an incredible sendoff that I was completely overwhelmed by. I was told that a conservative estimate of attendance was about five-hundred people, including my family, members of our community and Avalon, along with hundreds of boating friends.

Because of my connections with the boaters, Maureen did not want my retirement party to be just a gathering of employees and Island friends, but rather she wanted it to include as many of the regular Isthmus visitors as possible. She went all out in organizing the party, bringing our good friend Jeff Stress to the Island to emcee the 'roast' that was part of the retirement celebration.

There were several people who took the Catalina Express to the Island solely to attend my going away party. In addition, I was extremely pleased to have friends and colleagues from the Island, Doug Bombard, Ron Doutt, Packy Offield, Gail Hodge, George McElroy,

Geoffrey Rusack, Dr. Ann Muscatt, Rudy Piltch, Billy Delbert, Dan Teckinoff, and their families, along with others who had held key roles in my professional career, and in the community. In addition, the hundreds of boating friends, yacht club members and representatives who shared my special day, all helped to make it a moment in time that I will never forget. I was given several very nice retirement gifts, including the customary 'Gold Painted Buffalo Chip' from our friends Rudy and Melba Piltch, to hang on the wall in our new home. Our good friends Tom and Robin Moody from Cherry Cove Yacht Club presented us with a marvelous photo album commemorating the party, and the harbor staff gave me a wonderful photo album featuring Island memories.

Afterward, we spent the remainder of the evening with my family, my brothers and sisters, nephews and nieces, Maureen and our wonderful sons, Trevor, his fiancé Lauren and Troy. I realized something special that night; I am a very lucky man.

During the next two months we finished packing and shipping our belongings to the mainland. We were very fortunate to have the convenience of being able to store most of our belongings on a temporary basis at the USC warehouse on Terminal Island while we slowly and methodically moved our belongings off the Island.

After twenty-one years and more than one-thousand weeks, I submitted my last weekly article for the Catalina Islander Newspaper in late July. For the first time in all those years, I wrote the article in a first person format, thanking and acknowledging the many people I had worked with and bidding farewell to my readers. It had been a terrific experience for me, not always easy to meet the deadline, but it gave me a feeling of accomplishment and gratification to know that I had provided a small amount of community spirit and involvement in my effort to cover the 'news' of Two Harbors for the residents of the

Island, and for the thousands of mainland readers that have an affinity with Catalina Island.

I rented a small moving van in early July and moved our first truckload of belongings to our new home in Grants Pass, Oregon. Trevor, Maureen and my brother Dave went with me and stayed for about a week, helping me start the renovation process of our new home. I stayed in Grants Pass for about a month, working on the house, painting and doing as much as possible to make it livable.

Maureen stayed on the Island and continued to work. In early August, we held a big yard sale, getting rid of some of our thirty-two years of accumulated 'junk'. Some of the stuff that we sold was a little hard to leave behind, but they were not things that we needed for our new lives.

On August 6, 2010, we climbed aboard USC's vessel, *Miss Christy* and left our Island home of thirty-two years. As the *Miss Christy* chugged steadily toward the mainland, I kept looking back at the Island, thinking, reflecting, and remembering.

The churning wake left a milky path of white foam on the surface, and as I stared into the briny deep, I felt the pulse of the ocean reaching into the depths of my soul. I was both sad and happy. I felt somewhat empty, yet somehow fulfilled. My life as I had known it and lived it, was over. A new life was ready to begin. As the outline of the Island faded into the enveloping shroud of the omnipresent marine layer, I could feel a tear coursing down my cheek. I was leaving the place of my dreams, my past, and my home.

I knew that I would be back. Maureen was still working for the Marine Science Center. I was still under contract as a consultant. My sons and future daughter-in-law were still there, and the magical paradise known as Catalina Island would always be out there waiting for my return.

Epilogue

WE SETTLED INTO OUR NEW home in Grants Pass, grateful to have Maureen's sister Barbara, and her husband Dennis Brown living only a few miles away. They helped us with the transition from the Island to a 'big city'.

I continued to work on the house, painting, replacing doors and trim, patching the ceiling where we had removed a 'popcorn' surface, and making necessary repairs. My brother Dave came up from his home in Oceanside to help me with the renovation for about a month. His electrical talents along with his knowledge of renovations proved invaluable.

I joined an 'old-guys' slow-pitch softball league called The Relics, and began playing softball twice a week from late spring into early fall. I also started playing volleyball regularly, both at the local YMCA and at pickup games at a local gym. Maureen continued to work for USC, proving herself as a knowledgeable and valuable asset when Roberta Marinelli became the new director of the Wrigley Institute. Nearly two years later, Maureen is still employed by USC on a half-time basis, working remotely, much as she did while on the Island. She makes trips every four-to-six weeks to the Island to work hands-on and on some of those trips I go along with her.

Our son Troy graduated from Cal Maritime with a Bachelor's Degree in Marine Engineering and is now a Coast Guard licensed third engineer, finishing in the top three of his class. He secured a position with MSC, the Military Sealift Command, a privately operated maritime operation that supplies the military worldwide. He paid off his student loans within the first two-months of his employment.

Trevor and Lauren were married in September of 2011, exchanging vows at the Banning House Lodge, where Maureen and I were married thirty-three years previously. Trevor continues to work for USC as a boat captain and waterfront coordinator, and his little bride (and our new daughter-in-law) Lauren, holds the position of Lab Manager at the

Marine Science Center. Trevor and our 'third son' Logan Gardiner got together and bought my boat, and so now when I return, I can use it whenever I want.

We left Catalina behind physically, but mentally and emotionally the Island of Romance is, and will always be our home.

Printed in the United States
By Bookmasters